Liberating the United Nations

# Liberating the United Nations

## *Realism with Hope*

**Richard Falk** *and*
**Hans von Sponeck**

*Foreword by*
**Dr. Walden Bello**

*Afterword by*
**Ahmet Davutoğlu**

STANFORD UNIVERSITY PRESS
*Stanford, California*

Stanford University Press
Stanford, California

Printed in the United States of America on acid-free, archival-quality paper

Library of Congress Cataloging-in-Publication Data
Names: Falk, Richard, author. | Sponeck, Hans-Christof, Graf, 1939– author.
Title: Liberating the United Nations : realism with hope / Richard Falk and
    Hans von Sponeck.
Description: Stanford, California : Stanford University Press, 2024. |
    Includes bibliographical references and index.
Identifiers: LCCN 2024003573 (print) | LCCN 2024003574 (ebook) |
    ISBN 9781503638211 (cloth) | ISBN 9781503639133 (paperback) |
    ISBN 9781503639140 (ebook)
Subjects: LCSH: United Nations. | United Nations—Reorganization.
Classification: LCC JZ4984.5 .F35 2024 (print) | LCC JZ4984.5 (ebook) |
    DDC 341.23—dc23/eng/20240216
LC record available at https://lccn.loc.gov/2024003573
LC ebook record available at https://lccn.loc.gov/2024003574

Cover design: Michel Vrana / Black Eye Design

*To all those dedicated to Saving Humanity*
*and Planet Earth (SHAPE)*

*In the hour of darkness and peril and need,*
*the people will waken and listen . . .*

HENRY WADSWORTH LONGFELLOW,
"The Ride of Paul Revere"

The challenges of our age are problems
without passports; to address them we
need blueprints without borders.

KOFI ANNAN, UN Secretary-General

# CONTENTS

RUSSIA

Alaska
*(US)*

Greenland
*(Den.)*

C A N A D A

U N I T E D
S T A T E S

Hawaii
*(US)*

MEXICO

see detail

MARSHALL
ISLANDS

ECUADOR

FSM

NAURU

BRAZIL

KIRIBATI

SOLOMON
IS.

PERU

TUVALU

BOLIVIA

SAMOA

PARAGUAY

VANUATU

Cook Is.
*(NZ)*

French Polynesia
*(Fr)*

CHILE

FIJI

Niue
*(NZ)*

New Cal.
*(FR)*

TONGA

URUGUAY

NEW
ZEALAND

ARGENTINA

BAHAMAS

CUBA

MEXICO

DOMINICAN
REPUBLIC

ANTIGUA & BARBUBA

BELIZE

JAMAICA

HAITI

GTM

ST. KITTS & NEVIS

DOMINICA

HONDURAS

SAINT VINCENT &
THE GRENADINES

ST. LUCIA

BARBADOS

EL
SALVADOR

NICARAGUA

GRENADA

COSTA RICA

TRINIDAD & TOBAGO

PANAMA

VENEZUELA

COLOMBIA

GUYANA

French
Guiana
*(Fr.)*

SURINAME

The boundaries and names shown and
the designations used on this map do
not imply official endorsement or
acceptance by the United Nations.

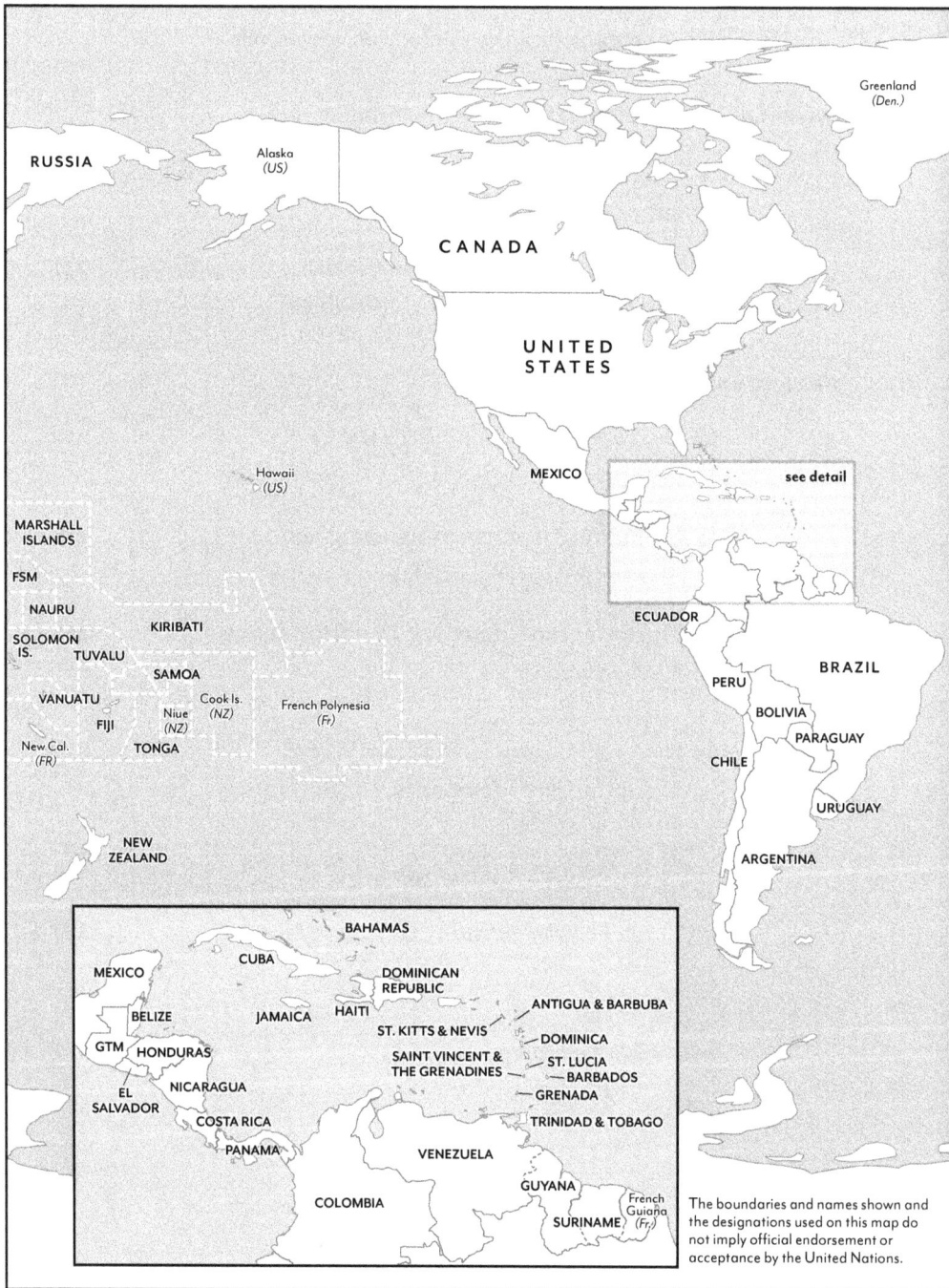

**MAP 0.1** Geopolitical world map

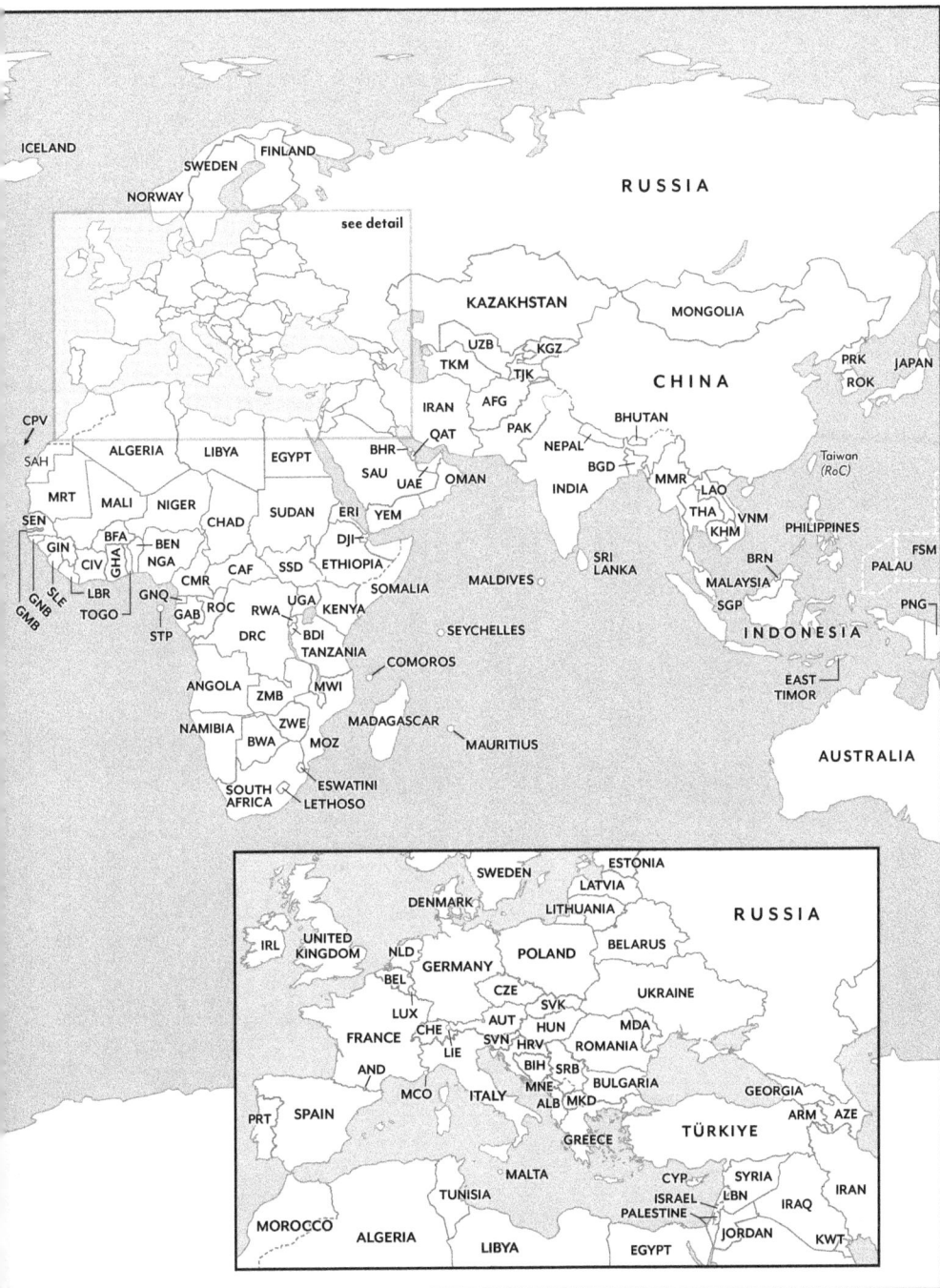

# The United Nations System

**PRINCIPAL ORGANS**

**GENERAL ASSEMBLY**

**SECURITY COUNCIL**

**ECONOMIC AND SOCIAL COUNCIL**

**SECRETARIAT**

**INTERNATIONAL COURT OF JUSTICE**

**TRUSTEESHIP COUNCIL[6]**

## General Assembly

### Subsidiary Organs
- Disarmament Commission
- Human Rights Council
- International Law Commission
- Joint Inspection Unit (JIU)
- Main committees
- Standing committees and ad hoc bodies

### Funds and Programmes[1]
- **UNDP** United Nations Development Programme
  - **UNCDF** United Nations Capital Development Fund
  - **UNV** United Nations Volunteers
- **UNEP[2]** United Nations Environment Programme
- **UNFPA** United Nations Population Fund
- **UN-HABITAT[2]** United Nations Human Settlements Programme
- **UNICEF** United Nations Children's Fund
- **WFP** World Food Programme (UN/FAO)

### Research and Training
- **UNIDIR** United Nations Institute for Disarmament Research
- **UNITAR** United Nations Institute for Training and Research
- **UNSSC** United Nations System Staff College
- **UNU** United Nations University

### Other Entities
- **ITC** International Trade Centre (UN/WTO)
- **UNCTAD[1,2]** United Nations Conference on Trade and Development
- **UNHCR[1]** Office of the United Nations High Commissioner for Refugees
- **UNOPS[1]** United Nations Office for Project Services
- **UNRWA[1]** United Nations Relief and Works Agency for Palestine Refugees in the Near East
- **UN-WOMEN[1]** United Nations Entity for Gender Equality and the Empowerment of Women

### Related Organizations
- **CTBTO** Preparatory Commission for the Comprehensive Nuclear-Test-Ban Treaty Organization
- **IAEA[1,3]** International Atomic Energy Agency
- **ICC** International Criminal Court
- **IOM[1]** International Organization for Migration
- **ISA** International Seabed Authority
- **ITLOS** International Tribunal for the Law of the Sea
- **OPCW[3]** Organization for the Prohibition of Chemical Weapons
- **WTO[1,4]** World Trade Organization

### HLPF
High-Level Political Forum on Sustainable Development

### Peacebuilding Commission

## Security Council

### Subsidiary Organs
- International Residual Mechanism for Criminal Tribunals
- Military Staff Committee
- Peacekeeping operations and political missions
- Sanctions committees (ad hoc)
- Standing committees and ad hoc bodies

## Economic and Social Council

### Functional Commissions[8]
- **ECA** Economic Commission for Africa
- **ECE** Economic Commission for Europe
- **ECLAC** Economic Commission for Latin America and the Caribbean
- **ESCAP** Economic and Social Commission for Asia and the Pacific
- **ESCWA** Economic and Social Commission for Western Asia

(Functional Commissions)
- Crime Prevention and Criminal Justice
- Narcotic Drugs
- Population and Development
- Science and Technology for Development
- Social Development
- Statistics
- Status of Women
- United Nations Forum on Forests

### Regional Commissions[8]

### Other Bodies[10]
- Committee for Development Policy
- Committee of Experts on Public Administration
- Committee on Non-Governmental Organizations
- Permanent Forum on Indigenous Issues
- **UNAIDS** Joint United Nations Programme on HIV/AIDS
- **UNGEGN** United Nations Group of Experts on Geographical Names
- **UNGGIM** Committee of Experts on Global Geospatial Information Management

### Research and Training
- **UNICRI** United Nations Interregional Crime and Justice Research Institute
- **UNRISD** United Nations Research Institute for Social Development

### Specialized Agencies[1,5]
- **FAO** Food and Agriculture Organization of the United Nations
- **ICAO** International Civil Aviation Organization
- **IFAD** International Fund for Agricultural Development
- **ILO** International Labour Organization
- **IMF** International Monetary Fund
- **IMO** International Maritime Organization
- **ITU** International Telecommunication Union
- **UNESCO** United Nations Educational, Scientific and Cultural Organization
- **UNIDO** United Nations Industrial Development Organization
- **UNWTO** World Tourism Organization
- **UPU** Universal Postal Union
- **WHO** World Health Organization
- **WIPO** World Intellectual Property Organization
- **WMO** World Meteorological Organization
- **WORLD BANK GROUP[7]**
  - **IBRD** International Bank for Reconstruction and Development
  - **IDA** International Development Association
  - **IFC** International Finance Corporation

## Secretariat

### Departments and Offices[9]
- **EOSG** Executive Office of the Secretary-General
- **DCO** Development Coordination Office
- **DESA** Department of Economic and Social Affairs
- **DGACM** Department for General Assembly and Conference Management
- **DGC** Department of Global Communications
- **DMSPC** Department of Management Strategy, Policy and Compliance
- **DOS** Department of Operational Support
- **DPO** Department of Peace Operations
- **DPPA** Department of Political and Peacebuilding Affairs
- **DSS** Department of Safety and Security
- **OCHA** Office for the Coordination of Humanitarian Affairs
- **OCT** Office of Counter-Terrorism
- **ODA** Office for Disarmament Affairs
- **OHCHR** Office of the United Nations High Commissioner for Human Rights
- **OIOS** Office of Internal Oversight Services
- **OLA** Office of Legal Affairs
- **OOSA** Office for Outer Space Affairs
- **OSAA** Office of the Special Adviser on Africa
- **SRSG/CAAC** Office of the Special Representative of the Secretary-General for Children and Armed Conflict
- **SRSG/SVC** Office of the Special Representative of the Secretary-General on Sexual Violence in Conflict
- **SRSG/VAC** Office of the Special Representative of the Secretary-General on Violence Against Children
- **UNDRR** United Nations Office for Disaster Risk Reduction
- **UNODC** United Nations Office on Drugs and Crime
- **UNOG** United Nations Office at Geneva
- **UN-OHRLLS** Office of the High Representative for the Least Developed Countries, Landlocked Developing Countries and Small Island Developing States
- **UNON** United Nations Office at Nairobi
- **UNOP[1]** United Nations Office for Partnerships
- **UNOV** United Nations Office at Vienna
- **UN YOUTH** United Nations Youth Office

Published by the United Nations Department of Global Communications 23-00013 – July 2023

### Notes:
1. Member of the United Nations System Chief Executives Board for Coordination (CEB).
2. The United Nations Office for Partnerships is the focal point vis-à-vis the United Nations Foundation, Inc.
3. IAEA and OPCW report to the Security Council and the General Assembly (GA).
4. WTO has no reporting obligation to the GA, but contributes on an ad hoc basis to GA and Economic and Social Council (ECOSOC) work on, inter alia, finance and development issues.
5. Specialized agencies are autonomous organizations whose work is coordinated through ECOSOC (intergovernmental level) and CEB (inter-secretariat level).
6. The Trusteeship Council suspended operations on 1 November 1994, as Palau, the last United Nations Trust Territory, became independent on 1 October 1994.
7. International Centre for Settlement of Investment Disputes (ICSID) and Multilateral Investment Guarantee Agency (MIGA) are not specialized agencies in accordance with Articles 57 and 63 of the Charter, but are part of the World Bank Group.
8. The secretariats of these organs are part of the United Nations Secretariat.
9. The Secretariat also includes the following offices: the Ethics Office, United Nations Ombudsman and Mediation Services, and the Office of Administration of Justice.
10. For a complete set of ECOSOC Subsidiary Bodies see un.org/ecosoc.

This Chart is a reflection of the functional organization of the United Nations System and for informational purposes only. It does not include all offices or entities of the United Nations System.

FIGURE 0.1. UN Organigram. For a full-color chart see https://www.un.org/en/delegate/page/un-system-chart.

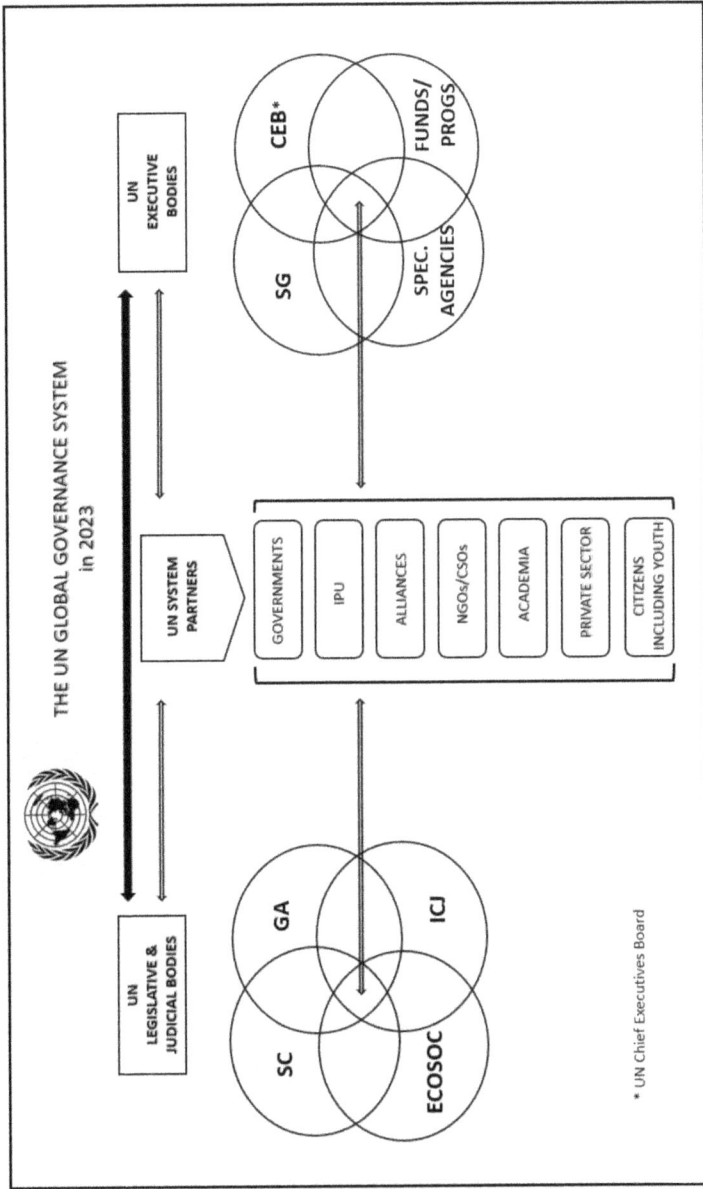

**THE UN GLOBAL GOVERNANCE SYSTEM in 2023**

UN LEGISLATIVE & JUDICIAL BODIES

UN SYSTEM PARTNERS

UN EXECUTIVE BODIES

GA
SC
ICJ
ECOSOC

GOVERNMENTS
IPU
ALLIANCES
NGOs/CSOs
ACADEMIA
PRIVATE SECTOR
CITIZENS INCLUDING YOUTH

CEB*
SG
FUNDS/PROGS
SPEC. AGENCIES

\* UN Chief Executives Board

**FIGURE 0.2.** The UN global governance system in 2023. *Source:* Anna von Sponeck.

# PREFACE

# Overcoming UN Marginalization— an Urgent Imperative

As we write, the United Nations is more needed than ever before and yet less relevant as a political actor than at any time since its establishment in 1945. Our intention in this book is to interpret this disturbing paradox, and what may be done to overcome it. This present set of circumstances is most relevant in the context of the war/peace agenda but applies increasingly to such crucial domains of global policy as climate change, ecological stability, health, human rights, regulating trade and investment, global migration, poverty alleviation, sanctions, and demilitarization/denuclearization.

In the background is the story behind the formation of a global organization more than a century ago in the aftermath of World War I. The League of Nations was originally put on the global agenda due to the insistence of the visionary American leader, President Woodrow Wilson, who believed that war was a barbaric and thoroughly outmoded way of resolving disputes among sovereign states and was hailed by the peoples of Western countries as a farsighted leader devoted to world peace.

It needs to be recalled that the European colonial system, although under challenge after World War I, still exerted direct and indirect control over most of the world's peoples, who were not represented at the peace talks in 1919 or invited to participate as members of the envisioned international institutions. Wilson did not challenge European colonialism but opposed only its extension to the fallen Ottoman and Habsburg empires after 1918.

After World War II it was recognized that Wilson had been ahead of his time in proposing an institutional framework with the proclaimed goals of establishing effective limits on unacceptable state behavior, somehow representing the peoples of the entire world, and engaging sovereign states geopolitically according to their status and capabilities as well as juridically to reflect their sovereignty. The public assumed and some leaders believed that the wartime alliance of victorious states over European fascism and Japanese imperialism would carry over to establish workable, equitable, and sustainable postwar peacetime arrangements. The devastation caused by the recently concluded war combined with the sense of worse to come, given the development of long-distance guided rocketry, culminating in the advent of the nuclear age at Hiroshima and Nagasaki. These developments gave new momentum to the recognition of an intensely practical need to establish viable global alternatives to war in reaction to serious conflicts among sovereign states.

However, as with the League, dominant global political actors seemed unready for endowing a new architecture of world order with necessary capabilities. The East/West tensions and a shared reluctance to establish a global institution with capabilities to override sovereign rights of states meant that retaining Western control over the essential workings of world order was given the highest policy priority. Even in the face of a rising tide of anti-colonial non-Western nationalism, the West continued to dominate lawmaking procedures and balance of power mechanisms on the global stage. Western statecraft remained protective of national prerogatives, especially control over national security, including military capabilities and the retention of military capabilities. This pattern reflected in part a reaction to the failed attempt at war prevention under the auspices of the League of Nations. There was greater support for a viable set of global institutions among political leaders in 1945 than in 1918, yet it was still woefully insufficient to enable the UN to become an effective war prevention institution in a global context of an emergent Cold War and unbreakable attachment to state sovereignty.

The opening words of the Preamble to the UN Charter signal a priority given to war prevention by the founders: "We the peoples of the world determined to save succeeding generations from the scourge of war have established the United Nations." The Preamble's inspirational sense of mission was largely absent from the substantive provisions of the Charter in which allocations of functions and roles of the various components of the UN system are specified. This priority was expressed by the legal limitations on war-making to instances of self-defense against prior armed attacks and authorized by the Security Council. Over the years the impact of these war prevention moves has been diluted by the periodic militarist behavior of leading states and by the right of veto possessed by the four winners in World War II plus China. The UN has also suffered from the obstacles to reform arising from changes in the global setting.

The UN was given an ambitious mission without any demonstrated willingness to create a global organization that reflected the civilizational diversity of the world. West-centrism at the UN was accentuated by freeing the five most powerful countries from the shackles of accountability. The UN was organized on this essentially *geopolitical* basis, which should have from its beginning lowered public expectations about its potential when it came to peace and security, as well as trade, investment, and human rights.

Despite these discouraging realities, all was not bleak. As European colonialism collapsed in country after country, the UN gained new degrees of legitimacy as non-Western membership and Global South activism increased. The UN continued, however, to disappoint many people around the world due to the paralyzing impacts of the East/West impasse in crucial policy domains, especially peace and security. What was gained by growing UN support for assertions of the right of self-determination and permanent sovereignty over natural resources was lost due to the emergence of a new phase of geopolitics that severely limited the role of the UN. Its core reality became the American/Soviet rivalry and its offsetting alliances and the accompanying nuclear arms race. It became clear to the public that security still depended on constantly enhanced military capabilities and the diplomatic ingenuity and prudence of leading sovereign states. Under these circumstances it is hardly surprising that a security regime emerged that was tied to deterrence and crisis management rather than respect for law, UN peace-oriented procedures, and a serious commitment to disarmament.

The US emerged from WW II as internationally more powerful and influential than the Soviet Union. It used its political leverage to try to gain control over initial UN operations. This gave rise in some quarters to a perception that the UN was an instrument of Western statecraft rather than an actor whose policies were guided by universal norms.

Disillusionment with the UN was premature and not fully justified. Few governments wanted the UN to fail in the manner of the League. The UN has succeeded in retaining the participation of even those states subject to strong opposition within the organization. Unlike the League, withdrawing membership from the UN never seemed a serious option for states that sharply dissented from UN majority viewpoints. Over the years, Israel and its main supporters have often complained loudly about Israel-bashing at the UN, but Israel has never seriously threatened withdrawal from the organization. The UN, despite its weakness and shortcomings, has been accepted as an indispensable part of the architecture of international relations. It is now almost inconceivable to imagine the world without the UN. At the same time, and it is a disturbing realization, it is equally hard to imagine the creation of a UN in the early twenty-first century framed as ambitiously as the UN was in 1945, much less an organization reframed to reflect the globalist policy priorities and world hierarchies of the 2020s.

There have been significant UN achievements, innovations, and adaptations over the years that exhibit institutional flexibility and resilience. The political independence of many countries in Asia, Africa, and Latin America created a more cosmopolitan UN that at least temporarily lent increased importance to the General Assembly as a principal organ of the UN that seemed more genuinely dedicated to world order values and global justice than did the Security Council. The increased prominence of its Afro-Asian membership achieved a collective identity via the formation of the Non-Aligned Movement, This initiative of the Global South sought noninvolvement in Cold War geopolitics and an increased appreciation of policy priorities involving global reform of the world economy, stressing a more equitable policy framework with respect to trade and investment. This led in the 1970s to a concerted effort at the UN, including calls for a new international economic order and the enthusiastic endorsement of the right of development as a primary sovereign prerogative.

These changes at the UN also led to anxieties in the North about adverse policy consequences of a more democratically oriented UN. There were worries about the challenges being directed at a market-driven world economy. This resulted in a backlash orchestrated by Western governments, with private sector backing, amounting to a North/South conflict configuration added to the East/West Cold War tensions. Although differently motivated, both the Soviet Union and the US joined forces to marginalize the General Assembly's role in relation to peace, security, and economic policy.

Another effect of the anti-Western turn at the UN was for these states to move outside the organization to shape global policy, especially with respect to the world economy. Powerful non-governmental free market initiatives were institutionalized by the private sector in the West. One influential pro-market response was the Trilateral Commission established in 1973. Undoubtedly the most effective response was that fashioned by corporate and banking interests, assuming its organizational identity as the World Economic Forum, which met annually with great fanfare in Davos, Switzerland. These initiatives sought to sidestep challenges to capitalism mounted by the Global South at the UN, as well as in other policy arenas, and to advance programs of their own. Among the countermoves to overcome challenges to neoliberal ideas of trade and investment was the intergovernmental formation of the so-called Group of Seven (G7), which was later enlarged to accommodate complaints of exclusion from the Global South and important emerging country economies including Saudi Arabia and India. The result was that the G7 shared the policy stage with the parallel Group of Twenty (G20). This accommodation of diversity lent both policymaking forums somewhat greater legitimacy and at the same time partially outsourced the policy role of the UN in the economic sphere.

Undoubtedly, the most significant unanticipated development in the activity of the UN was its involvement in areas of international concern and growing importance other than the headline issues of war/peace and the world economy. The UN as constituted and further expanded until it became accurate to refer to "the UN System," a myriad of agencies and commissions that function quasi-independently yet still beneath the broad umbrellas of the main organs of the UN and the overall administrative authority of the Secretary-General. These global issues are illustrative of the benefits of cooperation and shared knowledge with respect to health, culture, human rights, food, environment, education, children, and especially development.

The UN also proved its importance annually when world leaders traveled to New York City to deliver national policy statements and to meet with counterparts, the organization providing a leading space for media attention and high-level diplomatic interaction and even more importantly, enabling off-camera meetings with adversaries that sometimes paved the way to diplomatic accommodations and a reduction of tensions. In these respects, the UN attained a major relevance to the structure and processes of world order in a period of complex global developments in which the control of communications and management of economic interdependence were accorded as much attention as was the attainment of military dominance. To be sure, this role for the UN was not what its most ardent founders primarily had in mind when the Charter was drafted or the future contemplated. The UN was established for the overriding reason of helping to prevent a future major war, and such issues as development and human rights were initially seen as subordinate to this principal preoccupation, Yet over the years these latter concerns led the UN to make its most singular contributions to advancing human well-being.

It is sobering to take notice of a striking fact: despite intense conflict and close calls, no major war between geopolitical adversaries has occurred since the UN was established in 1945. No one can be sure that this would have been the case had the UN never been brought into existence.

## After the Cold War

There were high hopes that after the fall of the Berlin Wall in 1989 and the collapse of the Soviet Union a few years later that the UN could begin to function as intended with respect to peace and security.

These hopes became more well-grounded during the 1990 Gulf Crisis following the Iraqi conquest of Kuwait, when the UN Security Council seemed to function in a manner responsive to the Charter by imposing sanctions and authorizing the use of force to restore Kuwaiti sovereignty, rather than in an atmosphere dominated by the rivalry that was so paralyzing during the Cold War decades. Yet when military operations against Iraq began under US leadership, these hopes soon evaporated since the scope, course, and nature of the undertaking was controlled by Washington rather than the UN. This strengthened the impression that the UN in a war/peace setting is used as a geopolitical tool to give a cover of legitimacy to a military undertaking and not as an expression of world order values relating to the rule of law and observance of the UN Charter. As a result, although the approval of the use of force against Iraq in 1990 showed the possibilities of consensus in a war/peace setting, the implementation of the authorization began to erode trust among the leading governments and gave rise to a renewed concern that the UN was being used to provide an initial rationalization for the use of non-defensive force (remembering that the UN Charter only gives states a delimited right of self-defense under Charter Article 51), but once operations got underway, the control shifted to reflect the geopolitical priorities of the Western states that supplied the weapons and military personal for the actual operations.

When in 1991 sanctions were replaced by a military operation in confronting Saddam Hussein's conquest and annexation of Kuwait, with the support of all five permanent members of the Security Council, this expression of geopolitical consensus led the then American president, George H. W. Bush, to proclaim "a new world order." This mood soon dissipated, because the United States never seriously contemplated ceding independent authority in the peace and security agenda to the UN.

The failure of world leaders, especially those in Europe and the United States, to seize this golden opportunity to seek necessary and desirable global reforms after the Cold War ended with the collapse of the USSR. Unlike after the two world wars, the end of the Cold War was not treated by the East/West powers as an occasion to act with resolve to prevent some future recurrence of calamity or to enhance the capabilities and authority of the UN to address such new and intensifying world order challenges as climate change, migration, poverty, transnational disease, and criminality. There was no sense of urgency. No major leader articulated a rationale for global collective action. The main winners in the Cold War—the US, the UK, and France—saw the collapse of the Soviet Union and the end of strategic rivalry as not only a gain for world peace but an opportunity to consolidate their geopolitical and ideological primacy. This focus produced a series of misleading interpretations as to why the West won the Cold War and what to expect in the next phase of world politics. Fukuyama's *The End of History*, Huntington's *The Clash of Civilizations* and Kaplan's *The Coming Anarchy* epitomized the zeitgeist of the 1990s, with a notable failure of influential members of the political class in the West to come forward with any kind of constructive vision of what might be done to improve the ethical, legal, ecological, and institutional sides of world order on behalf of human well-being.

Instead, increasing the GNP of individual states and their private sector elites became the centerpiece of global order, with growth and development set forth as primary goals for North and South alike. The *real* new world order involved the spread of market-oriented constitutionalism to the four corners of the earth. In other words, it was neoliberal capitalism not humane global governance that led the way to the transformed priorities of the post–Cold War world order, and this again situated the UN on the sidelines of world order for reasons quite different than earlier.

In retrospect, there was a failure to take advantage of the end of the Cold War to upgrade the UN by making it politically and fiscally more independent, to seek serious nuclear disarmament and overall demilitarization, and to take steps to minimize violent geopolitics, as well as to promote human security by addressing the existential concerns of humanity relating to the mitigation of poverty and other forms of avoidable human suffering and the denial of fundamental human rights associated with meeting material needs of people. Seen in retrospect, the decade of the 1990s was a missed opportunity with tragic results. The peoples of the world are now enduring the harmful effects of this shortsighted economistic mindset in a variety of ways that could have been avoided. Transformative initiatives if successfully undertaken would have transformed the entire atmosphere of world order in a manner that would have led the UN to conform more closely to the expectations that existed at the time it was established in 1945. These failures of oversight serving the global interest are manifestations of severe deficiencies of the current world order that imperil the human future as much as does the danger of new wars.

Despite this discouraging failure to take advantage of the favorable situation existing in the early 1990s, the UN did take some positive steps. The organization led an effort to set forth a normative agenda for the peoples of the world, first in the form of the Millennium Goals, rearticulated as the Sustainable Development Goals (SDGs) to be realized between 2015 and 2030. Such an agenda has its focus on human security aspects of international life that would benefit from dedicated efforts by governments, international institutions, and civil society. Attempts were made to implement the SDGs by engaging civil society organizations in the work of the UN as never before.

The end of the Cold War provided an unusual opportunity to consider favorably a variety of constructive and entirely feasible proposals for endowing the UN with enhanced capabilities, authority, and responsibility, more detachment from the vagaries of geopolitics, and increased accountability to the global rule of law by all states. Among these options were Charter reform, altered patterns of permanent membership in the Security Council, elimination or abridgement of the veto power, independent funding and fiscal authority, widening the authority of the International Court of Justice, and increased autonomy for the Secretary-General. None of these options were seriously pursued during those years in the decade-long gap between the Cold War ending and the real new world order preoccupations taking over. It was during the 1990s that the opportunity for global reform was lost to "the clash of civilizations," Middle East turmoil, and Afghan chaos. Then came the geopolitical fireworks of 2001 following the 9/11 attacks and most recently during the Ukraine War. The proxy struggles among the United States, China, and Russia for geopolitical alignment are casting a complicating cloud over the future of Ukraine.

This mood of complacency about global reform in general and UN reform in particular is expressed by the failure to heed the proposals in numerous reports about ways to strengthen the UN. These reports have been gathering dust on library shelves due to the lack of political will on the part of leading member states. Also lost was the hope of bringing civil society actors into the global governance dynamics, which could help to create greater transparency and accountability for UN operations, as well as to promote the democratization of global governance.

There was a second chance for taking steps to strengthen the UN in accord with the approach of the millennial year of 2000, but here also the political will to do so was too weak at intergovernmental and civil society levels. This disappointing mood was expressed by Bill Clinton, America's president from 1992 to 2000, when he delivered an uninspiring message to the UN on the eve of the new millennium which set the tone with the dismissive admonition to "do more with less." In such an atmosphere it is not surprising that the end of the Cold War did little to enhance the governance role and capabilities of the UN.

The last century ended without the UN being able to take advantage of relative calmness in international relations, epitomized by the absence of strategic tensions among major states, although there were troubling regional conflicts brewing in South Asia and in the Middle East. Even this assessment may be too favorable. Two trends were working against reliance on the UN: first, the organization was perceived as hostile to Israel, world capitalism, and some aggressive moves in Western foreign policy; and second, the West, especially, the US government, was retreating from its embrace of liberal internationalism, seeking in various ways to substitute itself for the UN as the principal anchor of a global peace, security, and constitutional order.

This is a more important consideration than it first appears. Given gross power and wealth disparities, a law-governed world order will depend on the five permanent members of the Security Council (P5) coming to a genuine recognition that respect for and the bolstering of the authority of international law and the UN serves their short-term interests as well as their longer-term visions. Until geopolitical actors grasp this shift in realistically conceived national interests, the world will move from crisis to crisis with no positive outcome in sight. Yet achieving this shift will require a repudiation of those aspects of geopolitical governance and the private sector making global militarism and predatory capitalism alive and basically untouchable. In essence, moves away from the unipolar management of global security, as has been the case since the early 1990s, should be understood as giving rise to greater multipolarity in the management of peace, security, and development.

## Continuing Decline

The relevance of the UN continued to diminish in the early decades of the new century. As mentioned, after the Cold War the aggressive warfare against Iraq in 2003 and Ukraine in 2022 left the UN on the sidelines despite the core norms of the Charter being violated by two of the five permanent members of the Security Council. The UN played a facilitative role in sponsoring the Paris Agreement on climate change in 2015 but seemed helpless three years later when the United States withdrew. Despite the imperative of cooperative problem-solving to address issues of global scope from the perspective of the public good and human well-being, statism dominated responses to the COVID pandemic (2020–2023), global migration, and the destabilizing effects of growing inequalities within and among states. The UN has *voice*, especially through the pronouncements of the Secretary-General, yet lacks *will*, conceived of as fulfilling goals of the Charter, respect for international law, and imposing accountability on wrongdoers. As such, states and geopolitical actors retain near exclusive authority for the management of global security according to political criteria.

## UN Crisis

This disturbing pattern of the UN's decline has reached unprecedented crisis levels. The disturbing developments described above have been accentuated in recent years. From the perspective of strengthening the UN and respect for international law, the most alarming global trend is the rise of autocratic patterns of political leadership even in countries with long traditions of democratic governance. This kind of political leadership, often backed by public opinion, tends toward ultranationalist foreign policies highly skeptical of according respect to external obligations and also rejects the value of international institutions such as the UN and the EU.

A further pressure from similar sources is associated with global migration, pushing many national societies to scapegoat immigrants, refugees, and asylum seekers. Such often cruel responses produce tight societal embraces of exclusionary versions of national identity. As a result, universalist values associated with humane governance are cast aside as is the acceptance of external standards associated with international law, human rights, and UN authority. The UN is contemptuously looked upon as irrelevant by contemporary versions of right-wing populism, and the reality of global-scale problems is denied.

What makes this situation even more disturbing is the negative quality of global leadership. With 196 formally independent countries, the world needs both the coordinating mechanisms of the UN and enlightened forms of global leadership by dominant states to shape a consensus on matters requiring unified global action.

There are contrary geopolitical trends that could evolve in ways that would renew confidence in the UN as an institutional matrix with an indispensable role to play if humanity is to meet the looming challenges of global scope and longer time horizons. Such trends could bring new vitality to the UN as reflecting a series of global developments, including de-Westernization, the rise of transnational civic activism, intergenerational responsibility, and a renewal of support for human rights and greater ecological sensitivity as more universally reflecting values without threatening civilizational diversity.

## Our Undertaking

It is against such a background that we offer this book. It tries its best to document the failures of the UN without overlooking its positive contributions to peace and justice. Our intention is to make a case for supporting the UN as an indispensable feature of twenty-first-century world order. Our effort is to explore feasible ways to strengthen the UN so that it might better serve the purposes of the UN Charter while being mindful of global challenges that have emerged over the decades, some of which are now reaching crisis proportions. The world has changed in fundamental technological, geopolitical, social, cultural, political, ecological, and ethical ways over the course of the seventy-five-plus years that the UN has been in existence, and yet the UN structure remains largely frozen in the global setting that was present at the time of its founding.

As analyzed, the world is currently experiencing a dysfunctional ultranationalist backlash against all forms of internationalism, including the UN. We believe that there will arise a new movement for revitalizing democracy, a stronger UN, and a more benevolent global leadership, and we write with faith that in the end prudence, rationality, empathy, expanded time horizons, and mechanisms facilitating cooperation and imposing accountability will emerge. Ecological and geopolitical forces cannot any longer be adequately accommodated by a state-centric world order, and as this reality manifests itself, new cycles of internationalist thought and action will arise, perhaps in the form of a global movement that involves the collaboration of transnational civil society activists and those governments better attuned to the demands and needs of humanity, entailing safeguarding the long-term viability of the earth's natural habitat.

The deforestation of the Amazon Rainforest, worldwide wildfires, floods, severe heat waves, prolonged civil strife and chaotic conditions in several parts of the world, and the drought in Africa's Sahel region as well as the global COVID-19 pandemic are giving stern warnings about the kind of future that will confront humanity if fundamental relations between human activity and its natural surroundings are left unattended or are irresponsibly addressed by territorial governments and global corporate conglomerates. The UN provides the only architecture of problem-solving that is potentially not subordinated to the territorializing priorities of sovereign states or to the geopolitical ambitions of the most influential political actors on the global stage at a given time. For this architecture to work in the manner originally intended and now urgently needed requires that a great effort be made by the most enlightened forces of the political class that has set policy for globalization-from-above to become receptive to the demands, warnings, and grievances of an aroused multitude representing forces of globalization-from-below. In this spirit of informed realistic hopefulness, which functions as a thin veneer covering diagnoses of despair, we offer this book.

*Richard Falk and Hans von Sponeck*

# FOREWORD

## by Dr. Walden Bello

*Former Independent Member of the Philippine House of Representatives, Writer, and Activist*

How critical is the United Nations, a product of the twentieth century, to the maintenance of global order in the twenty-first century? To this query two eminent international relations scholars, Richard Falk and Hans von Sponeck, bring a perspective that is sympathetic to the UN but is at the same time very much aware of the different ways that the lofty mission assigned to this body at its founding in San Francisco seventy-eight years ago has been thwarted, derailed, or watered down.

No government has ceased to be a member of the UN, nor has the UN crashed in the same way its predecessor, the League of Nations, did in the late 1930s. Its peacekeeping forces make up a thin blue line separating contending forces in many parts of the world. It has become the principal arena for arriving at an intergovernmental solution to the climate crisis. And its General Assembly has become an indispensable institution for political and ideological debate, with resolutions that, though they may be breached in practice by powerful states like the US and Israel, nevertheless serve as the last word when it comes to legitimacy.

And yet, as Falk and Sponeck acknowledge, when it comes to resolving conflicts, geopolitics reigns, with the Security Council, the UN's ultimate decision-making body, either paralyzed by the veto power exercised by each of the Big Five or simply ignored by the global hegemon, as in the case of US's unilateral invasion of Iraq in 2003. And when it comes to governance of the global economy, the UN was outmaneuvered early on by the Bretton Woods institutions—the World Bank and the International Monetary Fund—which, while formally part of the UN System, actually serve the interests of the United States and other big capitalist powers.

According to liberal internationalist theorists like John Ikenberry, the UN at its founding in 1945 embodied aspirations and institutions derived from the ideology of liberal internationalism that had accompanied the spread of democracy since the late eighteenth century. This was a complex and conflictive process in which its values and institutions were entangled with capitalism, empire, hegemony, and racism. Yet while it has been compromised by its historical association with these forces, the matrix of liberal democracy and liberal internationalism has shown a capability of being "dis-embedded" from them to offer a better way of organizing relations within states and among states. This has been the source of its dynamism.

Dis-embeddedness can, however, never be complete, for the liberal democratic/liberal internationalist matrix cannot escape power relations. In other words, US hegemony props up the current global order of which the UN is a member, and this accounts for the dilemmas, contradictions, and powerlessness on which the UN often finds itself impaled. Liberal internationalism's mix of universalist values and great power hegemony may be hypocritical, but for committed liberal internationalists like Ikenberry, it is the best that people can hope for since a world order based only on norms and institutions of liberty, justice, and equality would be utopian.

This liberal internationalist order is, however, under severe stress at present. One cannot understand the state of play of the UN without placing it in the context of the current crisis of this broader system underpinned by global capitalism and US political and military power. The most striking manifestation of this crisis has been the dizzying rise of China to global economic prominence, such that, though it has not yet displaced the United States as the world's biggest economy, it has become the center of global capital accumulation, accounting for 28 percent of all growth worldwide in the five years from 2013 to 2018, more than twice the share of the United States. The emergence of China has had a massive ongoing impact on global geopolitics and on the multilateral system of which the UN is a prominent part.

The rise of China presents both challenges and opportunities for the United Nations.

On the one hand, just like the US-Soviet rivalry during the Cold War, it has the potential of providing the countries of the Global South more space both outside and within the UN to push their interests collectively with less fear of unilateral retaliatory measures from the United States and more opportunities to draw economic benefits from both sides. To a great extent, this process is already ongoing, with more and more governments in the Global South beating a path to Beijing for economic assistance instead of to the World Bank and the International Monetary Fund, thus reducing the power of the bank and the fund to dictate their economic policies.

One the other hand, China, probably being among the most "Westphalian" of contemporary states, cannot be counted on to support initiatives driven by human rights concerns such as the evolving UN principle of the "right to protect" that limits the principle of national sovereignty to prevent genocide or massive violations of democratic rights. Thus, while most members of the UN and even the Association of Southeast Asian Nations (ASEAN), known previously for its strict adherence to noninterference in the affairs of one's neighbors, have treated the Myanmar military junta that grabbed power in 2021 from Aung San Suu Kyi's National League of Democracy government as a pariah, China has not cut off economic aid and diplomatic support for the generals under the principle of noninterference.

The challenge is to further dis-embed the United Nations and the multilateral system from Western hegemony while avoiding its becoming entangled with or subordinated to the interests of another hegemon. The goal is to make the UN and the multilateral system more and more relatively autonomous from global power relations. Falk and Sponeck are, of course, aware that a complete disentanglement of the UN from the dynamics of global power relations is not possible. They are, however, more hopeful than Ikenberry and others about the UN's being able to achieve a significant degree of autonomy from the play of power relations. Their perspective of "realism with hope" sees the very problems that seem so intractable, such as climate change, as providing the goad that can make an accumulation of "incremental" political and institutional reforms translate eventually into a major opportunity for institutional transformation.

Falk and Sponeck treat us to a lively discussion of possible reforms in four critical areas. The first is whether the Security Council's Big Five will be able to come together to deal with problems with massive transborder consequences, such as climate change and war. The second is whether the Secretary-General as the "world's most legitimate moral authority figure" will be given the political space to play a more active role in connecting the UN with the strivings and aspirations of the peoples of the world. Third is how the resources can be brought together to address massive problems that demand responses of the scale of the Marshall Plan or the space race. Fourth is how to fashion a more integrated and efficient institutional response to threats to international peace and security that would involve coordinating the capabilities of the Security Council, the General Assembly, and, in some instances, the International Court of Justice.

Whatever may be their regard for it, there are few international actors that would consider the UN dispensable. That already gives us a leg up compared to other eras when it comes to the creation or transformation of global relations. A conjunction of the right circumstances, the existence of political will, and the state of play of geopolitical relations provided the opening for the creation or transformation of global institutions after the Second World War, when the UN was founded, and during the 1950s and 1960s, when the United Nations both helped bring about and was significantly reshaped by decolonization. Richard Falk and Hans von Sponeck's solid and sympathetic scholarship gives us hope that a creative conjuncture of the right events can happen again.

# PART ONE

## AN EVOLVING NARRATIVE

# ONE

# Profiling the UN

## THE ORIGINAL FRAMEWORK, ADAPTIVE MIRACLE, AND THE CHALLENGES AHEAD

### The UN as a Polycentric Hierarchical System

The United Nations is a complex organization consisting of many rather autonomous parts with distinct substantive mandates. See figure 0.2 for an overview of the UN System. It is a dynamic group of actors that have evolved over time with respect to both worldwide reputation and operational balance sheet of achievements and disappointments. Sometimes, the UN shows the world how important it has become, as it did during the COVID-19 pandemic when the moral authority of the UN Secretary-General, António Guterres, rose above the partisan clamors and nationalist behavior of the leaders of sovereign states.

As well, the world public came to realize during the pandemic that the UN is more than the Security Council and General Assembly. It understood the crucial role played by the World Health Organization (WHO) as a source of reliable and objective information, guidance, authority, and material assistance, which was invaluable for the least developed countries throughout the health crisis. The WHO also was generally regarded as a trustworthy framework for considering issues of global concern from the perspective of human interests. In this regard, it is illuminating that the coronavirus disease became designated a "pandemic" rather than a challenging epidemic only when the WHO declared it to be such on March 11, 2020.

Yet even in this moment of internationalist recognition and dependence, there was a pushback, expressed by the US government's harsh criticism and defunding of the WHO. These measures of disapproval were followed shockingly by its temporary withdrawal from the WHO in the midst of the pandemic. These clumsy, vindictive, self-destructive policies of the Trump presidency seemed partly intended to shift blame away from the deplorable initial responses to the health challenge by the political leadership in the United States. It was one of the most irresponsible geopolitical temper tantrums of all time, second only to the reckless temerity of blaming this lethal disease altogether on China, which is not to deny the unacceptable Chinese handling of the *outbreak* of the disease in Wuhan in late 2019. Failures of states to cooperate in response to the pandemic in a manner sensitive to the global scope of the crisis and the disparities in coping mechanisms among sovereign states increased the suffering attributable to the disease. It is also an important reminder of the need for states to reimagine their national interests as they relate to the United Nations, as well as to recognize the imperatives of cooperation to address collective goods problems of global scope.

Overall, the UN has had ups and downs during its more than seventy-five years of existence. As mentioned, when an international crisis exists that affects the well-being of humanity as distinct from specific countries, the UN is often the last best hope for a collective response that enjoys support worldwide, but even here the organization has often disappointed its most ardent supporters, including failures at the level of action. This happened during the coronavirus pandemic and to a less clear extent in fashioning a robust cooperative approach to the threats posed by climate change, an effort that did lead to the widely heralded Paris Climate Change Agreement of 2015. Yet at other times, the marginality of the UN while violence rages, famines threaten, and genocidal onslaughts occur leads many persons, as well as media commentary and governmental policy to dismiss the UN as an indispensable actor when it comes to addressing the biggest challenges of world. We regard such dismissal as unfair and as inaccurate as uncritical endorsement of the UN in spite of its mixed record.

*Limits of Authority, Capabilities, and Political Will
versus Unlimited Expectations*

The UN from its inception was not given the authority to address situations internal to sovereign states and was assigned no direct responsibility for world order challenges of global scope such as population pressures, planetary pollution, and migration trends. Its security writ was limited to the international sphere of interaction among states, although as globalizing effects became problematic and interdependence more pronounced, the lines separating national, international, and global concerns seemed to become unavoidably blurred.

In this regard disappointing results happened throughout the internal long war in Syria (2011–21), during which more than 500,000 civilians were killed in the country, millions more displaced internally and regionally, several ancient cities devastated, and international crimes frequently occurred. The UN failed to stop the violence or halt reliance on criminal tactics. Such dramas of inaction occur whenever there exists a political impasse at the geopolitical level of world politics on a vital matter, most evident in UN settings when the five permanent members of the Security Council (P5) are split, which was the case with respect to Syria when the P5 members intervened on opposite sides. Sometimes when geopolitical actors agree on policy, effective action is possible under UN auspices, as happened in authorizing the Gulf War of 1991 in response to Iraqi aggression against Kuwait.

Even during the Cold War years, the rival superpowers and their allies sometimes did manage to act together, most notably with respect to crisis management of the risks posed by the dangers of nuclear war. In this spirit, the United States and the Soviet Union issued an important joint statement in 1985: "Nuclear war cannot be won and must never be fought." Unfortunately, the war planners and weapons labs in both countries continued the search for superior nuclear weapons and war plans that sought victory rather than settling for a permanent strategic stalemate.[1]

Less prominent inaction, although also disturbing, is UN inaction in those circumstances where human ordeal is not linked closely enough to strategic interests to generate the political will to commit resources, and possibly lives, to stopping massive suffering in what is perceived to be a geopolitically marginal context. Typical geopolitical evasions are expressed by the realist meme "we have no dog in this fight" and applied to bloodshed in the Balkans or by a presidential decree forbidding US bureaucrats from using the word *genocide* to describe the obviously "genocidal" massacres that took place in Rwanda in 1994. The prohibition was imposed to lessen humanitarian pressures within and outside the US government to act, whether on its own or through the UN, to stop the killing.[2]

At other times, geopolitical forces suspend disagreements to facilitate a consensus on action that produces chaos rather than bringing peace. In such circumstances the UN can become an instrument of the very war-making it was established to prevent. This happened in 2011 when the Security Council compromised, authorizing a limited humanitarian use of force in Libya to protect the civilian population of Benghazi from an alleged threat of genocide by government forces.[3] When it came to implementation, NATO, the UN's delegated agent of enforcement, pursued an unauthorized regime-changing course of action. This was a clear expansion of the Security Council mandate and a violation of trust by the several states persuaded to abstain because of the strictly limited mission authorized by the UN Security Council resolution. Maintaining an atmosphere of trust among geopolitical rivals at the UN, especially within the Security Council in situations where a use of force is authorized, may be as important for UN legitimacy and effectiveness as it is to seek political compromises or find common ground between parties to a conflict.

The UN's public image suffered, especially in the Global South, from the failure of the political organs of the UN to challenge punitive national and international sanctions imposed on Iran and Venezuela during the ravages of the 2020 pandemic. In this sense, as much as we believe that the world needs a more empowered and respected UN, it is important to recognize that up to the present there have been some occasions and issues on which the UN has responded admirably, but more often it has not been able to fulfill the core Charter goal of war prevention.

The UN as presently constituted cannot be expected to do any better than what these geopolitical actors permit or undertake themselves. It is clarifying to appreciate that such geopolitical limitations on UN authority resulted from deliberate and fundamental features of the original design of the UN. This design is expressed through voting rules applicable at the Security Council and in relation to a variety of Charter provisions, including the selection of the Secretary-General, amendments to the Charter, and convening a conference of the membership devoted to global reform. It seems that wartime cooperation during the struggle against fascism in Europe and imperialism in Asia misled the public, and even the founders of the UN, as to what to expect from the new organization. This wartime optimism vanished soon after the Allies achieved victory. Only fears of World War III and worries about the recurrence of the Great Depression induced moderation of conflictual impulses. The UN was born and evolved through the decades in such an adversary atmosphere.

### The Organizational, Structural, and the Operational Reality

It is useful to think of three different initial dimensions of the UN System: institutional/ organizational, structural, and operational.[4] Roughly distinguished, the *institutional/organizational* dimension is descriptive of the many distinct platforms and organizational arrangements that together make up what has come to be called "the UN System," drawing a primary distinction between "political organs" and "specialized agencies, funds, and programmes"; the *structural* dimension is concerned with the constitutional arrangements that distribute functions and roles to the systemic units, but also specifies how states become members and how members participate, with attention to the tensions between "sovereign rights," "geopolitical autonomy," and "UN authority"; the *operational* dimension is descriptive of the practice of the UN in a wide array of situations over the course of UN history and how that practice reflects and alters expectations associated with structure and policy outcomes.

#### INSTITUTIONAL/ORGANIZATIONAL OBSERVATIONS

The public understanding of the UN then and now is overwhelmingly focused on the central war prevention undertaking set forth in the Preamble to the Charter, yet as we shall show this is a misleading form of reductionism with respect to an appraisal of the significance of the UN and what it would mean for the political well-being of the world's people if the UN did not exist or were to disappear. The management of the world economy was always given a substantive importance approaching that accorded the war/peace agenda, but for a variety of reasons, it was largely assigned a different organizational track, referred to as "the Bretton Woods Institutions," especially the World Bank and IMF (and the later World Trade Organization organizationally situated outside the UN System). The managerial challenges associated with the world economy gave rise as well to the less formally structured frameworks operating outside the UN, becoming known as the Group of Seven (G7) and Group of Twenty (G20). These policy platforms outside the UN were further complemented by private sector and civil society organizations, most significantly the Trilateral Commission, the World Economic Forum, and the World Social Forum.

The governing elites of leading capitalist countries after World War II had worries that the Great Depression of the 1930s would recur unless the world economy was better managed. In contrast were initiatives arising from Global South concerns that the promotion of profits and plunder by corporate and financial influence would continue to shape the world economy. These institutions also developed structures and procedures pertaining to funding and weighted voting, exhibiting the hierarchy of influence among market economies.

There is less awareness in the media and public opinion about what was well understood by UN founders—to wit, that world peace depended on more than prohibiting force, that it required a less dramatic set of undertakings, especially considering the diversities of states that made up UN membership, such as their differing priorities, civilizational identities, and resource endowments. This meant that if the UN was to succeed, it had to promote creative linkages among peace, security, and development, as well as deal with the peacetime challenges of health, employment, education, culture, law, and human rights in a functional manner that was as far removed from geopolitical tensions as possible.

This turn toward "realism" can be seen differently and more ambiguously. The veto was the main nonnegotiable price paid for vital assurances of Great Power membership and participation. It likely explains the perseverance of the UN despite many stressful periods as a global actor and the somewhat surprising fact that almost every state, large or small, maintained its membership and took advantage of its participation through good times and bad, an experience contrasting with the League of Nation's loss of participation by Great Powers. This is part of the reason why the hopes surrounding the establishment of the League were doomed from the start.

Another line of explanation for burdening the UN with the P5 veto was to accommodate the Soviet Union, whose leader made clear that Soviet participation in an organization with a Euro-American voting majority was dependent on assurances that the UN would lack the capability to override the strategic interests of the P5. The veto has been used over the years by Western powers to avoid Charter constraints and UN majorities, but in 1945 its central role was to secure Soviet participation without which the whole undertaking would lack credibility from its inception.

Yet it is most uncertain whether the road not taken would have turned out better. The League of Nations experience suggests that if the Great Powers cannot control the game they will not play. At least the UN has created multiple games within its organizational architecture. Although the biggest games of all, the war game and the transnational economic game, have essentially remained subject to geopolitics beyond the regulatory reach of the UN or international law, multiple other games such as disaster relief, health, cultural heritage, and multilateral cooperation with regard to the global commons and the environment have engaged all states in generally mutually beneficial ways. Dramatic increases in interconnectedness, complexity, and transnational networking associated with digitization of communications and relationships, as well as shifts in the locus of political conflict, challenge the UN. To make the UN effective given these globalizing conditions presupposes a gradual empowerment of the UN to shrink the influence of geopolitics. Such adjustments are imperative if the UN is to satisfy the growing demand for globalized solutions to issues associated with armed conflict, economic development, ecological sustainability, and more broadly, human security.

As conditions changed, the organizational profile of the UN evolved in response. Sustainable development and human rights became more important, while upholding labor standards and promoting cultural life diminished in significance. These assessments are constantly changing as policy priorities shift in response to changing conditions. Although the hope had been to shield the specialized agencies of the UN System from political controversy, the ironies have been that important member states, especially the United States and Israel, have more often expressed their frustrations in relation to the UN Human Rights Council, UNRWA, UNFPA, UNESCO, and even WHO than to the Security Council and the General Assembly. Such displeasure is expressed verbally and, more tangibly, by withholding funding and suspending participation, at least for long enough to exhibit displeasure or to reflect the viewpoint of a particular national leadership.

As suggested above, changes in the global setting shift the spotlight of attention with respect to organizational relevance. Until the coronavirus pandemic struck the planet in 2020 as an invisible meteor, for the public the WHO was a relatively unknown UN specialized agency and inadequately appreciated even by health specialists a source of indispensable information, especially for the less developed countries. WHO also disseminated best practices pertaining to serious health challenges. Specialized agencies can become arenas of intense controversy when policy divergencies emerge in relation to internationally controversial issues, especially involving countries that are accustomed to being a law unto themselves. In this regard the *functional* approach to international relations that had hoped to create a system of apolitical problem-solving agencies relying on science and expert opinion to give the range of international institutions a set of capabilities that could perform without the distraction of political tensions of member states was badly hampered by disturbing trends toward the politicization of knowledge.

## Structural Considerations

The structural character of the UN can be comprehended in two principal ways by the organizational chart (figure 0.2) that depicts the various components of the UN System. It also shows their relationships to the extent set forth in the constitutional framework provided by the UN Charter. Both organizationally and operationally the UN System has changed over time, reflecting an impressive ability to adapt to changed needs and take account of new knowledge about global dynamics, altering our understanding of coordination and cooperation and the distribution of authority within the UN, as for instance, among principal organs of the UN, such as the Security Council, the General Assembly, the Secretary-General, and the International Court of Justice.

In a crude sense, the Security Council is the UN decision-making body that gives overt weight to inequalities in status and capabilities among member states. When the P5 agree, the Security Council possesses almost unlimited potential authority. When the P5 disagree strongly, the Security Council is generally paralyzed, lacking the authority to even offer an opinion critical of Charter violations.

The General Assembly is more of a public forum that reflects the sovereign equality of all member states and provides an arena for non-Western countries, especially the developing world, to express their grievances and seek greater policy influence by the exercise of their recommendatory authority. In theory, if the Security Council fails to act in response to a situation threatening world peace, the Uniting for Peace resolution vests in the General Assembly a residual role at times of international emergencies to propose and authorize action to restore peace and security.[5] In practice, the P5, despite their differences with one another, are hesitant to support a wider application of UN authority than is present in the UN Charter, which indirectly challenges their future control over the peace and security agenda. It is rarely commented upon, but retaining geopolitical prerogatives has seemed more important even to the NATO members of the P5 than empowering the General Assembly with residual authority to act.

The Secretary-General plays executive and administrative roles within the UN and can express political opinions on matters of global concern, especially as comments on unfolding global crises. The Secretary-General is elected to a five-year term, which can be renewed once for another five years, following a recommendation by the Security Council and a vote of the General Assembly.

Finally, the International Court of Justice (ICJ) provides the UN with the highest source of judicial authority on the world stage. The Court is available to resolve legal disputes among states, but without authority to take up cases unless the state parties give consent in advance or in relation to a particular dispute, which is rarely given. ICJ authority does not automatically produce compliance as governments do not consistently implement its decisions even after participating in the process, making enforcement a problem that is available to be called upon if a Security Council consensus so directs. Yet if this happens, dangerous friction may be the consequence.

The ICJ also has the capacity to respond to legal questions put to it by UN organs and agencies by rendering Advisory Opinions, which seem authoritative from a juridical standpoint but are not legally binding and have a poor record of engendering political respect. Advisory Opinions have added influential jurisprudential understanding of important contested issues in international life such as the legal status of nuclear weapons or of the Israeli separation wall in Occupied Palestine.[6] These ICJ outcomes are important contributions within spheres of *symbolic politics* and often exert influence on civil society activism, but when it comes to altering the behavior of states or the UN itself, the results to date have been disappointing. By labeling ICJ responses to requests for Advisory Opinions as "advisory," or non-obligatory, the Statute of the ICJ deliberately disempowers the UN from insisting on respect for international law by all its members, sending an unfortunate message to the world.

Part of the complexity of the UN is due to certain contradictory elements in its makeup and behavior. The Preamble conveys a grandiose picture of the role of the UN, but when we come to the Articles or provisions of the Charter that set forth the roles and functions of the main organs of the UN, we are confronted by the centrality of member states, as represented by national governments, in the functioning of the UN and the absence of any sense of representation or procedures for meaningful participation, much less transparency and accountability to the people of the world. A fundamental contradiction is present in the Charter between national sovereignty of states as the highest source of authority in the UN governance structure and respect for international law as overriding the political will of states. It suggests that the UN has an unacknowledged mandate to hold only the weak and less dangerous states accountable to the Charter and international law but fails to even make legal attempts to constrain the strongest and most dangerous states should they or their friends engage in aggressive warfare or other forms of unlawful behavior.

Although this feature of the UN helps explain its disappointing record with respect to constraining the behavior of the P5 and their close allies, it is an accommodation to the realities of a world order in which governance depends so heavily on the quality of geopolitical leadership. The formative ideas about the UN were that it needed to accommodate geopolitics and state sovereignty, while at the same time aspiring to universality to enhance its effectiveness and legitimacy through the inclusiveness of its membership.

Another major limitation of the UN resulted from the inconclusiveness and diminished legitimacy arising from the acceptance of European colonial arrangements, which in 1945 continued to disenfranchise and underrepresent many national societies in Asia and Africa. Their indirect representation via colonial authority deprived the UN of legitimacy in most of the non-Western world, but this was overcome by stages as anti-colonial struggles achieved a string of successes resulting in the replacement of colonies by independent states that were admitted to the UN. As the winds of change gained force, the UN itself renounced colonialism and sided with the struggles of colonized peoples for political independence, invoking their inalienable right of self-determination. It was one of the important unanticipated characteristics of the UN to demonstrate political flexibility by modifying its identity in ways to make good on the claim of representing the peoples of the world. Impressively, the UN managed to achieve these results despite Cold War tensions. The admission of former European colonies as new members had an impact, none greater than partially redirecting the energies of the UN to the development agenda. The later addition of environment protection to the list of primary UN concerns illustrated a different kind of adaptation to changed conditions of global significance. As earlier commented upon, despite the difficulty of formally amending its Charter, the UN was able to respond to changing world order challenges of a substantive nature, although limited in policy formation by clashing governmental interests.

What the UN was often unable to do was to make fundamental *institutional* adjustments. It has been unable to alter the composition of the Security Council and the size, composition, and prerogatives of the P5, which has stuck with the geopolitical landscape of 1945 rather than adapting to the redistribution of global power in the 2020s. The UN has been able to alter its institutional treatment of some issues, however. For example, it upgraded the Human Rights Commission to become the Human Rights Council with a higher status within the UN System, and it established the UN Environmental Program in response to rising concerns about carbon emissions, pollution, pesticides, and toxic waste.

*Operational Considerations*

As a political actor conducting a wide range of activities, the UN is at once a tightly regulated and constrained bureaucracy and an international force that can act without constraints or supervision if it has the political wind behind it. Often, the relevance of the UN has seemed to revolve around the personality of the Secretary-General, demonstrated especially through signs of willingness to resist geopolitical pressures and the exertion of leadership responsive to the purposes and principles of the UN Charter. Bolder Secretaries-General sometimes paid the price by not being reelected or being sidelined, and in one instance, that of Dag Hammarskjold, being assassinated. It was Hammarskjold more than any other UN Secretary-General who demonstrated the potential for "innovation," in peacekeeping contexts as ways to circumvent to some extent the political paralysis associated with Cold War tensions. Yet Hammarskjold was by no means just a tool useful for extending the Western worldview to peace and security concerns. His demise occurred due to his attempts to uphold the radical economic nationalism of the Congolese leader Patrice Lumumba. By and large, UN Secretaries-General have been creatures of the geopolitically shaped organization, deferential political figures who know what red lines not to cross so as to avoid antagonizing the UN's most influential members, who hold the power of the purse and are adept at applying back-channel pressures.

UN peacekeeping operations as they evolved over the decades have often not been considered worthy of media or public attention even though they have effectively stabilized delicate ceasefires and volatile borders over long periods. For instance, the UN presence on the Lebanese-Israeli border has discouraged flare-ups in that highly sensitive part of the world, and the UN peacekeeping operation at the Pakistani-Indian border of Kashmir has prevented potentially dangerous confrontations over the years. What is clear is that UN operations reflect political considerations and often depart from their original mandate, which is a strength with respect to flexibility but sometimes a weakness with respect to accountability and fidelity to the expectations established at the time the mandate was agreed upon.

There are further issues of lawless geopolitics undertaken with direct or indirect UN blessings. Operationally, especially when enforcement is delegated to members with strong foreign policy goals connected with the issues, exceeding the scope of formal authorization for the use of force can strengthen the cynical impression that the UN can only be effective with respect to war/peace concerns when it puts its operations under the unsupervised control of P5 actors. This happened to a certain extent with respect to the tactics and war-making objectives determined by the US in the first Gulf War of 1991, creating a controversial gap between the UN role and its geopolitical implementation, leading many commentators to insist that future operations be linked more closely to Security Council supervision.

Also, the UN has been criticized for authorizing operations that seem to deny targeted states their sovereign rights. Such a criticism was made in light of the imposition of sanctions on Iraq following its invasion of Kuwait in 1990. These sanctions caused massive civilian casualties over the course of the next twelve years. As has been persuasively observed, any use of comprehensive post-conflict sanctions is punitive in effect rather than war-preventive, mostly punishing innocent civilians. Such sanctions are typically imposed in circumstances, as was the case in Iraq after the war, in a society already devastated by damage sustained during a recent war and struggling to recover.

In the subsequent Iraq War of 2003, the United States initiated a non-defensive war and long-term occupation without receiving the required prior authorization from the Security Council, despite its concerted effort to persuade the Security Council members of its justification for a use of force. Although the US-UK coalition defied the UN Charter and ignored the rejection of its arguments by the Security Council, no action was taken in support of UN authority and respect for international law. Not even a resolution of censure was adopted. The UN actually cooperated with the US government once the attack ended and the contested occupation of Iraq commenced. This UN acquiesence in the face of such a fundamental flaunting of its authority, reinforced by the evidence discrediting the major US justification (involving allegations that Iraq was hiding its possession and illicit development of weapons of mass destruction) for attacking Iraq. In effect, a double rejection of UN authority was present—attacking and occupying Iraq without any basis for claiming self-defense or receiving authorization from the UN.

### Stakeholder Perspectives

#### GOVERNMENTS OF SOVEREIGN STATES

Ever since the Peace of Westphalia in the middle of the seventeenth century, sovereign states have been the basic building block of world order, although until the collapse of empires and European colonialism, many people in the world were not represented in ways that reflected their values, interests, and identities. It should be recalled that the League of Nations did not challenge European colonialism, presiding over the colonialist conversion of the Ottoman Empire that collapsed at the end of World War I into the halfway house of the mandate system in which European colonial powers self-servingly "administered" territorially delimited societies throughout the Middle East and Africa. Supposedly, these mandates were to be administered as "a sacred trust" on behalf of the international community and not as colonies. Although formalized in this idealistic manner, in actuality, these mandates were governed as if the mandate-holder was endowed with colonial authority. As earlier noted, the collapse of European colonialism may have been the most important transformation of international society during the twentieth century. The collapse of European colonialism was accelerated by the effects of World War II, especially the weakening of France and the UK.

The collapse of European colonialism reflected historical, geopolitical, and normative factors and their political interrelations. After World War II, the Soviet Union became a great power in international life. Its championship of the anti-colonial movement combined with the ambivalence of the United States exhibiting the tensions between its own anti-colonial origins and its core alliance relations with the UK and France. As well, the right of self-determination, while not yet legally formalized, achieved prominence in stature ethically and politically, giving non-Western nationalism a sense of self-confidence that rose to greater heights when struggles, such as in Indochina and Algeria, demonstrated that European military superiority did not make its colonial domination invincible if confronted by a determined challenge in the form of persevering nationalist resistance. The geopolitical significance of this shift in the balance of forces as between intervention and national resistance in the middle of the twentieth century is a lesson yet to be learned by the West, particularly by the United States. This decolonizing historical trend helped shape the character and perception of the UN during the first thirty years of existence for several reasons.

Many non-Western countries were admitted to the UN, enlarging the overall membership significantly while highlighting the growing participation, global grievances, and unrealized claims of non-Western States. In the Cold War context, admission to UN membership depended less on the criteria set forth in Article 4 of the Charter than on the negotiation of bargains struck between the two main geopolitical antagonists: the US and the Soviet Union. Neither wanted to bolster the strength of its ideological rival, and yet both wanted to extend UN participation to all sovereign states that seemed to qualify for membership. The UN Charter in Article 4(1) sets forth criteria governing membership in the following language: "Membership in the United Nations is open to all other peace-loving states which accept the obligations contained in the present Charter and, in the judgment of the Organization, are able and willing to carry out these obligations." The word *other* referred to states other than those that were original members by virtue of their participation in the establishment of the UN. Article 4(2) outlines the procedure for formal admission that ensured the superpower gatekeepers would not lose control: "The admission of any such state to membership in the United Nations will be effected by a decision of the General Assembly upon the recommendation of the Security Council." Membership was not to be gained by establishing "peace-loving" credentials but by meta-legal political criteria.

An illustrative costly mistake by the UN, although it could be rationalized in many ways back in 1948, was to admit Israel as a member before the grievances of the Palestinian people were resolved and Palestine's claims of statehood were given, at minimum, an equivalent status to those of Israel. A different kind of mistake, although quite understandable from a geopolitical perspective, was to confer membership upon Belarus and Ukraine, although both political entities lacked the independence associated with sovereignty, resembling not states active in international political life but more the kind of constitutional units that make up a federal state, which is generally neutered internationally. True, these political entities attained independent statehood following the implosion of the Soviet Union in the early 1990s.

This exclusivity given by the UN to states highlights the unquestioned state-centric nature of world order in 1945. Would it be the same if the UN had been established in 1995 or today? Could an argument be made that the organization would be more legitimate and more effective if membership had been granted to other political actors—for instance, regional organizations such as the European Union or the African Union? Or might the selection of a civil society organization or large cities in each major sector of UN activity (human rights, arms control and disarmament, environment, development, international law) be helpful in debate and give more voice to international public opinion. The idea of an urban-centric parallel world order composed of global cities has recently gained interest and support, suggesting a less nationalistic, non-military, more people-oriented political configuration that deserves inclusion within a UN renovated to meet twenty-first century challenges and opportunities. Another idea with an appeal in civil society contexts would be the establishment within the UN of a Global Peoples Assembly, drawing inspiration from the European Parliament.

One strong characteristic of the UN as a political actor is the strength of its commitment to universality of membership by states. No state has withdrawn, except Indonesia briefly, and no state has been expelled or suspended from membership during the seventy-five years of UN existence. Even states that are habitually attacked at the UN such as Israel and North Korea have never publicly threatened withdrawal, although Israel has used defunding and temporary withdrawal from specialized agencies to express its anger. The one time the Soviet Union boycotted the Security Council because of the council's refusal to allow the Beijing government to represent China after 1949, the boycott backfired as the Security Council gave its formal blessings to the military defense of South Korea. If the Soviet Union had been present, it could have blocked that action. Soviet officials acknowledged their tactical mistake and resolved never to be ever again absent from Security Council proceedings.

As might have been expected and was taken into account in shaping the constitutional structure, some kind of balance had to be struck between the juridical equality of all states and the realities of geopolitical inequality. Giving the veto to the P5, combined with the requirement that major administrative decisions (Charter amendments, selection of Secretary-General, membership) cannot go forward without a Security Council recommendation, even when finally determined by the General Assembly, was a clever procedural way of minimizing the appearance of deferring to geopolitical priorities. A current debate persists as whether the viability of the UN depends on the necessity and desirability of accommodating geopolitics to the same extent as during the Cold War. At present, there are growing signs of a second cold war with China and possibly Russia as adversaries of the US. This dangerous development has yet to materialize fully and remains in the realm of conjecture. Another quite different possibility is that the first geopolitical alliance of world history will emerge in response to planetary challenges. Such an alliance, informal in the beginning, would be dedicated to addressing the eco-species crises of our time. If this happens, it would enlarge the political capabilities of the UN in new ecologically driven directions and create pressures for institutional reforms.

## CIVIL SOCIETY

The participation of civil society actors and representatives in UN activities, except for cooperation with the Economic and Social Council (ECOSOC), has been generally informal and indirect. It often takes the form of organizing valuable so-called side events within the many arenas of the UN System. These events may include representatives of member states. They may involve friendships with diplomats, experts, and de facto consultancy relationships with UN civil servants and diplomatic representatives. Civil society actors often bring special knowledge to bear or give advice and recommendations on sensitive subjects, even preparing draft presentations. Accredited non-governmental organizations (NGOs) and their representatives frequently perform lobbying functions on issues of human rights, environment, arms control and disarmament, and peace and security, and play informal advisory roles that are especially useful for understaffed delegations. There is also the danger of new patterns of manipulation. Many well-funded NGOs serve as instruments for the promotion of special interests acting in tension with Charter purposes and principles.

In recent years, smaller UN member countries have become active in ACT, a forum of some twenty small UN member countries, among them Costa Rica, Ireland, New Zealand, Singapore, and Switzerland. Their objective is to consult with each other on critical Security Council reform issues and to press for greater "accountability," "coherence" and "transparency" (ACT) in Security Council activity. In doing so, they often seek contact informally with civil society groups. Another innovative initiative with links to NGOs has to do with informal meetings of members of the Security Council convened under the "Arria formula" (named after the Venezuelan ambassador to the UN Diego Arria, who introduced this formula in 1992). These informal meetings are convened at the initiative of one or several members of the Security Council in order to hear the views of individuals and organizations on matters within the Security Council's competence, satisfying the demand for increased influence by states without geopolitical status. These issues will be discussed in more detail in chapter 8.

At the same time, the present civil society role should not be overstated, nor is it reasonable to claim that the access provided to civil society serves to represent the policy agendas of the peoples of the world as distinguished from the formal gatherings of governments under UN auspices. As matters now stand, the civil society role in the context of the overall workings of the political UN is a rather minor add-on that is only occasionally noticed and rarely plays a role in shaping UN responses to major agenda items. The contrast between civil society and UN perspectives was observable at the civil society event held annually during the 1990s in the Italian city of Perugia with the pointed title "The United Nations of the Peoples." This alt-UN had an agenda and a protocol that called attention to differences in priorities and operational atmosphere as evident across the board of global concerns, covering everything from the casual dress code to content and style of presentation pertaining to responsible "diplomats," emphasizing gaps between society and the state. Also notable was the chasm between Perugia's civil society populism and the elitist annual meetings of the World Economic Forum in Davos at which CEOs of mostly Western corporations paid large fees just to gain admission. UN Secretaries-General and heads of state never came to Perugia but they welcomed invitations to speak in Davos. In this important sense, civil society participation has been divided between issue- and people-oriented NGOs working in the trenches of UN activities and the business world's luxurious meetings and gala dinners in Alpine penthouses. As the UN is always on the lookout for new funding sources, the economic elites have leverage that translates into policy and action, as with the "blue-washing guidelines" and "public-private partnerships" that were nurtured by the UN as halfway houses between establishing corporate responsibility standards and a PR campaign to deflect criticism of corporate irresponsibility with regard to environmental, safety, and health issues.

There are other concerns that point to global reforms that might give civil society a more formal role within the various arenas of the UN System. Often the undertakings of the Security Council are held in closed, non-transparent sessions without even a nominal civil society presence in the form of observers. Two overlapping issues are present. The first is the desirability of greater transparency in UN operations, especially the Security Council's. The second is an upgrading of the role of civil society to enhance the legitimacy and accountability of the UN and expose the unhealthy intrusion of geopolitics upon the lives of world citizenry. Various suggestions have been made over the years. Perhaps the most promising has been a series of institutional proposals for some sort of civil society permanent organ representing the peoples of the world, the membership of which would be directly elected by citizens in participating countries rather than appointed by governmental action. The most influential proposals have been modeled on the European Parliament. Varying ideas exist as to whether such a body should be organizationally situated within the UN System or outside for the sake of independence. Also, differences of opinion among advocates arise as to whether this World Parliament of the People should be empowered to make recommendations that must be taken up by the General Assembly or assigned to the most relevant organ within the UN. There is a range of other complex issues that civil society leaders will have to clarify such as whether a global parliament should be given certain quasi-legislative roles, such as a role in ratifying the selection of the Secretary-General, initiating investigations of alleged serious human rights abuses, and offering recommendations across the same spectrum of issues as the UN General Assembly.[7]

So far, these proposals have languished on the sidelines, and in the present context, they are considered by many as naïve and unrealistic. There is little or no political will evident among the governments that would have to accept institutional innovations by consenting to any modification of the UN framework. If a peoples' parliament was established outside the UN, then its attempts to exert influence could probably be deflected more easily and even ignored and rejected, yet it might be less inhibited in expressing its viewpoint and thus achieve more media attention. The experience of the European Parliament, although mixed, is positive enough to keep the idea of such a parliamentary body near the top of the global reform agenda. Although cooperation between civil society and the United Nations has evolved over the years, much more needs to be done. In the years ahead, the role of the UN as protector of "the peoples" needs to be clarified and strengthened in various sectors of global decision-making. Multilateralism without meaningful civil society participation is neither viable nor beneficial. Non-governmental networks of actors demand and deserve greater access to all UN activities and should be selectively accorded formal roles in various UN proceedings, including summits on global policy issues. Of course, NGO participation must itself be scrutinized and regulated by reference to Charter purposes and principles. It is important to avoid allowing NGOs to become vehicles for lobbying by special interest groups, especially with strong private sector links. While regulation is necessary, dialogue and NGO diversity are to be encouraged.

### The Global Setting

As the prior discussion has made clear in several respects, an understanding of the UN is best achieved by taking into account fundamental changes in the global setting that either offer opportunities for the UN to be effective or close off paths due to the imposition of blockages of various sorts. Challenges come and go, and the UN agenda needs to be sensitive to such shifts in policy focus. Additionally, there are more or less permanent factors such as state-centrism and geopolitical leverage that have continuously (mis) shaped UN action and perceptions. A succession of changes in the global setting have also played crucial roles in giving the UN somewhat different public profiles over the course of its seventy-five-plus years of operational existence. This interpretative perspective can be best depicted by snapshots of a series of stages identified by reference to their salient features:

## (1) ESTABLISHING THE UN (1944–1946)

The most notable feature of this period when conferences of diplomats representing their governments were held in Yalta, Dumbarton Oaks, Bretton Woods, and finally San Francisco were discussions of how to approach the challenge of war prevention after World War II ended. In the background of the UN planning process was the recognition that the League of Nations was a flawed governance innovation that had failed to live up to expectations coupled with the consensus view that a global institutional framework was more indispensable than ever and could be improved through learning from past mistakes. In this regard the new organization rejected the League idea of a constitutional framework that presumed continued cooperation among the Great Powers. While this cooperation had been integral to the Allied victory over fascism in World War II, it could not be expected to endure in peacetime. These Great Powers, above all the United States and the Soviet Union, needed to act within a global framework that would encourage participation in conflictual times as well as during periods of Great Power harmony. The US, as well as the Soviet Union, needed psychological reassurances that their territorial sovereignty would be respected and that their stature as global leaders would be acknowledged. The UN founders allayed sovereignty concerns by conferring an unrestricted right of veto and tried to ensure US participation by physically locating UN headquarters in New York City, the financial capital of the world. Such a decision had the side benefit of legitimating capitalism as the dominant engine of growth and development. The ambivalence toward European colonialism was also expressed by substituting the Trusteeship Council for the Mandate System as a compromise between colonial claims and the emergent right of self-determination as challenging the legitimacy of colonial claims of territorial control.

The main public image of the UN as entrusted with war prevention at the dawn of the nuclear age was given rhetorical support in the Preamble but fell short of credibility in the distribution of functions and authority in the Charter and the unfolding UN operations. However, vesting hopes for world peace in the UN never persuaded political elites shaping the foreign policies of the strongest and wealthiest states. To this day, political elites adhere to an outmoded "political realism" that constructs history mainly on the basis of wars won or lost, with little belief that law and morality matter much except to regulate routine transnational interactions. Henry Kissinger, a preeminent US realist practitioner, complains in his book *Diplomacy*, devoted to statecraft, about staff members who annoyed him by acting as if law and morality should be taken into account when developing

American foreign policy. Overall, the UN has had its ups and downs when it comes to peace and security, never satisfying either legalistic idealists, who expected the UN Charter to prevail over the vagaries of world politics, or realist cynics, who dismissed the UN as a waste of time and quite irrelevant when it comes to national security.

## (2) THE COLD WAR YEARS OF DECOLONIZATION (1946–1989)

For many years, the West regarded the global setting as almost totally reflecting the Cold War tensions between the US's Western alliance and the Soviet bloc, centering on the control of Europe with secondary attention given to the divided polities of Korea and Vietnam, where two deadly proxy wars occurred. This geopolitical impasse achieved a certain stability at the UN and outside it due to the mutual fear of the outbreak of a third world war, which in all likelihood would be fought with nuclear weapons. The non-Western world experienced the period differently, centering on the liberation of societies governed by European colonial powers, especially in Asia and Africa, which produced long and costly wars that often were lengthened and intensified by Cold War concerns about postcolonial ideological orientations and international alignments. In effect, the decolonization process could not be disentangled in many settings from the geopolitical and ideological rivalry that dominated international relations after 1945.

The effects of this reading of the Cold War years had a decisive influence on how the UN evolved in this formative period after its establishment. Three main impacts can be distinguished. First of all, a political impasse at the UN on almost all major peace, security, and conflict issues, created the public impression that the UN was paralyzed by the standoff between the US and the Soviet Union. This generalization was subject to a few exceptions, but it is largely accurate. Secondly, the altered geographical composition of membership resulting from the success of the worldwide anti-colonial movement brought political independence and membership in the UN to many Asian and African countries. Such a process added a North/South axis of conflict to the East/West axis at the core of the Cold War, with a resulting shift in focus at the General Assembly from war prevention to development. This shift led to calls and proposals for a new international economic order, climaxing in an emergency session of the General Assembly in 1974 during which strident voices from the Third World, enlarged to take the Latin American experience into account, challenged many of the unfair features of the Western-dominated regimes governing trade, investment, and credit arrangements. Latin America, although liberated from European colonial rule in the nineteenth century, struggled hard to mitigate the exploitation of its resources and developmental hopes by US imperialism during the pre-UN period and even for many decades after. In this sense much of Latin America acted in solidarity with the Non-Aligned Movement initiated by China, India, and Indonesia at the Bandung Conference. The result was a backlash organized within and beyond the UN with the purpose of insulating market-driven economic development from socialist thinking and Third Worldism, reaching a shrill high point during the right-wing political leadership of Ronald Reagan and Margaret Thatcher in the 1980s. The UN became a target for verbal assaults by ambassadors representing the capitalist West who spoke openly about "irresponsible majorities" at the General Assembly composed of mainly tiny countries, insisting that such UN initiatives were giving misleadingly provocative guidance to global economic policy. It was even alleged by free marketeers that the UN had become a socialist-oriented group of institutions that did not reflect the values and interests of the leading dues-paying members of the organization. To offset what was regarded in the staunchest capitalist circles as an organized onslaught directed at the world economy, financial and corporate elites joined forces within the UN to do battle outside the UN as well as within its confines. Extremely influential non-governmental organizations were established to turn the tide of opinion, including the Trilateral Commission and the World Economic Forum. Ultimately, the new international economic order failed to materialize, with many governments in the South co-opted and corrupted and others discouraged by the futility of their efforts.

The third cluster of developments at the UN during the Cold War was to some extent reactions against the tensions generated by the first two clusters. It involved the steady growth in the activities, role, and variety of UN agencies devoted to such issues as health (WHO), children (UNICEF), agriculture and food (FAO,WFP, IFAD) culture and education (UNESCO), development (UNDP) and trade UNCTAD), human rights and displaced people (UNHRC, UNHCR), labor and industry (ILO, UNIDO), and environment (UNEP), as well as closely aligned institutions for civil aviation, maritime affairs, meteorology, and telecommunication. This diversification of activities, reflecting also expanding budgets and personnel, led the UN to be recognized as a nexus of functional undertakings serving the global public good and corrected the view that the UN should be written off as a dismal failure similar to the negative assessment of the League of Nations. The UN also succeeded in becoming the arena of choice to provide auspices for lawmaking treaties on such issues as public order of the global commons, including oceans, the Arctic and Antarctica polar regions, space, arms limitations, and more recently climate change. In addition, the UN organized global conferences, especially during the 1990s that brought valuable attention to global issues, such as women, social and economic challenges, human rights, environment, and population policy. These events became important sources of UN influence. Such gatherings sought common ground among the growing number of sovereign states active on the world stage, producing declarations and recommendations that were more progressive than what Western governments were often willing to implement. Despite obstacles, these UN mega-conferences had policy impacts and gathered information useful for many governments.

Overall, this diversification of undertakings and institutional identities made the UN of great practical importance to most of its members, especially to newly independent countries with less governmental experience and trained personnel and fewer resources. As it became more useful and reflective of human security needs, it developed a more adversarial relationship to hegemonic and ideological expectations of the P5, and so the war within the war went on inside the operational and substantive arenas of the UN.

### (3) THE ASCENDANCY OF NEOLIBERAL GLOBALIZATION (1989–2001)

At first the fall of the Berlin Wall (1989), epitomizing the end of the Cold War, seemed to open up a brighter future for a more peaceful world and an enlarged future role for the UN with respect to peace and security challenges. With the geopolitical impasse ended between the US and the Soviet Union, it would seem that the Security Council could take charge of implementing the fundamental prohibitions on the use of force that had always been viewed as the litmus test of the effectiveness of the Charter. The US government, headed by George H. W. Bush shared this optimism about post–Cold War P5 cooperation and opposed peace-oriented interpretations of what this meant in operational terms. The first revelation of what the new situation would mean for the UN came in 1990 when Iraq invaded, occupied, and annexed its neighbor Kuwait. The US turned to the UN to mobilize a collective international response in support of Kuwait's right of self-defense. US diplomats supported the view that with the Cold War over, the UN could at last, and for the first time, function as was envisioned in 1945, when it was established as a bastion against "wars of aggression." President Bush highlighted this raised expectation of UN performance by proclaiming "a new world order" in which global governance would henceforth be cooperatively administered in accord with the rule-based structures of international law and the implementing procedures of international institutions working on the basis of good faith rather than ideological rivalry.[8]

Yet all that glitters is not gold! A good example is the First Gulf War in 1991, which was heralded at the first undertaking under the banner of the new world order. The banner frayed, so this was also the last such undertaking. However, in 1991 the US-UK coalition, supported by Arab countries and backed by reliance on all "necessary" force that reversed Iraqi aggression, restored Kuwaiti sovereignty. This outcome was proclaimed a victory for the UN and international law and led to a new belief that the Charter's emphasis on prohibiting territorial expansion by force could be upheld by a response organized and implemented through the UN.

Yet not all observers applauded. There were concerns about the failure of the military operation entrusted to an American-led coalition of states to be more closely administered by the UN. More fundamentally, there was a concern as to whether the UN in the aftermath of the Cold War was becoming an *instrument* of US foreign policy rather than an objective arbiter of a rule-based system of world order. This view derived, in part, by some evidence that UN diplomacy refused to negotiate a pullback from Kuwait despite Saddam Hussein's apparent readiness to do so if he received a pledge that Iraq would not be attacked.

At least during the Cold War, the ideological impasse kept the UN from being instrumentalized to satisfy P5 transatlantic geopolitical undertakings. Unlike the First Gulf War, neither the United States in Vietnam nor the Soviet Union in Afghanistan had ever sought the backing of the UN for their unlawful interventions. The differences between rule-governed and geopolitically managed enforcement regimes may be a matter of degree, yet clarifying the distinction in UN practice is of paramount importance when describing what kind of political actor the UN was becoming at each stage of its evolution. Overall, the UN performance in relation to the First Gulf War illustrated the political utility of the UN Security Council when Great Power competition is paused, but did it justify being labeled the launch of a "new world order"? We think not, taking into account the US's subsequent abandonment of the claim itself, fearing it would get the country caught up in human rights and other war/peace undertakings in which its strategic interests were insufficient to justify a costly involvement and providing an occasion to show itself and the world that it retained freedom to maneuver in response to geopolitical challenges. As formulated by George H. W.

Bush, the new world order seemed to reflect the willingness of the most powerful states to accept a rule-based approach even when it went against their interests.

What is sad, as well as more revealing, is that the end of the Cold War presented the best occasion since the UN was brought into existence to move the organization toward realizing the promise implicit in the phrase "new world order" if understood to refer to rules and neutral principles. Instead of the geopolitical leadership shown by Bush in mobilizing support for a response to Iraqi aggression, when it came to making principled global governance under UN auspices the new world order, there was a return to the old, familiar modalities of the balance of power and geopolitical management of intergovernmental security. Neither George Bush nor his successor, Bill Clinton, exhibited the slightest commitment to strengthening either the legitimacy or the effectiveness of the UN, which would have been widely commended by the peoples of the world. For instance, on legitimacy, the P5 could self-limit or even renounce their right of veto or propose reforms as to the composition of the P5 or seek to connect funding to more independent revenue sources by imposing a tax on luxury cars, international flights, and hedge fund transactions. On effectiveness, permanent UN standby military capabilities for implementation of ICJ judgments and Security Council decisions could have been provided or a new process of electing and empowering the Secretary-General established or a serious effort made to seize the moment to negotiate a phased nuclear disarmament treaty that would abolish such weaponry of mass destruction. None of this happened or was even proposed. This open window of opportunity would close as the new century got underway and was slammed shut by the 2001 9/11 attacks on the World Trade Center and the Pentagon in the United States. The guiding ethos inhibiting reform efforts seemed a questionable application of the adage "if it ain't broke, don't fix it." Later chapters show that the UN was broke in more than one sense and badly needed fixing. And even if it had not been broken, it could have been improved.

In light of the coronavirus pandemic, the need for a more robust UN is again being widely recognized, perhaps as never before, and not just for matters of health. Yet the requisite leadership and evidence of a commitment is missing from the discourse of governing elites. Civil society activism is more attuned to the opportunity for enhanced cooperative UN efforts but is not yet sufficiently mobilized to push a globalizing policy agenda based on the premises of humane global governance and the priorities of *human* security. In effect, problem-solving involving UN backing for global cooperative solutions is widely supported, but so far there is no significant change in the UN role in war/peace situations. The UN remains on the sidelines when claims are put forward that the UN should authorize military attacks or interventions on behalf of human rights even in the face of crimes against humanity and genocide.

There was another development that worked against reinforcing the regulatory architecture of the UN System, and this concerned preoccupations with the management of the world economy. The 1990s became the decade in which there was a notable shift from geopolitics to geo-economics. Instead of Cold War preoccupations with conflict zones, the focus of global policy became trade and investment as shaped by the victory of the capitalist West in the ideological struggle. The measure of success was the rate of economic growth, the extent of technological innovations, and the degree to which governments facilitated the efficient use of capital, letting markets, not national borders, determine the locus of production as increasingly interconnected and globally administered by digital networking. This bundle of developments was understood as privileging markets and capital and subordinating national labor forces and peoples` social concerns. This overall policy configuration became known to the world as "the Washington consensus," or more generically as "neoliberal globalization," and its worldwide acceptance was widely appreciated as the consequence of the West winning the Cold War. More than two decades later, questions are being raised as to whether from the perspective of people, the West's victory over the Soviet bloc seems increasingly hollow. Such an assessment reflects the view that the main feature of the new global setting was to give predatory capitalism a green light while learning to live with ecological complacency. The UN seemed sidelined even more than it had been during the Cold War. In a superficial sense, the world economy *after* the Cold War became less people-friendly and more prone to inequalities arising from the workings of markets and trade. The alternative of socialism no longer moderated and somewhat tamed the predatory temptations of capitalism, which if left ideologically unopposed, as was the case in this time of illusion, epitomized by Francis Fukuyama's triumphalist claim that with the victory of liberalism over socialism the world was reaching "the end of history."[9] The price of such hubris continues to be paid by the peoples of the world in a frightening variety of ways, ranging from prolonged civil strife and famine to deliberate fires inflicting damage on the great rainforests of the world. While these developments occur, those who retain visionary hopes for peace and justice struggle against despair.

There was a second chance for a renewal of the UN mandate as the millennial year 2000 approached. The UN itself sponsored studies on such themes as expanding the Security Council, restricting the veto, achieving sustainable development, increasing the participation of civil society, and acting to achieve the Millennium Development Goals set by the UN. NGOs put forward a wide array of proposals seeking a stronger and more democratic UN. Unfortunately, once more as at the end of the Cold War, global leadership was busy elsewhere. The best the US could offer was to have its president tender avuncular advice to the UN: "do more with less" and "do not set your sights too high!" The Soviet leader Mikhail Gorbachev did put forth strong messages of support for a more globalized and humane world order centered in the UN, but few governments heeded guidance from a declining superpower, even as proposed by an internationally greatly admired leader. The year 2000 came and went, and as far as the UN was concerned, nothing happened—very little smoke and no fire. Even economic policy was being organized geopolitically with greater reliance placed on the G7 meetings, later enlarged to become the G20, which meant that the Washington-based Bretton Woods institutions were being superseded and circumvented by ad hoc arrangements with little structure and outside the UN's remit.

## (4) RE-SECURITIZATION OF INTERNATIONAL RELATIONS (2001–2020)

The 9/11 attacks of 2001 on the World Trade Center in New York City and the Pentagon in Washington created a sharp set of contradictory international reactions with major impacts on the UN. The American decision to respond to these mega-terrorist events, targeting its symbolic domination of the world economic and security structures, by recourse to war rather than relying on criminal law enforcement was a momentous choice with many adverse consequences for the entire world, including for the UN and for the US itself. The conservative leadership of the United States at the time was at once frightened by this exposure of vulnerability of the homeland to low-tech forms of political violence and seized the occasion to look upon the attack as an opportunity to gain political backing for active projections of its military superiority, especially in the Middle East. The projects of preemptive intervention in foreign societies and of regime-changing interventions to reach geopolitical goals of "democracy promotion" and containment of political Islam converged with nothing much expected from the UN beyond nods of approval and post-conflict cooperation. Adhering to international law or respecting UN authority were seen in Washington as out of touch with the realities of the twenty-first century that called for effective counterterrorist tactics without deference to legal or moral constraints.

On the level of conflict, whether via rationalizations for the wars in Afghanistan (2002–) or Iraq (2003–) or sending drones and special forces to dozens of countries in the far corners of the earth, the world as a whole had become the central new battlefield of geopolitical encounter, and neither principal antagonist was a state in the Westphalian sense. Terrorist groups struck wherever in the West or elsewhere they could find soft targets, while the West used its technological sophistication to track and destroy terrorist suspects. In such a political environment, the UN was again paralyzed and diplomacy circumvented. International boundaries were being ignored by both sides in a struggle that pitted two political and ideological actors against one another, neither of which was a sovereign state in the conventional territorial sense. The US had the properties of "a global state" with hundreds of military bases around the world and navies in every ocean, while al-Qaida was an extremist movement that could be anywhere and yet nowhere. The rules and concepts of international law were ignored by both sides. The liberal West engaged in torture, detentions without trials, deadly drone attacks on foreign targets of its choosing, covert and overt interventions in foreign countries, and economic coercion, while its extremist adversaries struck where they could, often deliberately targeting civilians to maximize the impact of its violent tactics. Unlike the First Gulf War, the UN could not be mobilized for counterterrorism undertakings because neither China nor Russia, nor much of the non-Western world were prepared to give approval to such blatant disregard of national sovereignty. There was also widespread concern about indirectly endorsing new forms of postcolonial imperialism under the guise of security. Geopolitical actors could ignore or defy the UN when it came to substantive policy, but they could always enlist the symbolic support of the UN with respect to implementing norms governing legitimate behavior.

At the same time, developments in the Middle East produced various kinds of more traditional war/peace challenges involving violent internal struggles for the control of a particular state, including instances of proxy warfare when other states aligned with one side or the other. The UN was established to address wars between states, not within them, although the language in Article 2(7) of the Charter created some space for interpretation: "Nothing contained in the present Charter shall authorize the United Nations to intervene in matters which are essentially within the domestic jurisdiction of any state or shall require the Members to submit such matters to settlement under the present Charter; but this principle shall not prejudice the application of enforcement measures under Chapter VII." The intention was to insulate issues internal to sovereign states, including even prolonged civil strife, from any interference by the UN, and this practice has mainly guided international practice, although it has not been complemented by meaningful restraints on intervention by states. The proxy war of twelve years in Syria, which combined internal, regional, and international struggles, also ignored the underlying principle of international law that the government of a country is legally entitled to receive assistance but its opponents are not. This bias toward constituted governments seems to follow the logic of a state-centric world order, but when the geopolitical stakes are high or the legitimacy bias favoring the government is offset by its severe human rights violation in an internal struggle for power, intervention occurs on both sides without generating serious legal friction. The characteristic conflicts in this period have proved to be a virtual no-go zone for the UN, both because consensus on a course of action has been impossible to achieve in the Security Council and there was not sufficient political support for the UN to be given the capabilities to play a conflict-resolving role credibly. The UN did make halfhearted offers of good offices, hoping to balance its role as respecting the Charter affirmation of nonintervention in internal conflict and its existential duty to protect vulnerable people. It sought to give more clarity to this balance by formulating in 2005 a novel conception, "responsibility to protect," but its implementation of the norm to date seems more expressive of geopolitical preferences than the high ideals of protecting the weak.

The Arab Spring and its aftermath manifested a regional expression of this world order disposition toward nonintervention by states and by the UN. The one UN exception, Libya in 2011 (as earlier noted), damaged the UN's reputation for constructive humanitarian initiatives by supporting an initial limited authorization to use force and then doing nothing at all once this mandate was grossly and deliberately exceeded by Operation Freedom Falcon entrusted to NATO. This geopolitical manipulation of a humanitarian initiative, invoking a responsibility-to-protect rationale, was seen as carried out in bad faith by important governments. The UN was reduced to becoming a spectator during the conflict, and then given the role of a post-conflict handmaiden to manage clean-up tasks and provide care for civilian victims. The UN's role throughout the devastating post-2011 decade of conflicts in Iraq, Syria, and Yemen is illustrative.

A parallel development during this period was the de-democratization of many UN members by way of the rise in all regions of the world of right-wing populism and top-down authoritarianism. This dual movement of governance at the national level helps explain the retreat from all forms of internationalism, including economic globalization, multilateral treaty

making and most types of global cooperation. This rise of chauvinistic nationalism exhibited its influence during the coronavirus pandemic through
disappointing refusals to share knowledge and medical and protective
equipment and most of all through the statist and divisive distribution of
medicines and vaccines. The type of ultranationalist political leadership
that has come to dominate the political life of many countries works against
reliance on the UN. During the health crisis of 2020, the World Health Organization gained a fragile prominence, as did the UN Secretary-General,
but the political organs of the UN remained mostly missing in action. What
minimal actions the UN took were of an exhortatory nature. More publi-
cized was the US's spoiler role in 2020 when it single-handedly stymied
a Security Council endorsement of the Secretary-General's extraordinary
call for a global ceasefire to last for the duration of the pandemic and possibly longer. Who can know what might have emerged from such an experiment in ad hoc peacemaking?

It seems rather clear that the UN will remain sidelined with respect
to the peace and security framework so long as geopolitical actors pursue
their agendas without heeding the UN. As long as the atmosphere of ultranationalist self-reliance persists and is not reversed by a political renewal
of internationalism or disrupted by some kind of breakdown of minimal
global public order, we can be sure that the UN will come under little
pressure to follow a rule-governed agenda shaped by the UN. Whether the
change of leadership in the United States in 2021 can produce renewed
confidence in the UN and globalism is presently unanswerable. Pressures
for enhanced global cooperation on climate change and post-pandemic efforts to create world health capabilities are combined in the search for effective responses to future worldwide disease hazards.

## (5) WILL THE PANDEMIC AWAKEN SUPPORT FOR THE UN? (2022–?)

It is tempting to suppose that the UN will be strengthened in the aftermath of coronavirus pandemic, but is that one more display of wishful
thinking by multilateralists? Rationality will prevail. Not only health but
an array of challenges require action to protect *global* interests, which are
more than the sum of national interests or the acknowledgement of hegemonic primacy. But can we be certain or even confident? A stressful period
of economic recovery will overshadow other interests for many years and
likely cast a nationalist challenge over the formation of policy.

There are some encouraging ways of looking at the UN's future. Although the proposal of a global ceasefire by the Secretary-General did not
seem to gain much traction with respect to ongoing conflicts, it did win the

support of fourteen of the fifteen members of the Security Council and, more meaningfully, the endorsement of twelve armed groups engaged in conflicts, including in Afghanistan, Iran, and Yemen. It also led to widespread public appreciation of António Guterres as the world's leading voice of moral authority. And had not the ultranationalist Donald Trump been the US president at the time, who knows what might have happened?

Similarly, the importance of the World Health Organization (WHO) became obvious to almost everyone in the world aside from Trump. The authority of the WHO was globally recognized, even by United States authorities. When the WHO declared on March 11, 2020, that outbreak of the COVID-19 disease was indeed "a pandemic," it was universally accepted, and the declaration was a game changer in the sense that the scope and seriousness of COVID-19 was authoritatively established.

Yet what seemed eminently sensible and rationally persuasive in the midst of the pandemic seems unlikely to prevail in its aftermath. Governments remain captive to special national interests, and special interests are driven by short-term, generally selfish political and economic interests. The well-being of the nation and its citizenry no longer guides governmental action even in countries that regard themselves as democracies and hold periodic elections. Also, societal habits and traditions associated with restoring the "old normal" remain strong, and momentous behavioral and institutional changes would seem to require either the widespread perception of the pandemic as a catastrophe of a gravity comparable to a world war or the result of a transnational populist surge of the sort not seen before in global history. Maybe such sea changes were prefigured by the rise of organized labor in the mid-nineteenth century in reaction to the early miseries wrought by the Industrial Revolution, which led to the negotiation of new social contracts between the state and society, as well as between labor and business.

The aftermath of the pandemic will exert some immediate influence on the future of the UN in response to the play of these forces, but international memories are notoriously short, and governments are quick to forget the worries of yesterday in their preoccupation with today's concerns, a tendency accentuated by the media's obsession with what is happening now. Besides, the world's peoples and leaders can be quickly distracted by the onset of new crises, with the effect of not benefiting from past mistakes. There is an innate tendency to look ahead and ignore the past, which in practice means accepting preoccupation with the present. This ahistorical mentality does not augur well if we proceed from a strong conviction that it is of utmost importance that the UN fulfill its potential to guide humanity toward a sustainable and benevolent future.

We can only hope that the lessons not learned and the opportunities not taken at the end of the Cold War and during the observances of the millennium year will be better heeded in the future and the opportunities for constructive reforms will be explored and acted upon in a positive fashion. If the UN begins to be appreciated as satisfying the needs of humanity in a time of mounting global challenges, then the unfolding of the history of this period may yet be redeemed from tragedies wrought by past failures and saved from further slides toward collective calamity. This is our hope.

## A Concluding Observation

Looking ahead, we highlight four institutional issues that will illuminate the struggle of the UN to strengthen its global role:

—Can the P5 find enough common ground to enable the Security Council to act in humanity's interest with respect to principal global challenges and to avoid the geopolitical gridlocks of the past?

—Will the UN Secretary-General as the world's most legitimate moral authority figure be given the political space to play a more active role in connecting the work of the UN with the strivings and aspirations of the peoples of the world?

—Will the critical importance of UN specialized agencies be recognized by sufficient funds to support ambitious programs addressing major global challenges, bringing the resources of knowledge communities and experts to bear in problem-solving contexts?

—Will it become possible to fashion more integrated and efficient response capabilities for the Security Council in coordination with the General Assembly and in some instances, the International Court of Justice in ways that impact on various operational undertakings and challenges?

Without neglecting the shortcomings of the UN or the uncertainties and complexities of international life, we believe the legitimacy and effectiveness of the UN will attain new heights if satisfactory progress is made with respect to these four dimensions of its undertakings. And if not, we can expect that the UN will remain trapped in its present shadowland of underperformance and underappreciation.

# TWO

# From the League of Nations to the United Nations

## Versailles

A review of the global order at the time of the First World War reveals that European and American leaders wanted to make sure that future international relations, if not controlled by a Western agenda, at least would be consistent with Western political and economic interests. This essentially hegemonic goal had far-reaching consequences for the peace negotiations in Versailles and the subsequent establishment of the League of Nations.

World War I ended in France on November 11, 1918, with the armistice at Compiègne confirming the military defeat of Germany. Much of Central Europe was destroyed. Millions of soldiers and civilians had died; many more were maimed; infrastructure damage was enormous; and the empires of Germany, Austria-Hungary, Russia, and Turkey were collapsing.

In mid-1919, European political leaders, among them Lloyd George, Georges Clemenceau, and Vittorio Orlando, the prime ministers of Great Britain, France, and Italy, and US president Woodrow Wilson came together in Versailles to debate the kind of world they hoped to emerge from WWI. Vladimir Lenin's 1917 Decree on Peace was taken into account a year later by Woodrow Wilson in outlining fourteen principles for peace in a future world that would follow the war that had been supposed "to end all wars." Wilson called for an end to secret treaties, a reduction of national armaments, and the adjustment of all colonial claims. In essence, he advocated the ending of colonial rule, as well as solving all territorial disputes in Europe by peaceful means. Above all, Wilson championed the idea of creating an association of nations that would provide mutual guarantees for political independence and territorial integrity for all member states.

Georges Clemenceau had invited allies to come to Versailles to discuss geopolitics and to meet with German representatives to agree on punitive measures against Germany, including reparation payments, new German national boundaries, and the termination of German claims to its colonies. Among the territories ceded to France at the peace talks in Versailles was Alsace-Lorraine. Versailles had symbolic significance as a location because it was there in 1871 that France had been forced to accept the transfer of Alsace-Lorraine to Germany at the end of the Franco-Prussian War of 1870–71.

This history of French-German relations would eventually complicate the cooperation between these two countries when Germany joined the League of Nations in 1926. Restrictions on German rearmament would generate friction and resentment. However, in 1919, winners and losers alike were exhausted, anxious for a new beginning in international relations and therefore ready to support a peace treaty. Such a treaty was signed on June 28, 1919, in Versailles. It was a punitive peace agreement that humiliated Germany and gave rise to Nazi extremism.

An especially difficult issue at Versailles had been the future status of German overseas territories. There was agreement that Germany had to relinquish control over its colonies, but there was disagreement as to which countries should take responsibility for their administration on behalf of the League of Nations. In the end, agreement was reached to have member states function as administrative mandate authorities for the former German colonies in West, Central, South-West, and East Africa and the South Pacific and Micronesia. These territories were apportioned among Belgium, France, Japan, and Great Britain and the latter's dominions of New Zealand, Australia, and South Africa. The German-leased Jiao Zhou Bay in northeastern China had already been taken from Germany by the Japanese during WWI.

It is important for the understanding of the dynamics of the League of Nations and the UN as its successor that responsibility for the former German overseas territories lay in Western hands, with Micronesia the only exception. Japan became the mandatory authority for these islands in the Western Pacific. Because it was not a member of the League, the United States was not given any mandatory responsibilities for the former German colonies.

However, in 1944 when the US had captured and occupied areas in the Pacific, Japan was forced to give up its League of Nations mandate authority for Micronesia and other Pacific territories. At that time, the US declared that for "strategic" reasons it sought control over some of these Pacific territories. These included the Bikini Atoll, where in 1946 the US began testing nuclear weapons, causing indigenous Marshall Islanders great harm from radiation.

In 1947, the UN Security Council confirmed unanimously (RES/21/1947) that the United States would be given the administering authority for what became known as the Trust Territory of the Pacific Islands (TTPI). As one of the WWII victors and a permanent member of the Security Council, the US had convinced the eight other members of the Security Council to support its objective of militarizing the TTPI by "establishing naval, military and air bases and to erect fortifications." The US also made the Security Council agree that the TTPI mandate would not be altered, amended, or terminated without the consent of the US as the administering authority. Even though the TTPI came to an end in 1994 when Palau, the Marshall Islands, and Micronesia gained their formal independence and joined the UN, they retained their close political and strategic ties with the US, reflected in their UN voting record for the priorities of Washington, which often were far removed from the interests of the Pacific Island peoples. The low profile of the US in shaping the League had given way to increasing American assertiveness during the UN's formative years.

During the Versailles summit, Woodrow Wilson's idealistic vision for a world living in peace had been contested by his European partners. As political realists and colonialists who, in the aftermath of a devastating war, dominated diplomacy in Europe, they insisted on a geopolitical framework for multinational cooperation. The US Senate, for very different reasons, which had to do with traditional federalist resistance to subscribing to sovereignty-encroaching internationalism, refused to ratify the Treaty of Versailles. Additionally, senators were angered by Wilson's failure to consult more with them about US postwar policy. It was felt that he departed from traditional American foreign policy that resisted involvement in world affairs outside the Western Hemisphere and the Pacific. For them, multilateralism as a political orientation did not exist. Despite this, the Great Powers of Europe wanted to "coordinate national policies in groups" based on shared interests and values.[1] They were searching for an institutionalized structure to protect these mutual interests and in doing so were prepared pragmatically to adopt a globalized multilateral agenda, the first of its kind.

The idea of creating a "league of nations" had already been raised by the UK in 1915 and thereafter kept gaining political traction. A commission was set up at Versailles to draft a covenant for the envisioned institution. There were months of acrimonious debates about which political actors should be eligible to join the league, how peace was to be maintained, the kind of disarmament that would be needed, and what obligations to maintain collective security were to be considered. The most disconcerting cluster of issues had to do with the responsibility for the administration of territories of European states that were losers of World War I. It was decided that such territories could become League of Nations members on condition that they "shall give effective guarantees of their sincere intention to observe their international obligations"! In accepting the Covenant, the League of Nations was formally established on January 10, 1920.[2]

The Covenant decreed that member nations would "take any action that may be deemed wise and effectual to safeguard the peace of nations" (Art. 11), "formulate plans for [the] reduction of [national] armaments" (Art. 8), discourage "the manufacture by private enterprise of munitions" (Art. 8), agree "to respect and preserve . . . the territorial integrity . . . of all Members of the League" and "the means by which this obligation should be fulfilled" (Art. 10), submit disputes between members of the League "to arbitration or judicial settlement" (Art. 13), and face possible expulsion should they "resort to war in disregard of . . . Articles 12, 13 or 15" (Art. 16).

League states considered themselves a defense alliance. They accepted the supremacy of the Covenant in relation to other international agreements if these were inconsistent with the League's Covenant (Art. 20). Many of the provisions contained in the Covenant would eventually be incorporated into the UN's Charter.

What this small community of signatory nations had established became a test run of institutionalized internationalism during the League's twenty-six years of stormy existence. Its existence and failures helped clarify the requirements needed for global order to be sustained through collective security arrangements, rather than by the maneuvers of the Great Powers. In 1920 the participating nations established the first League Assembly of thirty-two members and a League Council. The Council would include six so-called Principal Allied and Associated Powers: the British and the Russian empires, France, Japan, Italy, and the United States. The proposal was weakened, ironically, at its inception by the failure of the United States, initially the main proponent of the League, to join the organization as a member.

Ultimately, the Council consisted of France, Italy, Great Britain, and Japan as permanent members and Belgium, Brazil, Spain, and Greece as

elected members selected to represent the Assembly in the Council. Somewhat complacently, Article 4 of the League's Covenant stated that four Assembly members would "be selected by the Assembly from time to time [at]
its discretion." This was a clear indication that leadership of the League
rested with the "Council of the few" rather than with the Assembly of all
member states, a structure that would be replicated in a somewhat more
explicit form in the United Nations.

The League Secretariat was to be established in Geneva. Sir Eric Drum-
mond of the United Kingdom was elected by the Paris Peace Conference's
plenary session on April 28, 1919, to be its first secretary-general. The
League was explicitly associated with a European-dominated state-centric
system with a hegemonic relationship with the non-Western world, formalized through colonialism but also exhibited in a variety of unequal relations between the West and the rest.

At the same time, the Court of International Justice (CIJ) with its headquarters in The Hague was created to render decisions among states involving international law and to resolve doubts about legal questions put to it by
principal organs of the League. Its conclusions were formally categorized
as "advisory" rather than "obligatory," expressing the still lingering reluctance of sovereign states to submit their national interests to the discipline
of international law. While this court was conceived and proposed by the
League of Nations, it was formally independent. The US, not a member of
the League, also never became a member of the CIJ. An American judge,
however, was among the initial eight judges elected to serve on the Court.
During the years of its existence (1922–1946), the CIJ dealt with twenty-
nine cases involving mostly territorial disputes, minority issues, cross-
border trade, and travel. The UN International Court of Justice (ICJ), as the
successor to the League's CIJ, would be given a similar mandate to provide
advisory opinions and lacking obligatory force.

A major reason why the US had not supported the CIJ was the League's
rejection of the US demand to have a right of veto in court cases involving
the "domestic jurisdiction" of the US. Although the US is not a member of
the International Criminal Court (ICC), a non-UN institution, because of
its refusal to be held accountable by applicable international law, it is a
member of the UN ICJ because the Charter makes all UN member states automatically parties to the statute of this court. For several decades, the US
even agreed to a limited acceptance of the compulsory jurisdiction of the
ICJ except for disputes involving its internal affairs. This intermittent acceptance of ICJ authority was withdrawn in the mid-1980s after Nicaragua
submitted a complaint protesting the US mining of its harbors during an

internal struggle between the Contras, right-wing rebel groups supported by the US, and the Sandinistas, the ruling Marxist party.

Ever since the League of Nations came into existence and global multilateralism became a part of international relations, US diplomacy has often taken a rejectionist approach to international treaties and has generally tried to marginalize the work of the ICJ unless it could take advantage of a situation in which the ICJ was almost certain to interpret international law as supportive of US foreign policy goals. This was the case in early 1979, after radical students took over the American embassy in Tehran and held US embassy personnel hostage. The US sought vindication of its claims by recourse to the ICJ in what became known as "the hostage case." The UN court, by unanimous vote, pronounced that it was satisfied that the allegations of fact on which the US had based its legal assertions were well founded and in accordance with the statute of the ICJ.

In the early years of the UN, the US government was often supportive and sometimes instrumental in creating new international law. For instance, it displayed impressive leadership in overcoming obstacles to the adoption of the seminal UN Law of the Seas Convention in the 1980s and the preparation of the Comprehensive Test Ban Treaty for nuclear weapons. Yet, at the same time, the US Senate consistently failed to ratify even these important international agreements as they were thought to compromise sovereign rights or strategic interests. The US argument at the time of the League and subsequently in the UN has been partly based on the idea that no external party has a right to get involved in US domestic affairs, that territorial sovereignty is supreme, and where national security policy is involved, the US is unwilling to constrain its discretion to act on behalf of its national interests. This explains why even the UN Convention on the Rights of the Child and the UN Convention on the Elimination of All Forms of Discrimination against Women have still not been ratified by the US. The US authorities play this seemingly incoherent and self-serving role of championing international treaty making and rule-governed conduct for others but prefer, especially in the peace and security area, to rely on archaic realist arrangements like "balance of power" and "deterrence" rather than on international law, an implicit recognition of the primacy of geopolitics.

The multilateralism that developed at the time of the League of Nations was essentially Western, or at least Western-oriented, and tainted by large-scale European colonial rule throughout the Global South. This geopolitical reality would intensify during WWII and was reflected in the agendas of US and Western European powers after combat ended. Aware of the

structural and procedural weaknesses of the League of Nations, these victorious states were determined to create a new multilateral body with much
more authority than the League of Nations had possessed and, at the same
time, would be a political actor whose role they could control to reflect their
interests and values. Such a strategy of ideological domination that had
prevailed in the League earlier in response to the Russian Revolution of
1917, reemerged soon after 1945 in the form of an East/West confrontation
that soon hardened into the Cold War. The Soviet Union shared with the
United States a distrust of the League/UN approach to world order, prefer-
ring reliance on their capabilities to uphold security and pursue their wider
strategic ambitions.

Even before the end of World War I and the founding of the League of
Nations, Western powers had been planning, often in secret, for the extension of a colonial approach to the post-Ottoman Empire in the Middle East.
Mark Sykes, Middle East advisor to the British war cabinet, and François
Picot, French consul-general in Beirut, had been tasked by their governments to define mutually acceptable British and French spheres of interest in the Arab parts of the collapsed Ottoman Empire. An agreement to
this effect had been signed in 1916, to which Imperial Russia had given its
prior consent in exchange for assurances that Russian shipping within the
Black Sea and through the Turkish Bosporus strait would not be hindered.
To encourage cooperation, Arab leaders were promised European support
in their quest for future political independence. The end of the Ottoman
Empire was the beginning of formalized Western domination of the Arab
Middle East, but, as with the former German colonies, European colonialist
ambitions were compromised to the extent that the allocations embedded
in the Sykes-Picot Agreement were changed from imperially controlled colonies to internationalized mandates, supposedly creating essentially a fidu-
ciary "sacred trust" relationship with the League. At the time, these deals
were seen as political compromises between European colonialism and US
nationalism on the one hand and rising non-Western support for the emerging right of national self-determination on the other. A direct repudiation of
the colonial order did not occur, but arrangements were made that reflected
views that the independence of new states should become the goal rather
than the establishment of new colonies in the remains of the empires that
had fallen due to the outcome of World War I.

In the early years of the twentieth century, the Russian people's growing
dissatisfaction with feudalism and the autocracy of Tsar Nicholas II led to increasing social unrest and political protests culminating in the revolutions
of 1917. Russia, due to its preoccupation with internal post-revolutionary

political ferment, withdrew from the war against Germany and like the United States, did not become a founding member of the League but clearly for quite different reasons.[3] Lenin's Decree on Peace and the Second Congress of Soviets defined the Soviet Union's foreign policy in a manner that rejected Western ideas of world order. The focus was on the importance of global peace, disarmament, and cooperative coexistence with other countries and on Soviet commitment to the maintenance of Russian influence over elements of its former empire while formally renouncing colonialism and favoring self-determination. Pan-Slavism became another unifying element that the Soviet Union relied upon to express and strengthen its non-Western orientation. These various conceptions of world order are helpful for an understanding of Soviet and Russian positions at the UN, as well as the bilateral clashes with the West.

As far as Central Asia and Caucasian territories were concerned, Russia managed to keep control over them. Over time these individual territories were absorbed by the Union of Soviet Socialist Republics, becoming known as Soviet Socialist Republics (SSRs). They became an important element for USSR leaders when negotiating with their Western counterparts over national representation at the United Nations in 1945. They argued that all SSRs should be considered as full members in the UN General Assembly to offset the imbalance resulting from the large number of Western nations in the original General Assembly. Voices in the United States sarcastically argued that in that case, all the then forty-eight US states should also be represented in the United Nations. Western leaders finally agreed, with some reluctance, to admit three of the sixteen SSRs (Ukraine, Belarus, and of course, Russia) with full UN membership.

The fate of the Austro-Hungarian Empire was very different from that of the Ottoman Empire. It involved many ethnic and linguistic groups that regarded the 1914–18 war as opportunities for greater autonomy or preferably independence. These groups welcomed Wilson's fourteen-point peace plan because it specifically endorsed a limited right of self-determination, confined to the political circumstances of these two empires. His peace plan did not include a general condemnation of colonialism as articulated by the Soviet Union. Serbs, Czechs, Slovaks, Slovenes, Croats, and others were also encouraged to seek political independence by immigrant communities in the United States coming from these areas. In signing the Covenant of the League of Nations as newly emerging states, these ethnically constituted political actors were more concerned with upholding their unexpectedly achieved sovereignty and maintaining their political survival than with adhering to Western ideas about statehood. Many of these issues would resurface in the early 1940s, when in the footsteps of the League of Nations, the structure and charter of a post-WWII United Nations were conceived and negotiated. This process took place in an international atmosphere strongly influenced by the failures of the League of Nations.

In contrast to the United Nations, the League of Nations had never reflected a universal membership and as a result could not hope to possess an authentic global voice. Even during its most vigorous period, only two-thirds of existing independent states joined the League. The United States never joined, and for various reasons, Italy, Spain, Hungary, the Soviet Union, and Japan had been League members for only short periods of time. Germany joined the League in 1926 but Hitler's Germany left it in 1933. France, despite being a founding member of the League, was at no time convinced that the League would be effective in protecting the country from an attack by Germany. In this spirit, Prime Minister Clemenceau remarked: "I like the League, but I do not believe in it!" France withdrew from the League after Nazi Germany had occupied the country in 1941.

In view of the continuous fluctuation of membership and the absence of several key global powers, the League had little political leverage and lacked military enforcement capabilities. It was therefore not equipped to deal effectively with critical peace and security concerns. The Great Depression of 1929–30 further weakened the cohesion of the League by accentuating nationalist concerns, including economic protectionism. A major procedural impediment when it came to crisis management was the League's voting requirement that all decisions had to be unanimous. A single member country's disagreement with a League proposal prevented any further consideration. As an example, the League's Council proposed imposing economic sanctions on Italy for its occupation in 1935 of Abyssinia (Ethiopia), which constituted a serious violation of the League's Covenant. This proposal was not adopted because the UK as well as France were opposed, still believing that Italy was a counterweight to Nazi Germany. Narrow national self-interests prevailed over the primary peace and security responsibilities of the League. The League was also unable to prevent military confrontations between member states such as when Japan invaded Manchuria in 1931 to protect its economic and political interests from clashing with those of China and the Soviet Union or when Hungary occupied Carpatho-Ukraine in 1939 to recover lands it had lost in 1920 to Czechoslovakia under the Treaty of Trianon. The most dramatic and consequential failure of the League was its inability to convince Germany to abandon its war plans that led to WWII.

The civil wars in Ireland, Spain, Slovakia, and Poland were considered outside the purview of the League since no right of involvement in domestic disputes was included in the League's Covenant (Article 15). For the same reason, the League could not get involved in the Spanish Civil War even after General Franco's insurgent forces had received direct military support from Nazi Germany. Respect for state sovereignty and non-interference in a country's internal affairs formed the League's basis for conducting international relations. The innovative concept of R2P, the international responsibility to protect human rights and human security of people in countries engaged in internal strife, did not exist, and it remains to this day controversial and problematic and, at best, experimental. It was not until 2005 that the UN General Assembly took a firm position to give national sovereignty a human face by deciding that external intervention in a country's internal affairs could be justified on humanitarian and moral grounds when a government could no longer assure the benevolent survival of its people.

An observer of the initial years of the League concluded in 1924 that "the future of the League of Nations ultimately will depend on the strength of its moral powers. The League can achieve much if it is acting in the spirit of justice and humanity." The language used in the League's Covenant expresses an idealistic appeal for cooperation among sovereign states rather than addressing the realistic consequences of geopolitical strategic ambition and continued impunity with respect to accountability. The Covenant encouraged member states to "respect" and "preserve" sovereignty, to note "matters of concern," to take "wise action," to "act in good faith," to express "grave objections," and to identify "evil effects." Safeguarding world order by such pious appeals to sovereign states made the organization incapable of achieving the ideals of the League, caused an understandable wave of cynical disbelief with respect to the claims of international law and the authority of international institutions, and led to a permanent discrediting of future efforts to achieve a durable institutional basis for world peace.

The League's persistent inability to settle disputes and prevent wars, especially WWII, and the facts that over the years sixteen countries had decided to withdraw from the League and a major power, the Soviet Union, was expelled because of its pact with Nazi Germany and invasion of Finland clearly demonstrated that there was an urgent need to replace the somewhat "platonic" League with a new international organization that would have robust decision-making powers and implementing capabilities to promote peace and security for all in a post-WWII world. This seemed well understood by the leadership of the United States and the United Kingdom, and yet ultimately, even more definite actions were taken to impair the performance of the UN if it were to be similarly challenged. Connecting the dots seventy-seven years later between Hiroshima and Nürnberg, it was obvious that the wrong lessons were learned from the failure of the League to safeguard the peoples of the world from the ordeal of war. The blame should be placed less on the League and the UN than on the P5, who irresponsibly abuse their special status in the Security Council. This virtual acknowledgment of the primacy of geopolitics when it comes to addressing conflicts involving major states is a serious flaw, although one consciously undertaken in the design of the UN even more than in the League. But was it a flaw or a recognition of the realities of international relations as of 1945 that persists in the third decade of the twenty-first century?

## WWII and Preparations for a Future UN

Already in 1941, when the UK was a participant in the war against Germany and the US had not yet joined the WWII allies, their leaders, President Roosevelt, and Prime Minister Churchill, were concerned about new but anticipated geopolitical developments. They met to work out a US-UK strategy that envisaged political supremacy and disclosed their intention to convey their anti-fascist intentions to Stalin, the general secretary of the Communist Party of the Soviet Union. These Western wartime leaders wanted to discuss with Stalin the global order and the institutional arrangements they believed were needed to replace the ineffective League of Nations. Their intention was to reach agreement about how best to preserve peaceful relations in a post-WWII world. They also wanted to ensure the continuity of Western leadership of the world, yet they realized that this could not happen without including the Soviet Union. Especially Churchill was aware that this was a naïve goal, as Western leadership could not possibly be combined with Soviet inclusion, given the anticipated conflicts involving the future of Europe and the struggle of the Global South to achieve self-determination and political independence.

In preparation for such an important West-East exchange, the two Western statesmen had met off the Canadian coast in August 1941 on board the British destroyer HMS *Prince of Wales* to draft what became known as the Atlantic Charter, a UK-US declaration somewhat anticipating the constitutional framework embedded in the subsequent UN Charter. The Atlantic Charter was published on August 14, 1941.

Roosevelt and Churchill included eight articles in the Atlantic Charter. Among these was Article 3, which stressed the importance of self-determination—an article to which Winston Churchill, the notorious colonialist, agreed to most reluctantly and with a nullifying twist that in the end kept faith with his colonial past. Churchill never renounced British colonialism. He insisted that the British Empire, including its colonies, were to be exempted from this provision. However, the two leaders had readily agreed on other articles, especially Articles 5, 6 and 7, which called for improved global economic and social conditions for all, freedom from fear and want, and freedom of the seas.

In September 1941, the Atlantic Charter received important support from the London-based Inter-Allied Council, an association of governments in exile, including Free France, and the USSR. A few months later, in January 1942, further approval of the Atlantic Charter was given, again in London, by the UK, the US, the USSR, China, and twenty-two other governments in the Joint Declaration by Members of the United Nations. Meetings of leaders from the UK, the US, the USSR, and others followed in Moscow and Teheran confirming, yet again, their support for the Atlantic Charter. These two conferences concluded: "We are sure that our concord will win an enduring peace. We recognize fully the supreme responsibility resting upon us and all the UN to make a peace which will command the good will of the overwhelming mass of peoples of the world and banish the scourge and terror of war for many generations."

Two years of careful lobbying by the governments of the UK and the US for a post-WWII multilateral structure for peace and security led to international support for a Western-led and Western-oriented institution to succeed the League of Nations. In the autumn of 1944, the US government invited the UK, the Soviet Union, the Republic of China (Taiwan), and other sovereign states to come to Dumbarton Oaks near Washington, DC, to agree upon the next steps in negotiating the establishment of a global body that already in the 1943 Moscow meeting had been called the United Nations.

During the six-week conference (August 21 to October 7, 1944), with the war still going on in Asia, the United States and other Western participants had to face several dimly anticipated hurdles. Stalin's Soviet Union would not agree to Chiang Kai-shek's Republic of China participating in the conference. The Soviet Union and the US disagreed on the admission of certain countries, such as Poland and Argentina, to the future United Nations. Additionally, the Soviet Union had put forward a demand that all sixteen Soviet Socialist Republics be admitted as full members in the General Assembly. There were also disagreements over the adoption of voting procedures in the envisaged UN Security Council. The most sensitive element for the US, given its global power and leadership aspirations, was how to manage the combination of its role within the UN structure and outside it. At that time, the imminent defeat of the Axis powers was no longer in question, but somewhat more uncertain was the timing of the defeat of Japan.[4] Meetings of allies had the dual purpose of discussing how the war was developing in Europe and the Far East and beginning to plan a global security structure for the time after combat.

A crucial conference in Malta in early 1945 addressed such sensitive issues as colonial territories and trusteeship matters, criteria for UN membership, and the establishment of an international judicial body. This was followed by the decisive meeting in February 1945 on the then Soviet peninsula of Crimea. The three global powers, represented by Stalin, Roosevelt, and Churchill, met in Yalta to finalize a common political agenda on the establishment of the United Nations. France, to its dismay, was not included and neither the Republic of China nor the People's Republic of China were invited to be present. Even though Stalin was clearly concerned over the imbalance between the number of Western and Eastern states in a future UN General Assembly, he withdrew his earlier demand for admission to the UN of all Soviet Socialist Republics (SSRs). Roosevelt and Churchill in exchange agreed that in addition to Russia, two of the fifteen other SSRs, Ukraine and Belarus, would also be admitted to the UN as full members.

The three political leaders also decided to establish a UN Trusteeship Council responsible for the administration of national communities deemed not yet ready for sovereign statehood, most prominently the former German colonial territories. Stalin also confirmed that the Soviet Union would become an ally in the war against Japan. In turn, he received Western assurances that the Soviet Union would get back some territory that Russia had lost in the 1904–1905 Russo-Japanese War. Stalin informed the Western leaders that the Soviet Union would attend the forthcoming UN Conference on International Organizations in San Francisco in April 1945.

The three statesmen were leaders with very different geopolitical priorities, ambitions, and ideologies. They disagreed in many ways but seemed to share a common goal: a commitment to achieve a world without major wars as reinforced by minimization of international conflicts. Without their foresight and vision, their pragmatic steadfastness and their willingness to compromise, the creation of the United Nations in 1945 would have been impossible. The ideological barriers and the different expectations of the three leaders, which would later significantly limit the UN's performance in many domains of the international order, were put aside. This was perhaps an ironic benefit of "the fog of war," that made even these sophisticated statesmen happily less attentive to what divided them than to what united them, given the devastation and massive casualties of World War II. Such welcome harmonies did not long survive.

Yalta ended a long chain of enabling conferences stretching over many years. During these years, Eastern and Western global powers had each positioned themselves to ensure their politically preferred roles in a post–Second World War order. This pragmatic element conditioned and balanced the visionary dimension and made the UN a reality rather than a utopian dream. In the process, it produced a framework as suitable for geopolitical machinations as it was for the pursuit of peace and justice. This dualism is what makes agreement about the nature of the UN so elusive. Some see the Charter as a war prevention structure applicable to all states; others see the UN as a geopolitically dominated structure that lacks the capabilities to prevent violations of the Charter by P5 countries, especially those acts of statecraft that threaten to engulf the world in the most terrible of wars.

International financial and economic policies were concurrently part of the policy agenda agreed upon by Washington, London, and Moscow. The US and the UK wanted to ensure that the world economy would be market-driven and remain in Western hands. With this in mind, the US government invited global leaders to come to Bretton Woods in the United States in July 1944 to discuss global monetary, financial, and economic matters. Including somewhat surprisingly the Soviet Union, the overwhelming majority of the forty-four participating governments came from the Western Hemisphere. Again, neither Communist China nor the Republic of China were invited.

Postwar diplomacy was influenced by the shared conviction that the Great Depression of the 1930s had occurred because of the absence of global arrangements to govern the world economy based on mutual benefit. It was believed that such regulatory arrangements were needed, especially in periods of economic stress, in order to avoid adverse developments bearing on trade, investment, currency stabilization, and socio-economic progress.

The outcome of the Bretton Woods Conference constituted a victory for Western, especially US, interests. It concluded with agreements to create the International Monetary Fund (IMF) promoting global monetary cooperation and the International Bank for Reconstruction and Development (IBRD), later renamed the World Bank. Initially the bank was involved only in financing European postwar reconstruction but eventually expanded its mandate to provide countries in the Global South with loans for economic development and assistance in poverty programs. These two new institutions, both part of the UN System, had their headquarters in Washington, DC, signifying both the American ambition to control the world economy and the acquiescence of others. Participation in the IBRD was based on a nation's paid-in capital, and in the IMF on assigned and differential capital quotas. These quotas and the resulting number of votes a nation would have within the IMF and the IBRD were determined by its relative economic and financial strength and could be changed only by agreement of their respective boards. These weighted voting schemes were designed to allow the US and its Western allies to maintain a majority of votes. This Western orientation of the Bretton Woods institutions has persisted and has prompted increasing criticism, especially from the governments of the Global South and anti-neoliberal critics of economic bias favorable to the Global North.

As earlier indicated, the 1944 international meetings at Dumbarton Oaks and Bretton Woods were convened in preparation for replacing the League of Nations with a new global institution, the United Nations. These proceedings became major political, financial, and economic building blocks for a Western-dominated, US-led framing of globalization. This approach was unsurprisingly resisted by the Soviet Union and its allies. These states would make largely futile efforts to challenge this slanted shaping of the evolving new institutions.

It soon became clear that the Soviet bloc, lacking the political and economic influence to compete with the West in global settings, adopted increasingly uncooperative and often oppositional stances. In the process, the question of who owns the UN became a key issue that has remained salient and controversial throughout the years, although rarely posed so directly. Western political leaders, more than others, had made full use of what has become known as the "penholder's advantages"—a term describing self-appointed initiatives in the UN for the drafting of concept papers and resolutions. A former German ambassador to the United States aptly pointed out that "the one who presents the text, who stakes out a position early . . . is the one who determines the game!"[5] This power of the penholder has prevailed throughout the negotiations of the transition from the League of Nations to the United Nations and has remained a frequent tool for influencing results of complex negotiations within the UN System. However, phrasing the issue in this way begs the question of how penholders are selected or appointed.

Following the Yalta agreement in early 1945 between the "Big Three," forty-four nations came together in San Francisco for two months (April 25–June 26, 1945) to do the hard work of producing a concrete UN Charter text. The costs of participation were borne by the US government. The purpose was to work out the details of a constitutional and operational framework for the new institution. The United States, as host, was well prepared, both strategically and substantially, to lead the process that resulted in the finalization of the UN Charter. Alger Hiss of the US State Department, a controversial figure in American political life because of his alleged ties to Communism, served as the executive secretary of the 1944 Dumbarton Oaks Conference, and the year after, became the secretary-general of the UN Charter Conference in San Francisco. The UN emblem and the UN flag, displayed on this occasion, had been designed for the new organization by two US architects, Oliver Lincoln Lundquist and Donald McLaughlin.

Ever since the 1919 Versailles peace conference, and in consultation with the UK, its closest ally, the US had continuously taken stock of the outcome of subsequent East/West conferences. It had assessed geopolitical developments and analyzed the performance of the League of Nations— "nothing was left to chance . . . by the experts in Washington."[6]

The US understood that the League of Nations had endorsed a series of world order principles ranging from disarmament to territorial sovereignty and collective security that were often not reflected in either agreed rules of international order or the behavior of states. League members did not in practice uphold their previously declared "sincere intentions to observe their international obligations" as specified in the League's Covenant. This led to a discrediting gap between agreed guidelines and actual patterns of conduct.

The requirement of unanimity meant that a single dissenting vote in the Assembly of the League would defeat a resolution supported by a majority of other members. The language used in the League's Covenant had more to do with idealistic appeals for cooperation than facing the realistic adverse consequences of geopolitical impotence and impunity—that is, the lack of capabilities and political will to preserve the peace. The Covenant did nothing more than encourage member states to "respect" and "preserve" sovereignty, to note "matters of concern," to take "wise action," to "act in good faith," to express "grave objections," and to identify "evil effects." Such injunctions for good conduct were far from sufficient to achieve the desired results. Seeking to safeguard world order by relying on pious appeals to sovereign states was incapable of achieving the ideals of the League and caused a backlash of disbelief with respect to the claims of international law and the authority of international institutions. This gap between the aspirations of the public after the experience of a devastating war and the continuing state-centric/geopolitical nature of political consciousness governing the behavior of political elites exposes the root cause of the failure of the League. Such a gap has continued to exist and has deepened since the creation of the UN.

The post-WWII challenge was not only to avoid repeating the failings of the League but had the added urgency of war prevention resulting from the use of atomic bombs in the closing days of the war. The West wanted to make use of US power, prestige, and influence to build a US-led, Western-oriented, rule-based United Nations able to do what the League had not been able to do. Senator Connally was quoted in the *New York Times*, April 21, 1945, as saying: "The US has a peculiar responsibility. It has the lofty duty to perform in leading the peoples of the earth away from the concepts of rule by the sword!" US foreign policy has exerted varying degrees of influence to avoid the economic and political radicalization of nationalist elites in Asia, Africa, and Latin America during their various struggles for sovereign statehood. Even during World War II, there had been a US apprehension about the next stage of global relations, pitting the capitalist West against the socialist East, with the newly independent nations of the South caught in the ideological crossfire.

The League of Nations had clearly failed in its primary mission of enhancing global security and preventing wars. An awareness of this fundamental weakness of the League is both reflected and ignored in the UN Charter adopted at the mid-1945 San Francisco Conference. As it turned out, the United Nations, as the successor institution, would have a global outreach and universal participation that the League of Nations never achieved. It also was given a constitutional basis for establishing enforcement capabilities that had not existed before. As will be shown, when it came to practice, however, the UN, just as the League, had no provision for the restraint, much less the punishment of any state, especially the most powerful, if they violated international law relevant to peace and security, as embodied in the Charter. The UN also lacks the procedural mechanisms to withstand or even mitigate geopolitical rivalries and sovereignty-oriented approaches to national security. The capabilities to protect peace and guarantee physical security embedded in the Charter have never been adequately operationalized. The UN's failure to fully utilize its peacekeeping potential has given rise to the US insistence on retaining almost exclusive sovereign control over uses of international force in those few instances when it was authorized by the UN.

Not only the United States but also Europe remembered the reasons why in 1919 President Wilson had not succeeded in obtaining Congressional support for US membership in the League of Nations. The US had become sidelined internationally in the crucial years between the two twentieth-century world wars. President Roosevelt wanted to make sure that he would gain bipartisan support from the US Congress, especially the Senate, as well as from the American public for the central idea that it would be in the best national interest of the US to support the creation of a strong United Nations, and in doing so, overcome its traditional posture of isolationism and become the respected leader of an evolving global order. But this was a Faustian bargain that had large international costs as well as important national benefits, especially the assurance that US sovereignty and strategic priorities would never be made subject to UN authority.

## UN Charter Conference in San Francisco

Negotiations in San Francisco were based on the conclusions of the 1944 Dumbarton Oaks Conference and the policy decisions agreed upon in Yalta in the spring of 1945. The forty-four delegations faced a wide array of challenges that needed to be addressed. Among these were conditions for UN membership, the role of the General Assembly, middle-power representation in the Security Council, self-determination, decolonization and independence, the fears of smaller nations of being dominated by the big powers, the East/West representational balance in the General Assembly, and trusteeship management.

The single most contentious concern among all delegations, however, related to the conferral of the right of veto on the permanent members of the UN Security Council. The five nations to be confirmed by the conference as "permanent members" of the Security Council (the so-called P5), however, were anxious to maintain the appearance of "world power unity," while others feared and objected to the emergence of a "dictatorship of the few." This issue has persisted in various forms unto this day. "The world is greater than Five," coined by Turkish President Recep Tayyip Erdoğan, has become a popular battle cry underpinning contemporary calls for UN reforms.

The Soviet Union, reflecting its perceived minority status, wanted to reduce the authority of the General Assembly and enhance the power of the P5 in the Security Council so that it would not find itself subject to "a tyranny of the majority." The US, on the other hand, insisted on a distinction between "procedural" and "substantive" voting in the Security Council, limiting the right of veto to issues of substance. In the end, the Soviet Union had its way in assigning to the General Assembly no more than an advisory role in matters of peace and security, and the United States obtained agreement for veto voting by the P5 based on the distinction it had proposed. Some 3,500 participants debated, lobbied, and pressured at different levels, even threatened during efforts to influence the bargaining process that produced the construction of a global institution to which all states wanted to belong. US President Truman in his address on April 25, 1945, to the UN General Assembly reminded world leaders: "If we do not want to die together in war, we must learn to live together in peace." This compassionate call for unity of purpose unfortunately has not translated into the decision-making dynamics of the Security Council.

During seventy-eight years of the UN's existence, the refusal of permanent members of the Security Council to act as a team to reform decision-making in the Security Council has persisted. The existence and misuse of the veto has remained the single most important factor in restricting UN efforts at crisis prevention, management, mediation, and resolution. There has always been a measure of constitutional incoherence between affirming the authority of international law while giving the most powerful states a constitutional right to avoid its applicability. As we have said, the UN Charter itself confers a geopolitical right of exception, which vests authority to put to one side both the restraints of international law and accountability procedures for its violation.

Cynics have reasonably asked what sort of organization imposes its rule of law on the weak while granting the strong an exemption without restrictions. The situation reduces to accountability for the weak and impunity for the strong. Such a reality is not a political arrangement based on the rule of law where equals are treated equally but rather a hierarchy of power in which formal equals—sovereign states—are treated unequally reflecting a geopolitical ranking by the Charter in relation to the most vital issues under the purview of the UN.

At the end of the two months conference in San Francisco, five world powers and forty-five other nations had finally agreed to the UN Charter with its nineteen chapters. It was concluded in a high-spirited mood of optimism, with the constitutional document described as a charter of peace, a blessing for the earth, a great adventure, a dream of humanity come true. In the final plenary of the conference, US president Truman, visibly moved, told the delegations, "No matter how great our strength, we must deny ourselves the license to do always as we please." The Charter's Preamble and Article 1 reminded governments and civil society "We the peoples of the United Nations [are] determined" to maintain international peace and security, to collectively outlaw international threats and aggression, and to promote friendly relations through the promotion of economic and social advancement of all people. The world order would be determined from now on by a multilateral agenda. The UN, open to "all peace-loving nations," it was stated, would be dedicated to promoting the public good of the world's peoples. The UN Charter entered into force six months later, on October 24, 1945.

In the following chapters of our book, we hope to shed some light on this continuing struggle to fulfill the vision of the UN Charter. For this vision to become reality will depend on two sets of developments: first, the recognition that adherence to international law serves the interests of all states, including the P5, and second, the political will to forego or greatly restrict the right of veto. At present, an outmoded form of "political realism" pervades the highest levels of government in the most powerful states. Therefore, for the UN to live up to its ideals will require an ideological struggle that challenges deep-seated ideas about security in the anarchical society of nations.

## Challenges Ahead

Of course, the dilemma exposed was real. To gain and retain participation of states, it was necessary to provide assurances that their adversaries would not use the UN to bully or take advantage. Such reassurances could not be provided to the Soviet Union, sure to be outvoted on most contentious issues without the safety belt of the veto. It must be remembered as well that the failures of the League were attributed in part to the concerns of major states that their interests were being trampled upon by feared tyrannies of the majority. None of the major states showed any willingness to entrust the General Assembly, where sovereign equality prevailed, with a right of decision. We are left, then, with this dual understanding: the peoples of the world need and desire an effective and legitimate UN to fulfill the expectations of a world without major wars. Such a cautionary assessment is further confirmed by the persistent refusal of the West to seek a strengthened UN. Sovereignty and geopolitics, as much as ideological rivalry and economic disparities, make hopes for a UN strong enough to prevent war and atrocities, as well as to promote global sustainable well-being, beyond the reach of attainable politics. The UN continues to play its part in a largely state-centric, geopolitically dominated, ecologically dysfunctional world order. Our exposition and advocacy of what we call "visionary realism" is intended to depict a perspective necessary for human survival and ecological coexistence. We need to acknowledge that such goals contrast in motivation and intention from the pieties of statesmen who had founded the League of Nations in 1920 and the UN in 1945.

# THREE

# Multilateralism during the Cold War and Beyond

The Yalta consensus of 1945 reached by Stalin, Roosevelt, and Churchill about power sharing at the future UN and the joint maintenance of peace and security was sidelined almost as soon as the Security Council and the General Assembly, the political organs of the UN, were established. Explanations for this development must be found in order to understand the early ineffectiveness of the Security Council and the General Assembly. They will help to identify what reforms should be undertaken to create a United Nations able to tackle the unfolding challenges facing the global order. Poverty, climate change, sustainable development, biodiversity, extremism, digitalization, pandemics, and migration as universal concerns, therefore, deserve to become key priorities in the evolving reform debate.

The hope after 1945 was that fundamental East/West differences of historical experience and ideology would not interfere with the common objective to build an institutional framework designed to protect the community of nations against war while facilitating socio-economic progress, as well as addressing later concerns about ecological stability. We are convinced that this ambitious undertaking, although obstructed, remains realistic as a goal because it is necessary for human survival. The continuing quest for the maximization of extraterritorial power and influence, however, has continued to be the dominant objective in Moscow, London, and Washington, and that has become increasingly difficult to hide from the public. Years of multilateral diplomacy prior to the establishment of the UN could have been relied upon by all sides to address these obvious and fundamental contradictions between the geopolitical interests of the parties and the multilateral purposes and principles of the UN. Unfortunately, this did not happen.

Once the UN Security Council and the General Assembly had become operative, it would have been important to appraise the progress of work in these two political organs continuously and to review the extent of cooperation between them concurrently to assess whether their adherence in practice to the provisions of the UN Charter was acceptable. These concerns involved primarily the rights, obligations, and benefits of membership for all; peaceful means of settling international disputes; and the absence of threats and use of force against any state in accordance with the UN Charter (Articles 2, 24, and 51), including the Security Council's special responsibilities in this respect. The extent of nonadherence to the Charter resulted in disappointing consequences for the efficacy of the UN. Individual victors of World War II were convinced that "power" was on their side, ignoring the contrary flows of history. Therefore, they avoided any self-scrutiny and preferred to keep silent. However, other UN member countries, non-governmental organizations, civil societies, and scholars had a responsibility to call attention to the obstacles the Security Council faced in dealing with peace and security matters and identify steps to redress this dysfunctional pattern of behavior. Unfortunately, this did indeed not happen.

From 1945 to 1965, there was a steep increase in UN membership, from 51 to 117 nations. All this happened under the watchful eyes of the US and Soviet governments. Most of the newly independent countries in Africa, Asia, South America, and the Middle East, such as Ghana, Indonesia, Trinidad, and Jordan, were poor, had inadequate administrative structures, and lacked indigenously trained human resources. The developing world, however, was acutely aware that level playing fields relevant to their development priorities did not exist, that there was a distinctly tenuous relationship between the US and the Soviet Union, and that a treacherous road lay ahead for them if these conditions persisted. They, therefore, were among the first countries to lobby for institutional reforms of the United Nations. One way of overcoming the formidable disadvantages of the countries from the Global South, their leaders argued, was to form, in and outside the UN, alliances and pressure groups, mainly with other newly independent countries.

These countries also welcomed a US initiative to create a mechanism for the General Assembly to overrule the Security Council in cases when an international emergency had arisen and unanimity on how to respond to it was not forthcoming among the permanent members of the Security Council. In this spirit, in the context of the Korean War, the General Assembly passed in November 1950 the Uniting for Peace resolution (A/RES/377), with an overwhelming majority of fifty-two votes for to five votes against and two abstentions. The Soviet Union, together with four Eastern European countries within its recognized sphere of influence, voted against this resolution but could not prevent its adoption. The prime motivation for the US proposal of such a resolution had been to limit possible future Soviet vetoes in the Security Council of peace and security initiatives not to their liking. Between 1946 and 1950, the Soviet Union had already vetoed fifty-one Security Council proposals, while the US and the three other permanent members had not vetoed a single resolution. This would change significantly in later years, as US policy on various controversial issues became less insulated against disapproval or potential sanctioning, encouraging the US to exercise its Security Council right of veto.

## Emerging Alliances

The Non-Alignment Movement (NAM), founded in Belgrade in 1961 as a new multinational alliance, is today, aside from the United Nations, the largest grouping of states with an avowed goal of avoiding the dangerous distractions of bipolar realities of the Cold War. Jawaharlal Nehru of India, Josip Tito of Yugoslavia, Kenneth Kaunda of Zambia, Gamal Abdel Nasser of Egypt, Kwame Nkrumah of Ghana, Sukarno of Indonesia, and U Nu of Burma, as NAM's leaders representing all parts of the world except Latin America, were determined to create a third power bloc in the UN with the hope that such a coalition would make a difference in global-order discourse. Committed to securing the independence of developing countries from undue great power influence, NAM was prepared to promote the political and economic leverage of the South in relation to development goals, to confront the remnants of colonialism as well as the new challenges associated with neocolonialism, and to support disarmament. The UN was regarded as the best available platform from which to influence geopolitical developments. Speaking at the UN in 1960, Kwame Nkrumah, the president of Ghana and one of the NAM leaders, put it this way: "I look upon the United Nations as the only organization that holds out any hope for the future of mankind." Another NAM leader, Gamal Abdel Nasser, the president of the Egyptian Arab Republic, told the UN on the same occasion: "Imperialism is trying to use the UN as a mask to conceal its designs!" Two years later, in 1962, US president Kennedy tried to reassure the developing world that "our basic goal remains a peaceful world community of free and independent states—free to choose their own future and their own system, so long as it does not threaten the freedom of others." The qualification "so long as it does not threaten the freedom of others" enabled partisan misinterpretations and provocative behavior because of its imprecise wording.

During this period, US lawmakers observed with concern the increase in UN membership and challenged an alleged "tyranny of the majority" within the UN. They argued unabashedly that the emerging new majorities in the General Assembly would lead to a multilateral agenda focussed on development and human rights. It was widely understood that they were worried that their nationalist objectives of expanding the global influence of the US and its interest in securing the ascendancy of a market-oriented world economy would now encounter strong resistance, including promotion of reforms deemed "socialist" in conservative Western circles.[1]

## The Early Years of the Cold War

Self-serving interpretations of Security Council resolutions became part of the tool kit of power politics, especially for the P5. Ambiguous wording was often the only way to build a consensus that was able to obtain a majority of General Assembly votes and to prevent a veto from P5 members. This led the Security Council to give a misleading impression that it was acting in unity when in fact, it was often dangerously divided.

A review of the Security Council's handling of the 1962 Cuban missile crisis, as an example, shows that the US and the Soviet Union reacted to draft resolutions on Cuba either by supporting a consensus resolution or abstaining, not voting at all, or being recorded as being absent. This was deceptive because US/Soviet Cold War rivalries prevented any agreement in the Security Council to end the Cuban crisis; instead the crisis was overcome, with the help of good luck, by a geopolitical compromise negotiated between the two reigning superpowers acting on their own outside the UN. These big powers seemed oblivious to their war prevention pledges at Yalta while the world trembled.

Instead of thinking multilaterally, these two superpowers ignored the UN Charter and acted bilaterally to protect their respective national and regional interests and uphold their clashing global ambitions. The limitations of the UN as a credible conflict mediator in such circumstances became evident in ways that damaged its reputation. Each side blamed the other as being the cause of the conflict. The US accused the Soviet Union of its secret "offensive military build-up" in Cuba and reminded the Security Council of the American right of self-defense, as supposedly authorized in Article 51 of the Charter. Actually, the US claiming the right of self-defense was an expansion of the narrowly circumscribed right embodied in the Charter that was limited to responses taken after a *prior* use of force against sovereign territory. The Soviet Union, for its part, condemned the encroachment by the US on "the freedom and independence of a small country" like Cuba and blamed the US for "trampling behind the back of the Security Council upon the principles of the UN Charter" through its earlier deployment of nuclear missiles in Turkey threatening the Soviet Union.[2]

## South/North and East/West Cleavages

Statements by representatives from both developing and developed countries in the early years of the UN were testimonies not only directed at existing East/West rifts but also of serious South/North discords, especially when it came to matters of trade and investment. Political inexperience on the part of the developing world had generated false expectations that their pleas for a reformed global economy would be sympathetically heard and even receive substantial support from developed countries facilitating their socio-economic development. The South also sensed early on what the NAM leader, Ghana's president Nkrumah called the "great dangers at the UN." One of his countrymen, Acting Prime Minister Lamptey in October 1971 almost pleaded, "The big powers should put an end to the struggle for supremacy in the third world." These hopes and fears of the developing world were marginalized at the UN by the overwhelming dynamics of the East/West divide and the competitive nature of Big Power relations. It was not just the voices from the South that expressed frustration about geopolitical trends. Such concerns had become global, although in the North with a focus on the dangers of major warfare.

Eleven years earlier, in 1960, the Security Council had passed an unusual resolution entitled Question of Relations between the Great Powers (S/RES/135). It criticized P5 members for their failure to agree on how to maintain international peace and security. The resolution appealed to the permanent members "to make every effort to restore and strengthen international good will and confidence." Special reference was made to "the mounting danger of the continuation of the armament race." This resolution was supported by four of the five permanent members of the Security Council. The USSR, joined by Poland, did not reject the resolution but abstained.

In these early years, the US and the USSR, despite rising tensions, often tried to cooperate in the Security Council. Open confrontation between these two leading states was the exception. The Cuban missile crisis constituted the most ominous example of such an exception. Even though the USSR often resorted to casting a veto, P5 members preferred to signal disagreement by abstaining or being absent rather than by casting a veto and thereby abruptly ending Security Council debates on matters of peace and security.

Initially, individual victors of WWII were convinced that power, as well as history, were on their side and that it would be possible to ensure that Security Council policy would be shaped to reflect their distinct governmental interests. In response, the UN General Assembly with the support of non-governmental organizations and academia could have pointed to the structural unpreparedness of the emerging organization when confronted with the growing East/West power competition. The Security Council could have taken steps to cooperate with the General Assembly to redress the existing dysfunction. This did not happen. In these early years of the UN, there was no government or groups of governments willing and able to challenge Cold War politics in ways that might have allowed the UN to play the roles envisioned by the architects of the UN back in 1945.

Russia had significant power in its geographical area of influence but was preoccupied by complex geopolitical developments in several Soviet republics. Moscow, however, lacked the financial and human resources needed to compete with the US in shaping the UN agenda in a global setting that at the time was largely Western or Western-oriented. Washington, in contrast, had the necessary resources and diplomatic leverage. It used these instruments of influence to shape and control the emerging multilateral political, economic, and financial systems, all physically and psychologically situated in the West. The World Bank and the IMF had been set up to operate in Washington, the UN was headquartered in New York and Geneva, the International Court of Justice was in The Hague, and the UN System of agencies was predominately spread across Western Europe and North America.

## The Role of UN Secretaries-General

In the early years of the Cold War, the UN Secretaries-General were widely perceived as symbols of the ideals of the UN, as diplomats, civil servants, and spokespersons for the interests of the world's people. Powerful member states in the Security Council, however, were more inclined to view a Secretary-General not as a policymaker but as the UN's chief administrative officer, as stipulated in the UN Charter. In both the East and West, there was a strong reluctance to accept the Secretary-General as a formal political bridge-builder and mediator with respect to geopolitical rivalry.

The calls from around the world for Secretaries-General to show values-based leadership with humility, integrity, and dignity in relations with nations were discreetly disregarded. Member governments, especially the US and the USSR, generally perceived these calls as unrealistic and politically irrelevant. References by Secretaries-General to the dangers of shortsighted selfishness in political decision-making and their criticisms of governmental indifference to East/West disarmament, the dangers of a nuclear arms race, and global socio-economic inequality were all deemed inappropriate in Washington and Moscow. The support of Secretaries-General for a new international economic order was not welcomed in the industrialized world. Concerns expressed by Secretaries-Generals about US and USSR involvement in regional conflicts and the observation by one Secretary-General (Waldheim) that "power politics remains the prevalent mode of international behavior" received a cold-shouldered response.[3] Secretaries-General advocating "respect for international law" and daring to remind the world of humanity's hopes for peace and justice for all were not welcomed by P5 governments, nor was their insistence that human rights were universal. There was a tacit agreement between the USSR and the US not to get Secretaries-General, as nonelected international civil servants, involved in "their" political affairs. Gone was the spirit of Yalta, and territorial sovereignty and the pursuit of national interests prevailed over promoting human and global interests.

During the years of the first five UN Secretaries-General,[4] there were national political leaders who wanted to relegate them and their executive staff to no more than useful backstage diplomats possessing no formal political mandate. Independent decision-making by Secretaries-General in security and crisis-related matters, as foreseen in the UN Charter (Article 100), regretfully did not exist then nor does it today, although Secretaries-General have varied greatly in their abilities, energy, and willingness to engage controversial behavior of P5 states and their close allies, especially during their first term.

## The UN Civil Service

The idea of a permanent UN civil service was not at all popular in countries with long traditions in foreign affairs. They feared UN "meddling" would interfere with their own bilateral diplomacy. "There was a tendency to look at international civil servants as clerks and second-class bureaucrats, at best, and at worst, as interlopers," writes a former Undersecretary-General.[5]

In 1946 the United Nations, while still located in London, had initially recruited some three hundred staff members, mostly of British nationality. Quite appropriately, fifty of these first-generation UN civil servants had already served in the League of Nations. Their experience in multilateral affairs was considered important for the fledgling UN civil service. Their knowledge and experience in a wide range of areas was helpful in establishing the initial UN institutional frameworks for WHO, UNICEF, ECE, ICJ, UNDP, and the World Bank and the IMF.

Six months later, when the UN headquarters had been moved from London to New York, the number of UN staff had increased to three thousand, with a concentration of New York residents. Ever since, the UN System has grown exponentially in efforts to meet its expanding worldwide activities. Staffing on "as wide a geographical basis as possible" (UN Charter, Article 101[3]) was technically possible, but could not be implemented in the early years of the UN since many countries did not yet have adequately trained men and women or, for political reasons, governments were not willing to release nationals for such international assignments. The UN Secretariat was staffed at that time largely by individuals from the US and Western Europe. Only a handful of UN staff came from the Soviet Union, Eastern Europe, and newly independent countries. At senior levels, there were at first very few women. Gender balance was not part of the staffing policy in the early period of UN existence. Seventy-six years later, the UN reports progress: in 2022, 125,436 staff worked in the UN System worldwide, and 46.2 percent were females.[6]

## UN Crisis Prevention, Peacekeeping, and the Security Council

The UN Charter identifies the maintenance of peace and the strengthening of collective security as major UN objectives. Member countries are asked to make available national armed forces (Article 43) for the purpose of maintaining international peace and security, and a Military Staff Committee was supposedly going to advise and assist the Security Council on the military requirements for peace and security (Article 47). The Security Council as well as the General Assembly were preoccupied from the very beginning of the UN with major political and security concerns involving South Asia (India/Pakistan) and East Asia (Korean Peninsula), Central Africa (Congo) and the Middle East (Israel/Palestine and Egypt). Therefore, the Security Council could have benefited from an active Military Staff Committee operating as intended. However, distrust and conflict between the USSR and the US, aggravated by disunity within the P5, explains why the Military Staff Committee has not yet been able to function in accord with its intended advisory role.

In response to the Arab-Israeli War of 1948, the Security Council carried out its first peacekeeping operation by establishing the UN Truce Supervision Organization (UNTSO) to observe the Israeli-Arab armistice agreement (S/RES/50 [1948]). Unarmed UN military observers were deployed to the Middle East to preserve peace in the area, relying on nonviolent military forces. Under arrangements like the UNTSO mission, the United Nations Military Observer Group in India and Pakistan (UNMOGIP) was formed in 1951 as another major peacekeeping operation and charged with monitoring the cease-fire line of control along a five-hundred-mile corridor separating Indian and Pakistani Kashmir (S/RES/91). UN peacekeepers, in both the UNTSO and UNMOGIP missions, came almost exclusively from Western countries. As a third example, the Security Council responded in 1960 to the violence that had erupted in the Republic of the Congo due to tribal conflicts and ethnic regionalism. These clashes were linked to demands to end Belgian colonial rule in the country. At that time, the Council decided to mount an intercontinental multinational peacekeeping force, the first of its kind, to the Republic of the Congo (S/RES/143); UN peacekeepers were sent from Europe, Africa, Asia, and North America (Canada). As permanent members of the Security Council, the US and the USSR were deeply involved multilaterally in the Congo, but as Cold War protagonists, they also pursued their adversarial national interests in the country.

The war between North and South Korea (1950–53) is also relevant to further document the diversity of the global conflicts with which the UN Security Council was confronted by in the initial years of its existence and to show how early fundamental East/West differences surfaced among the permanent members of the Security Council. Communist North Korea had received political, material, and military support from two communist allies, the Soviet Union and the People's Republic of China (PRC), while the Western-oriented South Korea obtained major assistance from the United States and its allies. This resulted in a proxy war between the US and the USSR and the PRC. Although the Security Council played its mandated mediation role through various resolutions in efforts to resolve the conflict between the two Koreas, the UN never became a party to any legal agreement that the US had concluded bilaterally with the government of South Korea. The misleadingly named UN Command (UNC) was an American invention purporting to internationalize a military operation controlled by the US. In 1994, Secretary-General Boutros Boutros-Ghali in a letter to the foreign minister of the Democratic People's Republic of Korea (North Korea) Kim Yong-nam, conveyed his view that the Security Council "did not establish a unified command as a subsidiary organ under its [UN] control but merely recommended the creation of such a command specifying that it be under the authority of the United States. Already in 1974, the General Assembly, objecting to the UNC designation, had passed a resolution asking the US to end the use of this misnomer. Over the years, three Secretaries-General, Boutros Boutros-Ghali, Kofi Annan, and Ban Ki-moon, declared that there was no basis for the US claim of UN involvement in post-armistice military operations in South Korea. The US government and its military command-ers in South Korea ignored these appeals, and the government in Seoul, anxious not to cause friction with the US, its principal ally, did not object. Even today, and without any overt criticism from other UN member coun-tries, the US government still maintains a large contingent of troops in South Korea under a legally nonexistent "UN command," with American soldiers displaying UN insignia and US military installations flying UN flags. The US claim of operating in South Korea under UN auspices is false but exhibits the strong unilateral influence of the US in relation to its most sensitive operations. The assumed partners for peace in the UN Security Council became adversaries in war on the Korean Peninsula. In 1953, the US, the PRC, and North Korea but not South Korea and without UN partici-pation signed an armistice agreement. Despite the lengthy passage of time, a peace treaty has yet to be signed.

The voting in the Security Council about the four conflicts mentioned above shows that in the early years of the UN, there was no consistent East/West divide. In the case of the UNTSO operations in the Middle East, both the USSR and the US supported the Security Council decision to set up a peacekeeping force. Regarding UNMOGIP (the UN observer mission for Pakistani- and Indian-held territories in Kashmir), the US and Pakistan supported this initiative while the USSR and India abstained. The US and the USSR agreed to the formation of a UN military force for the Congo but disagreed with its implementation. In the 1956 Suez Canal crisis, the USSR joined the US in demanding a cease-fire. Ideology and geopolitical interests rather than multilateral convergence determined US and USSR participa-tion in the UN Security Council.

Developments in the 1950s, 1960s, and 1970s reveal the deepening East/West divide and the multilateral power imbalance between the US, the USSR, and China since 1971, when the PRC had been accepted by the UN as representing China, taking account of its "one country, two systems" policy. There was also an emerging split between the Soviet Union and the

PRC affecting the global order. The two countries had jointly supported Ho Chi Minh's communist North Vietnam and Kim Il Sung's communist North Korea, but over the years developed growing disagreements over the application of the doctrines of Marx and Lenin. Both countries wanted to be seen as leading opponents of colonialism and supporters of the developing world's anti-imperialist demands. In the conduct of its international relations, the PRC additionally presented itself as a developing country and strongly objected to the USSR's promotion of peaceful coexistence and détente with the West. The PRC also resented the USSR's lack of support in its efforts to end the Tibetan uprising in 1959 and in its border dispute with India in 1962. China observed with suspicion the intensifying military ties between the USSR and India and, consequently, began to cooperate more closely with Pakistan economically and, more significantly, in nuclear energy research and development, especially after India had successfully carried out a nuclear weapons test in 1974. Security cooperation between Pakistan and China, as two nuclear powers, has continued. Agreements for power plant constructions in Karachi and Mianwali (Punjab) have been signed between the two countries, and nuclear cooperation has intensified following the 2008 nuclear technology agreement between India and the US. The existence of Pakistan and India as two nuclear powers, with China and the US as their respective allies, constitutes a significant new international concern for global security.

Until the end of the Cold War in 1989, the two pillars of the communist world, the USSR and the PRC, wanted to jointly construct a network of non-Western, anti-imperial alliances but frequently differed when it came to defining the direction and agreeing on details. The weight of the Cold War and the fragmented Communist world certainly adversely affected the ability of the UN to fulfill public expectations, especially with respect to international peace and security. As a result, the political UN became almost fully occupied with East/West controversies, which explains why there was neither the will nor the material resources to address adequately global development concerns and non-security-related issues.

## The Operational UN Technical and Capital Assistance

The UN System began providing technical assistance to developing countries in the 1950s. The few non-governmental and civil society organizations that existed at that time were working mostly in parallel to the UN. There was only marginal cooperation and coordination. Through their work in disease control, primary education, rural water supply and sanitation, food crop development, institution building, and other sectors, UNICEF, FAO, WHO, WFP, UNESCO, and the UN System became well known and generally respected by the beneficiaries in the villages and townships of Africa, Asia, and Latin America. In contrast, citizens in the Western world and the Soviet Union and its allies had little knowledge of the UN's development work in the Southern Hemisphere. They were more aware of the political aspects of East/West relations and the Cold War. They had seen and heard their leaders at the Security Council and the General Assembly advocating the advantages of communism or the capitalism for the peoples of the world. A curious dichotomy of knowledge about the United Nations as a political actor and as an operational presence existed in different societies around the world. These differences eventually would significantly impact the global perceptions of the legitimacy and effectiveness of the UN.

The UN gradually increased its global outreach, adding peacekeeping and preventive diplomacy as major and new undertakings besides technical and financial development assistance. The UN Development Programme (UNDP), as the largest multilateral provider of technical assistance in the world, set up field offices in the early 1960s in Africa, Asia, and Central and South America. The World Bank, the focal point for multilateral capital assistance, did the same but at a much slower pace. In these early years of UN System development assistance, cooperation between the World Bank representing Western interests and the UNDP with its global orientation was clearly defined but not without disagreements. The UNDP had the responsibility for pre-investment and technical assistance; the World Bank provided follow-up capital assistance. The World Bank (or the International Bank for Reconstruction and Development as it was called in the beginning) initially had lending portfolios predominantly in Western European countries such as France, Denmark, and the Netherlands, concentrating in the years after 1945 on post-conflict national reconstruction, with only a modest involvement in the Global South.

As the network of UN System field offices expanded, a new approach to staff recruitment at the country level was required. Local professional staff was added to international country teams as local knowledge and culture became recognized as important. Increased UN membership also called for broadening the geographical base of recruitment beyond the original Western sources. It was an unwritten understanding between the permanent powers in the Security Council, but also welcomed by many other governments around world, that UN field offices would deal solely with their technical assistance and financing mandates and not have any political role in their contacts with national and local governmental authorities.

UN civil servants who crossed these boundaries were quickly removed from their posts by the UN Secretariat, usually under pressure from the respective governments. Also, UN staff were continuously reminded by their administrative superiors that the sovereignty of member states should be always respected.

The International Court of Justice was available to issue "opinions" on legal matters if requested by the Security Council and the General Assembly. This rarely happened, especially since the Security Council was always more engaged by the political rather than the juridical aspects of global dynamics. The Security Council failed to recognize and take seriously the indivisibility of peace and security and socio-economic progress. This wall of separation and isolation between the Security Council and the UN operational system during the years of the Cold War had a profoundly negative impact on peacebuilding, preventive diplomacy, and the overall effectiveness and reputation of the UN as an institution of global governance. These issues of function and operational priorities have remained topics of debate.

## NGOs/CSOs

As the UN's network of field offices continued to expand, the NGO movement was anxious to align itself more closely with the work of the UN. This was facilitated by the consultative relationship between the UN and its Economic and Social Council (ECOSOC) and international, regional, sub-regional, and national non-governmental organizations (NGOs) as had been foreseen in the UN Charter (Article 71). In 1946 Western NGOs started to apply for a consultative status with ECOSOC. A French, a Belgian, and a Greek NGO became the first to obtain such a status. Special efforts were made by ECOSOC to encourage NGOs from the developing world to join the NGO community and from developed parts of the world to establish relationships with the UN.

Beginning in the early 1970s, the United Nations planned and implemented a wide range of major global conferences in such critical areas as human rights, social development, education, women's rights, the welfare of children, and human habitation. Non-governmental and civil society organizations (CSOs), initially again mostly from Western countries, significantly helped prepare these meetings, participated actively, and promoted their follow-up.

Over time, Western predominance of NGOs/CSOs began to give way to a geographically more balanced civil society partnership with ECOSOC.

Applicants were increasingly regional, national, and local institutions from the South. This became important for the developing world since only NGOs with consultative status could attend UN meetings, contribute to ECOSOC's agenda and, at the request of ECOSOC, carry out special studies. On a modest scale, NGOs from all parts of the world began also to implement projects in partnership with the UN System, but being generally sensitive to human rights and gender dimensions of sustainable development, they often faced considerable opposition from conservative national authorities, while raising awareness of these previously downplayed concerns.

The NGO/CSO communities wanted to broaden their engagement not only with the operational system of the UN but also with the political UN, in particular the Security Council and the General Assembly. Yet even though the UN Charter makes provision for such cooperation, the Security Council and the General Assembly were not ready to encourage such contacts until much later and even then, only in an informal manner without much discernible impact. It was not until 2002, when UN Secretary-General Kofi Annan appointed a panel of eminent persons to consider how the relations between the UN and civil society could be strengthened that increased civil society UN participation received much attention. In doing this, Annan challenged the political UN and member states to clarify how they would like UN cooperation with civil society and the non-governmental community to evolve. He wanted the UN to "become a more outward looking organisation" and "to connect the global with the local" in all parts of the world. Referring primarily to the Security Council, he suggested extending "the UN from being a diplomatic forum to being the focal point for wider global politics."[7] Until then, UN Secretaries-General had not been prepared to propose initiatives of this kind. They accepted the prevailing practice that made it the sole prerogative of the Security Council to address such fundamental policy matters.

## UN Multilateralism amid Continuing Geopolitical Rivalry

The geopolitical dynamics of 1989 lead to one unequivocal conclusion: dramatic changes took place in Europe during that year. These changes would have momentous impacts on global governance, multilateralism, and the relations between countries and regions. At the time, the fall of the Iron Curtain and the Berlin Wall, symbolic images of the deep ideological divide between Western and Eastern Europe, as well as the rejection of communism as an ideology by most of the peoples of the Warsaw Pact countries, were major political developments. It, however, took many years for Europe and beyond to become fully aware of how this would shape the geopolitical landscape. What happened in 1989 continued to preoccupy European governments and citizens in their efforts to establish a satisfying European niche in the post–Cold War emergent global order.

East/West Cold War competition appeared over. Western capitalism had defeated Eastern communism. Two US intellectuals, Francis Fukuyama and Samuel Huntington, reacted with publications that had a major impact on the public debate. Fukuyama argued in his influential 1992 work *The End of History and the Last Man* that the universalization of Western liberalism was justified because democracy constituted an "end point of mankind's ideological evolution" and there was no acceptable alternative system. In 1993, Huntington replaced "ideology" with "civilization" in a *Foreign Affairs* article, "The Clash of Civilizations?" warning that Western domination could not be assumed after the Soviet collapse and that clashes along inter-civilizational borders involving the Muslim world should be anticipated. He insisted that cultural differences between nations and regions had to be taken into account if a Western-oriented future world order was to come into being.

These two influential thinkers and their followers could not imagine that global-order development during the twenty-first century might be determined neither by ideology nor by civilization but by the power of the poor and underprivileged. It took three decades and a virus to make the world aware of the fragile nature of the neoliberal existential model of socio-economic development as well as the unwillingness of its main Western protagonists to accept any responsibility for universal social and economic progress in accordance with the UN Charter and the two UN Covenants on human rights.

November 9, 1989, the day the wall separating East and West Berlin fell, was to become a date of critical importance in the history of international relations, not just for Germans who understandably celebrated the resulting prospects for immediate reunification. After twenty-eight years, impatient East Germans were told at a hurriedly organized press conference by the leadership of the Socialist Unity Party of Germany that Germans could now at last freely travel across any of the borders separating the Eastern German Democratic Republic from the Western Federal Republic of Germany. "Es wächst zusammen, was zusammengehört" (what grows together belongs together) were the memorable and moving words of the then West German foreign minister and future chancellor Willy Brandt.

These dramatic developments signaled the beginning of a worldwide political, economic, and social transformation of tectonic dimensions initiated by civil society in the Soviet Union and Eastern Europe. For US president Ronald Reagan, the "evil empire" and "godless communism" had reached their deserved end. The Western world had not expected this dramatic transformative event associated with the Soviet implosion. German chancellor Helmut Kohl was in Warsaw a day before the Berlin Wall came down, giving his opinion to the Polish president Lech Walesa that "it would take many years before Germany would be reunited."

Not only Kohl but also Reagan, Gorbachev, and Thatcher were all caught completely off guard by this surprising occurrence even though it was known to them that social unrest in East Germany and in other parts of the Warsaw Pact area, including the Soviet Union itself, had been intensifying. Two years earlier, President Reagan, while visiting Berlin, had implored the Soviet leader in dramatic language at a public demonstration in Berlin, "Mr. Gorbachev, tear down this wall!" When the Berlin Wall did come down, Gorbachev sent a message to the East German leadership that he approved of the border opening. Speaking at the UN General Assembly on December 8, 1988, he had expressed the Soviet Union's support for the UN, praising its ability to act as a unique international center of global unity vital for the maintenance of peace and security, and in this context he made a radical call for the demilitarization of international relations. To add credibility to this affirmation of internationalism, Gorbachev simultaneously announced the withdrawal of Soviet tank divisions from East Germany, Czechoslovakia, and Hungary. He ominously told the General Assembly, "Let everyone show the advantages of their social system." UK prime minister Margaret Thatcher enigmatically told the General Assembly on the eve of the fall of the Berlin Wall, "We need our reason to teach us today that we . . . must not try to be the lords of all we survey." US president-elect George H. W. Bush reacted guardedly to the tearing down of the wall by telling a press conference, "We salute those who can move forward with democracy" but, according to one journalist, cautiously sidestepped any effort to declare "victory" in the Cold War.

There was not, however, much enthusiasm among Western leaders about the prospects for a reunited Germany. Margaret Thatcher and her French counterpart François Mitterrand undoubtedly subscribed to the French Nobel Prize laureate François Mauriac's adage "I love Germany so much that I am glad there are two of them!" "I am not an emotional kind of guy" was the disappointing admission of George Bush. Mikhail Gorbachev, on the other hand, a forward-looking political realist who understood what he saw in Eastern Europe, considered these developments unavoidable and in the interest of a "new" Europe in which its Eastern and Western parts could live together in peace.

The year 1989 had started for the Security Council and the General Assembly with the usual array of global-order concerns. It was faced with the intractable East/West disagreements on human rights, including the right of development, the reform of the global economic order, and the elusive rights of the Palestinian people. The surging anti-apartheid campaign in South Africa, the impending independence of Namibia, civil strife in Cambodia, external interventions in Central America, the Antarctic treaty system, sanctions against Somalia, and the activities of al-Qaida and the Taliban were the never-ending challenges on this long UN agenda.

A major event at the time was the withdrawal of Soviet troops from Afghanistan. On February 15, 1989, the last Soviet soldiers had crossed the Amu Darya River from northern Afghanistan into Soviet territory at Termez in Uzbekistan. The war between the Afghan government and the Islamist mujahideen had been a major proxy war between the Soviet Union and the US. Ten years earlier, the Soviet government had agreed to supply troops and armaments to the government of the People's Democratic Party of Afghanistan. The US government, in turn, had clandestinely provided military supplies and intelligence to the mujahideen in cooperation with Saudi Arabia, Pakistan, and the UK. Nine years earlier, in 1980, the Soviet Union had vetoed Security Council Resolution 462, which called for the withdrawal of Russian troops from Afghanistan. In the General Assembly, 104 of 152 governments, including those of the US, the UK, Arab countries, and China, had supported the application of the Uniting for Peace resolution,[8] "strongly condemning the recent (Soviet) intervention." The Great Game of the nineteenth century between tsarist Russia and British India over the control of Afghanistan was continuing but with a different cast of characters. Following earlier proxy wars fought at the expense of North and South Korea and later of North and South Vietnam, the war in Afghanistan was yet another stark example of the deep East/West divide and the growing difficulty facing the Security Council in fulfilling its mandate to uphold global peace and security.

There, however, had also been some collaboration in the Security Council between the US and USSR in providing humanitarian assistance for countries in the Caribbean and the Sudan and in efforts to enhance UN cooperation with other intergovernmental groups such as the Organisation of Islamic Cooperation (OIC). Both the US and the USSR supported the 1988 UN-negotiated cease-fire between Iran and Iraq and agreed in the Security Council to the deployment of UN Blue Helmets[9] and to finance the presence of the UN Iran-Iraq Military Observer Group. Most importantly, the US and the USSR continued their bilateral disarmament talks after signing the Intermediate-Range Nuclear Forces (INF) Treaty in 1987 to reduce dangers posed by the deployment and possible use of medium and shorter-range missiles. The two governments agreed to the subsequent destruction of several thousand ballistic and cruise missiles. The UN Secretary-General at the time, Javier Perez de Cuellar, concluded that during the presidencies of Ronald Reagan and Mikhail Gorbachev, Cold War tensions between the two powers eased and the UN role in international affairs increased.

The UN atmosphere of cooperation in New York, reached a dramatic high on November 9, 1989, when suddenly nothing appeared more urgent on the East River than monitoring events in the two Germanys. In response to the fall of the Berlin Wall, the two Germanys spontaneously agreed on November 15, 1989, to propose jointly an extraordinary General Assembly resolution (A/RES/44/21). It called on all states "to intensify their practical efforts towards ensuring international peace and security . . . through cooperative means in accordance with the Charter of the United Nations" and "to consult and cooperate within the framework of the United Nations, the Security Council, [and] the General Assembly . . . to implement and strengthen the principles and the system of international peace, security, and international cooperation laid down in the Charter."

The easing of tensions through joint East/West initiatives at the UN was welcomed around the world as it conveyed the reassuring messages that both sides wanted to avoid further confrontation. It demonstrated the weight the Security Council possessed whenever it was able to act in a unified manner. Presidents Reagan and Gorbachev had shown statesmanship and foresight at a critical moment in East/West relations. It was tempting to believe that in a post–Berlin Wall world, there would be no more tensions in Europe of the kind that had so deeply influenced international relations ever since the early days of the Cold War. The prospects seemed good for a global and regional political warming, reinvigorated multilateralism, and a United Nations finally able to make a difference in the shaping of geopolitical dynamics.

Such cooperation at the UN was in line with the spirit of the Helsinki Accords of the Conference for Security and Cooperation in Europe (CSCE). It took a year from the date the Berlin Wall fell in November 1989 before the CSCE member countries came together in Paris November 19–21, 1990, to negotiate the Charter of Paris, also known as the Freedom Charter. Despite the still ongoing Cold War, thirty-two countries from Western and Eastern Europe plus the US and Canada adopted on that occasion an agreement that confirmed the inviolability of existing frontiers, the peaceful settlement of intergovernmental disputes, no interference in internal affairs, and respect for the right of self-determination of the peoples. Apart from preventive diplomacy and security considerations, a wide range of cooperation was envisaged in trade, science, and technology and somewhat surprisingly, considering that the date was 1990, the protection of the environment. The guarded reference to "freer" rather than "free" movement of people undoubtedly reflected a reluctant concession by the USSR and its allies to allow limited cross-border travel.

During this period, multiparty elections were held in Hungary, Czechoslovakia, and Poland, which were good indicators of the political transformation, both structurally and ideologically, that was taking place in Eastern Europe. An ambivalent France and UK were not able to prevent a speedy German unification process. Three weeks after the fall of the Wall, West German chancellor Kohl had presented a ten-point plan for the future of the two German states. Kohl made it plain that any contemplated reunification would be on West German terms: "The German people must regain their unity through free self-determination" and "the future German architecture must fit into the future architecture of Europe." France, the UK, and the US would have likely added that German reunification should proceed not only on West German but on Western terms.

Following free elections in East Germany on March 18, 1990, the German-German Unification Treaty was concluded in East Berlin on August 31, 1990. Important for the stability of the future of the "new" Europe was also the signing in Warsaw of the German-Polish Border Treaty on November 14, 1990, with the united Germany accepting that it had lost territories on its eastern border, including Gdansk (Danzig).

An important precondition for the signing of the Paris Charter for a new Europe or, as President Gorbachev called it, for a "common European house," had been the settlement of the "German question," which would allow the formal unification of the two German states. This happened on October 3, 1990, when the German Democratic Republic joined the Federal Republic of Germany, ending forty-one years of separation of the German people. The two Germanys, which had been represented at the UN as separate nations since 1973, notified the UN Secretary-General that they had merged into a single UN member state on that day.

Only when these steps had been taken, did Eastern and Western governments agree to come together in Paris for the CSCE conference, a summit of historic importance for global peace and security. CSCE countries observed that "the era of confrontation and division in Europe had ended" and that "Europe had liberated itself from the legacy of its past." On this occasion, CSCE member states confirmed that they "supported fully the UN and recognized with satisfaction the growing role of the UN in world affairs." The world was amazed that Western and Eastern countries alike had decided to "build, consolidate and strengthen democracy as the only system of government of our nations . . . with the aim of making democratic gains irreversible." It was stressed that this would be achieved with the help of the United States, Canada, and the Soviet Union as co-signatories.

Against the backdrop of an Eastern Europe that, politically and economically, had steadily weakened, it is not entirely surprising that the Soviet Union agreed to include in the Paris Charter a commitment to "strive for a new quality in our security relations while respecting each other's freedom of choice," adding "security is indivisible" and "the security of every participating State . . . [would be] inseparably linked to that of all other States." What was meant by "new quality" was not explained nor how such a linkage to "all States" in West and East would work.

Preceding the Paris Summit, a NATO meeting had taken place in London in May 1990 that indicated that the North Atlantic Alliance no longer considered Warsaw Pact countries as enemies. NATO therefore was ready to scale down its defense expenditures and downsize several of its programs in preparation for the Conventional Forces in Europe (CFE) agreement with the Warsaw Pact. Such an accord was signed at the beginning of the Paris summit in November 1990. With the end of the USSR, the Warsaw Pact, however, was dissolved.

The outcome of the 1990 CSCE summit in Paris for the Europe of the future and the East/West agreement on a future United Nations that had been reached in 1945 at Yalta had significant critical elements in common: they reflected the inherent imbalance of power in the international discourse in favor of the West and they made it clear that only with US leadership, Western political, economic, and security interests would be guaranteed regionally and globally. US penholder preparedness and persistent lobbying at the UN, the European Union, and the CSCE, as well as bilaterally throughout the years had paid off. The Paris summit opened global floodgates, this time not for governance in the Southern Hemisphere but for a free Europe as a partner in a Western-centric global political, economic, and cultural order.

The Charter of Paris was not signed in a void. The good intentions of 1990 had their context. Forty-four years of geopolitical dynamics had brought political independence to many, created an impressive body of international law, fostered a spirit of shared responsibilities for human well-being, seen impressive scientific and technological advances, and achieved some arms control and disarmament. There were signs that a global order was emerging with many promising features but also many deficiencies. Great Power compromise produced the INF treaty, but only when the two Great Powers wanted to protect their own interests and not because it intrinsically was the right thing to do. Neither side, however, had absorbed into their national thinking the ethos of Article 2(4) of the UN Charter, which demands that UN member countries "refrain in their international relations from the threat or use of force against the territorial integrity or political independence of any state." What did change was that the Yalta spirit of cooperation had morphed into an open rivalry for power. WWII did not become forgotten history. New wars, new genocides, and new forms of military warfare had emerged. Iraq's invasion of Kuwait in August 1990 was a stark reminder that the potential for wars had not diminished, neither in the Middle East nor elsewhere.

During all these years, UN Secretaries-General had consistently emphasized the positive developments that had taken place in international relations. Again and again, they reminded UN member states that crises could be solved when there was adherence to Charter principles, and in this spirit, they cautiously prodded the Great Powers to cooperate with each other. Secretaries-General were regarded, especially by the weaker members and unrepresented peoples, as beacons of hope, optimism, and idealism. Secretary-General Perez de Cuellar observed in 1990, at the very beginning of the post–Cold War period, that the "UN was no longer paralyzed by the bipolar struggle to fulfill its historic Charter mission" and that the "age of the United Nations had come." But he also warned governments and world public opinion that "the transition to a new pattern of international relations would be neither easy nor risk free." As a result, Secretaries-General, with their voices of caution, were continuously subjected to uncompromising back-channel pressures by individual governments.

Within the UN and bilaterally, 1991 was the year during which the Great Powers cooperated in disarmament, in containing conflicts, and in encouraging others to solve their crises peacefully. Following nine years of negotiations, the US and the USSR were able to sign in July 1991 the Strategic Arms Reduction Treaty (START), a treaty on the reduction and limitation of strategic nuclear weapons. Earlier in the year, the two countries had jointly decided to discontinue their weapon deliveries to all Afghan parties. In the Security Council, they had condemned Iraq's invasion into Kuwait in 1990, yet, in 1991 the Soviet Union did not join the US and its allies in approving Operation Desert Storm. The USSR supported the "coalition" against Iraq only so far as the restoration of Kuwait's sovereignty was concerned and not when it came to the use of force designed to change the internal politics of Iraq.

The Security Council and the General Assembly were the UN settings where Great Power nationalism remained the defining factor when it came to global developments. The disarmament resolutions in these two bodies about, for example, the production of fissionable materials suitable for weaponizing, the banning of nuclear weapons, and the prohibition of chemical and biological weapons, as well as resolutions for the promotion of human rights for all, including the rights of the Palestinian people, failed to obtain support from either the US or the USSR.

Globalization, having spread exponentially during the latter years of the Cold War, caused increasing polarization. Alliances had been encouraged by the Great Powers during the Cold War and persisted after it ended. Voting patterns in the General Assembly reflected this.[10] Developing countries joined by Russia and China were on one side, and NATO countries joined by former Warsaw Pact members and a few industrialized Asian states were on the other side.

Developing countries had always demanded that the needs of the South be given priority by the United Nations. The Security Council, preoccupied with security matters, left the debate of international development cooperation to the General Assembly, ECOSOC, the United Nations Development Programme (UNDP), and the World Bank and the International Monetary Fund (IMF). It was in those venues that newly independent nations of the Global South had their best opportunity to foster an understanding of their lack of funding and trained human resources, their poor health and education standards, and their concerns about developed countries' unfair trade and investment practices. They wanted the UN and the world to know that they were determined and able to turn this around, if given a fair chance, as well as to receive some redress for past exploitation.

The comparative data for longevity, income, and education that have been collected by the UNDP, the World Bank, and the IMF, the three major UN institutions concerned with economic development, show that while there were improvements between 1990 and 2021–22 for developed and developing countries, but, as can be seen in table 3.1, the wide North/South gap remains. Unless substantial increases in resources for sustainable development are made available to these countries and a major reduction in global corruption occurs, there will be little prospect that the Global South

**TABLE 3.1.** The North/South Gap: Indicators of
life inequalities, 1990 and 2021–2022.

| | Life expectancy, years | | Adult literacy, percentage | | Annual per capita income (PPP), US$ | |
|---|---|---|---|---|---|---|
| | *North* | *South* | *North* | *South* | *North* | *South* |
| | Japan | Ethiopia | Italy | Burkina Faso | United States | Tanzania |
| 1990 | 78 | 42 | 97 | 14 | 17,615 | 405 |
| 2021–2022 | 84.8 | 65 | 99.9 | 34.6 | 64,765 | 2,664 |

*Sources:* UNDP Human Development Reports 1990–2022.

could contribute to a stable and peaceful global order. Concurrently, the Security Council would have to devote much more time to promoting human security in more tangible ways than has been the case.

After the Cold War, the prospects for intensified multilateral development cooperation with a focus on poverty alleviation and sustainable development improved significantly. In 1990 in a foreword to the first UNDP human development report, the UNDP administrator William Draper, former chairman of the US Import-Export Bank, referred to the "irresistible wave of human freedom sweeping across many lands" and went on to insist that "people must be at the centre of all development." Such a sentiment exhibited the growing critical UN reaction to the World Bank's structural adjustment programs, which, UNICEF argued, should be supported only if development policies had a "human face." Yet again, this reflected the fundamental differences between the Western-oriented World Bank–IMF worldview and the global-minded UN as to how best to carry out fair and effective development.

## Guarded UN Optimism at the End of the Twentieth Century

The last decade of the twentieth century, nevertheless, started with a mood of optimism. Secretary-General Perez de Cuellar in his yearly statement referred to 1990 as a "watershed in UN history" and a "significant opportunity to meet new tasks and challenges." These challenges led to a range of major conferences on such varied themes as the least developed countries, the welfare of children, education for all, the impact of climate change, and of course, human rights as well as a special General Assembly session on international cooperation. There also seemed to be a general willingness among P5 countries to strengthen global security through disarmament. This mood recalls the joint statement made by the US and the USSR in

Geneva in 1985 that "nuclear war cannot be won and must never be fought."

The follow-up to such assurances, however, made it again clear that the entrenched Cold War mentality had basically not changed, especially in Washington. What ensued was not nuclear disarmament but a dangerous and costly nuclear arms race and a global security system ultimately still resting on the apocalyptic premise of "mutually assured destruction" (MAD) that underpinned the deployment of large numbers of nuclear warheads. In 1989, a General Assembly Resolution (A/44/117) calling for a worldwide nuclear freeze was adopted by a large majority but opposed by thirteen governments including the US, the UK, France, other NATO countries, Japan, and Israel. A similar voting pattern, invariably involving US opposition, prevailed in such areas as economic rights for all, extended support for developing countries and their protection against political and economic coercion, decolonization, and the establishment of zones of peace in different parts of the world. The geopolitical dynamics of the 1990s showed that Perez de Cuellar's "watershed" began to look more like a narrow mountain pass controlled by Western interests. The new tasks and challenges for the UN, especially the P5, in the areas of peace and security, disarmament, and human rights were largely controlled by US foreign policy interests supported by the UK and increasingly challenged by China and Russia. France preferred to support multilateral decision-making in dealing with such issues as terrorism, weapons of mass destruction, and Iraq sanctions to give UN policies a greater degree of international legitimacy. As a result, at the UN during these post–Cold War years, France and the United States were often at odds.

At the end of the Cold War, it was clear that a global consensus for leveling the playing field of the world economy still did not exist. Russia found itself politically and economically challenged domestically by virtual chaos and thus preoccupied with the reorganization of its own immediate political landscape, especially in central Asia, and not motivated to or capable of playing a strong role supportive of multilateralism. China, even though its economic power was rapidly increasing, preferred to retain a low profile on the world stage. President Deng Jiao-ping's advice for China's internal development to "cross the river by feeling out the stones with our feet" also became China's approach internationally. Deng's counsel for China's foreign relations to "keep a cool head and maintain a low profile and never take the lead but aim to do something big" guided Beijing's diplomats at the UN and elsewhere.[11] China wanted to be nonconfrontational and continue to behave as a developing country. It sought to give the impression that it had no geopolitical ambitions of its own and refrained from military engagement aside from upholding its own border security. In voting at the General Assembly before 1989 and since, China, has consistently sided with countries of the South.

UN Secretary-General Boutros-Ghali, sharing the optimism of his predecessors, observed in 1992 that the end of the struggle of two competing global political systems at least raised hopes for a renaissance in facing long neglected challenges of resolving international conflicts confronting the UN. What he called a "historic meeting" of the Security Council, which was attended by heads of state and government, confirmed a new commitment to the United Nations in dealing with ongoing crises in the Middle East, between Ethiopia and Eritrea, between Greek and Turkish factions in Cyprus, and between Armenia and Azerbaijan over Nagorno-Karabakh. As a particularly important and positive UN achievement, Boutros-Ghali singled out the adoption of the 1992 Framework Convention on Climate Change at the Earth Summit in Rio de Janeiro. His proposals for a levy on arms sales and air travel to improve UN funding for human development, however, failed to get the needed support, a telling reminder that world order remained state-centric and subject to geopolitical manipulation.

At the end of the Cold War, there had been some hope that the lessening of East/West tensions would result in a peace dividend. Secretaries-General Perez de Cuellar and Boutros-Ghali used this opportunity to remind governments that the demands on the UN System were continuously increasing without an equivalent increase in financial resources. More generally, both Secretaries-General called for a sizable increase in available resources for international development. The trends of the 1990s showed, however, a strikingly different picture. Boutros-Ghali concluded in 1995 that "sadly, the record of world affairs of the past few years has belied expectations. Old conflicts continue, new wars, mostly intra-country, have started and voluntary development assistance is declining." While the global defense budgets had indeed decreased from US$1.49 trillion in 1990 to $1.07 trillion in 1999 according to the Swedish International Peace Research Institute (SIPRI), the resources for development had also decreased. OECD Development Assistance Committee (DAC) data show for 1999 an overall official development assistance of 0.22 percent of global Gross National Income (GNI), down from 0.27 percent in 1995 and 0.33 percent in 1990. The US official development assistance (ODA) contribution in 1990, at 0.2 percent already one of the lowest of developed countries, had fallen in 1999 to a meager 0.12 percent. Years of pleading by Secretaries-General for developed countries to increase their aid programs and repeated recommendations by the General Assembly to focus on poverty reduction and Great Power disarmament did not result in more financial support for sustainable peace. The modest General Assembly target of 0.7 percent of GNI, as the recommended contribution for industrialized nations to low-income countries, had become an even more remote and unrealizable goal.

P5 vetoes in the Security Council had been cast throughout the years by national and regional interests, alliance commitments, and ideological considerations rather than by joint efforts to prevent or solve international crises. In the early years, the Soviet Union had made frequent use of self-serving vetoes while the US, with majority backing, seemed determined and able to mobilize UN support for its geopolitical priorities. The USSR often objected to the admission of new member states and disagreed with actions favored by the Security Council in conflicts involving the Congo, the Korean Peninsula, and the wars in Vietnam and Afghanistan. On the other hand, the US vetoed resolutions critical of Israeli Palestine policy and was not embarrassed to admit that it would only support UN resolutions when both Israel and the Palestine Authority agreed to them, which never happened.

This self-serving use of the veto in the Security Council did not change in the post–Cold War period, and the same pattern characterized Great Power voting in the General Assembly. It is striking, however, to realize that despite being politically isolated, the United States frequently cast dissenting votes in the General Assembly, often as the only dissenter, on a wide spectrum of international concerns. US administrations, Republican and Democrat alike, differed only by degrees when voting took place in the General Assembly. Party affiliation did not seem to make much difference, whether on global security, regional peace, international law, disarmament, nuclear proliferation, sanctions, independence for colonial territories, human rights, the Palestinian/Israeli conflict, or many other issues.

## Difficult Years for Multilateralism

US ambassadors serving at the UN have often had a single brief to say no unless there was evidence that the proposed actions were consistent with US national interests. In 2000, the Republican chairman of the US Senate Committee on Foreign Affairs, Jesse Helms, an extremist figure in American politics, made this clear when he attended a UN Security Council meeting.[12] In his hard-hitting nationalist address, he warned the UN against trying to "impose its utopian vision onto the United States." He pointed out that "if the United Nations is to be 'effective,' it must be an institution that is needed by the great democratic powers of the world." He reminded the UN that "the American people will never accept the claims of the United Nations to be the 'sole source of legitimacy on the use of force in the world.'" He bluntly threatened the UN that American financial support was dependent on UN cooperation with the US, which, if decoded, signifies subservience.

The UN had become accustomed to receiving such messages from Washington but had learned to circumnavigate many of the obstacles US governments put in its way. The power of finance had been used by the US governments to influence decision-making and the appointment process within the UN but also to assert its influence throughout the whole gamut of international relations. The General Assembly, in turn, responded by regularly tabling resolutions, objecting to "unilateral economic measures as a means of political and economic coercion against developing countries." Such a UN pushback did not lead the US to reconsider its rejectionist approach to global demands. In explaining the failure of the UN to live up to expectations, perhaps no factor has been more significant than for the leading state among the P5 to go its unilateral way on key symbolic issues, such as maintaining sanctions on Cuba, and not deferring to the will of large majorities in the political organs of the UN.

Even though at the end of the Cold War, there had been optimistic initial forecasts of increasing international cooperation, it turned out that these were difficult years for multilateralism. The UN's agenda was crowded with acute worldwide peace-and-security-related conflicts. There was the Panama conflict in 1990; the first Gulf War in 1991; the disintegration of Yugoslavia and the resulting turmoil in the Balkans, especially in Bosnia in 1992; the Rwanda genocide and Haiti's civil war, both in 1994; and NATO's intervention in Serbia in 1995 and the Kosovo War in 1999, as well as multilateral sanctions against Iraq. In other words, the end of the Cold War did not produce a more stable world order, which caused public disappointment that indirectly and unfairly weakened support for the UN.

Despite the unanticipated but required Security Council preoccupation with crisis management during the 1990s, UN reforms were needed and should have been treated as a priority at the UN. The advocacy of UN reform won support from many governments and from the UN itself. "A World in Need of Leadership" was the title of a 1990 presentation by two senior UN officials, Brian Urquhart and Erskine Childers, who argued for an improved UN image and for secure funding of the UN. Concurrently, Denmark, Finland, Norway, and Sweden, four of the most multilaterally minded UN member states, had developed a Nordic project for UN reform that they put forward as a contribution to making the UN a more effective organization. The project was limited to socio-economic issues and institutional management reform, which conveyed the disturbing implicit acknowledgment that peace and security were beyond the reach of the UN given the continuing prevalence of geopolitics. This expression of "Nordic realism" explains why two major reform challenges were not included in the Nordic initiative: structural reform of the UN, especially of the Security Council, along with the need to integrate UN peace and security policy within the broader policy contexts of international cooperation and economic development.

The geopolitical climate of the early 1990s seemed to provide an excellent opportunity to begin a serious and comprehensive review of the geographical imbalances of membership in the Security Council, the use of veto, the relationship between the General Assembly and the Security Council, and accountability for violations of international law. Despite what seemed like a favorable international climate for attempting such basic reform initiatives, it turned out that the political will to do so was absent to varying degrees among the P5. Secretaries-General had repeatedly argued that peace and security would become sustainable only when development with a human face was a core part of the UN agenda, yet the Great Powers failed again and again to adjust structures and programs of action accordingly. The US refused to lead any UN reform effort, focusing on a geopolitical agenda that exhibited a preoccupation with control over the Middle East and bestowed legitimacy on and minimized the regulation of neoliberal globalization, which came to be referred to as the "Washington consensus" in recognition of its ideological affinities with US foreign economic policy. The UK prime minister at time, Margaret Thatcher, called neoliberal globalization "the only game in town," pungently designating it as TINA (there is no alternative).

The unpredictable timing of payments by member states and the resulting cash-flow problems obstructing the regular work of the UN, including peacekeeping operations, continued as before during the 1990s. In view of its permanently volatile financial situation, the UN found itself often unable to pay its bills on time. The General Assembly had established in 1995 a working group to look for solutions but failed to find an approach that was generally acceptable. Even the Security Council urged member states to "honor their financial obligations." A year later, unpaid obligatory contributions had reached US$3 billion, an amount higher than the UN's annual budget. Seventeen member states had lost their right to vote, in accordance with Charter Article 19, because of their arrears. Luxembourg, on behalf of the European Union, had written to the UN expressing concern that the United States, as the major contributor,[13] had substantial arrears that were the main cause of the perennial financial crisis.

Besides the persisting financial shortages facing the organization, Secretaries-General also had to deal with structural shortcomings: the difficulties of the Security Council in reaching consensus within its own ranks and the hesitation of the UN operational system to improve coordination in the delivery of assistance at the country, regional, and interregional levels. Particularly challenging were the initiatives by Secretaries-General to enhance cooperation between the UN and the Bretton Woods institutions. Despite energetic efforts, synchronization of their policies did not get very far. Joint implementation of development assistance was complicated because of ingrained organizational mindset differences, incompatible sets of rules, cost differentials, and the fact that the UN provided grants while World Bank assistance consisted of credits and loans. One good example of coordinated global action was the fight against the HIV/AIDS pandemic, for which the UN and the World Bank had joined hands in 1994 with other UN agencies to establish UNAIDS, an interagency program to fight HIV/AIDS.

## The UN Operational System

The UN field system, with offices in practically all UN member countries of the South and elsewhere, nevertheless continued to make good progress in building up an integrated UN country presence. Often joint UN offices were established, a common development assistance framework was formulated, sometimes even with an agreed UN System budget, and increasingly led by a single official, the UN Resident Coordinator, representing the Secretary-General and the UN System, with the de facto exclusion of the World Bank and the International Monetary Fund. In this context, Secretary-General Boutros-Ghali, always stressing the unique cumulative experience of the UN System, insisted that more use should be made of the UN's local experience in helping the Security Council with preventive diplomacy. This bold proposal was noted by the General Assembly but ignored by the Security Council. Neither the P5 countries nor governments in the developing world would accept that UN personnel working in the fields of development and humanitarian protection should play any role, even an informal one, in areas that were perceived as linked to national sovereignty. This once again confirmed the subordination of the UN worldview to the logic of state-centrism further accentuated by geopolitical overlays.

How sensitive governments could be to what they considered external interference is illustrated by an initiative that the UN Resident Coordinator in Pakistan and heads of UN agencies in Islamabad (except the World Bank representative) had taken in publishing an open letter on human develop-ment in 1993.[14] The letter reiterated that "development was much more than economic growth" and was "first and foremost about people." It was a dip-lomatically cautious statement to avoid negatively affecting the strong part-nership that existed between Pakistan and the UN. The letter emphasized that the UN team did not want to appear "disrespectful of national sover-eignty" and wanted to confirm the UN's "deep commitment to the progress of Pakistan and the welfare of its people." As soon as the letter appeared in Pakistan's media, the foreign ministry expressed its misgivings to the UN Resident Coordinator about this initiative, concluding, "If we did not know you and your colleagues as well as we do, we would have asked you to leave our country!"

Less controversial was Secretary-General Kofi Annan's call in 1997 "to bring us closer to the peoples we serve." He made no secret of his frus-tration with the inadequate performance of the UN Department of Public Information in bringing the UN closer to the people. Annan sought a fun-damentally reshaped UN media role. He had joined the UN at a junior level and worked his way up to become the first Secretary-General appointed from within the organization and was therefore well placed to point out in a major report entitled "The UN: Global Vision, Local Voice" that "we must ensure that the tale of UN activities is told with more vigour, purpose, and greater effect. The UN cannot achieve the purposes for which it has been created unless the peoples of the world are fully informed of its aims and activities." This struck a chord with many UN staffers in the field who were receiving the weekly diplomatic pouches (or "garbage bags," as some disre-spectfully called them), which contained stacks of UN press releases about global political matters of concern to the Security Council and the General Assembly but of no relevance to the lives of local people struggling to cope with their daily survival.

## The UN in the Last Decade of the Twentieth Century

For the UN, the last decade of the twentieth century was not a period of predictability and stability but rather one of unpredictability and surprise. Secretary-General Kofi Annan talked about a period of tension and diffi-culty for the UN. "The global order displays all the symptoms of disorder of the Cold War years," he said, "because the causes have not disappeared during the post–Cold War years." Wars and military confrontations had continued, and the development of new nuclear weapons capabilities had not stopped. Complex and costly peacekeeping remained necessary in Africa, Asia, and Latin America, and serious human rights violations including genocides, mass killings, torture, and executions in all parts of the world could not be prevented and occurred with disturbing frequency and impunity.

Decision-making in the UN became increasingly hampered by the impact of accelerated Westernization and unilateral power displayed by the US in its participation in the Security Council. In the first three years of the 1990s, President Bush, a Republican, was forced to work with a Democrat majority in both houses of the US Congress, and during the following seven years, President Clinton, a Democrat, had to deal with a Republican majority, but there seemed to be no difference in US policymaking at the UN. This bipartisanship when in came to the UN can be confirmed by a review of Security Council and General Assembly resolutions during the 1990s. National unity prevailed over party politics in matters of foreign policy, just as it had during the Cold War.

The perceived Western victory of 1989 reinforced US exceptionalism and geopolitical freedom of action. In the mid-1990s, neoconservatives created the Project for a New American Century (PNAC), a think tank that produced a blueprint for global US dominance, including a statement of principles proposing an aggressive hegemonic and anti-multilateral US foreign policy. PNAC called for "significant increased defense spending" and for "challenging regimes hostile to US interests and values." In a separate report entitled *Rebuilding America's Defenses*, it was argued that "fighting and winning of multiple simultaneous major theatre wars should be a core mission" of the US.

There was bipartisan congressional acceptance that the United States by virtue of its economic, financial, and military power had the political right and even obligation to exercise global leadership. It therefore should not come as a surprise that in 1998, the US House of Representatives and the US Senate, both with a Republican majority, passed the Iraq Liberation Act, which Bill Clinton, a Democratic president, signed into law, declaring that the US should support regime change in the Iraq of Saddam Hussein. In geopolitical terms, the UN found itself controversially interpreting the impact of the Soviet collapse in creating a unipolar illusion that the US could satisfy the larger geopolitical ambitions of being the sole provider of global security without risking war. Throughout the Cold War the UN was often neutralized by the political impasse between the two most powerful

P5 member states. After the Cold War, the US attempted to use the UN as a policy tool to support its more controversial national foreign policy goals. Both postures undermined the UN of the Charter as conceived by its founders.

In the 1990s, international relations had reached a plateau: the "new" Europe and non-Western industrialized countries such as Japan and South Korea generally supported US unilateralism; Russia, Central Asia, the Group of 77 (G77), the Arab League, and the wider developing world had few options but to accept the status quo; and civil society was mute, and global peace movements, anxious to challenge this turn toward militarism and away from peacemaking, were too weak to make a difference. NATO, a creature of the Cold War, allowed the US-led Western alliance to behave aggressively beneath a military security umbrella. In 1991, NATO's secretary-general Anders Rasmussen, from Denmark, stressed that as a defense organization, NATO's primary role was to guarantee the security and territorial integrity of the then sixteen member states. At that time, there was no reference to authorizing NATO out-of-area operations. However, the affirmation of "a new strategic environment" and "multi-directional risks requiring new functions for alliance forces in crisis and war situations" led to militarist convictions that NATO's European origins no longer precluded the possibility of involvements beyond its continental borders. Strategic changes announced by NATO in 1999 referring to possible "non-Article 5 crisis response operations"[15] confirmed this supposition. Critics maintained that NATO was a Cold War defensive alliance whose treaty mandate no longer corresponded to the security environment of Europe, and the spirit of the Charter of Paris.

NATO's 1999 military operations in Kosovo against Serbia were not only an *out-of-area* war in disregard of UN Charter Articles 2(4) and 51 but also demonstrated that NATO, as a regional organization, had ignored its subsidiarity responsibility to the United Nations as specified in the North Atlantic Treaty Article7. This naturally was of great concern to the UN. NATO's repeated public confirmation that "nuclear weapons remained essential to preserve peace" and US voting in the General Assembly on this subject worried UN Secretary-General Kofi Annan and worried UN staff even more. Throughout the 1990s, there had been a consistent US opposition to a "nuclear arms freeze," to the "ending of the nuclear arms race" and to a "nuclear free world," as expressed in US voting at the General Assembly.[16] Out of 153 countries, the US was the one country that opposed the 1999 General Assembly resolution that called for the prohibition of attacks on nuclear facilities (A/RES/45/58J). The US insisted that policies governing nuclear issues be subject to primary control by national governments, with the UN having no supervening authority. Around the world, this was perceived as a frightening display of geopolitical unilateralism, exhibiting an astonishing disregard of nuclear dangers.

Another Western building bloc, the European Union, had made significant progress during the 1990s in defining its scope as a power with a singular voice at the UN. The treaties of Maastricht (1993), Schengen (1995), and Amsterdam (1999) formalized the freedom of movement of people, goods, and services of member states. Europe was becoming a "neighborhood" with a common monetary policy and the euro serving as its currency and with joint concerns for socio-economic welfare, and security, as well as defense and environmental challenges facing the Continent. While globalization with a Western face was accelerating, Secretary-General Boutros-Ghali reminded the world that the "gap between untold economic prosperity and the growing numbers of marginalized and poor people was deepening."[17]

At the end of the twentieth century, the global balance sheet for peace and security, disarmament, sustainable development, and human rights identified a somber picture of serious contradictions, national selfishness, and an unwillingness to accept compromise and convergence of interests and values as preconditions for global progress. The political UN, primarily the P5 countries in the Security Council, had failed to cooperate as a team in upholding their multilateral mandate. The UN could not function as a coherent body because it was unable to integrate its political, legal, social, and economic responsibilities, which were being obstructed in multiple ways, especially by the United States, the UN's original architect and principal member. This obstructionist posture of the US can be explained by changes in the global setting since 1945, when American leadership outside the Soviet bloc was virtually uncontested and generally appreciated as constructive. With the end of European colonialism and the collapse of the Soviet Union, the world changed, and so did the US. There was greater diversity of views on development and global security, implicitly an endorsement of multipolarity, while on the contrary, the United States saw the path open to the worldwide dissemination, by force, if necessary, of the US neoliberal orientation as sustaining its management of unipolarity.

At the end of the millennium, the UN still had to deal with a wide range of complex and unresolved reform challenges, including the financing of the UN. In 1999, the UN Secretary-General administered, as in previous years, an embarrassingly inadequate operating budget of US$2.5 billion to finance UN core activities in the eight headquarters situated in the US,

Europe, Asia, Africa, and Latin America. During the same year, New York's police commissioner had an operating budget of $7.4 billion.

At the beginning of the twenty-first century, it had become obvious that the reform of the United Nations had to be addressed if the organization was to function as a guardian and conflict mediator for global peace and a force for justice. The Security Council's geographical representativeness and the veto would have to become major issues of reform to create an organization that operated in conformity with the Charter, its foundational vision. The canvas of UN reforms, however, needed to be significantly broadened beyond these high-profile concerns. The relations between the Security Council, the General Assembly and the International Court of Justice; the enlarged authority of the General Assembly; the role of civil society; and the linkage between peace, security, and human development would have to be included in the UN reform agenda. UN member countries needed to accept that *political accountability*, intractable as it was, had to become an integral part of the decision-making process in the UN, without which the rebuilding of trust between nations would not grow to facilitate a more meaningful transfer of rights and responsibilities to the UN.

In the decades before and after the millennium, there had been two extraordinary windows of opportunity for such reforms of the United Nations. First, the end of the Cold War in 1990, with peace in Europe, had created a profound atmosphere of receptivity to major proposals for change, and second, at the beginning of the twenty-first century, there had been another natural occasion for bold actions in the furtherance of global cooperation regarding peace, human rights, social and economic justice, and environmental protection. However, there was neither visionary leadership nor populist pressure to take such overdue and desirable steps. This failure of political will was summarized by US president Clinton's demoralizing injunction as the millennium approached: "The UN must learn to do more with less."

# FOUR

# The UN Global Policy Agenda for the Twenty-First Century

## East/West and North/South Disagreements

The East/West optimism about the future of multilateral cooperation that prevailed at the time of founding the United Nations in 1945 became increasingly eclipsed during subsequent years because of North/South tensions. The world, however, was made to believe, yet again, that the US and Russia and their respective followers would at last succeed in bridging the gap between these two so unequal partners and promote socio-economic progress for all in accordance with UN Charter principles. Years of the multilateral debate and experience with international cooperation had created a wealth of knowledge for governments and the UN to facilitate the translation of the two Covenants of political, civil, economic, social, and cultural rights into measurable implementation to make sure that nobody would be left out, as Secretaries-General continue to insist. The prospects for tangible universal socio-economic progress for all, promising as they seemed, have not materialized.

At the beginning of the third decade of the twenty-first century, it is important to consider the geopolitical context as it has evolved since 2000 because it reflects an ever-widening range of security, economic, and social developments within and between countries. These developments have impacted all 193 member nations as they interact at national and international levels.[1] The UN can claim the legitimacy that flows from the universal membership of sovereign states, yet its operational efficiency is burdened by the accompanying complexity, with many diversities of circumstances and deep clashes of interests making the identification of common ground often a daunting challenge.

During this period, globalization accelerated in all its facets. More people than ever before were traveling; increasing numbers had to flee their homelands due to wars or climate change; more goods were being exchanged between countries, regions, and continents and capital flows across borders were greater than ever before; more transnational economic and political crimes were taking place; and new alliances among like-minded countries were formed and old ones were re-formed. On every continent, more and more people, young and old, participated in debates about the world's future and were taking to the streets to express their political views, and yet, at the same time more autocrats were voted into power imperiling genuine democratization.

This current and evolving geopolitical reality presents many formidable challenges to the UN agenda but also provides expanded opportunities to play a greater role in addressing the common problems of our interconnected world. Not a single element of these complex, interwoven and unplanned global changes can be ignored any longer, and no country, not even the most powerful, is able to handle these challenges on its own.

It must be recognized that multilateral decision-making does not take place in a vacuum. This is particularly relevant regarding China, France, Russia, the UK, and the US, the five permanent members (P5) of the Security Council, the prime decision-makers in the UN for the execution of global peace and security policy. During the past seventy-eight years, the individual policy preferences, priorities, and concerns of these five countries have always had a decisive bearing on the character of global dynamics. During the 1945–1990 Cold War, for example, it was the US and Russia (then the Soviet Union) that dominated the global policy agenda at the UN. Subsequently, the UN has been caught increasingly between the vagaries of US global leadership, the more multilateral geopolitics led by China, and, more recently, Russia's invasion of Ukraine.

## The P5 and Their International and National Priorities

We call attention to several salient features of the twenty-first-century preoccupation of the P5 that help to explain how they are acting within the UN. Turkey's leader Recep Tayyip Erdoğan has questioned the hegemonic relationship of the P5 with his slogan "The world is bigger than five." So long as the Security Council veto persists and geopolitical priorities prevail over respect for the UN Charter and international law, the world certainly is larger than five. But whether within the UN System, particularly within the Security Council, there exist ways to make the UN operate more in accord with the values and interests of the peoples of the world and non-P5 preferences on global security issues seems doubtful, at least for the time being. For this reason, we have identified in table 4.1 major foreign and internal policy concerns for each of the P5 members.

For the United States, following the "America First" unilateralist policies of the isolationist Trump administration, the Biden administration's foreign policy has returned to acting "multilaterally if we can, unilaterally if we must." The assumption is that America's security at home and abroad is guaranteed and, more questionably, with it, its global leadership position. Involved is also the reconfirmation of US confidence in NATO; the retention of worldwide US military footholds; the building of likemindedness with its allies, especially its guardian role with Israel; adherence to the 1989 Washington consensus on free-market trade and deregulation, coercively, if necessary; the assurance of Western dominance in the World Bank, the IMF, and the International Finance Corporation; and the domination of US might in the Security Council. Current policies within the US have to do with social polarization and the widening gap between extreme wealth and extreme poverty; the eroding well-being of the middle class; the depressed and racist conditions of the African American and Latin American communities and other minority groups; the quality of public education; the high national debt; the severely deteriorated national infrastructure; the dysfunctional federal and state governance structures; and a Supreme Court split along political party lines.

For the United Kingdom, internationally important is the protection of its territorial integrity, with special reference to Northern Ireland; the defense of its remaining overseas colonial territorial interests; the maintenance of its increasingly disputed leadership in the Commonwealth; the fostering of the special UK-US relationship; the adjustments to its abrasive EU exit and to post-Brexit isolation; the active participation in NATO; and the support of multilateral diplomacy. Internally, the UK is concerned about the cohesion of the four nations of England, Wales, Scotland, and Northern Ireland; social harmony between the various ethno-religious groups; the tackling of income inequality and poverty, especially for minority groups; and the reestablishing of trust of disenchanted electorates.

The Russian Federation's focus internationally still has to do with the adjustment to post-USSR developments, especially in Central Asia and the

**TABLE 4.1.** The P5 and their international and national political priorities, 2023.

| | International priorities | National priorities |
|---|---|---|
| China | One country, one system; Taiwan, bilateral matter; global leadership; multilateralism; support for the developing world. | Strengthening national power structure; Han nationalism; minority groups; social controls; rich-poor gap; increasing domestic markets; youth employment. |
| France | Europe as unified global power; European defense force within NATO framework; multilateralism and strengthening of UN; supporting OSCE and the ICC; leading implementation of climate change agreement. | Resolving unrest within civil society among trade unions and activists concerning labor conditions, retirement, and social welfare, especially minorities; adjusting government structure. |
| Russian Federation | Post-USSR foreign relations; rebuilding international standing following annexation of Crimea and invasion of Ukraine; restoration of global power status; new alliances and strengthening security and economic relations with China; protection of interests in the Arctic Circle. | Stabilization and autocratic governance; relations with opposition; rich-poor gap; rehabilitation of public service system; brain drain; corruption; management of war in Ukraine. |
| United Kingdom | Protection of territorial integrity; leadership of Commonwealth; US-UK relations; post-Brexit policies; active participation in NATO; multilateral diplomacy. | Cohesion of England, Northern Ireland, Scotland, and Wales; social harmony with ethnic and religious groups; income inequality and poverty; reestablishing trust of the electorate. |
| United States | Balance of multilateral and unilateral policies; global leadership including within UN Security Council; relations with China; military footholds abroad; cooperation with allies, especially NATO countries; special relations with Israel. | Social polarization and widening gap of wealthy and poor; eroding well-being of middle class; race relations; national and state gun laws; quality of public education; high sovereign debt; state of national physical infrastructure; federal/state governance structure. |

*Source:* Wikipedia.

Baltic states; the restoration of its status as a global power; the encouragement of new alliances such as the Commonwealth of Independent States, the Eurasian Economic Community, and the Collective Security Treaty Organization; the difficult rebuilding of its standing abroad following its 2014 takeover of the Crimea; and its 2022 illegal invasion of Ukraine, a war for which, as we write, there is no end in sight. Foreign policy priorities also include increasing collaboration with China, especially in trade, energy, and military ties, as well as participation in the China-led Shanghai Cooperation Organization and in China's Belt and Road program; the protection of its interests in the Arctic Circle area, of which 60 percent lie within Russia; and the fragility of the country as an export-dependent oil and gas supplier. Internally, Russia wants to stabilize its autocratic governance structure in response to the increasing popular discontent with the harsh treatment of the opposition. Other challenges with political implications include the oligarchy-versus-poverty divide; the decaying public service system; the continuing brain drain; all-pervasive corruption; and most importantly, the call-up of reservists for the war against the Ukraine.

Internationally, primary concern of the People's Republic of China (PRC) relates to the maintenance of its "one country, two systems" policy related to Hong Kong, Macau, and Taiwan, the Republic of China; its relations with Taiwan are a strictly bilateral matter, including special economic, trade, and travel relations. The PRC's major foreign policy objective is to prepare itself as an upcoming superpower. This is no longer a covert effort, as had been the case when Deng Xiaoping headed the PRC government during the last decades of the twentieth century; now it is openly proclaimed by President Xi Jinping. Part of this quest for international leadership is to secure access to needed natural resources and to protect this access through a network of maritime and land-based commercial/military hubs stretching from Western China to Southeast and South Asia and from Central Asia to the Middle East and Western Europe. Apparent are China's hardline sovereignty and security positions regarding its border with India and its presence in the South China Sea. Within the UN, China has consistently supported the developing world. Internally, China's preoccupation includes the defense of its national power structure, Han nationalism, and the rights of Buddhist Tibetans, Muslim Uighurs in western China, and other minorities; the government's social controls; the closing of the rich-poor gap, especially, the rural-urban life-quality differences; the enhancement of its domestic market; and the increasing youth unemployment.

Priorities for France, internationally, have to do with Europe as a unified global power; the development of a "strategic culture" within the European Union relating to the formation of a European defense force as well as support for transatlantic security within the NATO framework; and strong advocacy of strengthening the UN. In 2019, France, in cooperation with Germany, founded the informal Alliance for Multilateralism with participation of some twenty developed and developing countries. France, however, rejected Germany's proposal to replace the French permanent seat in the Security Council with an EU seat. Supporting the Organization for Security and Cooperation in Europe (OSCE) and the International Criminal Court (ICC) remains a French foreign policy priority. France wants to retain its leadership for global climate action following the 2015 Paris Climate Summit, which with the return of the US post-Trump, is again supported by all P5 countries. France furthermore strongly backs the UN 2030 Agenda for sustainable development and the expansion of its international business and trade interests consistent with the provisions of the Paris climate agreement. Internally, the French government is addressing the increasing unrest within civil society, trade unions, and activist groups like the Gilets jaunes (Yellow Vests), all exhibiting intense dissatisfaction with labor conditions, retirement, and social welfare, especially for disadvantaged minorities, and demands for reforming the country's governance structures.

The priorities of the five permanent members outlined above have influenced their decision-making in the Security Council. They started to realize that the worldwide impact of climate change and natural catastrophes involving floods, drought, wildfires, and harvest uncertainties, and of course, pandemics, such as COVID-19,[2] are beyond their immediate control and cannot be stopped by military might, economic power, or the building of walls. Most ominously, extremism, terrorism, and epidemics have expanded to all corners of the earth and have become the most serious challenges facing the UN Security Council.

These complex and often countervailing pressures represent a formidable challenge for the entire United Nations System, governments, and people. The General Assembly cannot escape its responsibility to review the causes leading to the persisting and fateful gridlock in the Security Council that has stymied effective decision-making and seriously shaken public confidence in the problem-solving capacities of the UN. The key to unblocking this state of dysfunction will be the willingness of the General Assembly and especially the permanent members of the Security Council to act internationally without hidden agendas of national self-interest. This would result in convergence and compromise for the benefit of the world's eight billion citizens. Not pursuing such a course of action would mean that Charter law would continue to be ignored with catastrophic consequences for citizens everywhere.

## Challenges for Secretaries-General

It is impressive that the three Secretaries-General who served the UN during the first twenty years of this century—Kofi Annan from Ghana, Ban Ki-moon from South Korea, and currently, António Guterres from Portugal—have staunchly stood up for maximum global cooperation in all areas of UN responsibility from peace and security, disarmament, and human rights to sustainable development. Earlier Secretaries-General would have endangered their election to a second term or as in the case of Secretary-General Boutros-Ghali, who, critical of the NATO war against Yugoslavia, forfeited reelection.

Kofi Annan reminded us that a Secretary-General office had as many doors as there were UN member states, a reference to the diversity of demands and expectations he faced daily from all corners of the world. He did not shy away from making bold statements to government leaders reminding them in 2002 that "today's real borders are not between nations, but between the powerful and the powerless, the free and the fettered, the privileged and the humiliated." We share his belief that the UN could deal with such a reality as it has the means and the capacity, if only the political will could be found. During his years in office, he accepted that most often the political will did not exist to prevent conflicts that should never have happened in the first place, as in Afghanistan, Iraq, Syria, Sudan, Libya, and elsewhere. An exasperated Annan exclaimed to *Time* magazine in February 2013: "Could you imagine if the UN had endorsed the war in Iraq what our reputation would be like?" Those responsible for that illegal war did not care. Dialogue, mediation, offering his good offices to solve inter- or intra-country conflicts were for Annan fundamental UN leadership principles. He told audiences again and again that "arguing against globalization is like arguing against the laws of gravity." Annan initiated a wide range of important reviews of critical areas of global concern,[3] which confirmed that in his many years of UN service preceding his Secretary-General appointment, he had impressively absorbed the ethics and experiences of multilateralism and knew how to shape the better world he had in mind. The Nobel Committee in Oslo recognized this by honoring him with the 2001 Nobel Peace Prize, stating that the "only negotiable route to global peace and cooperation goes by the way of the UN." There is no doubt that his thoughts on peace will remain immensely valuable to guide future UN reform initiatives.

Kofi Annan did not expect the opposition he faced while leading the organization. Yet, with a smile he once observed, "The Lord had the wonderful advantage of being able to work alone." At the end of his term in 2006, Annan concluded, "In the twenty-first century the mission of the UN will be defined by a new, more profound awareness of the sanctity and dignity of every human life, regardless of race or religion." He was right, but the vision we share with him is as far as ever from realization despite the growing evidence that a stronger UN is the only way to have justified hope for a positive future for humanity.

Unlike Kofi Annan, his successor, Ban Ki-moon, had no UN civil service background. He came from national foreign service that included an assignment to the South Korean UN observer mission in New York.[4] He needed time to get to know the UN System beyond the politics of the Security Council and the General Assembly. Yet, international security challenges, especially the then acute conflicts in Syria, Palestine/Israel, Iraq, Libya, Sudan (Darfur), and Afghanistan as well as the intricate P5-plus-Germany talks with Iran on nuclear cooperation, the threats posed by North Korea, and Russia's annexation of Crimea took much of his time. It is hardly surprising that as a former South Korean foreign minister, he associated global leadership with the legal and moral obligation to rid the world of nuclear tests and nuclear weapons.[5] Ban became deeply frustrated by the failure of the independent Conference on Disarmament and the UN Disarmament Commission to make any progress, especially with nuclear weapons disarmament.[6] The one modest exception was the recommendation by the General Assembly in 2017 for confidence-building measures for conventional weapons reduction. The UN Climate Change Conference and the resulting 2015 Paris Agreement for a global response to the threat of climate change were for Secretary-General Ban "a monumental triumph for people and our planet." He was convinced that the way our earth was being treated constituted a recipe for "global suicide." In his opinion, a climate "revolution" and maximum efforts to meet the UN's sustainable development targets had to take place.[7]

Ban would frequently observe that he was reminded of the need for a strengthened UN and was convinced that people wanted a global agenda. At the same time, in his mild manner, he warned that multilateralism must harness both power and principles and that full accountability prevailed when all were held accountable. Ban nevertheless was sometimes por-

trayed, as a somewhat weak Secretary-General, as he had difficulty han-
dling pressures exerted by Washington, for example, regarding insulating
Israel from UN censure, as one of us experienced while serving as Special
Representative on Palestine.

In 2017, António Guterres followed Ban Ki-moon as UN Secretary-
General. It was the first time in UN history that there had been more than
one candidate: seven women and six men, ten from Europe, one from Oce-
ania, and two from Latin America. As a candidate, Guterres had submitted a vision statement to the UN in which he stressed the importance of
international law, collective action, the dignity and worth of the human
person, and the creation of a sustainable world.[8] He referred to the importance of understanding mega trends such as nationalism, climate change,
and human migration and the nature of conflicts and holistic approaches
as major challenges he would expect to face as a Secretary-General. Once
elected, he gave a wide-ranging interview in New York in which he argued
that "in a world where power relations are unclear and where impunity and
unpredictability tend to prevail, what we see is that the capacity of prevention and conflict resolution of the international community as a whole, but
also of the UN in particular, are today severely limited."[9] He warned the
Trump administration that "if the US disengages from many issues confronting the international community, it will be replaced," adding "if the US
gets involved in . . . mediation, that, of course, will be welcome, if they are
able to do so in an effective way." Such blunt words from a UN Secretary-
General addressed to a major global power had not been heard since the
early days of the UN. During his first term, Guterres devoted much time to
translating the vision of a Secretary-General candidate into the targets of a
serving Secretary-General. In a confused world of harmful contradictions,
he forcefully repeated what his predecessors had also advocated: "no one
should be left behind," and to succeed, the UN had to intensify its preventive diplomacy and "build up the nexus between peace and security, sustainable development, and human rights." Bringing together UN political
missions and UN interagency development programs to integrate diverse
UN responses is evidence of the important new focus Secretary-General
Guterres has introduced into operational activities.

As with Ban Ki-moon, Guterres has proved susceptible to geopolitical
pressure on Israel; for example, early in his term, he ordered the removal
from a UN website of a study commissioned by the Economic and Social
Commission for Western Asia (ESCWA) in Beirut that concluded that Israel
had imposed an apartheid regime on the Palestinian people. The action
by Guterres was a response to the American ambassador at the UN, Nikki

Haley, who, referring to the report, had made veiled threats about the implications for UN funding. US criticism prompted the resignation of the head
of ESCWA, Rima Khalaf of Jordan, who had refused to carry out the direc-
tive to remove the report from the UN website. This incident illustrates the
inhibiting impact of geopolitics on even the UN's freedom of expression
when issues are politically sensitive.[10]

All nine Secretaries-General who have served the UN during the past
seventy-eight years have had much in common: a commitment to the principles of the UN Charter and to humanity, integrity in the discharge of their
mandates, and perseverance in their demands for disarmament and for
human rights for all. The Secretaries-General have all struggled to manage
insufficient financial resources compounded by late payments of assessed
contributions, while having to deal with an ever-increasing agenda of tasks
identified by member governments. They all have been aware that as un-
elected officeholders without political power, they are often ignored when
national and geopolitical interests supersede multilateral demands for joint
initiatives.

If it were possible for the Secretaries-General to have the chance to
share their combined UN experience, they would probably all agree with
the first UN Secretary-General, the Norwegian Trygve Lie, when greeting
his successor from Sweden, Dag Hammarskjöld, in New York in 1953: "Welcome to the most impossible job on this earth." At the same time, they most
likely would also concur with the current UN Secretary-General, António
Guterres, who sixty-seven years later expressed his faith in the UN, saying,
"We must make sure that when someone sees the Blue Flag, she or he can
say 'I am protected.'"

Those who reject such UN idealism, and there are many, as unhelpful or
even counterproductive in tackling global problems conveniently overlook
the fact that such idealism does not have to be disconnected at all from a
realistic appreciation of UN limits. Secretaries-General in looking to the
stars have kept their feet on the ground most of the time. They certainly
have been aware that UN multilateralism needs a well-calibrated dose of
both vision and realism. They have rightly argued that there should not be
an alternative for the path toward human progress and environmental protection. Credible proposals for reforms of the Security Council, the General
Assembly, and the mandates of Secretaries-General as well as the UN System's operational responsibilities are already available in large measure,
having long awaited the attention they deserve. In an over-armed world
of confrontation, mega-crises, anti-globalization, and inward-looking,
often autocratic nationalism, governments must accept that demands of

Secretaries-General, as the prime representatives of "we, the peoples," should no longer be ignored, even if reforms cannot be fully implemented.

## The General Assembly and the Annual Heads of State Meetings at the UN

Year after year, heads of state attending the General Assembly's annual autumn meetings tend to adorn their speeches with the language of conciliation, peace, and universal justice. They promise their support for preventing or ending wars and other conflicts, to abide by the rule of law, to fight impunity and uphold accountability, and for those in a position to share their national wealth, to make more resources for development available. The official rhetoric on these occasions suggests to the public a readiness to take the steps necessary to make the long-awaited shift from swords to plowshares and to give peaceful coexistence a chance. There have been exceptions. As observed before, Trumpism belittled the UN, rejected multilateralism as an enemy of "America First," and reduced US financial and diplomatic support, so crucial for the work of the UN. Despite such aberrations, the UN System has not been relegated to a fringe role. The UN, however, was made to bear the costs of the invisible wall Trump and a subservient US Republican Congress tried to construct between the US and the UN between 2016 and 2020.

Despite annual grandstanding at the General Assembly, wars and misuse of power are continuing almost as if the UN does not exist. The politics of confrontation among nations seem relentless and unstoppable. The language in the Security Council and the General Assembly has become more belligerent and positions have hardened in areas of global concern, peace and security, preventive diplomacy, crisis management, and even development cooperation and climate change. There is a distinct unwillingness of some member states to act in the global interest through compromise and convergence. The two recent decades of UN history show this dramatically. Voting in the General Assembly and the Security Council reflects year after year a worrisome canvas of serious geopolitical disagreement and rising nationalism.

On behalf of the Non-Aligned Movement in 2004, Malaysia spoke in the General Assembly of the "gradual erosion in recent years of the role of the UN as the primary interlocutor" in matters of peace and security and of the consequent urgency for strengthening the UN, as had been "emphasized by almost every leader at the current session of the General Assembly." The resolution, if it were adopted, would constitute "a strong political platform for the maintenance of peace and security."[11] The US considered the resolution premature and criticized the text for "reaffirming some principles of international law and not others," without presenting any evidence in support of such an assertion. According to the US, the resolution also "mischaracterized the role of the UN in the management of the international economic system. . . . Economic and social development of any country would only take place when that country takes on that responsibility." No details were given. Some abstaining countries made statements that shared the view that the UN needed strengthening but they felt that there had not been enough "actual and textual" negotiations to reach a consensus. The resolution was approved by ninety-three countries from the Southern Hemisphere plus China and Russia; it was rejected by the US and Israel; and forty-seven nations abstained, including France, the UK and other EU and former Warsaw Pact nations, plus Australia, Canada, and Japan. The votes confirmed once again the fragmentation of the General Assembly along North/South lines. The unspoken subtext of divergence concerned issues of power and geopolitical flexibility.

## UN System Multi-sectoral Country Operations

In 2000, there were twenty peacekeeping operations with a total of 90,905 Blue Helmets deployed mainly in Africa and the Middle East but also in Asia and Central America. In 2020, the geographical distribution had not changed much but was reduced to fourteen operations with a smaller overall contingent of 69,122 UN peacekeepers. More important, since the end of the Cold War, peacekeeping was no longer a self-contained operation dealing with interstate conflicts without links to the wider UN presence in a country or region[12] but had become a multidimensional mission with new partners and cross-sectoral responsibilities helping to implement peace agreements, post-conflict military demobilization, and the reintegration of combatants into their respective societies. In 2005, a joint Security Council–General Assembly decision created the UN Peacebuilding Commission, a subsidiary organ of the Security Council, to accompany and help to backstop UN political missions.[13] Secretary-General Kofi Annan had been pleading all along with UN policymakers to facilitate such links between security, development, and human rights and to adopt holistic strategies for the UN as a global service provider. Special political missions had been carried out as early as 1948, when Swedish diplomat Folke Bernadotte had been appointed by Secretary-General Trygve Lie as a UN mediator in Palestine to work along with the UN Truce Supervision Organization.[14] The time had come to give new life for such initiatives.

Political missions rapidly increased in number and scope. They were deployed in such crisis areas as Central and Western Africa, the African Great Lakes region, Ethiopia/Eritrea, Haiti, Nepal, Sri Lanka, and elsewhere. In cooperation with the Security Council Peacebuilding Commission, they focused on conflict prevention, peacemaking, and peacebuilding but gradually expanded their roles as crises became more complex and required an even greater canvas for UN cooperation. It was timely that in 2012 the General Assembly requested Secretary-General Ban to prepare a status report on such special political missions.[15] The report observed that partnerships between political and peacekeeping missions and UN country teams concerned with economic and social development were critical for ending crisis conditions.

The degree of success of such operations was quite uneven. To illustrate: while stability had returned to Burundi and Liberia in 2014 and 2018 respectively and the UN could close its special political missions in these two countries, the extremely complex and volatile political and security conditions in the Democratic Republic of the Congo, Yemen, and Syria continue to require UN good offices, special political missions, and country team support to work with all parties to conflicts in these countries.

The Security Council and the General Assembly, in cooperation with the Secretaries-General, have come to terms with the need for connectivity between the UN's peace and security missions and its development mandate. The improvements in the UN System's structural coherence and the coordination of its political, economic, and social programs in multisectoral circumstances should be recognized as valuable and far-reaching accomplishments and milestones of UN reform that tend to be unappreciated outside the circle of those dealing with the UN directly. This also partly explains why the UN fails to be given the credit that is due and instead receives blame for policy frustrations over which it has no control.

## The Challenge of Compromise in UN Negotiations

Looking at the wider UN political and security agenda for 2000 onward reveals how difficult it will be for the United Nations to live up to its core responsibilities. Unless profound reforms are carried out, the UN will remain unable to compromise when it faces policy differences. In making this evaluation, we argue that the UN was constitutionally hampered from the outset and that many of its most visible shortcomings are more a reflection of the irresponsibility of member countries than UN institutional incompetence.

Part of the difficulty arises from the direct and indirect encroachment of geopolitics on the work of the UN, particularly relating to peace and security, human rights, and the world economy. This encroachment has mainly to do with P5 influence, particularly that of the United States. For most of the period since the end of WWII, the US has been the leader on matters of global policy and the role of the UN and other global and regional intergovernmental institutions, and it pays the largest share of the assessed UN budget. It should therefore not come as a surprise that the US receives so much critical attention.

The United States, more than any other major nation, has over the course of the last century advocated an approach to world order that can be described as "liberal internationalism." It accords a major role to global cooperation between international economic and political institutions and gives only selective attention to international law. Such an outlook has often invited cynicism as the US has tended to confuse its geopolitical foreign policy priorities with its internationally expected approach to global leadership.

As the discussion of the clash between the Western countries and the rest of the world on issues of disarmament, especially nuclear disarmament, illustrates, the US is at times in virtual isolation or joined by only a few other supporters. It is not a leader in finding compromises on contentious topics of international concern, as it has consistently rejected all attempts to delegitimize its reliance on nuclear weapons or to curtail their role in global security. This controversial issue reached a climax with the Treaty on the Prohibition of Nuclear Weapons (TPNW) finally entering into force in early 2021 after years of negotiations and being ratified by fifty countries in defiance of a refusal by the US, France, and the UK to take part in the negotiating process. The three governments issued a strong statement rejecting the normative and policy positions taken by the TPNW. At the same time, the UN had received strong civil society support for such a treaty. Compliance with this treaty is almost certain to remain high on the agenda of antiwar and antinuclear actors around the world. Their collaborative efforts had already contributed to the adoption by the UN of the treaty banning antipersonnel land mines in 1997 and the establishment of the International Criminal Court in 2002.

Responses of UN member states to General Assembly resolutions in the field of nuclear disarmament, as a key issue for global peace, are symbolic

of the larger picture of a frustrating negotiating environment as the following examples of geopolitical division illustrate. In 2000, a resolution
on nuclear disarmament (A/RES/55/33T) calling for irreversibility in applying nuclear disarmament and strengthening the Treaty on the Limitation of Anti-Ballistic Missile Systems (ABM Treaty) was submitted to the
General Assembly. Supporting this resolution were 109 countries, including China; 39 countries were opposed, most notably France, the UK, and
the US; and 20 countries, including Russia, abstained. Two decades later,
in 2019, an identical resolution (A/RES/74/45) was passed with a similar
voting outcome. Noticeable, however, was that the resolution expressed a
much deeper sense of urgency out of "concern for the humanitarian consequences of any use of nuclear weapons" and called for an international
agreement to end ongoing efforts to improve existing nuclear weapons systems. This time, 120 countries gave their support, 41 were opposed, and
22 countries abstained. Throughout the twenty-two years of the new millennium, this schism in the General Assembly has continued. Neither the
Conference on Disarmament nor the Disarmament Commission have been
able to make much difference. Apart from some improvements of control
for small arms and light weapons, there has been a disturbing absence of
progress in all other areas of disarmament.

Although more and more countries have ratified the UN Comprehensive
Test Ban Treaty (CTBT), it can come into force only when all countries with
nuclear reactors have done so. Ratification from the US and the People's Republic of China is awaited. Initially, China insisted that disarmament not
be delinked from arms control, nonproliferation, and test bans and that a
pledge of no first use be included, but it finally decided to sign the treaty. The
government explains that for "bureaucratic reasons," ratification has yet to
take place. This undoubtedly has to do with the US failure to ratify. The US
initiated work on the CTBT, signed the treaty, and then failed to ratify it, as
it has often done before—for example, regarding the International Criminal
Court. This failure to ratify is explained by the American concern to keep
up with new nuclear technology, and like China, because by the worry that
the "other side" has yet to ratify—a true catch-22.[16] This makes the prospects
for the treaty to come into force soon practically nonexistent.[17]

Besides the continuing failure to agree in the General Assembly on a
nuclear weapons treaty, there also have been no signs of consensus in other
key areas of the nuclear debate. Year after year resolutions were passed in
the General Assembly by large majorities, with only a few countries casting
dissenting votes. The US often stood alone as the one country not support-

ing major initiatives for peace and disarmament. The picture that emerges reveals a most serious UN dysfunction: a majority of General Assembly members vote for a resolution important for global peace and security, some member states abstain, and a minority of P5 members vote against the resolution, and nuclear disarmament fails to take place.

There are other examples of key disarmament resolutions giving evidence of a divided General Assembly and the ultimate failure of adoption because of geopolitical power:

The Advisory Opinion of the International Court of Justice (ICJ/546 [July 8, 1996]), for example, refers to "the unanimous opinion of the Court [including a US judge] that there exists an obligation to pursue in good faith and bring to a conclusion negotiation leading to nuclear disarmament in all its aspects under strict and effective international control." This was subsequently (e.g., A/RES/51/46D [December 10, 1996]) ignored by the General Assembly.[18]

Similarly, the General Assembly repeatedly tabled resolutions to prohibit the development and manufacture of new types of weapons of mass destruction. Each time, this resolution was supported by a large majority against the negative vote of the US, the only objecting country, with Israel abstaining.

The Declaration of the fourth disarmament decade and the convening of a special session of the General Assembly devoted to disarmament involved two resolutions supported by more than two-thirds of the General Assembly membership. In both instances, these two resolutions were rejected by the US as the only country casting a dissenting vote.

Year after year, the UN General Assembly has adopted with two-thirds majorities resolutions aimed at decreasing the operational readiness of nuclear weapon systems. In 2010, for example, such a resolution (A/RES/65/71) was supported by 157 General Assembly members, 22 countries abstained, and 3 (the US, the UK, and France) opposed it.

For nineteen consecutive years, the General Assembly considered the resolution "Risks of Nuclear Proliferation in the Middle East." Three-quarters of the UN member states including three permanent members (the UK, Russia, and France), voted for this resolution, noting that Israel remains the only state in the Middle East that has not yet become a party to the Treaty on the non-proliferation of nuclear weapons (the NPT) (e.g.,

A/RES/51/48 [January 8, 1997] and A/RES/54/57 [December 31, 1999]). The United States and Israel, joined at times by the Marshall Islands, Micronesia, and Canada, rejected this important resolution every year.

The serious damage done by using depleted uranium (DU) in the wars against Iraq (1991), Serbia (1999), and allegedly in Ukraine (2023) has been confirmed by medical research and by military and civilian victims. General Assembly resolutions in 2010 and in following years were adopted by a large majority; the resolutions requested governments that had used DU-containing munitions to provide information on locations of use and to consider recommendations of the IAEA, UNEP, and WHO to "mitigate potential hazards to human beings and the environment from the contamination of territories with depleted uranium residues" (A/65/55). The US and UK governments, as major DU users, denied at the time that DU was dangerous, and together with France and Israel rejected these resolutions. One of us served in Iraq and saw the evidence in the Mother and Child Hospital in Basra of the genetic effects of DU on newborns in southern Iraq in the 1990s. WHO staff in Geneva confirmed that the US government thwarted in 2000 a planned WHO mission from gathering information in the area on the effects of DU used by the US military during its 1991 Operation Desert Storm.

Even in the General Assembly debates about the relationship between disarmament and development, a consensus for action had not been reached by 2021. Year after year, the same softly worded resolution was put before the General Assembly making the obvious point that a "symbiotic" relationship existed between disarmament and development and that disarmament could make resources available for much-needed sustainable development undertakings. These resolutions also requested the Secretaries-General to reappraise this relationship in the light of global changes. Initially, the US was the only country voting against these resolutions. Since 2007, these resolutions have been accepted by acclamation. They were passed but have not yet led to any tangible actions.

Throughout the decades, many governments, regions, and alliances have warned of the dangers of militarization, especially nuclear arms development, and have been eager to protect themselves. They welcomed the General Assembly initiative to create zones that would be free from nuclear arms. A majority in the General Assembly have supported these efforts, facilitated by Article 7 of the Nuclear Non-Proliferation Treaty. This article makes provision for groups of states "to conclude regional treaties in order to assure the total absence of nuclear weapons in their territory." Today, these

Nuclear-Weapon-Free Zones (NWFZs) exist for the South Pacific, Latin America, Africa, and Southeast and Central Asia. Some P5 countries, all nuclear powers, oppose NWFZs, even reserving for themselves the disruptive right to transport nuclear weapons through such nuclear-free zones. Unresolved has been the establishment of such zones in the Middle East and the Indian Ocean–South Asia areas. In both cases, a main reason is that nuclear countries such as Pakistan, India, Israel, and China are not willing to give up the nuclear power they consider vital for their national survival. Israel has additionally indicated that it would consider an NWFZ only when nuclear demilitarization is linked to a comprehensive peace settlement with Palestine and peaceful relations are established throughout the Middle East. While these are not reasons for preventing multilateral mediation to be considered, it reminds us how complicated it will be to negotiate matters of national security in either region. It took nine years of tough diplomatic bargaining to agree in 2015 to the Joint Comprehensive Plan of Action (JCPOA) by Iran and the co-negotiators, the US, the UK, France, Russia, China, and Germany. The outcome was hailed as a "historic accomplishment and a testament to the value of diplomacy." Three years later, however, the aberrant US leader Trump decided to withdraw from this agreement, thus making the world again a more insecure planet.[19] As of 2021, the Biden administration has started to reengage with Iran bilaterally and is currently reviewing under what conditions the US may return to the negotiations with Iran.

The Middle East has been a major regional flashpoint for global insecurity from the very beginning of the UN. In 1956, the UN, with US support, succeeded in ending the Suez Crisis by upholding the Egyptian government's decision to nationalize the Suez Canal zone and by inducing the UK, French, and Israeli militaries to withdraw their troops and stationing Blue Helmets in their place in the Sinai Peninsula. The deployment of UN peacekeeping forces in subsequent years helped to contain conflicts in the Middle East. The UN, however, has been unable to prevent five subsequent wars in the area, including the 2006 military confrontation between Israel and Lebanon, and to date has failed to broker a lasting peace deal between Israel and the Palestinian Authority.

The disunity within the Security Council and the General Assembly in dealing with the Israeli/Palestinian crises reflects a paralysis and unwillingness to compromise analogous to that during the Cold War years. If there is any difference, it is that the disagreements among UN member states about how to improve security, promote peaceful coexistence of Israelis and Palestinians, and find constructive solutions for both sides have intensified and become even more intractable. When in March 2001 the

UN Security Council was yet again discussing the situation in Palestine, seven of the ten elected, nonpermanent members of the Security Council jointly submitted a resolution (S/2001/270) calling for the reactivation of the Middle East peace process and the adherence by Israel and the Palestinian Authority to agreements reached in Sharm El Sheikh and elsewhere. There was general agreement in the Council on ending violence but as the Ukrainian ambassador Volodymyr Vasylenko, president of the UN Security Council at the time, said, there was "no common ground" on how to achieve it. The vote: nine countries, including China and Russia, supported the resolution; four countries abstained, including the UK and France; and the US vetoed the resolution in response to Israel's objection to allowing the UN to exercise any influence over the diplomatic process and to sustain the US role as an authoritative party.

The picture was no different in the General Assembly. Between 2000 and 2020, there were many General Assembly resolutions supporting Palestinian rights within and outside the territory of the Palestinian Authority. They had to do with sovereignty of the Palestinian people, help for their welfare, especially for women and children,[20] Israeli occupation of Palestinian lands, the construction of a wall on Palestinian territory, the impact of Israeli settlements on the lives of Palestinians, and the humanitarian work of the United Nations Relief and Works Agency for Palestine Refugees in the Near East (UNRWA).

In the spirit of the many General Assembly efforts to improve conditions of life for Palestinians, an international civil society initiative was started in 2008 known as the Free Gaza movement, organized by groups abroad from all walks of life to make the international public more aware of the desperate human conditions in Palestine and to bring humanitarian goods to Gaza by boats. Most of the multi-ship voyages failed to reach the Port of Gaza because of illegal interdictions of these ships in international waters off the coast of Palestine by the Israeli navy. The most serious incident occurred in 2010, when Israeli naval commandos boarded the Turkish vessel *Mavi Marmara*, the largest ship of the humanitarian aid flotilla. Ten unarmed activists were killed and many more were wounded. While Secretary-General Ban Ki-moon called for a full investigation, the Security Council only "regretted" the loss of life but failed to even refer to illegality although the UN Human Rights Council confirmed the violation of international law. Impunity prevailed.

To summarize: All resolutions on Palestine were adopted by the General Assembly with large majorities but were opposed without exception by the United States, which argued that its decision reflected the policy of both

US Democratic and Republican administrations to support resolutions on Palestine only when both Israel and the Palestinian Authority would agree to a proposed UN resolution. There has been only one exception: Security Council Resolution 2334 of 2016, which the Security Council supported by a 14–0 vote. The US abstained, still causing much criticism of the Obama administration by pro-Israeli groups for refraining from casting a negative vote, which would have resulted in the resolution being vetoed. Australia and Canada often also joined the US in the rejection of General Assembly resolutions on Palestine because of their objection to what they perceived as the unfair singling out of Israel for criticism. Forgotten was that from the earliest time of existence, the UN had been given a special responsibility to find peaceful solutions for the Israeli/Palestinian conflict that would be acceptable to both sides.[21]

There is agreement that both Israelis and Palestinians have been committing serious crimes against each other, but there can be no doubt that the crude rockets of Hamas are not comparable to the diverse and sophisticated capabilities of the Israeli Defense Forces. Furthermore, Israeli settlement policy and continuous Israeli annexation of Palestinian territory have intensified Palestinian misery and constitute serious violations of international humanitarian law, human rights, and the law of war. Also, Israeli regulations limiting the freedom of movement of Palestinians and Israeli Arabs have resulted in de facto apartheid conditions prevailing in Occupied Palestine, as we have indicated earlier.[22] This is partly why most UN member states argue that the overwhelmingly disproportionate scope of the illegality and the crimes perpetrated by Israel justify the focus on Israel of these General Assembly resolutions. Palestinian observers have called attention to the fact that failure to adopt a resolution on Palestine in the Security Council means that a single permanent member could prevent the Council from carrying out its duties to preserve international peace and security in accordance with the UN Charter.

It is this reality that has led to decades of persistent but unsuccessful General Assembly and Security Council efforts to bring peace to the area. The government of Israel and the Palestinian Authority should remember the emotional exchange at the 1993 signing at the White House of the framework agreement for peace between the Israeli and Palestinian leaders. "We, who fought against you, the Palestinians, we say to you today in a loud and clear voice: Enough of blood and tears. Enough!" were the moving words of Prime Minister Yitzak Rabin, to which PLO leader Yasser Arafat responded equally movingly by saying "The land of peace yearns for a just and comprehensive peace."

The rift between nations about how to solve crises has not been confined to security and disarmament but extends into other areas of global
life that, one would assume or at least hope, enjoy a basic acceptance by
all UN member states that the purposes and principles of the UN Charter have universal applicability and that all members of the UN welcome
the strengthening of "international cooperation in solving problems of an
economic, social, cultural, or humanitarian character."[23] Relevant General
Assembly resolutions make it clear, over and over again, that the reality has
been different, as can be seen in the vote in 2001 on a General Assembly
resolution (A/55/1011) calling for "respect for the purposes and principles
of the UN Charter" and reminding the world of the dignity and worth of
human beings, the importance of the promotion and protection of human
rights for all, the need to remove obstacles, and the enhancement of international cooperation. This resolution was supported by 104 nations of the
South, joined by China and Russia; 15 countries abstained; and 52 states—
including EU and former Warsaw Pact countries, plus the US, Australia,
and Canada—rejected it. The main reason for opposing this seemingly apolitical appeal had undoubtedly to do with a disagreement over Article 103
of the UN Charter, which asserts that in cases where there is a conflict
between UN Charter law and other international obligations, UN Charter
law shall prevail. What objecting countries obviously have failed to accept
and follow is that as UN member countries, they should be aware of this
provision and respect it.

A year later, another human rights resolution was passed by the General Assembly along North/South lines that set forth many of the preconditions that needed to be met before there could be full enjoyment of human
rights in developing countries. The South, again joined by China and
Russia, supported this resolution. The US government noted its "concern
that the resolution did neither recognize the complexities of the issues nor
the importance of domestic measures," without providing any details. It
concluded correctly that the voting "reflected the deep divisions between
member states on the impact of globalization." The US, together with the
UK and France and forty-three other countries, most affiliated with the
EU and the OECD, voted against this resolution. The negative reaction of
the North was no doubt due to the resolution's call for transparency in financial, monetary, and trading systems and for open, equitable, rule-based,
and nondiscriminatory trade policies. The voting confirmed the tensions
surrounding the formation of global economic policy that led to the failure
of the Doha trade talks after many years of negotiations.

## The UN's Development Goals (2000–2030)

The eight Millennium Development Goals (2000–2015) and the seventeen Sustainable Development Goals (2015–2030), which all UN member states have adopted, include the key goal of the eradication of hunger. Secretaries-General and their staffs have considered this goal not only critical for humanity but achievable by 2030. Not lack of global availability of food but lack of access to food is seen as the major obstacle. Ever since 2001, a right-for-food resolution has become a standard part of the annual General Assembly agenda to remind member governments that "hunger constitutes an outrage and a violation of human dignity and requires the adoption of urgent measures at national, regional and international levels." Those following the debates in the UN General Assembly have been horrified that, with the exception of the years of the Obama administration when such resolutions were adopted by the General Assembly, the US rejected these annual reminders,[24] using such unreasonable arguments as "the United States has consistently taken the position that the attainment of any right for food or the right to be free from hunger as a goal or aspiration has to be realized progressively that does not give rise or diminish the respective responsibility of national governments to their citizens."[25]

The resolution on the rights of the child is another human rights resolution tabled at yearly intervals in the General Assembly since the beginning of the century. During the tenure of the George W. Bush administration, the US on several occasions was again the only country voting against this resolution.[26] The US also remains the only OECD country that has failed to ratify the Convention on the Elimination of All Forms of Discrimination against Women (CEDAW). Furthermore, the United States rejects all General Assembly resolutions supporting gender equality[27] because of concerns over its sovereign rights, accentuated by diverse values in the fifty US states on social issues with special regard to religious beliefs and family values. The picture that emerges is one of a country that is inward-looking, self-serving, and not willing to see itself as a member in a community of nations that accepts that compromise and convergence must be part of global coexistence.

Over the years, the General Assembly has regularly adopted resolutions, against the wishes of industrialized countries, supporting a global compact for a more just and more equitable socio-economic order for all based on the Charter of Economic Rights and Duties of States.[28] The General Assembly-adopted charter declares that "all states have the duty to conduct economic relations in a manner to take account of the interests of all states and should avoid prejudicing developing countries." The postcolonial South insisted on a new international economic order that was not weighted in favor of the most-developed Western countries. Equitable markets and greater benefits of trade and investment for the developing world remain the demands of the South. They also claim their right to regulate multilateral corporations within their countries, the right to nationalize foreign property, and the right to reject any form of political or economic coercion about national administration and international commercial relations. The annual submission to the General Assembly of resolutions against "unilateral economic measures as a means of political and economic coercion in relation to domestic governance of the economy against developing countries" was consistently opposed by the US but supported by China and Russia while France and the UK abstained. In an example of direct and unabashed political coercion, the US sought to obtain the support of Yemen for the 1991 war against Iraq. When Yemen refused to vote accordingly, US Ambassador Pickering told his Yemeni colleague Ambassador Abdalla Ashtal, "This was the most expensive vote you ever cast!" Soon thereafter, the $70 million US aid program for Yemen was canceled.[29] The US not only disagreed with Yemen's position but used its geopolitical weight to intimidate a weak and vulnerable member state.

The US angered the General Assembly by voting against similar resolutions, as only an OECD country would dare, defending its votes by stating that such resolutions constituted a "direct challenge to the sovereign rights of states for the free conduct of their economic relations" and that "unilateral and multilateral sanctions were legitimate means to achieve foreign policy objectives."[30] The G77, the Arab League, and the African Union, three important regional and interregional groupings, expressed their strong objections to such hegemonic claims. Many governments considered Washington's stand "outrageous, harmful and flagrant violations of the norms of international law and obstacles for the right to development," as delimited by the UN.

## West/South Dynamics

In a wider context, the negative position taken by the US should not come as a surprise. In the early 1950s, the US government and Western European countries such as the UK, France, Belgium, the Netherlands, and Luxembourg, joined by Australia and Canada, had negotiated the establishment of an international trade organization, but the US Congress refused to give its approval, fearing that it could work against internal US economic interests.

As trade has always been a key element in international relations, especially for the many newly independent nations, trade imbalances, inequities, and protectionism were regular topics in the UN General Assembly. Finally, the General Assembly agreed in 1964, without vote, to establish a new UN body, the standing Conference on Trade and Development (UNCTAD), as an organ of the General Assembly. Through a resolution (A/RES/1995[XIX], 1964), it wanted to make UNCTAD a center for "harmonizing trade policies" in accordance with the Purposes and Principles of the UN Charter. The UNCTAD secretariat in Geneva was given the mandate to handle all trade and relevant investment matters, with special responsibilities for the concerns of developing countries and their involvement in trade-related aid. With such a mandate, serious disagreements between the governments of the South and the North were pre-programmed for UNCTAD. Paul Prebisch, the Argentinian first head of UNCTAD, anticipated the accusation that this new UN body was favoring developing countries by pointing out that at UNCTAD, "we are striving to be always impartial. But as for neutrality, we are not more neutral to development than WHO is neutral to malaria!"

Developing countries were hoping that UNCTAD would be able to help them in reducing the considerable trade disparities between the South and the West. At the same time, Washington and other Western industrialized countries were not comfortable with such a focus. They wanted to make sure that the IMF and the World Bank, two Western-oriented UN institutions, would pursue multilaterally what the US already practiced bilaterally and that the terms of trade would favor the West rather than the South. Eleven years after UNCTAD had come into existence, the World Trade Organization (WTO) began, as a Western-preferred non-UN inter-governmental organization (IGO) endowed with much more decision-making power as well as more human and financial resources than were available to UNCTAD.[31] This, however, did not guarantee success. The WTO Doha Rounds of Trade, charged with the reduction of trade barriers, have been failing ever since they started in 2001 because the US and other Western economies have not been willing to give up their trade monopoly by cutting their farm subsidies and opening their agricultural and industrial markets. UNCTAD became the poor-man's trade organization, unable to compete with the much larger WTO supported by OECD countries. Here again is evidence of bloc mentality, this time in global trade relations, for which neither UNCTAD and WTO nor the General Assembly and the Security Council have been able to negotiate solutions.

The colonies of the twentieth century had become sovereign developing nation states in the twenty-first century, with only a few exceptions. These exceptions are the reasons why decolonization has remained an annual General Assembly topic of debate and disagreement. In 2010, a resolution (A/65/55) was adopted, with 168 countries in support and 3 countries (the UK, Israel, and the US) objecting, taking the position that the General Assembly was "deeply concerned that fifty years after the adoption of the Declaration of Granting Independence to colonial countries and peoples, colonialism has not yet been totally eradicated." In 2020, there were still about nineteen non-self-governing territories (NSGTs), all administered by Western powers. These include New Caledonia, Tokelau, the Falkland Islands, Gibraltar, Puerto Rico, Guam and eleven other island territories, and Western Sahara, which is currently under UN administration. These resolutions argue that colonialism in any form, including economic exploitation, is incompatible with the UN Charter and that the wishes for independence of the peoples of these territories should be respected. They also restate the inalienable rights of the peoples to their natural resources and ask the administrative powers to respect such rights.

Even today, US and UK representatives argue that they could not support such resolutions because of their "narrow definition of colonization" and their failure "to consider the complex reality of the Non-Self-Governing Territories (NSGTs)," and because, without providing details, "some elements in the texts were unacceptable." The US contention that complexities were ignored is incorrect since the reports on individual territories make clear references to ethnic and socio-economic differences. The UK made the tenuous concession that "there was a commitment to modernize the relationship with the people of the territories."[32] What the UK government means by "modernizing relationships with their territories" is unclear except that the UK wants to justify why it intends to maintain the status quo for the territories still under its control. The Chagos Archipelago, a non-self-governing territory in the Central Indian Ocean referred to by the UK as a British Indian Overseas Territory (BIOT) is an example. In the 1960s and 1970s thousands of Chagos Islanders had been forcefully removed by the UK from the archipelago. They were resettled, mostly in the Seychelles and Mauritius, to make room for a strategic military defense facility, leased by the UK to the US until 2036. A large air base exists there, which was able to launch air strikes against targets in the wars involving Afghanistan and Iraq. A UK ambassador to the UN, Karen Pierce, argued that this military facility would allow the UK and the US to play "a vital role in efforts to keep allies safe . . . notably by controlling terrorism, drugs, crime and piracy." The British government also pointed out in 2019 that it was "clear about its sovereignty over this territory and that it was designing a $50 million support package to improve the livelihoods in the Chagos Islands." There is no mention that during the same year, there had been a vote in the General Assembly with 116 countries demanding that "the UK unconditionally withdraw its colonial administration from the area within six months."[33] London simply ignored this vote, and questioning the right of the ICJ to pronounce on the status of the islands, it rejected the Court's opinion that the UK's continued administration of the Chagos Islands constituted a wrongful act with legal consequences.[34] When Mauritius announced a visit to the archipelago in early 2020, the US reacted strongly, stating it would consider such a visit a "provocation that will severely damage relations between the US and Mauritius."[35] It should be noted that a rejection of a legal position of the ICJ, a most authoritative multilateral judicial body, would damage the reputation and undermine the effectiveness of the UN. It would also confirm that the power of the authorities administering a non-self-governing territory such as Chagos still prevails, rather than law and morality.[36]

Another recurrent topic in the General Assembly has to do with the right to development for all, a subject of broad agreement, one would expect. At the operational level, however, it is beset by ideological and geopolitical tensions even though there has been this overarching acceptance by the UN that the advancement of human security, the freedom from fear, and the freedom from want must be UN priorities. During his tenure, Secretary-General Kofi Annan repeatedly stressed that "we will not enjoy development without security, or security without development and will not enjoy either without universal respect for human rights."[37]

## Evolving UN System Cooperation

Developing countries began to benefit from UN cooperation in 1949 when the Expanded Programme of Technical Assistance came into being. As most territories of the South were preparing for independence or had just become sovereign nations, UN development assistance in these early years, as we discussed in the preceding chapter, focused on public administration and institution building in such sectors as agriculture, health, education, and small-scale industry. More specifically, food production, disease control, primary and secondary school improvement, and vocational and management training in these areas were the clear priorities. Geological mapping of natural resources and data collection for national planning purposes had also become standard areas of UN assistance.[38] Although not capturing much media attention, this UN involvement in "basics" provided indispensable assistance to many countries during the early years of their independence.

Initially, there was little cooperation or substantive coordination within the UN System. WHO, FAO, UNICEF, ILO, WFP, UNFPA, and other UN entities provided their expertise in accordance with their mandates, with financing coming mostly from UNDP as the principal administrator of UN development funds. As governments improved their national administrative capacity and the UN System gained experience in development cooperation, the UN System began in the 1980s to gradually tailor the content and the structure of its assistance to a country's specific circumstances. Transfer of know-how through foreign technical experts,[39] training of nationals abroad, mostly in Western countries, and the supply of imported equipment increased. There were also beginnings of co-financing between the UNDP and the World Bank in infrastructure development such as dams, mines, harbors, roads, and industrial estates. Increased sensitivity for the cross-sectoral nature of development fostered UN interagency program and project linkages and in the 1980s, led to the appointment of senior field-based UN officials as UN Resident Coordinators who served concurrently as UNDP Resident Representatives and were directly responsible to the Secretary-General and the UNDP Administrator for overseeing UN programs. These joint UN-UNDP appointments unfortunately no longer exist, as will be discussed later.

It came as no surprise that including the World Bank, the IMF, and the International Finance Corporation in such coordination would prove difficult. The postulates of the UN System and the Bretton Woods Institutions were just too different. As of the mid-1990s, during the tenure of World Bank president James Wolfensohn, an Australian-American lawyer and financier, the Bank broadened its involvement to include lending and grant finance for social development. In this context, the UN System, particularly UNICEF and UNDP, often had to explain to World Bank representatives in the field that external actors should never forget that the challenge of development cooperation was to make sure it was not just development but *human* development. This was difficult for the World Bank to readily accept, with its business-oriented policies and initiatives.[40]

Since 2000, the UN Chief Executives Board (CEB), which includes the World Bank and the IMF and even the WTO, a non-UN institution, has encouraged all UN entities to integrate, where possible, their efforts at the country level. As a result, UN–World Bank cooperation has improved and the adverse attempts to make governments adhere to fiscal discipline, useful for foreign investors but undermining national efforts to address poverty and advance social infrastructure relating to health, education, and housing, have diminished.

In the course of time, many recipient countries reached levels of institutional self-reliance and therefore asked their external partners, especially the UN System, to abandon their foreign-centric forms of implementation and instead, reinforce national capabilities with international support, utilizing local expertise and local knowledge as much as possible. While these government demands were generally justified, the UN and other donors initially reacted with hesitation, arguing, often with justification, that the time had not yet come in many instances for such change. These different approaches also reflected different perceptions about the levels of achieved local competence and the role of the state in guiding development and disagreements about development priorities.

The UN System has adopted a policy of consistent follow-up to summits and global conferences, which significantly enriched the quality and scope of its assistance as it allowed much more comprehensive, innovative, and relevant attention to local governance, poverty reduction, and environmental protection.[41] Today, programs will be approved only if human rights, gender dimensions, sustainable development, and increasingly, the participation of younger generations are integral elements of them.

These significant reforms were carried out by the UN operational system without prodding from the political UN. The Security Council, the General Assembly, and ECOSOC had little to do with these changes even though they supported such steps in their debates about development. The detrimental disjunction between the political UN and the UN development system lessened but continued. Consequently, a reluctance remained within the UN Secretariat, especially in the Department for Political Affairs, and the Security Council to routinely interact with the UN operational system. At the country level, there has generally been little interest among P5 ambassadors to familiarize themselves with the UN's development work. There are exceptions, especially when matters of bilateral political interest are involved, such as movements of refugees or the internally displaced, drug trafficking, border area developments, minorities, and other country information of intelligence value.[42]

Secretary-General Guterres insisted, right from the beginning of his tenure, that preventive diplomacy and operational foresight in the areas of development and humanitarian assistance had to become major elements of the UN agenda. Such programs would have to be linked with human rights missions, conflict prevention, crisis management, and peacekeeping measures. Confrontations in Central Africa, the Middle East, Central

America, and elsewhere would no longer receive UN peacekeeping support without coordination with other UN operational activities on the ground. UN operations in Iraq between the 1990s and early 2000s serve as stark reminders of earlier fragmentation with serious consequences: fourteen separate UN entities concerned with development, humanitarian assistance, human rights, disarmament, finance, and border control were active in Iraq without any overarching strategy and coordination. Those in charge of these UN units never met. Even less-complex country operations involving development activities and peacekeeping, as in Pakistan, Lebanon, Chad, and elsewhere, have been carried out as separate operations. This changed when Secretary-General Annan established linkages between the UN Department for Political Affairs and the UN Development Programme. Secretary-General Guterres appointed UN Peace and Development Advisors tasked to work with UN Country Teams in peace promotion, conflict prevention, and development programs.[43]

These steps reflect important structural changes and made the operational UN much more efficient and effective in carrying out its peace, security, and development mandates. In the past, P5 resources available to the UN and the UN development system have always been modest. Table 4.2 contrasts global UN/UN System funds and OECD/DAC development funds with global defense budgets for 2000 and 2022 to show orders of magnitude. Governments would not have supported such initiatives because they perceived such linkages as encroaching on their decision-making territory. They appear to appreciate now that cooperation at the operational level does not negate their power at the political level but rather enhances the prospects of effective performance.

General Assembly resolutions on the right to development, annually submitted since 1986, continue to be important reminders of the provisions of the UN Charter and the UN Covenants that the right to development is universal and for everyone. They recognize that poverty and hunger are among the greatest global threats and should encourage developed countries to meet the modest 0.7 percent GNI target the UN has set for their contributions to international development. The resolutions also stress the significance of development partnerships with civil society. The most recent such resolution (A/RES/74/152, 2019) was approved by 138 developing countries, joined by China and Russia, and opposed by the US and 23 EU countries, while 26 countries, including Australia, Canada, New Zealand, Norway, South Korea, and 5 EU countries abstained. It is difficult to comprehend why such a resolution identifying so clearly the causes of underdevelopment should not find a consensus.

TABLE 4.2   Global development and defense budgets, 2000 and 2022.

| Year | UN | UN | OECD/DAC | Global |
|------|----|----|----------|--------|
| 2000 | Regular budget US$2.5 billion<br><br>Peacekeeping US$1.7 billion | System budget[a] US$24.1 billion | US$75.8 billion | Defense budget US$1.114 trillion |
| 2022 | Regular budget US$3.1 billion<br><br>Peacekeeping US$6.5 billion | System budget[a,b] US$65.8 billion | US$185.9 billion[c] | Defense budget US$2.113 trillion[d] |

a. Excluding BWIs
b. 2021
c. Increase over 2021 mainly COVID-related
d. 2021

*Sources:* Organisation for Economic Co-operation and Development; UN; Stockholm International Peace Research Institute.

## UN System Finances and Global Defense Budgets

The right to development becomes meaningless unless it is backed up by adequate resources. The UN's funding history is full of challenging and at times, even threatening moments, when Secretaries-General have had to use their administrative ingenuity to facilitate continued functioning of the organization by using reserves and borrowing.[44] Year after year, many member governments defaulted in paying their dues on time for the UN's regular and peacekeeping budgets, creating serious cash-flow problems. For 2019, $838 million in dues had been paid but $1.6 billion was owed. Four of the P5 members—China, France, Russia, and the UK—had paid their dues in full between February and May. The US had paid arrears for the year before (2018) but only in December 2019 and then made only partial payment for 2019. Because the US annual contribution of $590 million at the time constituted the miniscule amount of 0.0177 percent of the overall US federal budget (which in 2018 amounted to $3,338 billion), such payment behavior must be considered deliberate, politically motivated, and punitive.

   In contrast, Bhutan, a small and poor country in the Himalayas, exhibited its high level of "UN citizenship" by paying its dues on time and, at 0.0870 percent of its national budget. Table 4.2 shows that during the twenty-two-year period, the UN regular budget increased annually by an average of only 2.4 percent; during the same period, the UN peacekeeping budget increased annually by 19 percent, mainly a result of increases in peacekeeping operations. The most compelling comparison involves the OECD/DAC funds for development and the global defense budget. In 2000 and 2022 development funds amounted to, respectively, a sobering 4.8 percent and 8.7 percent of the defense budgets. The extreme inadequacy of resources available for development becomes even more apparent when compared with the anticipated cost of implementing UN Agenda 30 with its seventeen sustainable development goals for which Secretary-General Guterres has identified a current annual financing gap of between $2.5 trillion and 3 trillion.

Throughout the years, all attempts to introduce innovative new funding mechanisms for development, such as income from currency transactions, carbon-use taxes, special new IMF drawing rights, or even a global lottery, have failed as major governments fear that they would lead to a politically unacceptable UN independence. Holding a short funding leash points up the tensions between functional imperatives for the UN and the political constraints expressive of geopolitical leverage that partially explains why the UN has been denied the funding needed to realize its potential.

Funds and programs such as those of UNICEF, UNDP, UNFPA, and the World Food Programme, all committed to sustainable development, rely entirely on *voluntary* financial contributions. This introduces a serious element of annual uncertainty into important UN activities, recently compounded by the COVID-19 pandemic and the Ukraine crisis. In addition to a lack of adequate and foreseeable core resources, there is a trend toward more noncore resources.[45] These are voluntary contributions provided by donor governments for UN programs. Some donors do not want to accept that untied core resources constitute the bedrock for implementing the UN System's own policies. Such noncore finance violates the provisions of the UN Charter that indicate the "exclusively international character of the responsibilities of the Secretary-General and staff" and that governments should not seek to influence the UN, as a global service provider, in the discharge of its responsibilities.[46]

A much more complex UN reform challenge will be for the Security Council and the General Assembly to accept the need for institutionalized links between the political UN and the UN development system, and for ECOSOC to significantly expand its network of cooperation with civil society. Such collaboration would require UN policy adaptation and strategy reforms in accordance with UN Charter principles and purposes. Meetings among members of the Security Council, especially the elected members, the General Assembly, and non-UN parties would become more frequent as the value of informal consultations with the outside using the Arria meeting format is being recognized.[47] Consultations should be seen as small steps in the right direction while the General Assembly Open-ended Working Group on Security Council reforms continues to lobby for more fundamental constitutional reforms.

Political rifts, ideological differences, and annual reconfirmation of ingrained positions of national or regional interests without signs of convergence within either the General Assembly or the Security Council have unfortunately become routine. Unilateral decisions, even though they violate UN and other international law and are harmful to other nations, are still undertaken with impunity. Stagnation of decision-making in the Security Council and pervasive failure to implement General Assembly resolutions are strong indications that major structural and constitutional reforms will not take place in the foreseeable future. However, climate change, global polarization, nationalism, renewed militarization, pandemics, and the recent increases in poverty, hunger, and joblessness underscore the urgency of strengthening and reaffirming the United Nations during this third decade of the twenty-first century.

## PART TWO

## HOW THE UN COPES WITH CHALLENGES TO THE CHARTER, INSTITUTIONAL INTEGRITY, GEOPOLITICAL MANIPULATION

# FIVE

# Palestine Occupied: The UN Frustrated

## Points of Departure

The UN engagement with the question of Palestine over the Organization's lifetime is perhaps its most visible and lamentable failure. It has been costly to the reputation of the UN as a legitimate and effective political actor, as well as causing a prolonged ordeal for the Palestinian people. Concern about Palestine and its Israeli adversary preceded the establishment of the UN and has persisted throughout the entire history of the organization. There are no signs of the removal of Palestine from the UN agenda anytime soon, yet also no signs that the long deferred, denied, and inalienable right of the Palestine people to self-determination will be realized in the foreseeable future.

The unfolding narrative concerning the UN is complex, controversial, and significantly interconnected with broader features of Middle East politics as well as with several global policy challenges. This narrative also illuminates the frustrating limits on the UN capacity to live up to the expectations of its own Charter, but also is a demonstration of the importance and potential of the UN when it comes to seemingly intractable issues of law, justice, and peace. An objective assessment of the UN role with respect to the Israel/Palestine struggle tends to focus on the ordeal of the Palestine people and UN's futile attempt to implement its own proposals for a peaceful solution or to spare Palestinians the ordeal of having their right of self-determination denied and since the 1967 War of protecting Palestinians in line with the Geneva Conventions governing international humanitarian law. In contrast, Israel and Zionist organizations, especially in Europe and North America, attack the UN for bullying Israel and giving allegations of its wrongdoing disproportionate emphasis compared to its attention to other similar issues. This line of anti-UN criticism, rising to outrageous allegations of anti-Semitism, ignores the historical reality that the UN inherited a special responsibility for the future of Palestine when it accepted the termination of the British mandate for the territory.

Various efforts to resolve militarily the question of Palestine have given rise to several wars as well as periodic upsurges of large-scale internal violence (1948, 1956, 1967, 1973; and in Gaza 2008–9, 2012, 2014, 2021). It is impossible to consider here the entire story of the UN's efforts over the decades to address aspects of the Palestine conflict, which above all, is primarily understood as being a long and unresolved struggle between these two peoples claiming respective rights to the land between the Jordan River and Mediterranean Sea, with references to competing claims of territorial sovereignty, religious and ethnic prerogatives. The fate of Palestine confirms our central contention that the nature and extent of the UN's influence depends on many factors, but most of all, as here, it confirms the disillusioning reality that the primacy of geopolitics takes precedence over international law and considerations of justice whenever serious clashes of strategic interests occur.

As elsewhere in our treatment of the UN, we give favorable attention to the *symbolic* domain of political contestation. It is in this domain that the parties seek to legitimate their grievances and rights. It contrasts with the *substantive* domains in which power, not norms shape political behavior and even enjoy an ambivalent measure of legitimation by way of the veto power.[1]

Before too readily dismissing the outcomes in the symbolic domains as irrelevant because of their seeming inability to have direct impacts on behavior, it is helpful to consider the historical record, which when objectively reviewed reveals an unexpected result during the period that the UN has existed. Often in the last half of the twentieth century, symbolic victories eventually exerted control over the political outcome of this type of conflict. And what is surprising is that this happened far more often in self-determination struggles than when coercive superiority was able to bring victory to the side enjoying military superiority and battlefield victories. This counterintuitive pattern befuddles "realist" gurus and arms merchants who continue to act on the belief that historical agency mainly belongs to those with better weapons and smarter tactics for their use.

Israel and its geopolitical source of support, the United States, subscribe to this outmoded style of exerting their political will and so far successfully countering the broader historical trend.

Before discussing the specifics of the UN impact on the Palestinian struggle, it is necessary to recognize the complexity and distinctiveness of the Israel/Palestine struggle because several elements set it aside from all other conflict patterns during the long existence of the UN and need to be taken into account in assessing the UN role:

(1) Israel becoming a state in 1948 is appropriately considered the last major settler colonial project aiming at imposing an alien state on an indigenous population in the Global South. Israel was established at a time when comparable colonial states had either effectively subdued the indigenous nationalist opposition or permanently marginalized such opposition by ethnic cleansing of various types with genocidal overtones (e.g., the US, Canada, Australia).

(2) The Zionist project benefited from the colonialist pledge it received in the form of the Balfour Declaration in 1917, later incorporated into the Covenant of the League of Nations. Palestine became a hybrid normative reality after World War I. Britain was given unlimited authority to administer Palestine as a Mandate but agreed to view the well-being of the inhabitants as "a sacred trust of civilization."[2] In practice, during the early stages of the Mandate, Britain encouraged Jewish emigration so as to further its colonialist tendency to divide and rule native populations under its authority. With the passage of time the Zionist movement developed anticolonial tactics because of its statist ambitions, which stimulated Arab resistance to further Jewish immigration as well as to British rule. The British, as was their practice in the twilight of colonialism, relied on commissions to recommend solutions, and came up with the idea of the partition of Palestine, really a formalization of the divide-and-rule logic.[3]

Despite these efforts, Zionist ambitions in the late 1930s and 1940s were expressed by insurrectionary political violence designed to make Palestine ungovernable. These revolutionary tactics were successful, leading Britain to give up its mandatory role and transfer the authority and responsibility to determine Palestine's future to the UN, formally effective in 1948.[4]

(3) Support for establishing a Jewish sanctuary homeland/state received widespread governmental and civil society support throughout the

Global North, in response to the virulent anti-Semitism of Nazism culminating in the Holocaust. Partly due to this preoccupation and partly
due to Western Orientalism, the impact of such Zionist ambitions on
the non-Jewish majority population was subordinated and generally
disregarded in the case of Palestinian rights, despite the general endorsement at the time of the right of self-determination of a people
subject to colonial schemes.

(4) Unlike other settle colonial entities, Jews had for millennia maintained
a presence in Palestine, although it constituted a small minority below
10 percent when the Balfour Declaration was issued. This Jewish minority presence was reinforced by a biblical claim that present-day
Palestine was "the promised land" of the Jewish people; its founding
leader, David Ben-Gurion prophetically declared, "The Bible shall be
our weapon."

(5) The United States, the leading geopolitical actor, lent unconditional
support to the core Zionist goal of a Jewish state, which over the decades has evolved into a stronger strategic partnership with Israel
based on upholding Israeli security and supposedly shared values and
interests, especially in the region. Especially since 1967, this partnership rested on shared wider strategic goals in the Middle East politics,
which emphasized access to energy and nonproliferation and came to
include protecting Israel from critical symbolic initiatives at the UN
even when supported by a large majority of members.

(6) As if this geopolitical support arrangement was not sufficient, it is complemented and influenced by a powerful Jewish lobby that has been
effective in insuring that US and European foreign policy defers to Israeli priorities on crucial security questions that have varied over time
even when at odds with national interests.[5] Israel has exerted great
influence in Washington since 1979 on policy toward Iran in a manner
that has increased regional tensions and discouraged normalization
efforts that included addressing Iran's nuclear program. This dysfunctional reaction toward the Iranian Islamic Republic and complicity in
allowing only Israel to acquire nuclear weaponry in the region despite
the adverse impact on US national interests and the discriminatory departure from its championship of a global nonproliferation approach
are perhaps the most disturbing aspects of "the special relationship."
Despite this departure from international legal efforts to control the
spread of nuclear weapons and to seek denuclearization, the UN has

been effectively subordinated to the incompatible US geopolitical agenda.

(7) The Zionist project was committed to establishing a Jewish state, with special prerogatives for Jews, and at the same time it was dedicated to being a "democracy." Such dual objectives compounded the difficulties of settler colonialism with a racist commitment that was disguised to some extent by being combined with democratic features, including citizenship rights of non-Jewish residents of Israel.[6] Quite predictably the dominant Zionist tendencies to achieve and maintain racial supremacy produced both a movement of armed resistance and an oppressive governance regime that has in recent years been found to be a form of apartheid.[7]

(8) The well-documented allegations of apartheid against Israel have challenged the UN to take responsive action similar to that taken in response to South African apartheid. Up to now, the analogy has been ignored in relation to Israel in UN circles. The UN intergovernmental consensus has continued to evade its responsibility to act by reaffirming a commitment to the zombie two-state solution, which long ago vanished as a credible policy option. It is uncertain whether a civil-society consensus as to Israeli apartheid will affect the UN discourse and response in coming years. The report of the Human Rights Council Special Rapporteur on Occupied Palestine, Michael Lynk, did treat the apartheid issue as fundamental to achieving Palestinian self-determination in both Occupied Palestine and Israel.[8]

(9) Despite the involvement of the League of Nations with Ottoman Palestine, as well as the UN, Israel and the US complain repeatedly that the UN pays disproportionate attention to Israel, and its alleged wrongdoing, to such an extent as to constitute anti-Semitism. Such a pattern has produced UN-bashing reactions in the West that undoubtedly have eroded more general efforts to strengthen the organization, especially thwarting reforms designed to give the UN greater operational independence and funding robustness, including dooming any attempt to limit or eliminate the veto. We have emphasized in other chapters that UN behavioral impacts are confined by boundaries set by the P5. When major P5 states seek support in the Security Council and face resistance, they act outside its scope as NATO did in Kosovo (1999), the US in Iraq (2003), and Russia in the Ukraine (2022). Israel, confident of US support and protection, violates international law at will without

experiencing adverse consequences within the UN and arguably not outside either, given its dealings with Arab countries in the last decade or so.

(10) Unlike any other situation in the world, the UN legitimated Israel by admitting the new state to membership in 1948 despite the massive displacement of Palestinians, the settler colonial nature of the Zionist project, and the ethnic-racial discriminatory character associated with imposing a Jewish state in a non-Jewish society.

This summary of the complex background and unfolding reality acts as an introduction to a selective assessment of the UN performance with respect to Palestine and Israel over the course of more than seven decades.

## The Never-Never Land of Partition

One of the persisting frustrations of the UN and its membership concerns the treatment of Palestine after the UK gave up its role as the Mandatory Power in 1948. Britain had been designated by the League of Nations as the holder of the Palestine Mandate to administer the former province of Palestine in the Ottoman Empire until the end of World War I. Such an internationalization of Palestine was not the preferred British outcome, but having failed to gain diplomatic backing for acquiring Palestine as a British colony at the Versailles peace conferences that followed the war, the UK agreed to accept a compromise. It would exercise de facto control within the mandate framework established as a compromise as to the Middle Eastern portions of the Ottoman Empire between colonial claims of the UK and France and an outright grant of political independence as recognition of the right of self-determination. This solution reflected the twilight zone separating the collapse of European colonialism and the emergence of politically independent states fulfilling the promise of national self-determination, which became an uber-norm after 1945.

Despite the attempt of American statecraft to exclude colonial rule from the operation of the Mandates System as it administered territories such as Palestine that had been previously within the Ottoman Empire, strong colonialist features assumed prominence during the British administrative role in Palestine. Britain never abandoned its underlying colonial ambitions of control, which meant dominating the whole of Ottoman Palestine as a vital safeguard of its trade routes to Asia, especially India. Palestine also had strategic importance for Britain with respect to UK determination to maintain secure maritime rights over the use of the Suez Canal under all conditions. The UK approach to administering Palestine depended on its typical colonialist divide-and rule-strategy that accentuated hostility between the growing Jewish minority population and the long-resident Palestinian majority.

Furthermore, in a complex move subject to many interpretations, the British government had made a formal pledge already in 1917 to the World Zionist Movement by way of the Balfour Declaration (named after the British foreign secretary, Lord Alfred Balfour) to support the Zionist project of establishing a Jewish homeland in Palestine. Although colonialism was still treated as a legitimate form of political control by Western democracies, such a pledge to the Zionist civil society initiative seemed a rather crude assertion of authority by the UK to determine the future political development of Palestine. Although the Balfour Declaration violated the core feature of the principle of self-determination, it could be argued that such a principle was not yet internationally recognized as a *legally* binding norm, but had the status of a *moral* aspiration at the time that was enjoying growing *political* approval, especially from the US and even more so as a result of the Soviet takeover of Russia. The Balfour Declaration displayed colonial arrogance by supporting a project for the establishment of a Jewish homeland in a majority Arab society without even consulting representatives of the resident majority population, much less seeking their views by way of an internationally supervised referendum. In the twilight of the colonial era, this UK move motivated by some extraneous considerations, sowed the seeds of future regional conflict and disruption, as well as the beginning of the long ordeal of the Palestine people.[9]

These colonialist aspects of the British mandate that interacted with certain historical developments have greatly complicated the unfolding story of Palestine not only for Britain and the Palestinian people but for the region and beyond, including the United Nations. For one thing, Jerusalem was the symbolic center of the Arab world, a religious site sacred to the three monotheistic religions. Its control by a European country or settler colonial society was destined to clash with the priorities and expectations of Arab nationalism, the related ethos of Islamic regional exclusivism, and even Christian traditions. For another, establishing a quasi-colonial relationship in the twentieth century, when European colonialism was under mounting attack in Asia and Africa, as well as from the leaders of the Russian Revolution, was an undertaking that increasingly meant swimming against a strong current in world history. It was the American president Woodrow Wilson who had promised the world that the territorial units of the Ottoman Empire would assume an identity based on the principle of self-determination reflecting the identity and preferences of their resident populations, and not as in the past, as legalized plunder to be transferred from one European imperial master to another imperial master in the aftermath of an interimperial war.

There were other reasons to be worried about the future of Palestine as so prefigured. The very idea of establishing a Jewish homeland, especially as championed by Europe and the West in an Arab society with a Jewish population of less than 10 percent was an Orientalist plan that would inevitably run up against the opposition and resistance of the majority native population.[10] It was Orientalist in the most fundamental sense because it erased from political and legal consciousness the relevance of the grievances and concerns of the indigenous Palestinian population. This settler colonialist background became even more apparent when Arab Palestinians understood that Zionist ambitions extended far beyond the Balfour pledge of a Jewish homeland, envisioning the formation of a Jewish state in Palestine. Israel has until this day maintained indeterminate borders as a signal that its territorial ambitions remain as yet insufficiently fulfilled.

It was against this background that the UN entered the picture, having acquired the responsibility in the process of Britain's resignation of its mandatory role, driven by an acknowledgement that Palestine was becoming ungovernable at acceptable costs due to the anti-colonial opposition of both Jews and Arabs. As the UN would often do when faced with a problematic challenge, it established a commission of leading international personalities to propose a course of action. The UN commission, as in colonial times, without bothering to consult the population, concluded that the two peoples could not live peaceably together in a single national polity and recommended partition of the territory, with the city of Jerusalem acquiring a separate and distinct international status that would belong to neither Jews nor Arabs, which was also an acknowledgment of Christian and Islamic connections with the city.

In General Assembly Resolution 181(1947), the UN gave its blessings to the partition along these lines over the opposition of the Arab neighboring states by a vote of thirty-three to thirteen, with ten abstentions. This recommendation overrode the unified opposition of the Arab countries, including the representatives of the Palestinian people, while the Zionist leadership acting on behalf of the Jewish minority population accepted the UN proposals as a step toward attaining its more ambitious statehood goals, but only as a step, not an end point. Partition fell well short of the Zionist objective of achieving Jewish statehood in the entire "promised land," which expressed the full scope of the biblical sense of territorial entitlement and a significantly larger territorial claim than what the partition resolution had allocated to Israel even taking account the enlargement of Israel in the armed struggle that surrounded its establishment.

The 1948 War ensued in which better equipped, trained, and armed Jewish militia forces defeated the invading armies of Arab neighboring countries, ending in an armistice arrangement that left Jewish forces in control of 78 percent of Palestine, with Arabs controlling the remaining 22 percent, and Jerusalem under the divided control of Jewish forces and Jordan (in contrast, the UN partition plan had proposed a 55 (Jewish)–45 (Arab) percent split, with Jerusalem under a specially designed legal regime). Under these conditions, Israel was established as a sovereign state admitted to the UN shortly afterward with near universal backing, while the remainder of Palestine was supposed to be temporarily administered by Jordan and Egypt until a Palestinian state could be established.

Another notable dimension of the 1948 War was the permanent exclusion by force and fear of as many as 750,000 Palestinians, accentuated by the Israeli demolition of several hundred Palestinian villages. Called the Nakba by Palestinians, meaning "catastrophe," it was experienced as an exclusionary climax of being displaced by the Zionist settler colonial undertaking. Subsequent generations of Palestinians understand their plight as a continuation of the Nakba, conceived of as a process. The UN Security Council was muted during the early stages of this Palestinian tragedy as it continued to unfold, while the General Assembly seemed to produce increasingly futile cries in the wilderness. It is notable that the settler colonialist state of Israel was legitimated simultaneously with the delegitimating of colonialism worldwide, which is partly explicable as a legacy of World War II in which Euro-American priorities prevailed and the European colonial powers were permanently weakened as extra-European actors.

## The 1967 War, Security Council Resolution 242, Jerusalem, and Occupation

The 1967 War improved Israel's security in the region and represented a major advance on the path of the Zionist project to gain effective control over the whole of Ottoman Palestine. Israel as a government did not confront the UN with this outcome, and the P5 unanimously passed Security Council Resolution 242, which called for Israeli withdrawal from the territory occupied during the war, including East Jerusalem. At Israeli insistence, 242 did contain language about minor border adjustments. It also proposed a just resolution of the problems associated with the Palestinian refugees displaced in 1948 and after, which provided Israel with the grounds for permanently "delaying" implementation of the withdrawal core provision. The resolution was widely interpreted at the time as paving the way to a resolution of the refugee question, and border adjustments were completed. Israel did not object to 242, apparently feeling that it could manipulate its implementation, which, it turned out, the UN was helpless to challenge or even question. UN expectations were that the Israeli occupation was a temporary and would end within five years, if not sooner.

As a result of the 1967 War, Israeli forces occupied the West Bank, East Jerusalem, and the Gaza Strip, with a dividing line between Israel and Occupied Palestine, administered by Israel but supposedly accountable to the constraints of international humanitarian law as set forth primarily in the Fourth Geneva Convention of 1949 governing belligerent occupation.

Once more the UN stepped up to play what appeared to be a major role. By a unanimous vote, it set forth a framework for Israeli withdrawal from Occupied Palestine leading to a just resolution of the refugee crisis generated by the Nakba. Israel relied on ambiguous language in Security Council Resolution 242 about border adjustments to justify its refusal to withdraw.

There were at least three problems with 242 from the perspective of establishing a sustainable peace between these two peoples. First, 242 assumed the validity and legitimacy of the partition of Palestine without the consent of the resident population, but it was never acceptable to large numbers of Palestinians, especially to those who were consigned to what became permanent refugee status. Second, Israel under the sway of Zionism never gave up on the pursuit of its ultimate goal of acquiring sovereignty over the whole of biblical Israel, which meant that it would be extremely reluctant to give up control over the territory occupied in 1967. Third, the UN lacked the political will to take strong steps to implement 242, having limited enforcement capabilities and facing unwavering geopolitical support for Israel on the part of the United States and Western Europe.

Another development that occurred in defiance of 242 was Israel's unilateral proclamation that a territorially enlarged Jerusalem was now the unified and eternal capital of Israel. The UN has withheld recognition of the validity of Israel's claim to Jerusalem, and as recently as 2019 condemned the US movement of its embassy to Jerusalem.[11]

In this period, a majority of the UN membership became frustrated by Israel's failure to uphold the principles of international humanitarian law in the Occupied Palestinian Territories (OPT), as principally set forth in the Geneva Conventions. Annually, the General Assembly passed resolutions critical of Israel's practices and policies that undermined the spirit and letter of 242, especially the establishment of Jewish settlements in Occupied Palestine in obvious violation of Article 49(6) of the Fourth Geneva Convention. Although the UN continued to condemn Israeli behavior in the OPT over subsequent years, it did not have the capability to impose any adverse consequences. The United States purported to respect international humanitarian law with respect to the OPT, but its responses to Israeli violations came to nothing more than a quiet rebuff as "not helpful," or more commonly, as a matter of "security," allowing Israel great latitude in deciding how to defend itself against Palestinian resistance.

An important consequence of the 1967 War involved the changed status of Israel in relation to the US and Western Europe. Instead of being regarded as a burden that threatened the West's strategic dependence on Arab oil, Israel emerged as a strategic asset that led to its unconditional bipartisan support over the course of the next century, with the UN becoming more and more of a spectator. To the extent that diplomatic gestures toward a solution continued, the US superseded the UN as chief peacemaker, even enjoying Palestinian acquiescence. Such a role emphasized the weakness of Palestine as a political actor because such a negotiating framework did not offer credibly impartial auspices by which to search for peace.

## The UN Responds Symbolically

There is no doubt that the UN was disturbed and frustrated by the denial of basic rights to the Palestinian people and the imposition of discriminatory and punitive control over them, whether they lived under occupation, in refugee camps, or within Israel proper. Israel claimed security justifications and mollified world public opinion by continuing to act as if favored a negotiated peace. In fact, the Palestinians were chided as never missing an opportunity to miss an opportunity, which was meant to imply an Israeli readiness to go along with the two-state diplomacy while creating facts on the ground that made it less and less tenable, most obviously by expanding the settlements and accompanying infrastructure (e.g., bypass roads for Jews only) under whatever leadership was elected in Israel. It was not only Jerusalem and the continual expansion of the settlements that made objective observers skeptical about Israeli intentions, but also the language used internally, especially in Hebrew. The occupied West Bank, the last major territorial objective of the Zionist project was referred to not by its UN name but by the Biblical names Judea and Samaria. Palestinians were routinely referred to by Israelis as "Arabs," suggesting a Jewish refusal to accept the claim of Palestinian peoplehood, of being entitled to exercise the right of self-determination. From the perspective of the language of politics, Israel and the UN lived in parallel universes with respect to visions of preferred futures.

Among the UN responses was to accord significant attention to Palestinian grievances, especially those relating to violations of human rights. Over Israeli and US objections, a Human Rights Council (HRC) mandate was established for the OPT, the exercise of which was entrusted to a Special Rapporteur, who was expected to make two missions per year to the OPT and present thematic annual reports to the HRC and the Third Committee of the General Assembly. Much careful documentation of Israel's persistent violations of international law was presented by the Special Rapporteurs, who were well versed in international law and human rights. Their recommendations for bolder actions were ignored by the HRC and the political organs of the UN. Israel opposed the mandate altogether and stopped allowing entry of Special Rapporteurs to the OPT in 2008, thereby violating a UN treaty obliging members to cooperate with the UN in its discharge of official functions, but revealingly, there were no consequences.

## Palestinian Resistance: Armed Struggle and Nonviolent Popular Mobilization

If it is correct to regard Israel as some variant of a settler colonial state, then the Palestinian people enjoy a right of resistance within the limits of international law. Israel has treated all political violence as "terrorism," a criminal activity that lacks any legal or moral justification. In fact, Palestinian recourse to armed struggle and receptivity to armed intervention by Arab neighbors failed to improve Palestinian prospects for an acceptable political outcome to their long struggle and was substantially abandoned except in isolated instances and in interaction with Israeli provocations relating to Gaza.

Western liberals, particularly in the US, had long lectured the Palestinian leadership to challenge Israel by recourse to nonviolent forms of resistance as that would elicit positive responses from a morally inclined society such as Israel. In 1987 (and less clearly in 2000) the Palestinians organized a mass uprising based on a pervasive ethos of nonviolence exhibited mainly by noncooperation. It was called the intifada and was met not with calls for dialogue and reconciliation, but by Israeli repressive violence. Again, despite the global responsibility to achieve a fair peace, the UN was sidelined and without relevance. Palestinian frustrations erupted in a second intifada, which featured more violence on both sides, the Palestinians having acquired some light arms. These intifadas did spread an awareness of Palestinian desperation and gave rise to calls for renewed diplomatic efforts.

## Oslo Diplomacy

In the aftermath of the first intifada, a new framework for a "peace process" emerged in 1993 from secret informal contacts between Israelis and Palestinians in Oslo. It was presented as a breakthrough, culminating in the famous handshake between Rabin and Arafat on the White House lawn with a smiling Bill Clinton looking on triumphantly. This high-profile acknowledgment of the PLO as representing the Palestinian people seemed briefly promising as a replacement for treating the political leadership of Palestine as a bunch of terrorists. As a result of the Oslo framework, the Palestinian Authority replaced the PLO, was recognized as representing the Palestinians living in the OPT, and even as governing the urban areas in the West Bank. From the UN perspective, what was notable was its irrelevance to what was proclaimed as a peace process. The US was accepted by the Palestinian leadership as the sole intermediary, and what was rather damaging, the Palestinians accepted the US advice to defer their international complaints about continued settlement expansion, collective punishment, excessive force, and international law generally until the final stage of negotiations, which never came.

For more than twenty years, the Oslo diplomacy was considered the only game in town, although it became increasingly clear that the prospect of independent Palestinian statehood was not on the Israeli agenda, while settlement expansion, de facto annexation, and making the occupation a permanent status quo were the one-sided main outcomes of the reliance on the Oslo framework to secure a solution. The UN stood aside, a virtual spectator, except for reporting on these continuing Israeli violations in the OPT and the recurrent General Assembly and Human Rights Council resolutions critical of Israel's behavior. The UN was added to the so-called quartet to add a certain diplomatic weight to the Oslo process, but nothing changed. With Donald Trump's presidency, beginning in 2017 the delusional posture of the US as "honest broker" for seeking peace between the two peoples was abandoned, with the US supporting Israel's regional goal to confront Iran as well as according formal approval over the maximal version of the Zionist project, giving Israel virtually complete control over the West Bank and East Jerusalem, as exemplified by moving the US embassy to Jerusalem in recognition of its claim to unified control and the right to have its capitol in the city.[12] To the extent that Oslo diplomacy was initially welcomed as the path to Palestinian statehood, it was worse than a failure as the image of a two-state solution became widely understood as no longer realizable, and its retention as a mantra amounted to conceding Israeli ascendancy over the whole of Ottoman Palestine.

## Zionism as Racist, Israel as an Apartheid State

The UN was widely appreciated as helpful to the opponents of South African apartheid and overall, as an ally in the struggles against racism and colonialism. Despite strategic relations and ideological affinities with the US and the UK in the midst of the Cold War, these governments possessed strategic reasons for favoring the status quo yet still did not attempt to openly oppose the UN efforts to delegitimize South African racism or to lend support to the global solidarity movement. It poses the question as to why the UN has been so effectively marginalized in relation to Israel and Palestine. Some of the reasons are set forth in the ten points above that seek to identify the originality of the Zionist project, given the historical circumstances surrounding Israel's establishment. Additionally, it can be observed that Israel has reacted with more tactical skill and stronger geopolitical backing than was the case in relation to South Africa, as well as learning from the mistakes made by that apartheid regime. It also seems the case that the South African anti-apartheid movement enjoyed superior leadership, while the Palestinian leadership has been unimpressive, lacking in unity, and lending plausibility to Israeli claims that it has had no partner in the search for peace.

Not only has the UN been neutralized by Israeli pushback efforts, but the organization has been weakened generally and in particular with respect to its wider efforts to combat racism. The Israeli government in conjunction with activist, militantly pro-Israeli NGOs has mounted a counteroffensive based on allegations that the UN has allowed its platforms to be used for Israel-bashing amounting to institutional anti-Semitism. This whole process has been given an effective conceptual framing by the International Holocaust Remembrance Association, which has served Israeli whitewashing of criminality by associating criticism of Israel with anti-Semitism. The cumulative impact of these pushback efforts has been to put UN critics and criticism of Israel on the defensive and to divert media and diplomatic dialogue from urgent messages about Palestinian abuse to questions relating to the credibility of the messenger, with an even wider pernicious, inhibiting impact on UN civil servants and others. While serving the UN as Special Rapporteur between 2008 and 2014, coauthor Falk experienced the full force of such defamatory smears, being called "a notorious anti-Semite" and the like, which acted as a major distraction from his role as human rights investigator. This defamation, without any foundation in reality, has been repeated to harm the reputation of the current Special Rapporteur, Francesca Albanese, and to divert attention from her powerful evidence-based reports. It is a disgrace and at best a telltale sign of UN institutional insecurity that its highest officials to do not offer even verbal protections to the people doing unpaid work on behalf of the UN as exemplified by the Special Rapporteurs who have reported on Palestine.

This use of anti-Semitism not to identify hostility or hatred of Jews and Judaism but to deflect criticism of Israeli state behavior has hampered UN anti-racist efforts generally. UN officials and others associated with the Durban Process of opposition to all forms of racism have been repeatedly defamed by Israel and subservient NGOs such as UN Watch as "anti-Semitic" largely on the basis of harsh criticism coming from civil society initiatives connected with intergovernmental gatherings. UN High Commissioners for Human Rights, despite leaning over backward to avoid any appearance of a focus on Israeli wrongdoing, have nevertheless been discredited and put under pressure to cancel such events, which have been boycotted by several governments aligned with Israel.[13]

Of course, governments and their friends have every right to object to the UN if it acts unfairly or in response to geopolitical pressures, but the Israeli response is one of defaming the organization and its representatives because it is attacking a country with major geopolitical support and growing international influence. By so acting, the UN is weakened in its capacity to do the work expected of it and loses civil society backing either because it is alleged to be biased or it is blocked in positive work by P5 formal and informal opposition.[14]

## Recourse to International Institutions: The World Court and International Criminal Court

The South African anti-apartheid movement made excellent use of the UN to promote its goal of ending racism in its country, especially constructing its argument that the white supremacist regime was unlawful and even a species of crime. This argument, challenging the sovereign prerogative to establish a government according to its own national values on racial policy, was rejected by the International Court of Justice (ICJ). Although these judicial outcomes were "advisory" and nonbinding, their impact reinforced the claims that the South African regime was illegitimate as constituted. This encouraged solidarity activity as well as direct resistance and eventually produced a startling about-face by the ruling elite, releasing Nelson Mandela from prison, which led to a rather smooth transition to a constitutional democracy. In the South African case, it can be confidently declared that recourse to the UN made an instrumental contribution to the struggle against apartheid.

Even when one part of the UN actually lent support to the apartheid claims of South Africa, which the ICJ did in its 1966 majority opinion in the South-West Africa cases, another part of the UN, the General Assembly, reacted by accelerating the claims of South-West Africa to achieve political independence, which it did in the renamed political entity of Namibia.[15] The UN, in facing the challenge of South African apartheid, performed in the spirit of the UN Charter. It underscores the contrast with its role in upholding the basic rights of the Palestinian people.

This UN role of legitimating Palestinian basic grievances, while disappointing, given its inability to end the ordeal of prolonged occupation, ethnic cleansing, and apartheid, has nevertheless helped to keep the conflict alive and provide legal, moral, and political grounds for global solidarity activism throughout civil society. The strong 2004 Advisory Opinion in the Wall case, although defied by Israel, strengthened the international law basis for objecting to the separation wall built on the OPT and to the whole settlement phenomenon.[16] This institutional outcome gave aid and comfort to the Boycott, Divestment, Sanctions Movement that was the core activist initiative in civil society.

Subsequently, support given to Palestinian legal grievances by the International Criminal Court (ICC) was deeply upsetting to Israel, although it involved only a decision to proceed with an investigation of the Palestinian legal complaint alleging Israel's war crimes after 2014. Israel's highest officials denounced the decision as "pure anti-Semitism," and the Trump administration response was to impose individual sanctions on the Prosecutor and other ICC officials. Although it seemed unlikely in the extreme that any prosecutions of Israeli officials would ever take place, even though the evidence was abundant, still the decision was a Palestinian victory in the ongoing legitimacy war. A new ICC Prosecutor has shown little enthusiasm for conducting the authorized investigation, and it seems destined to remain in limbo indefinitely.

A comparison of the differences between the UN roles in the South African and Israeli contexts is illuminating. The major observation is that the

UN can be much more effective in addressing human rights abuses when P5 actors are not directly or indirectly involved in strategically important ways. A secondary observation is that even when the UN cannot influence objectionable behavior, it may still play an important role by keeping the struggle and hopes of an aggrieved people alive and by exhibiting influential support for grievance claims by its impacts within symbolic domains where legitimacy wars are waged and resolved.

## A Few Concluding Remarks

The failed efforts of the UN to bring about a solution of the Palestinian struggle for the right of self-determination and other rights has cast a shadow over the UN as an effective and legitimate institution ever since its establishment in 1945. There can be no denying this distressing conclusion.

Despite this failure, the UN has been an important arena for both Palestinians and Israelis in the pursuit of their antagonistic goals. The Palestinians have sought to have their legal, political, and moral grievances effectively addressed within UN settings. The Israelis have sought to discredit and deflect these efforts as encroaching on their sovereign rights and have mounted a counteroffensive alleging a bias against Israel amounting to anti-Semitism, which is a second version of a legitimacy war.

As in other settings, the solidity of geopolitical support for Israel exhibited over many decades by the US government blocks all efforts to reach an accommodation that could produce a just and sustainable peace between Palestinians and Jews.

In our judgment, this unresolved Palestine/Israel struggle is illustrative of why it is important to minimize the role of geopolitics, maximize respect for international law, and limit if not overcome the role of the veto. In thinking about UN reform, it is important not to undermine the positive work of the UN in many areas or to overlook the League of Nation's mistake of driving geopolitical actors out of the organization.

# SIX

# Iraq: Oil for Food—the Dilemma of Geopolitical Humanitarianism

On August 6, 1990, the UN Security Council announced comprehensive sanctions on Iraq in response to Saddam Hussein's occupation of Kuwait. These legally imposed sanctions were lifted thirteen years later after the US and UK governments and their allies, breaking international law, had invaded Iraq on March 19, 2003. Most Security Council members, including China, France, and Russia, had refused to support military action, which they considered unwarranted. Following its defeat, Iraq entered a period of eight years under US occupation (2003 to 2011) during which political, economic, and social conditions worsened.

Detailed and credible information about the catastrophic conditions of life in Iraq under UN sanctions, as summarized in table 6.1, has already been published.[1] The focuses of this chapter are (1) to review options the UN Security Council, the UN Secretariat, and the wider UN System have had in dealing with Iraq under sanctions; (2) to see whether the options chosen were consistent with the UN mandate; (3) to assess the impact of UN sanctions on people's lives; and (4) to suggest that the Iraq sanctions experience be added to the list of UN reform challenges.

It will be shown at four distinct levels how UN Iraq sanctions were carried out and what alternatives existed structurally, substantively, procedurally, and morally by (1) the Security Council, (2) the interaction between the Security Council and the Secretary-General, (3) the collaboration within the UN Secretariat, and (4) the cooperation between the UN and the wider

TABLE 6.1.    Iraq under UN sanctions, 1990–2003.

Facts of Misery

Severe malnutrition

Extreme child mortality

Water-borne diseases

Health system collapse

Large number of single-female-headed households and orphans due to Iraq/Iran War

Serious birth defects in southern Iraq due to US use of depleted uranium

Destroyed infrastructure (water, electricity, roads, bridges) (Gulf War, 1991)

Severe housing shortages and domestic violence

Educide[a] and large increase of illiteracy

Major upsurge in mental illness

Internal displacement of citizens

Destruction of farmland (rice and wheat)

Dilapidated oil industry

Frozen assets

a. Hans von Sponeck coined the term *educide* to reflect the planned destruction of Iraq's educational system under sanctions.

*Sources:* Hans von Sponeck, *A Different Kind of War* (Berghahn, 2006); Hans von Sponeck, "The Politics of the Sanctions on Iraq and the Humanitarian Exception," in *Land of the Blue Helmets*, ed. Karim Makdisi and Vijay Prashad (University of California Press, 2017).

UN System.[2] Such a review will bring out the deficiencies of UN involvement in the Iraq under sanctions and the reasons why UN Charter law was disregarded.

There is no doubt that the UN Iraq experience represents a significant lesson-learned opportunity, valuable for a discourse about the protection of people in countries under multilateral sanctions and for the UN reform debate.

In August 1990, after Iraq had invaded Kuwait, the Security Council reacted immediately with a warning, followed by the introduction of comprehensive sanctions imposed in response to Iraq's failure to withdraw its troops.[3] Neither the Security Council nor the UN Secretariat had been prepared to take concurrent measures to protect the people of Iraq. The Security Council furthermore was not willing to mobilize any resources to meet basic needs of the civilian population. The responsibility to protect was considered the exclusive obligation of the government of Iraq. The Council took this position without any attempt to verify whether under sanctions, the authorities in Baghdad had the resources to meet the basic needs of the Iraqi people. As the conditions in the country deteriorated rapidly, the UN Secretariat hurriedly launched general appeals for voluntary emergency contributions but without the benefit of detailed on-the-ground needs assessments; the US and UK governments disseminated misinformation about the human conditions in Iraq and its causes; the UN Department of Public Information lacked the courage to correct false bilateral information; and Western media focused mainly on the dictator, Saddam Hussein, as the supposedly sole party responsible for the plight of Iraqi civilians. All this had a significant and pervasive influence on public opinion throughout the world and greatly weakened the international willingness to respond to the UN Secretariat's call for humanitarian help.

In the remaining months of 1990, the Security Council warned the government of Iraq of serious consequences, should Iraq continue its occupation of Kuwait. Resolution 678/1990 indicated that "all necessary means," including military action, could be deployed, if Iraq had not complied by January 1991. This in turn led to an agreement between the Iraqi and US governments, rather than between Iraq and the Security Council, to meet to discuss the terms under which Iraq would be prepared to end its occupation of Kuwait and the US would agree to the lifting of sanctions. A meeting between Iraqi foreign minister Tariq Aziz and US secretary of state James Baker in Geneva on January 15, 1991, failed to reach common ground. A day later Operation Desert Storm, a US-led coalition, began military action against Iraq.

The Security Council had authorized military intervention to free Kuwait from Iraqi occupation but had failed to define the terms of such authorization and therefore was unable to prevent the destruction of the country's physical infrastructure for water, electricity, roads, bridges, communications, and other civilian facilities such as hospitals and schools. This destruction constituted a clear violation of the Hague Land War and Geneva Conventions.

The Iraqi military had to withdraw from Kuwait and was forced to sign an armistice agreement with the US on April 11, 1991. The Security Council took note of this agreement but left people's welfare in the hands of international non-governmental organizations operating under the authority of the UN Department of Humanitarian Affairs.

Postwar life in a significantly devastated Iraq, except for the Kurdish areas in the north, worsened rapidly. Without safe water and sanitation and electricity, diseases long absent from the country reappeared at an alarming rate. Iraq, food-dependent on external sources even before sanctions, saw malnutrition spread quickly to all parts of the country. Child mortality climbed to global peak levels. Two hurriedly mounted postwar UN Secretariat missions, led by Under-Secretary-General Maarti Ahtisaari (March 1991), and by UN Executive Delegate Sadruddin Aga Khan (July 1991), concluded that Iraq had been "relegated to a pre-industrial age." These two missions emphasized that "speed of assistance was vital" and meeting people's basic needs had "more to do with financing of imports than with actual sanctions prohibitions." Massive financial requirements, estimated at $22–25 billion, were needed to restore the country's infrastructure, including the oil sector, upon which the Iraqi population of some 18 million was dependent. Funds for the rehabilitation of the country had to be found in Iraq's own resources, the UN missions concluded, as such an amount was far beyond what was likely to become available internationally. The Security Council was empowered by two of its early sanctions resolutions (661 and 687) to start such a rehabilitation program by unfreezing externally held Iraqi assets, but it had no intention of doing so. The UN Secretariat's reminder that it was "a cardinal UN principle that an innocent civil society should not be held hostage to events beyond their control" was unheeded by the Security Council.

The UN System could therefore do little to avoid a human catastrophe, as it had neither the authority nor the resources to implement a UN humanitarian rescue operation on the needed scale. During the period 1991–96, the UN Department of Humanitarian Affairs[4] organized five UN humanitarian appeals in the hope of receiving at least $1.2 billion for immediate emergency programs but collected a mere $420 million. The general perception remained, especially in Western countries, that it was the responsibility of Saddam Hussein's government, to look after the Iraqi people, and therefore, neither governments nor the Security Council were willing to cover the resources shortfall to halt the deteriorating conditions in the country. Yet, as the suffering of civilians deepened year after year and became daily news around the world, international pressure mounted from people in the streets, non-governmental institutions, and the UN civil service to overcome the political impasse.

Following the defeat of the Iraq military in the US-led Operation Desert Storm in early 1991, the Security Council passed resolution S/687/1991, which upheld the continuation of UN sanctions until Iraq had "completed all actions contemplated." This consensus resolution, like earlier resolutions on Iraq, gave the impression of Council unanimity while in fact it was hiding fundamental disagreements within the P5. The government of Iraq rejected this resolution arguing that Iraq by withdrawing its troops from Kuwait had already "completed all actions contemplated" as foreseen by Security Council RES/660/1990. The Iraqi government therefore considered Resolution 687, which introduced new conditions, as a breach of agreement and refused to accept it. What the Security Council had done was to link the lifting of economic sanctions to Iraqi disarmament. In other words, the fate of the Iraqi people was to be determined by the politics of their government and the UN Security Council. Despite the seriousness of such a decision, de-linking, or even correlating progressive disarmament with a concurrent easing of UN sanctions, was completely out of the question for Iraq's main protagonists, the United States and the United Kingdom. Security Council decision-making was clearly dominated by unilateralist lobby power reflecting at best subsidiary concerns for humanitarian demands. This inhumane ping-pong diplomacy of the government of Iraq and the UN Security Council continued for five years and ended in April 1995, when the Security Council finally approved humanitarian relief for Iraq by establishing the Oil-for-Food Programme (S/RES/986/1995). It took another year before the UN Secretariat and the government of Iraq signed a corresponding Memorandum of Understanding for humanitarian assistance, which became operational in May 1996 (S/RES/356/1996). A further nine months passed before the first consignments of Security Council–cleared humanitarian supplies started to arrive in Iraq in January 1997.

The human costs (mortality, morbidity, malnutrition, mental health, abject poverty) of such delays were immense and stood in stark contrast with the generic recommendations P5 countries had outlined for the management of multilateral sanctions in general just a day before the Iraq-specific Oil-for-Food Programme (OFFP) had been approved by the Security Council. In this P5 note to the president of the Security Council, the US and the UK plus the other P5 members, China, France, and the Russian Federation, had urged that "unintended adverse side-effects of sanctions should be minimized"; the Security Council should "give due regard to the humanitarian situation" and "unimpeded access to humanitarian aid" be allowed; and procedures for the procurement of humanitarian supplies be as "expeditious as possible."[5] The P5 note also asked that future UN sanction committees should draw "on the experience . . . of different sanctions committees." This general declaration left no doubt whatsoever that all five permanent members of the Security Council were fully aware of the UN's responsibility for the protection of innocent civilians living in countries under multilateral sanctions including Iraq. The application of this collective big power acknowledgment of responsibility in the case of Iraq, however, was about as contrary to the actualities of UN sanctions management proposed by the P5 as it could possibly have been. There was a total absence in the Security Council of any sense of urgency for providing humanitarian assistance to Iraq.

Iraq was measured with a very different yardstick. US ambassador to the UN John Negroponte confirmed this when he briefed the US Senate Foreign Relations Committee in April 2004 on Iraq, saying, "Although the flow of humanitarian goods . . . was a matter of strong interest to the US Government, it should be emphasized that an even greater preoccupation [was] Iraq's WMD Program. . . . We concentrated our efforts on this aspect of the sanctions." This statement exhibits irresponsible gaps between the humanitarian rhetoric and the practice of geopolitical actors. Note also should be taken of the lack of due diligence by those P5 members that did not support the political mission of the US in Iraq.

Both Secretary-General Perez de Cuellar and Secretary-General Boutros-Ghali had pleaded with the Security Council to allow the Iraqi oil industry to produce as much oil as the dilapidated industry was able to produce. The additional funding required to meet minimum standards of survival would have to come from external sources or Iraqi sources held outside. The Security Council, referring to the two earlier UN missions to Iraq, decided to limit such oil sales to a ceiling of $1.6 billion for a period of six months, an amount that was grossly insufficient to meet basic civilian needs.[6]

## The Two Phases of Iraq Sanctions

During the thirteen years of Iraq sanctions, two distinct periods can be identified: 1990 to 1996, a period of amorphous, haphazard, and ad hoc handling of sanctions by the government of Iraq, the United Nations, and individual countries, and 1997 to 2003, when the Security Council and the government of Iraq reluctantly implemented a more structured humanitarian exemption. The suffering of the Iraqi people during both periods was accepted by the Security Council as "unfortunate but unavoidable collateral damage" and by the government of Iraq as the result of deliberate hostile acts from foreign powers. There was a sobering disregard of moral principles on all sides. These two periods are reviewed, in accordance with the four institutional levels identified earlier, to allow a comparison between the actual sanctions management and other options that were available but not considered.

*The Security Council*

At the time sanctions were announced in August 1990, the Security Council had the structural, substantive, and procedural authority as well as the moral responsibility to introduce measures to protect the civilian population from adverse impacts of the sanctions program it had introduced. It failed to apply these. At the same time, the government of Iraq showed an unsatisfactory willingness to meet the demands of the Security Council by disarming. Whatever happened was determined by political interests of both parties, with the Iraqi people paying the price.

In the early 1990s, the Security Council left resource mobilization to meet emergency needs of 18 million Iraqis entirely to voluntary efforts. The Council took no action to cover the gap between the voluntary contributions collected and the funding required to finance a minimal humanitarian exemption. It took sanctions decisions without examining data that would have allowed a more reliable needs assessment. Such data and experience were available from the UN Secretariat, the World Bank, and the IMF. The Security Council possessed the option to either release frozen Iraqi assets or mobilize donations from UN member states. It did neither. In passing Resolution 687 in April 1991,[7] linking the lifting of economic sanctions to disarmament, the Security Council also had the option to introduce a gradual easing of comprehensive economic sanctions linked to progress in Iraqi disarmament but did not do so. Such linkage would have made a significant difference for the Iraqi population.

The Security Council also had procedural and morally responsible options it could have included in its sanction policies but, pressured by the US and the UK, adopted measures that were often simply punitive. The Council decided in 1991 to allow, during periods of six months, the sale of Iraqi oil of up to $1.6 billion, knowing that such an amount was totally inadequate to meet minimal needs of the Iraqi people. It even deducted from an already severely inadequate amount 30 percent payable to the UN Compensation Commission for individuals, companies and governments for damages caused to them by Iraq's invasion of Kuwait.[8] The more humane alternative would have been to use oil revenue first for the survival of Iraqis with the understanding that victimized foreign workers would be compensated at the same time from unfrozen Iraqi assets or other sources. Governments and corporations, of course, would also be compensated but only when sufficient funds were available to meet humanitarian needs. This option, life-determining for many Iraqis, was not chosen. The Security Council, making matters worse, instead of limiting its role to overseeing sanctions policies, chose to micro-control UN operations, thereby delaying the procurement of urgently needed humanitarian supplies.

Bilateral disinformation, mostly disseminated by the US and UK governments, fostered the distinctly false impression that the Baghdad dictator was the sole cause of suffering of Iraqis living in areas under government control. Those residing in the locally autonomous Iraqi Kurdistan were handling the situation much better. Washington and London failed to mention that Iraqi Kurdistan with 13 percent of the country's population had been appropriated 19 percent of the oil revenue. The three Kurdish provinces of Dohuk, Erbil, and Sulaymaniyah also received support in cash not available to the government in Baghdad, and no UN supplies for the three Kurdish provinces were ever blocked by the UN Iraq Sanctions Committee.

The US government also disinformed by wrongly stating that food was withheld by the Iraqi government from Shia opposition groups in southern Iraq. The UN World Food Program's countrywide ration-card system used in administering the food distribution showed that this accusation was false. Equally false was the allegation that the Iraqi Ministry of Health was hoarding medicines rather than giving them to hospitals. At the advice of WHO, the Iraq Ministry of Health had been keeping stocks of medicines to be available in case of an epidemic.

The US and the UK argued that the government of Iraq was guilty of large-scale corruption. This indeed was the case. Convincing evidence existed that members of Saddam Hussein's Baath Party enjoyed appalling luxuries while the Iraqi people were starving. However, the outside world was never told that the government was forced to make a major part of the illegal funds available to pay the military and the civil service and to provide funds for the maintenance of the country's physical infrastructure, which due to the 1991 war was in a most precarious condition. The Security Council never wanted to acknowledge that any country, including countries under sanctions, could operate without cash. While it was proper to hold the government of Iraq fully accountable for the misuse of legally and illegally acquired resources, this in no way absolved the UN, supposedly a people's organization dedicated to promoting the global public good, from its moral and legal responsibilities to do whatever it could to provide humanitarian assistance in response to the desperate conditions in Iraq after the 1991 war.

The continuous and planned dissemination by key members of the Security Council of incorrect assessments of conditions in Iraq further delayed the distribution of supplies or blocked them from becoming available at all. False information made UN humanitarian efforts on the ground even more difficult. It also put into question the professionalism and objectivity of UN staff charged with implementing the inadequate Oil-for-Food Programme. In retrospect, it is amazing that the Security Council failed to make efforts to present the credible information that was available. These efforts should have included regular direct or indirect contacts between the Security Council and the UN in Baghdad. UNICEF, WHO, WFP, FAO, and of course, the UN Humanitarian Coordinator possessed detailed information about the actual conditions of life in Iraq.

It is most revealing that during the thirteen years of sanctions, except for a single short visit by the ambassador of Portugal, António Monteiro, chairman of the UN Sanctions Committee, there was not a single Security Council visit to Iraq during the entire period. Also, the UN Charter (Article 31) states that if a member of the UN "is a party to a dispute under consideration by the Security Council, it shall be invited to participate . . . in the discussion related to the dispute." The Security Council should have always taken this procedural option seriously, but in the case of Iraq, it did rarely do so. Because the Security Council Rules of Procedure have remained "provisional" since 1945, allowing the Security Council to decide whether a meeting should be formal or informal, Council presidents often opted for the latter. In such cases, non–Security Council members were not allowed to join. As most Security Council meetings on Iraq were "conveniently" declared as informal, Iraqi diplomats could only rarely participate in reviews of their country's situation.

The US and UK, as two permanent Security Council members, prevented Baghdad-based Humanitarian Coordinators from briefing the Security Council on the humanitarian conditions in Iraq. After two of them had resigned from the UN, the French ambassador to the UN, Alain Déjammet, requested that the Security Council invite them to jointly brief the Council about their Iraq experience.[9] This request was vetoed by the US and UK on the grounds that they "had only limited sanctions experience" and therefore "could not contribute much to the debate." Regular Security Council visits to Iraq and regular Security Council briefings from Baghdad-based senior UN officials would have been valuable procedural and substantive options as they would have produced important clarifications about conditions on the ground and could have allowed the Council to add a social safety net to the humanitarian exemption with much greater protection for the Iraqi people.

No country visits by the Security Council, only rare Security Council briefings from Iraq-based UN officials, and no more than intermittent opportunities for New York–based Iraqi diplomats to present their government's positions constituted a shocking failure of UN responsibility to defend the truth of the human plight in Iraq. Dialogue on Iraq was just not an option for a Security Council dominated by two governments intent on geopolitical punishment as a sequel to the 1991 war.

### Cooperation between the Security Council and the Secretary-General

The relationship between the UN policymaker, the Security Council of fifteen members, and the Secretary-General with his team as the policy implementer has been always complex and sensitive, especially between the P5 and the Secretary-General. In the context of the UN Iraq sanctions, Secretary-General Boutros-Ghali reminded the Security Council that when it imposes sanctions, "it should at the same time define objective criteria for determining that their purpose had been achieved" and "care should be taken to avoid giving the impression that the purpose of imposing sanctions is punishment rather than the modification of political behavior." On both counts, the Secretary-General's carefully worded advice was ignored by the Security Council. A precondition included in Resolution 687 (1991) for the lifting of sanctions was that "all actions had been completed." What actions, what criteria, what indicators? Members of the Security Council had the freedom to give their individual answers. P5 members had the power to veto the lifting of sanctions if they concluded that not all actions had been completed. Given the wording, this was easy to do at any time. However, they also had the obligation to humanize the application of the sanctions. What was lacking was a shared understanding of principles by all fifteen members of the Security Council and an absence of morality by some.

Over the years, it became obvious that the people of Iraq would be punished by comprehensive sanctions as long as President Saddam Hussein remained in power. Secretaries-General Boutros-Ghali and Annan had become fully aware that the toppling of the Iraqi government was the shared political objective of US administrations, whether Democrat or Republican. Initially, the Bush and Clinton governments had tried to hide this preference, giving covert support to the Iraqi opposition. In the late 1990s, however, the open calls by Washington for regime change increased and were formalized in 1998 by Democratic President Clinton signing into law the Iraq Liberation Act, which had been submitted for enactment by a Republican-controlled US Senate. Under these circumstances, a Secretary-General's scope of action had become extremely narrow. Critical Secretary-General statements on political positions of the Security Council would not be condoned and would have serious repercussions.

Secretary-General Boutros-Ghali failed to get a second term as the US threatened to veto any Security Council proposal for his reappointment. The US took exception to his opposition to a NATO air offensive against Serbia and more generally, resented that he had publicly declared that Americans were "making his work life difficult." Kofi Annan understood the political limitations of his authority and instead focused his attention on the humanitarian aspects of sanctions. In a meeting we had with Secretary-General Annan in October 1999, he offered advice in a warmhearted manner. It followed an interview about conditions in Iraq we had given to the *New York Times*, which had been harshly criticized by the US State Department. The department's spokesperson James Rubin declared, "The man in Baghdad is paid to work, not to talk." The Secretary-General said to us in this connection, "You can express your concern about factual inaccuracies of statements regarding sanctions made by members of the Security Council, including the US, and offer corrections, but never criticize Security Council policies." It seemed that Annan supported what had been said in the interview and shared our concerns about the Security Council's handling of Iraq sanctions but knew that as the Secretary-General, he did not have the option to express these concerns publicly. Such a limitation on the independence of the highest UN civil servant is illustrative of the serious deficiency in the functioning of the UN, if it is viewed as a Charter-based peace and security organization rather than a concoction of P5 geopolitics.

The Security Council turned regularly to Secretaries-General for the implementation of its policy decisions. In the case of sanctioned Iraq, this involved, for example, the establishment of the UN Iraq-Kuwait Observer Mission (UNIKOM) headed by generals of all five permanent members of the Council to monitor the demilitarized zone between Iraq and Kuwait.[10] This UNIKOM-UN collaboration is one of the rare examples of cooperation between the eight distinct Iraq-based UN units.

## The UN Secretariat

After Iraq's illegal invasion of Kuwait on August 2, 1990, the UN Secretariat's Disaster Relief Office and the UN Resident Coordinators in Kuwait and Iraq were expected to play their mandated emergency and humanitarian roles. There was immediate international criticism about the sluggishness of the UN response. This was not quite fair since no one, neither governments nor the NGO community nor the UN System, could have foreseen such a crisis. Criticism was much more justified about the political decisions the Security Council had taken without even consulting Secretary-General de Cuellar on the humanitarian consequences of sanctions. Resolution 666/1990 emphasized that "it is for the Security Council . . . to determine whether humanitarian circumstances have arisen" and whether there would be a consequential need to supply foodstuffs and medicines. Most likely because the UN Secretariat lacked Iraq-relevant data and had inadequate sanctions management experience, it was not able to convince the Security Council that such circumstances existed. As a result, serious "tensions between the Security Council and the UN's humanitarian machinery" developed but without impact upon the actions taken by the Security Council. At the same time, the government of Iraq introduced free food rations of 1,000 calories a day in all eighteen provinces, the maximum amount they could offer, and then only for a limited period.

During these initial years of Iraq sanctions, the UN Secretariat struggled to define coordination tasks and to issue guidelines for humanitarian inter-agency cooperation with UN partners such as the World Food Programme, UNICEF, WHO, FAO, and UNHCR. There is no good explanation as to why the UN Disaster Relief Office was not better prepared to respond more quickly to the Security Council decision of August 6, 1991, to impose comprehensive economic sanctions. The grim picture of human devastation that emerged in the following months, however, led Secretary-General de Cuellar to create in 1991 the Department of Humanitarian Affairs, headed by an Under-Secretary-General, to cooperate with governments, NGOs, and civil society groups to facilitate a program of humanitarian assistance for Iraq.

The Security Council had introduced cumbersome rules regulating Iraq's import of humanitarian supplies. All consignments of donations, wherever they came from, required the country of origin to give clearance and the Security Council Iraq Sanctions Committee to give its approval as well before any goods could be dispatched. Awaiting clearance, ships and trucks often were forced to retain much-needed supplies at Iraqi land and sea borders until they received permission to unload. Such delays resulted at times in spoilage and worsening of the human conditions throughout the country.

In this early phase of the crisis, the UN Secretariat had no option other than pleading with the Security Council to accelerate and simplify the goods-release process. Regrettably, the distance between the decision-makers in New York and the recipients in Iraq diminished any sense of urgency within the UN headquarters bureaucracy. Following the 1991 Operation Desert Storm and the adoption of Resolution 687 in April 1991, the Security Council had put forward proposals for a structured humanitarian exemption that the government of Iraq had rejected. As explained earlier, this resulted in a serious stalemate and a disturbing record of UN humanitarian inaction. People were suffering and the UN Secretariat had to content itself with accepting a continuing passive standby role while the Security Council and the government of Iraq battled to find a compromise for ensuring the welfare of the Iraqi people based on the unfortunate linkage of disarmament and economic sanctions. After six years of the toughest and most comprehensive sanctions ever imposed by the UN on a member country, the two sides finally agreed in April 1995 on a humanitarian exemption program. Such an exemption was to be totally dependent on the precarious state of the Iraqi oil industry and the sale of its oil in a highly volatile global oil market.

The Security Council passed a corresponding resolution, which referred ironically to its concern about "the serious nutritional and health situation of the Iraqi people . . . and the risks of a further deterioration"; this completely overlooked the fact that the Council itself had contributed to creating such conditions in the first place. This resolution made it clear that suffering would continue because sanction rules would apply not only to the government of Iraq but to every Iraqi citizen, as the following three examples show. An old Baghdadi man who needed to undergo major surgery in Amman and had the resources in his UK account to defray the costs was told by the UN that he could not access his account; the father of a young girl learning to play the flute was unable to order music sheets from abroad; Saudi Arabia, an enemy state, had decided to allot a quota to Iraqi nationals for the annual hajj pilgrimage and was even willing to give the International Committee of the Red Cross funds for Iraqi pilgrims during their stay in Mecca. The UN Sanctions Committee refused to give flight clearance for the Iraqi aircraft.

It took another year before the UN Secretariat was authorized to sign in May 1996 the Memorandum of Understanding (MOU) with the Iraq government to implement the long-awaited Oil-for-Food Programme (OFFP). Iraqis had to wait a further eight months before the first humanitarian supplies arrived in January 1997. It was the beginning of seven years (1996–2003) of UN "humanitarian" assistance—entirely paid for by Iraqi oil revenue. The Security Council opted to maintain the status quo of suffering in violation of international humanitarian law and moral propriety rather than reducing the level of suffering by covering resource gaps from non-Iraqi sources. OFFP imports of rice and wheat from distant places, such as Vietnam and Australia, could have been replaced in part by locally produced crops at significantly lower prices and providing badly needed income for Iraqi farmers. The savings for the OFFP would have allowed the import of more medicines or educational materials and spare parts for the water and electricity sectors. The US strictly opposed this option with the argument that it involved local cash transactions that could be used for rearmament.

During the thirteen years of sanctions, there were three key humanitarian Security Council Iraq Resolutions (687, 986, and 1284) and an MOU that defined the political and humanitarian details for the UN Secretariat's implementation of the Oil-for-Food Program. The options for implementing the OFFP were mainly determined by these three Security Council resolutions. Secretaries-General did have the authority to choose independently limited alternatives for running the humanitarian program.

According to the memorandum, the UN Secretariat and the government of Iraq would jointly prepare six monthly distribution plans as "temporary and supplementary" measures for "equitable," "adequate," and "effective" assistance to the Iraqi people in all parts of Iraq, including the three Kurdish provinces. The question of "supplementary" to what quickly entered the minds of UN staff in Iraq as there were practically no local food stocks, let alone medical supplies. The UN Secretariat understood that such a program could not be realized if the needed funding was fully dependent on what the Security Council had authorized.

Secretary-General Kofi Annan decided to travel to Baghdad in February 1998 to meet the Iraqi leadership to review all aspects of the sanction situation, including progress toward completing agreed disarmament arrangements and the humanitarian exemption. Having tacit Security Council approval to discuss the inadequacy of the funding for the OFFP, the Secretary-General announced in Baghdad that it was agreed with President Saddam Hussein to double the OFFP resources from $2.6 billion to $5.2 billion for the next six-month phase. Here was a Secretary-General with commitment and courage to bring about better terms for the Iraqi people—"better" as measured by basic needs. It is worth observing that even this doubling of available resources proved insufficient for meeting the basic needs of the Iraqi civilian population. And yet, US secretary of state Madeleine Albright did not hide her displeasure criticizing Kofi Annan's announcement.

References in both Resolution 986 and the corresponding MOU to respect the integrity and sovereignty of Iraq, standard phrases in all major Iraq-related Council decisions, had little meaning. The Security Council, for example, had decided to establish special OFFP rules for the three Kurdish provinces, which put Iraqi sovereignty and integrity in question.

This was done by making the bizarre argument that "the humanitarian conditions in the various Governorates had to be considered." All such a statement did was to rationalize the preparation of a separate OFFP distribution plan for the Kurdish north administered by the UN "on behalf of the government of Iraq." Iraqi Kurdistan, where 13 percent of the country's population lived, received 19 percent of the OFFP resources; unlike the Arab areas under Baghdad's control, cash payments were allowed in the Kurdish areas to finance housing, forestation, and road projects. Not a single OFFP relief consignment for Dohuk, Erbil, and Sulaymaniyah was ever withheld by the Sanctions Committee, in contrast to numerous denials for areas under Baghdad's control. For non-Kurdish areas, the UN Sanctions Committee had blocked, either temporarily or permanently, as much as $5 billion worth of much needed humanitarian supplies and equipment. Making a mockery of Iraqi sovereignty, British and American intelligence operatives traveled regularly from their locations in Turkey across the border to Iraqi Kurdistan without Baghdad's permission. Some even had the audacity, when we met accidentally in Erbil, to lecture us about the evilness of the Baghdad government, while overlooking the cruelty of the policies their governments were implementing in Iraq.

The country's integrity was repeatedly tested by the US, the UK, Israel, and others who wanted to de-link Iraqi Kurdistan from other parts of Iraq even though this was publicly denied by the two Kurdish leaders, Masud Barzani of the Kurdish Democratic Party and Jamal Talabani of the Patriotic Union of Kurdistan. Concurrently, there was in play Kurdish demands for a separate currency, separate car license plates, and an electricity supply independent from Baghdad. In the spirit of UN resolutions, we discouraged these efforts and instead tried to convince the Kurdish leadership to drop the currency and license plate demands and consider other options for electricity supply. After an initial reluctance in Baghdad and in Iraqi Kurdistan for the two sides to meet, they finally agreed to come together. A Kurdish team traveled to Baghdad for a meeting with officials from Iraq's Electricity Department, a meeting that we chaired. It ended with an agreement that Baghdad would supply additional electricity through the one electricity connection that still existed in Ninawa Governorate between the national grid and the Kurdish areas. This was a success—at least so we thought. We reported this accomplishment to the UN Secretariat in New York, convinced that we had acted as an impartial UN mediator. Instead of praise, we received a stern warning from Benon Sevan, the head of the UN Office of the Iraq Programme (OIP): "Your predecessor burnt his fingers; do not burn yours" was the written message. The option we had chosen was considered a political option and therefore supposedly not part of our remit. It did not fit the strategic interests of the penholder powers in the Security Council in New York. The leash constraining local decision-making by senior UN officials in Baghdad proved to be extremely short. Over time, it became obvious that the UN Secretariat was remote-controlled by the US State Department.

Secretary-General Annan, having delegated the management of the Iraq file to his deputy, Louise Fréchette, a former Canadian deputy minister of defence, seemed not fully aware of the degree of politicization of the humanitarian operations and the significant impact this was having on the effectiveness of the UN presence in Iraq. The independence of the UN civil service was under attack and led to a fragmentation within the team of UN decision-makers in New York. The OIP was removed from the Department of Humanitarian Affairs (DHA) and became a separate unit at the Secretariat, depriving it of the considerable experience of DHA staff familiar with crisis management in different parts of the world. A DHA staff member was told by his supervisor that he should stay away from the OIP "as people there are too political"! Such a separation certainly was not in the interest of implementing an efficient humanitarian exemption for Iraq. It also made no sense structurally. It occurred because a free-standing OIP was easier to control.

The New York tentacles of interference reached into the UN Office of the Humanitarian Coordinator in Baghdad with profound management consequences. The OIP had decided, allegedly under direction of the Security Council, in subservience to US policy, that two units in the Baghdad office, the multidisciplinary observer unit and the administration, should report directly to the UN Secretariat and not to the Assistant Secretary-General, as the head of office. A correction of this dysfunctionality, we were told, was not negotiable. When this was brought to the attention of Secretary-General Annan, he reacted with disbelief, saying, "This cannot be possible." It was clear that the UN Secretariat had the option of rectification but ended this anomaly only after the Secretary-General got involved and much damage had already been done. More generally, the OIP did not play the role of an honest broker as it was endlessly involved in an opportunistic balancing act, trying to please Washington, London, and Baghdad at the same time and in the process steadily lost credibility in all quarters and weakened the UN's humanitarian mission in Iraq.

An important function of the UN Humanitarian Coordinator in Baghdad involved regular reporting to the Secretariat on the implementation of the OFFP. Such reporting involved multifaceted presentations of the respective distribution plans and the impact of these plans on the welfare of the Iraqi people. There was an agreement that the UN Secretariat in New York could send staff to help in compiling these intricate informational reports. But there certainly was no agreement that the focus of these reports would be on UN performance rather than the adequacy, or inadequacy, of the resources needed for protecting civil society from the harm inflicted by UN sanctions. Our request for more balanced reporting did not change what ended up on the desks in New York. "The UN is doing a great job under difficult local circumstances; the government did not cooperate sufficiently" was the underlying message, which, of course suited Washington and London. More generally, our criticism about the inadequacy of the OFFP was countered by the OIP in New York with "The OFFP was never meant to meet all humanitarian needs."[11] Self-serving conclusions for those outside but also for some inside the UN in the incessant blame game were aggravated by the appointment of a UN reports analyst at OIP of a civil servant on loan from the UK Department of Defence. Such deployment, of course, cast serious doubt on the trustworthiness of UN programs when subjected to geopolitical pressures.

Most unfortunate was that among UN staff with the highest sense of integrity, some individuals working in the OFFP in Baghdad possessed neither the professional competence nor the morality to be on the UN Iraq team because of inadequate security checks. It was awkward and embarrassing that the Iraqi Foreign Ministry had to alert us on several occasions that the government had evidence that members of staff were apparently working as foreign agents and were to be declared personae non grata. The OIP in New York would ask us to intervene with the Foreign Ministry to reverse these decisions. Since there was compelling evidence of wrongdoing on the part of a UN staff member so charged, we chose not to do anything to influence the Iraq government decisions.

Unquestionably, the Security Council and individual governments had caused many managerial difficulties for the UN humanitarian programs in Iraq. The UN Secretariat, however, cannot escape justified criticism for succumbing to external political pressures. The Secretariat did have structurally, substantially, and procedurally genuine options that would have enabled it to implement its mandate more fully. What was needed in full measure but did not prevail was courage, moral commitment, empathy, perseverance, professional management, and UN Charter-mindedness of senior executives directly overseeing Iraq-based operations.

The security of all one thousand-plus national and international UN staff in Iraq was always taken seriously during Iraq's years of sanctions.

On December 15, 1998, for example, the US government informed the Security Council that in the evening of the following day, it would undertake Operation Desert Fox, involving air strikes on Baghdad. The Secretary-General had to decide swiftly how to protect UN staff. We had proposed that international staff be evacuated to Amman, except for a small number who would make sure the UN flag would continue to fly in Baghdad, and more important, that national UN staff be assured that the UN would not abandon them.[12] Kofi Annan agreed. He asked us to identify a group that should stay behind. This allowed twenty-eight UN staff, including medical, administrative and, of course, security personnel, to remain during the four nights of heavy bombing of Baghdad (December 16–19). Following these US air strikes, the Iraqi government decided that all UN staff of US and UK nationalities should be immediately withdrawn from the country. The UN in Baghdad lost some twenty fine colleagues, all victims of political irresponsibility.

In the new year, the US and UK air forces began to operate in Iraq's no-fly and fly zones under significantly enlarged rules of engagement. The intention was to further destabilize Iraq.[13] Because this escalation also affected the safety of UN staff in their work across the country, we asked the UN Security staff in the Baghdad office to keep a record of incidents caused by the recurring air strikes. We began to compile three monthly air strike reports for the Secretary-General and the Security Council. For 1999 these reports reflected that there had been 132 air strikes with 144 civilian deaths and 446 civilians injured as well as destruction of nonmilitary buildings and, on two occasions, oil installations. The reaction from US and UK Allied Commands at the Incirlik and Sultan Ahmed airbases, in Turkey and Saudi Arabia respectively, was invariably "We do not target civilian installations, but our pilots have to protect themselves against Iraqi aggression." This was a perfidious and untruthful justification since it was common knowledge that an Iraqi air force no longer existed and antiaircraft facilities were incapable of reaching high-flying foreign aircraft.

The director of the OIP, Benon Sevan, was outraged by our decision to compile such air strike reports. In contrast, the chef de cabinet of the Secretary-General, Iqbal Riza, wrote to us that these reports were "very interesting and useful to the Secretary-General's Office" and should continue. This serves as another example of the deep rift within senior management at the UN Secretariat in New York, impairing the UN's humanitarian efforts on the ground and certainly confusing us in Baghdad. As far as the Security Council was concerned, it merely took note of these air strike reports without taking any action.

During one of our visits to New York, UK ambassador Stewart Eldon reprimanded us in strong language that we were "straying off our mandate" and had "no business outside the area of our competence." We disagreed and told him that we reported to the UN Secretary-General and not to the Queen of England, and unless the Secretary-General were to ask us to stop compiling these reports of illegal air strikes, we would continue to submit such information. The ambassador was upset, and for opposite reasons, so were we. This incident prompted a joint letter by the US and UK ambassadors to the UN asking Secretary-General Annan to withdraw us from Baghdad. Annan refused to do so.

## The UN System

The government of Iraq decided that any UN organization that had left the country at the time of Operation Desert Storm in 1991 would not be welcome to return. Therefore, apart from the UN itself, only eight UN entities involved in implementing the UN humanitarian program were resident in Iraq during the years of sanctions: FAO, UNDP, UNESCO, UNICEF, WFP, and WHO. UNCHS for housing and UNOPS for demining were deployed in Iraqi Kurdistan only. In addition, UNHCR, mainly responsible for Iranian refugees, and UNIKOM, for control of the Iraq-Kuwait border, had offices in the country. The UN Guards Contingent in Iraq, a team of police officers, operated exclusively in Iraqi Kurdistan, providing logistical support for the implementation of UN assistance in the northern areas.

In early 1997, these eight agencies were asked by the UN to function as a team, led by a UN Assistant Secretary-General, in carrying out what became the largest humanitarian country operation in UN history.[14] The UN six-month distribution plans were implemented by this group with a clear division of labor, a deep sense of commitment, an unusual team spirit that was responsive to the daily manifestations of widespread civilian suffering, and, most importantly, the awareness that we had a common adversary in the wider world of UN politics that wanted to prevent the success of our combined efforts.[15] This is a harsh statement to make but it is borne out by the obstacles that confronted us. This tension between UN humanitarianism and bilateral geopolitics should not be surprising as it is a motif that I have seen not only in Iraq but also in earlier assignments elsewhere.

We were indeed anxious to function as a team when discussing implementation problems with interministerial groups of Iraqi officials, who were much more cooperative and people-minded than reported in the Western media. We regularly briefed the Baghdad-based diplomatic corps and visiting foreign civil-society delegations on the status of the OFFP and would have liked to do the same for New York–based Security Council and General Assembly members, but they never came to Baghdad. We prepared joint reports for the Council, the most important of which was a brief for the Security Council panel on the humanitarian situation in Iraq chaired by the ambassador from Brazil, Celso Amorim, who was serving as President of the Security Council at the time. On behalf of the team, we went to New York to convey to the Council our hope for more responsible oversight by the political UN over our work in Iraq. The Security Council had not only the authority but the responsibility to do all it could to facilitate an effective civil society survival program. It clearly failed to do so.

As a team, the UN System in Iraq did not hold back criticism of Security Council micromanagement, the unnecessary control over our work, and the destructive bilateral misinformation. The ever-increasing bureaucratization of the OFFP by the Security Council seriously hampered our efforts. In 1999, it took an average twenty-three separate administrative steps for an item, other than food and medicine, to reach the locality where it was needed. Only after exporters, foreign and defense ministries, the UN, the Iraq government, the supplier country missions at the UN in New York, the transporter of the goods, the UN Treasurer, and the Banque Nationale de Paris (holder of the UN Iraq oil account) had cleared an item could it be dispatched. This process usually took a full year. In Baghdad, we did not hide our outrage over the mounting and irresponsible blocking by the UN Sanctions Committee of much-needed humanitarian supplies. Even small-scale assistance given by the few NGOs that still operated in Iraq, such as CARE, the Middle East Council of Churches, Un Ponte Per Baghdad, Enfants du Monde, and the ICRC assisting with rural water supply, primary health care, and primary education lessened suffering for a few at the grassroot level. As one example, Ponte Per Bagdad, an Italian NGO, wanted to provide an isolated village north of Basra with small quantities of water purification chemicals (a request we had forwarded to the UN Sanctions Committee in New York with our full support) was turned down by the Sanctions Committee on the grounds that these chemicals were considered "dual use" items that could be used to build weapons of mass destruction! Occasional visits by the UN Sanctions Committee to Iraq undoubtedly would have convinced any fair-minded person that the UN in Iraq and the NGO community in the country knew what was necessary to do to ensure that there was no misuse. Such an option, which the UN Secretariat in New York could have easily chosen, was not considered as it was politically not "convenient" to do so.

As a UN team in Baghdad, we indeed were isolated.[16] The so-called UN Secretariat Steering Group on Iraq, chaired by the Deputy Secretary-General Louise Fréchette, had the option or more aptly, the fundamental responsibility to ensure coherence of UN sanctions operations in Iraq. We did not receive even once any information as to what this group in New York was all about and how it related to what we were doing in Iraq. Better coordination could have made a fundamental difference in the overall effectiveness of the UN System as a whole had this steering group instructed the UN humanitarian team and the disarmament group (both Baghdad-based), the UN Compensation Commission and the UN Special Rapporteur of the Commission on Human Rights (both resident in Geneva), and UNIKOM (located at the Iraq-Kuwait border) to come together in New York at regular intervals to brief the Security Council and the Secretariat about developments in Iraq and how UN operations could be improved at the political and humanitarian levels. It goes beyond the scope of this chapter to argue why such an approach would also have been possible and beneficial for an overall Iraq peace process. The fact to be noted is that it did not happen.

More specifically, there were no consultations at all between the Humanitarian Coordinator in Baghdad and Human Rights Rapporteur van der Stoel, a former Dutch foreign minister based in Geneva, on the impact of sanctions on human rights, despite an option to have such consultations. Stoel saw no value in such contacts and therefore rejected our suggestion that we meet. His successor, Andreas Mavromatis, a former foreign secretary of Cyprus, however, understood the importance of such contacts and chose to meet. We agreed that UN economic sanctions were perpetuating human rights violations in Iraq and deserved to be treated as an important part of his brief. His more balanced approach allowed him to come to Iraq for discussions with the Iraqi leadership, foreign diplomats, and the UN team, something his predecessor had been unable to do since the government had opposed his visits. This is yet another powerful example of options available to senior UN officials in carrying out their missions.

Contact between OFFP and the UN Compensation Commission also never materialized. From a humanitarian perspective there existed the option to give priority to the use of oil revenues first for the welfare of the Iraqi people and for the compensation of the foreign labor force that had lost their employment and income earned from working in Kuwait at the time of the Iraqi invasion. Compensation for claims by governments and companies could have been postponed until such time when sufficient revenue was available. Instead, the option chosen was a flat rate deduction of initially 30 percent, later reduced to 25 percent from the OFFP budget, regardless of the funding requirements of the humanitarian distribution plans.[17]

Even though the UN humanitarian and disarmament units were housed in the same building in Baghdad, there were hardly any working contacts between the "bunny huggers and the cowboys," as UN staff satirically named the two groups with such distinctly different mandates. Under one UN flag, there were two UN administrations, two medical services, two security details, two fleets of vehicles, and two entirely different mindsets. It was an unduly costly operation, but cost was of no concern to the UN since Iraq would pay for it. Whatever funds were needed for the UN administration were simply deducted from the humanitarian budget. Our request to carry out an integrated audit for the UN System programs in Iraq was not acted upon. There can be no doubt that such an audit would have uncovered many unnecessary expenditures, even fraudulent spending, as for example, for UN System staff at various head offices that only marginally dealt with Iraq. To cite one example of serious misuse: We had been informed in Baghdad by UN headquarters in New York that a new generation of computers was on the market and were on their way to us in Iraq. We were also told that our old computers should under no circumstances be handed over to the government of Iraq but should be destroyed. There was immediate agreement within the UN team in Baghdad that this was completely unacceptable. The old computers, purchased with Iraqi funds, were in good condition, and were not even UN property, as Iraq had paid for them. Government departments badly needed computers; for example, the Ministry of Health, having no computers, had to manage their stocks of medicines manually. It was one of the better kept secrets that we decided to pass on some of these computers to selected government departments without informing New York rather than destroying them, as we had been asked. We realized yet again how far removed New York was from Iraq's misery. Geopolitical pressures, disregard for Iraqi property, and a detestable lack of empathy help explain such outrageous behavior.

## The Great Game and the Iraqi People's Tally

UN reports out of Baghdad; rare Security Council briefings in New York by Iraq-based senior UN staff; major presentations by Secretaries-General, especially Kofi Annan, to the Security Council; the findings of the Security Council panel on the humanitarian situation (2000); and accounts from major international NGOs all pointed in the same direction. They painted a picture of human catastrophe that had evolved over thirteen years. After six and a half years of so-called humanitarian assistance from the UN, the Oil-for-Food Programme, on which some 70 percent of the population was dependent, received $43 billion out of the total Iraq oil revenue of $61 billion; 30 percent had been deducted for the UN Compensation Commission and 2 percent for UN overheads.[18] Only $28 billion worth of supplies could be utilized, mainly due to bureaucratic delays caused by the UN's sanctions machinery. For an estimated population of 23 million Iraqis during those years, this translated into $185 per person/year, or an appalling 51 cents per person/day.[19] In comparison, the salary of the head of the UN in Iraq averaged $350 per day, which was equivalent to what 175 Iraqis would get per day from the UN as "humanitarian" support. Shockingly, the help given Iraqis and such salaries were paid from the same source: Iraq's oil revenue.

The Security Council heard many voices from all parts of the world expressing serious reservations pertaining to the heavy-handedness of individual governments in the Security Council manipulating the UN in dealing with the Iraqi people. Among those highly critical of UN Iraq sanctions policy was Canada's foreign minister Lloyd Axworthy, who reminded the Security Council that there existed an imperative that "sanctions reflected the objectives of the international community and not just the national interests of the most powerful members." Brazil's ambassador to the UN Celso Amorim stated that "life for the Iraqis has become catastrophic and while the government of Iraq is not exempted from its own responsibilities, the bottom line is that even if not all the suffering in Iraq could be imputed to external factors, the Iraqi people would not be undergoing such harsh deprivations in the absence of the prolonged measures imposed by sanctions." Professor Marc Bossuyt, a respected judge in Belgium's Court of Arbitration, in a special report to ECOSOC on Iraq sanctions in 2000, came to the grave conclusion that "the sanctions regime against Iraq had as its clear purpose the deliberate infliction on the Iraqi people of conditions of life . . . calculated to bring about (Iraq's) physical destruction in whole or in part." His report alleged that members of the Security Council had violated the UN Genocide Convention of 1948. Nobel Peace laureate Mairead Maguire wrote to us: "The questions we must ask are 'what kind of people could do this to other human beings? Were those who ordered and carried out such acts insane and mad?'" These words frightened us as they accused the UN, especially those in the Security Council and those in the UN System who were the willing executioners, that we had collectively failed to uphold and to defend the UN's moral imperative of preventing injustice and of protecting the innocent. It took a while for us to realize that our determination to succeed in Iraq would make no difference. On the other hand, carrying on would have made us guilty of compliance and complicity with those who wanted the UN to fail in Iraq. The only option was to resign in 2000.

There were indeed structural, substantive, and procedural options that would have enabled a much more humane Iraq sanctions strategy, based on holistic policies and adequate financing, as well as de-bureaucratized implementation and credible monitoring. The UN and the government of Iraq had indeed options to administer a "humanitarian bubble" to protect the people against much of the fallout from the political, security, and disarmament controversy. Having lost the war of 1991 and feeling the immediate effects of UN sanctions, the government of Saddam Hussein should have accepted the conditions of the April 1991 Security Council Resolution 687 for disarmament and the humanitarian exemption. In the early years of sanctions, Iraqi leadership, however, cared more about its political future and chose to keep the fate of the Iraqi people as a bargaining chip.

In the mid-1990s, the government of Iraq finally concurred with Security Council demands and accepted an oil-for-food program that was to be "equitable, adequate and effective." It, however, was never more than a poorly functioning goods-supply program and was neither adequate nor effective and not at all equitable. Malaysia's permanent representative to the UN, Ambassador Tan Sri Agam Hasmy, underlined this poignantly in the Security Council when he said: "How ironic is it that the same policy that is supposed to disarm Iraq of its weapons of mass destruction has itself become a weapon of mass destruction."

The UN Security Council had a wide range of options, including the fundamental structural option of separating disarmament of Iraq as a state and the humanitarian protection of the Iraqi people; the UN Secretariat had the option of reintegrating the Office of the Iraq Programme into the Office for the Coordination of Humanitarian Affairs; the UN System could have easily created a unified sanctions management structure headed by the Secretary-General, with the mandate to compile for the Security Council and the General Assembly cross-sectoral reports on Iraq's disarmament, the humanitarian exemption, human rights, and compensation. Additionally, substantive and procedural options were available to the Security Council, the Secretariat, and the wider operational system to implement a holistic UN Iraq sanctions program in a manner consistent with the moral and legal imperatives of the UN Charter. Had this been the case, the history of Iraq under sanctions could have been written along very different lines, and the Iraq of the twenty-first century would have had a different fate.

The reality is different. It is futile to speculate about how many people would have survived thirteen years of sanctions and eight years of occupation. Suffice it to say that many thousands would be alive today had the UN and the US acted in a more principled and humane fashion. The UN certainly would have become recognized as a trustworthy global institution led by men and women with respect for international law and motivated by an ethics of empathy. At the same time, civil society around the world would have been reassured that for the UN people's lives mattered.

In the shadow of power politics, failure was inevitable. The UN was once again used as a convenient toolbox, as it had been in the Korean war, in Afghanistan, in Libya, and elsewhere. As the UN box did not contain the "right" tools for Anglo-Saxon designs, the US, supported by the UK, abandoned the UN and applied unilateral options leading to the 2003 unlawful invasion and predatory occupation of Iraq. The primacy of bilateral US geopolitical interests and military power combined with a horrendous dilettantism prevailed rather than the option of multilateral diplomacy and Charter-based actions.

This multidimensional failure in Iraq that we have studied, together with similar failures in other parts of the Middle East, in Asia, Africa, the Americas, and Europe, has motivated us to reflect on peace, humanitarianism, and humane geopolitics as offering a more viable and promising inventory of policy options for member states, which underscores for us the urgency of a reformed United Nations.

# SEVEN

# Syria: The Douma Deception—Institutional Integrity versus the Primacy of Geopolitics

Ever since the establishment of the United Nations, the Middle East—the bridge between Europe and Asia—has constituted a severe test of the viability of the organization as framed by Charter Principles and Purposes, The end of the Ottoman Empire and twilight of European colonialism in the mid-twentieth century and its replacement by the emergence of independent nation states brought to world attention the extraordinary endowments of ethnic, religious, cultural, and natural resources in the Middle East as well as the diversity of the communities living in the area. The evolving political landscape exhibited strong signs of nationalism, yet at the same time also possessed Pan-Arabist impulses. Baghdad, Cairo, and Damascus even at one time seemed drawn to the idea of a single "Arab nation" that included all countries that eventually would form the Arab League in 1945. British withdrawal from its mandatory role in Palestine and the establishment of the State of Israel in 1948 briefly strengthened the regional resolve to demonstrate the existence of a unified Arab identity. The Middle East quickly became a focus of UK, US, and wider geopolitical attention when in the 1970s and 1980s Arab governments began to replace Western corporate-based oil and gas exploration by nationalizing energy production. Iran had already done this in 1951, but at the cost of provoking a CIA-backed coup in 1953 that still has geopolitical reverberations.

We consider the region's complex socio-economic diversity, the rich oil and gas resources, and the unresolved Palestinian/Israeli conflict as the prime causes why today the Middle East must be considered as among the most crisis-ridden areas in the world. Except for the Sultanate of Oman, all countries from Israel and Palestine in the west to Iraq and Syria in the north, Iran in the east, and Saudi Arabia and Yemen in the south are currently involved in serious domestic or cross-border conflicts or both.

Five of the Arab League's current twenty-two nations, including Syria, are among the founding countries of the United Nations. Throughout the years, Syria has been an active UN member state, at the political as well as the operational level, including as an elected member of the UN Security Council in 2002–2003. In 2011, Syria's civil society, especially the younger generations, rose up in the spirit of the Arab Spring protest movements and immediately faced brutal reactions by the Syrian government, a one-party government that has been in the hands of the Alawite Assad family since 1971, governed until 2000 by President Hafez al-Assad and since then by his son, Bashar al-Assad. Syria was suspended in 2011 as a member of the Arab League because of the government's repressive treatment of its people but in May 2023 was restored to full Arab League membership.

It is outside the scope of this chapter to reflect in detail on the politics of the Syrian government since it joined the UN in 1945. Instead, we would like to address specific peace- and security-related developments in Syria since the beginning of the insurrectionary civil strife against the government of Bashar al-Assad in 2011 and to draw conclusions bearing on the UN's ability to meet its Charter-based responsibilities in relation to Syria.

Suppression of people's rights, sustained poverty and unemployment, corruption, and no prospects for change for most Syrians triggered the 2011 national unrest. Local dissent swiftly broadened the confrontation to involve such regional forces as the Muslim Brotherhood, which was also Syria's main opposition party, as well as an increasing array of state and non-state parties from inside and outside the Middle East that joined the conflict on opposite sides. Syrian civil strife acquired characteristics of an exceptionally complex proxy war.

Over the years, a bewildering network of anti- and pro-government actors has been active throughout the entire country in both urban and rural areas. Allegiances of outside parties have been shifting their support from one side of the conflict to the other in a few instances or have even extended their support to both sides. Disinformation, covert cross-border interventions, and false flag operations have made it even more difficult to assess credibly at any time the dynamics of the Syrian conflict, including the assessment of allegations about the use of chemical weapons by the Damascus regime.

Apart from the involvement of four P5 countries (France, the UK, the US, and Russia), Iran, Iraq, Israel, Jordan, Saudi Arabia, the UAE, Turkey, Qatar, and other Gulf countries have also provided various levels of overt and covert support, mostly to the Syrian opposition but also to the government and its armed forces. In addition, a plethora of militias and other armed groupings have taken part in Syria's internal conflict. These have included the Syrian Free Army, a defector militia, two Syrian Kurdish groups (the Democratic Union Party [PYD] and the People's Protection Units [YPG]), and the Kurdistan Workers Party (PKK), located in Turkey but principally operating from Iraq and affiliated with Kurdish groups in Syria and in Iraq.

## UN Involvement in Syria since 2011

The complexity of the Syrian crisis has presented significant challenges to the UN at both the political (General Assembly and Security Council) and operational (UN System) levels in carrying out their mandates of promoting a peace process for Syria and of protecting the civilian population in both government- and opposition-held areas of the country. Nevertheless, the Security Council and the UN Secretariat in New York and the UN Human Rights Council in Geneva together with the Syria-based UN country team of some sixteen entities resident in Damascus have been involved ever since the crisis began, making persistent efforts to promote the Security Council's and General Assembly's initiatives for Syrian-devised political solutions and for the UN System to provide humanitarian assistance and, against all odds, to help Syrian authorities in implementing the UN's sustainable development goals. Highly experienced UN officials such as Lakhdar Brahimi, a former Algerian foreign minister who had earlier served as UN Special Envoy for Iraq and Afghanistan, and Staffan di Mistura, who had had similar assignments in these two countries and Southern Lebanon, served successively as Special Envoys for Syria. Both were preceded by former UN Secretary-General Kofi Annan, who, as a Joint Special Envoy for Syria of the UN and the League of Arab States, had resigned in August 2012 after only a few months in this position, stating, "As an envoy, I can't want peace more than the protagonists, more than the Security Council or the international community." The Syria Justice Accountability Centre, a Syria-led human rights organization located in Washington, DC, declared, "Kofi Annan understood that he had no choice but to resign when none of the relevant actors were committed to serious engagement in a just and inclusive peace process."

Since the beginning of the crisis in 2011, the UN has been unable to generate meaningful political negotiations between the Syrian government and the opposition, even though the UN had equipped itself at the operational level with an increasingly refined framework for dealing with both humanitarian and political and security-related issues globally, regionally, and nationally. The absence of any political commitment by the Security Council, especially by the P5 countries, to find sustainable solutions to end the bloodshed and massive displacement in Syria explains the continued frustration of UN efforts on behalf of peace and security.

It is for this reason that the UN Secretary-General's Special Envoy for Syria, Geir O. Pedersen, a former Norwegian ambassador to China and to the UN and director of the Asia and Pacific Division in the UN Department for Political Affairs, is facing exactly the same dilemma as his predecessors but with one significant difference: the geopolitical polarization involving the entire UN membership has intensified, and the Cold War of the past century has returned in the form of colder and more ominous confrontations in the current century. These changes obviously have had their impact on the UN's efforts in Syria.[1]

At an EU meeting in Brussels in May 2022, Pedersen stated: "Over the years, my predecessors and I have continuously called for a nationwide cease-fire and a comprehensive Syrian-led and owned political solution—one that meets the legitimate aspirations of the Syrian people, that respects the Syria's sovereignty, unity, independence, and territorial integrity." The UN official concluded that the government and the opposition negotiating a new Syrian constitution were "far from a political solution," and this gap persisted after eleven years of a devastating Syrian civil war.

The UN Office for Disarmament Affairs (UNODA) had been added in 1998 to the UN Secretariat to support worldwide programs leading to "general and complete disarmament under strict and effective international control, with a primary focus for weapons of mass destruction and to foster disarmament measures through dialogue, transparency and confidence building."[2] In the context of Syria's civil war and the seriousness of the repeated use of chemical weapons in the country, the existence of UNODA gave the UN Secretary-General further authority for insisting that all Syrian and external actors operating in Syria adhere to the 1997 Convention on Chemical Weapons[3] and assist in implementing appropriate disarmament programs.

Besides UNODA's involvement with the Syrian crisis and the presence of a UN Special Envoy for Syria, Secretary-General Ban Ki-moon had additionally appointed in December 2013 the UN Mission to Investigate Allegations of the Use of Chemical Weapons in the Syrian Arab Republic to be jointly carried out with the Hague-based Organisation for the Prohibition of Chemical Weapons (OPCW), a non-UN international organization, and with the World Health Organisation (WHO). Two years earlier, the Independent Commission of Inquiry on the Syrian Arab Republic had been set up by the UN Human Rights Council to "investigate alleged violations of international human rights law including the illegal use of chemical weapons."[4]

We recognize the overlap between what the UN Secretariat in New York and the UN Human Rights Council in Geneva decided to do about chemical weapons issues in Syria. This overlap is explained by the fact that the Security Council determines to a large extent the UN's agenda in New York, while the General Assembly exerts a similar influence in Geneva via the UN Human Rights Council.

## The UN and the OPCW in the Context of Syria

The United Nations, especially the Security Council and the Secretary-General and his team, had established close working relations with the Organisation for the Prohibition of Chemical Weapons (OPCW) from the moment it had been founded in 1997. The OPCW mandate is "to ensure a credible and transparent regime for verifying the destruction of chemical weapons . . . while protecting legitimate national security and proprietary interests." OPCW was awarded the Nobel Peace Prize in 2013 for "its extensive efforts to eliminate chemical weapons." In its award statement the Swedish Nobel Committee pointed out that "recent events in Syria, where chemical weapons have again been put to use, have underlined the need to enhance the efforts to do away with such weapons."[5] This was a reference to an alleged chemical weapons attack in Ghouta on August 21, 2013. In this chapter we review in some detail the relationship that evolved between the UN and the OPCW and how both organizations handled integrity and neutrality while carrying out their respective mandates.

The call for UN sanctions on Syria by the EU, the United States, and somewhat more reluctantly by the Arab League failed because of vetoes from China and Russia in the Security Council. At the same time, however, an agreement was reached among the P5 that the UN should investigate all allegations contending chemical weapons were being used in Syria. They therefore fully supported Secretary-General Ban Ki-moon's chemical weapons initiative and the UN Human Rights Council's ongoing investigation of alleged human rights violations.

Unlike the deadlock in the Syria peace process, there has been intermittent cooperation over the years between Western P5 members and Russia and China about the civil war in Syria. An important example re-

lates to the Russian proposal of September 2013 for the international control of Syria's stockpile of chemical weapons and the subsequent joint US
and Russian efforts to work out with the government of Syria an international agreement for the elimination of this stockpile, setting a destruction
deadline of June 30, 2014, and agreeing to store some chemical weapons
materials outside of Syria. There had also been cooperation in counter-
terrorism operations against ISIS/Daesh, joint targeting of other terrorist
groups, and collision avoidance between the US and Russian militaries
operating in Syria.

In response to the attack in Ghouta near Damascus, where chemical
weapons had allegedly been used, according to the Syrian opposition, by
pro-Assad forces, a contention that was strongly rejected by the Syrian government. The US and the EU recommended that UN inspectors should investigate these allegations. The government of Syria, which had just joined
the OPCW, readily agreed to an investigation by the UN.

The report on the investigation, jointly carried out by the UN, the OPCW,
and the WHO in Ghouta and other locations, was published on December
13, 2013. It confirmed, but without attribution, that chemical weapons had
been used and civilians had died.[6] The government of Syria conveyed to
the UN Secretary-General its position that it had not been responsible for
the use of chemical weapons in the attack on Ghouta and that an extremist
anti-government militia was the responsible party. The US, the UK, France,
and Qatar disagreed, accusing instead the Syrian government of having
used the nerve gas agent sarin in carrying out the Ghouta attack. Russia in
turn called these accusations a "provocation planned in advance," intended
to discredit the Syrian government. Without direct reference to the incident, China expressed its full confidence that the UN was "conducting an
independent, objective, impartial and professional investigation."

A similarly disputed attack occurred four years later, on April 4, 2017,
in which chemical weapons were allegedly used in Khan Shaykhun, the
capital of the Idlip Governorate, a province bordering Turkey that had been
and still is a rebel-controlled stronghold. The report of the joint UN-OPCW
mission to the area was submitted by Secretary-General Guterres to the Security Council in June 2017,[7] indicating that due to security considerations,
the mission had been unable to visit the site and had relied instead on interviews by OPCW experts and various non-governmental groups, including
the White Helmets,[8] which suggested that "sarin or sarin-like" substances
had been used. There was again no confirming attribution by the UN of
the perpetrators. In contrast, Wikipedia stated that the joint UN-OPCW investigation had identified the CW attack as having been carried out by the

Syrian government. The conclusions reached by the Syrian opposition and Western P5 members supported by Israel and Turkey were that chemical weapons had been used by the Syrian Defense Force. The Russian Federation had called it a "staged" operation. Even though the government of Syria refused to accept responsibility for this attack, neither the UN nor the OPCW carried out a credible investigation. Despite this absence of convincing evidence of Syrian culpability, the US responded aggressively three days later, launching a cruise missile attack on a Syrian airbase.

UN and OPCW records provide indisputable evidence that the government of Syria had used chemical weapons in different locations *prior* to becoming an OPCW member state and a signatory of the Chemical Weapons Convention in 2013. It is equally evident that "other" parties on both sides of the political divide had also used chemical weapons.

Even though the Syrian authorities joined the OPCW in 2013 and had acceded to the Chemical Weapons Convention, declaring that they no longer possessed chemical weapons, and seemed to want to become a rule-abiding UN member state, the serious incidents in Khan Shaykhun (2017) and in Douma (2018) put such a claim in doubt. The UN-involved governments and civil society organizations rightly demanded evidence that the government of Syria had indeed not secretly retained chemical weapons and was not responsible for their use after 2013. There was agreement that only a rigorously independent and objective scientific assessment could result in holding those responsible accountable for these disturbing incidents, engendering the hope of justice for the surviving victims, as well as assurance that chemical weapons would not be used in the future.

## Syria's Chemical Weapons, UN Charter Law, and the Case of Douma

An investigation of the attack on Douma provides an opportunity to identify how the UN, governments, the OPCW, and civil society responded to this crisis that had so significantly impacted the security situation in Syria, the region, and beyond and affected global geopolitical dynamics. We devote the rest of this chapter to the alleged chemical weapons attack on Douma on April 7, 2018, for several reasons:

> to determine how the United Nations, as a "we, the people" organization, and the General Assembly, the Security Council, the International Court of Justice, the Human Rights Council, the Secretary-General, and the wider UN System reacted to the attack;

to understand how the UN's integrity fared in a violent situation where it clashed with geopolitical interests;

to identify the way OPCW, a non-UN international organization, cooperated with the UN in carrying out the Douma investigation;

to show how the public responded to claims made by OPCW officials alleging OPCW malpractice in its reporting on the Douma investigation and suggesting complicity on the part of OPCW's top officials. These allegations became public knowledge following a meeting in Brussels in October 2019 convened by the Courage Foundation,[9] a UK-based independent trust dedicated to the legal defense of whistleblowers and journalists. The Courage Foundation group included the virtual participation of the first OPCW director-general, Ambassador José Bustani.

In our review, we were guided by UN Charter law that gives the General Assembly the right to "call the attention of the Security Council to situations which are likely to endanger international peace and security" (Charter Article 11/3). Did the General Assembly do so and invoke the Uniting for Peace resolution[10] as an emergency response to the US-UK-French air strikes of April 14, 2018, following the alleged chemical weapons attack on Douma on April 7, 2018?

Did the Security Council of five permanent and ten elected countries react "in accordance with the Purposes and Principles of the United Nations" and "refrain . . . from the use of force against the territorial integrity or political independence of Syria" (Charter Articles 24/2 and 2/4)? How did the five permanent members react, collectively and individually, to the Douma incident? What role did the ten elected Security Council members play, if any, in shaping the Security Council response to Douma? Was there any attempt by the Security Council to "encourage the development of pacific settlements of local disputes through regional arrangements" (Charter Article 52/3)—for example, by invoking the services of the League of Arab States?

The General Assembly, the Security Council, and the Secretary-General have the right to request the International Court of Justice to give Advisory Opinions on legal issues. Did the General Assembly, the Security Council, and the Secretary-General make use of such an opportunity to clarify the international law issues associated with the attack on Douma?

As mediators and facilitators, Secretaries-General may bring to the attention of the General Assembly and the Security Council any situation in which in their opinion the maintenance of international peace and security are threatened (Articles 12 and 99). Why did this not happen in the light of the Douma controversy? UN Charter Article 100 obliges Secretaries-General and UN civil servants to "refrain from any action which might reflect on their position as international officials." Had this been the case in response to Douma? Secretaries-General have the moral authority to intervene within and outside the organization when peace, security, and people's welfare are threatened. Why did such interventions not take place in relation to Douma?

It was also of particular importance to us to understand how the UN and the OPCW had cooperated in dealing with Douma. In this regard, we took note of OPCW's "Internal Vision" that declares that the organization "manages through empowerment with accountability, equality, fairness and transparency"; encourages its staff "to say what they think"; and always conducts itself " with integrity."

### Civil Society's Response to OPCW's Douma Investigation and the OPCW and the UN Reaction

As more and more critical assessments reached the public that manipulation and suppression of scientific evidence by OPCW's Douma Fact-Finding Mission had taken place, pressure mounted to organize a public response as the Douma controversy, which was also creating doubts about the reliability of other OPCW fact-finding missions for Syria, including the treatment of the attack at Khan Shaykhun in 2017. A small group, meeting in early 2021 in Berlin, decided to form the Berlin Group 21,[11] whose sole purpose would be "to uphold the truth and to help to restore the credibility of the OPCW [as] an independent, objective and scientifically rigorous organization." This in turn led to the preparation of a Statement of Concern about the OPCW Douma investigation.[12] It was signed by twenty-eight internationally known individuals with legal, military, political, and intelligence backgrounds, among them four former OPCW scientists; OPCW's first director-general; Lord West of Spithead, UK former first sea lord and chief of naval staff; US colonel Lawrence B. Wilkerson, former chief of staff of Secretary of State Colin Powell; and two former senior UN civil servants. Two additional OPCW scientists and Douma inspectors (Brendan Whelan, a chemist from Ireland, and Ian Henderson, an engineer from Australia) who had become whistleblowers were ready to add their names but could not sign for legal reasons associated with their professional roles.

The Statement of Concern was distributed widely. Among the first to receive it were OPCW director-general Fernando Arias; all 193 OPCW state parties; Volkan Bozgir, the president of the UN General Assembly (2021); US ambassador Linda Thomas Greenfield, president of the UN Security Council for March 2021; Ambassador Nazhat Shameem Khan, president of the UN Human Rights Council; UN Secretary-General António Guterres; UN High Commissioner for Human Rights Michelle Bachelet; the chair of the UN Human Rights Council's Syria Commission of Inquiry, Paulo Pinheiro; and UN High Representative for Disarmament Affairs Izumi Nakamitsu.

OPCW Director-General Arias chose not to respond to the Statement of Concern. In fact, his office returned unopened the registered letter from Berlin Group 21 containing the statement. It was a citizens' request that he undertake a review of the OPCW Douma report that would involve all OPCW scientists who had taken part in the Douma investigation and participated in preparing interim reports and drafting the final fact-finding mission report for Douma, in order to resolve the allegations that OPCW management had suppressed and manipulated scientific evidence involving the chemistry, toxicology, and ballistics of the investigation.

As it turned out, neither the leaders of the General Assembly, the Security Council, and the Human Rights Council (HRC) at the UN political level nor the Secretary-General and other senior UN civil servants at the operational level reacted to the Statement of Concern they had received from a group of international citizens worried about serious, well-documented allegations involving OPCW and the resulting geopolitical implications. There was one exception. The chair of the HRC Syria Commission of Inquiry, Paul Pinheiro, confirmed receipt of the Statement but without offering a comment.

### The Ongoing Involvement of the OPCW and the UN with Douma

Although the unwillingness of the United Nations and the OPCW to engage with representatives of civil society was obvious, the issue of Douma remained a major subject of controversy within and between these two organizations. Despite the allegations, OPCW management continued to report to institutions like the Security Council, the EU Parliament, and OPCW state-parties meetings that the report of the OPCW's fact-finding mission had confirmed that there were "reasonable grounds that chlorine had been used" in Douma.[13] OPCW made no reference to the existence of several drafts and several groups of drafters of the report that have generated serious and to date unresolved disagreements within the organization and within the Security Council, primarily between the three Western P5 members (France, the UK, and the US) and the two Eastern P5 members (Russia and China). In public statements, OPCW director-general Arias stressed that the Douma "fact-finding mission investigation was conducted based on objectivity and due process" and he stood "by the conclusions of the final Douma report," according to an OPCW press release dated February 6, 2020. According to Arias, Inspector Henderson had not been a member of the fact-finding mission team, and Inspector Whelan had not completed the training needed to be deployed on-site in Douma. In contrast to these OPCW observations, public records suggest that Henderson had indeed been a member of the Douma fact-finding mission team and Whelan had been the chief drafter of the original fact-finding mission report.

Ever since the Syrian civil war started in 2011, the entire UN System had become involved at political and humanitarian levels. There was not a year when the General Assembly, the Security Council, and the Human Rights Council did not debate the Syrian crisis. Resolutions were put forward and passed in the hope of ending a crisis that has yet to end. Altogether Syria's chemical weapons before 2013 and its alleged continued possession and use of such weapons have remained a topic in resolutions on Syria but mostly without specific references to Douma. In the Security Council, however, Douma has become a regular monthly agenda item, but the Council remains unable to reach any agreement on steps to be taken to resolve the controversy.

In two documents, the General Assembly has provided details about the investigations of the UN's Independent International Commission of Inquiry on the Syrian Arab Republic about the political, security and humanitarian conditions in the country.[14] There were specific references in the Commission's report on Douma about a "vast body of evidence collected by the Commission [that] suggests a gas cylinder containing a chlorine payload had been delivered by helicopter" on buildings in Douma, but the report added that "the Commission cannot make yet any conclusions concerning the exact cause of death" of civilians.[15]

Regarding the air strikes of April 14, 2018, which followed the alleged April 7, 2018, chemical weapons attack on Douma, the UN Independent Commission stated that a period of seriously "increased international tensions" followed. Three years later, the Commission observed more critically that "the US-led coalition also conducted air strikes documented to have caused civilian casualties, failing to take all feasible precautions to avoid and minimize incidental loss of civilian life, injury to civilians, and damage to civilian objects in violation of international law humanitarian law."[16] In this 2021 Commission report, the General Assembly voiced criticism about what it called "ten years of Security Council inaction" (para.

99) and more specifically in relation to "Security Council supported restrictions of Syrian cross-border humanitarian aid" (para. 96).

The most recent update on the political, security, and human conditions in Syria is included in some detail in a General Assembly resolution of January 10, 2022 (A/RES/76/228), which yet again reminded member countries, as the General Assembly had done at yearly intervals before, that "the only solution to the current crisis in the Syrian Arab Republic is through an inclusive and Syrian-led political process under the auspices of the UN." Without specifically referring to Douma, the resolution requested OPCW to consider "additional procedures . . . to ensure the complete destruction of the Syrian chemical weapons programme."

The resolution is evidence of the links the General Assembly had developed with the Security Council, the Human Rights Council, and its Independent Commission, as well as the Secretary-General and his Special Envoy for Syria, reflecting a trend over the years toward more overarching approaches within the UN in dealing with complex and inter-sectoral crises like those confronted in Syria. At the same time, the voting on this resolution, with 93 countries supporting it, 16 voting against it, and 52 abstaining, also exhibited the prevailing geopolitical divisions in the General Assembly, a result that is consistent with similar voting on Syria in other UN bodies.

Secretary-General António Guterres and his predecessor Ban Ki-moon repeatedly expressed their disappointment that the Security Council had been failing in its obligation to deal with the issue of accountability for the use of chemical weapons in Syria. Following the Syrian Arab Republic's accession in September 2013 to the Chemical Weapons Convention, the Security Council requested the director-general of the OPCW to report monthly via the UN Secretary-General about Syria's compliance with the Chemical Weapons Convention. The Security Council furthermore asked the Secretary-General to provide information regularly on all UN activities in Syria.[17] Secretary-General Guterres has done so, criticizing not only the Syrian government and Syrian opposition groups for their "failure to protect civilians and their lack of support for the Syrian peace process, but also external parties for their participation." These included Russian, Turkish, and Western interventions. Addressing the air strikes of April 14, 2018, by the US, UK, and France, following the attack on Douma a week earlier, Secretary-General Guterres stated that when dealing with matters of peace and security, the Security Council should act consistently with the UN Charter and international law. He appealed for "the unity of the Security Council to avoid worsening the suffering of the Syrian people."

In the monthly meetings of the Security Council on conditions in Syria, the Under-Secretary-General and head of the UN Office for Disarmament Affairs, Izumi Nakamitsu, reminded the Council of "Syria's continuing failure to deal with outstanding chemical weapons issues: the gaps, inconsistencies, and discrepancies in Syria's declaration of its chemical weapons stockpile" and that OPCW had yet to receive from the Damascus government details about its possession of undeclared nerve agents. In her statements, she made no reference to the controversy surrounding OPCW's Douma investigation and the need for a reassessment of OPCW reports on Douma and the alleged manipulation of scientific evidence that led independent experts and journalists to doubt the truthfulness of the OPCW approach to the use of chemical weapons attributed to Syria and providing the rationale for retaliatory attacks by NATO powers.

### Adherence of the UN and the OPCW to UN Charter Provisions

Ever since 2011, the Syrian civil war and its political, security and humanitarian repercussions have occupied the General Assembly, with a special concern for the disarmament of the country's chemical weapons. The Assembly has cooperated closely with the Security Council, and consistent with UN Charter Article 11/3, has provided the Council with reports on disarmament and specific references to Douma. Repeated air strikes, involving also Douma, were carried out by the Syrian government and also by external parties, with serious implications for the Syrian people and for international peace and security. The Security Council failed to intervene and the General Assembly chose not to make use of its right to call for emergency meetings (Resolution A/377 of 1950) to de-escalate a given crisis.

Developments in Douma and elsewhere in Syria called for the Security Council to act as a team. However, it has consistently been fragmented, including between permanent and elected members acting in their own geopolitical and national interests rather than carrying out collectively what the Charter demands as the Council's common objectives of war prevention and restoration of peace in response to violent conflict. Resolution 2585 of July 9, 2021, involving crossline delivery of humanitarian assistance across Bab al-Hawa is the only Syria resolution the Security Council has ever passed unanimously since 2016. The controversy over the use of chemical weapons in Douma in 2018 and the alleged OPCW manipulation of scientific evidence in the course of its Douma fact-finding mission have yet to result in a Security Council process that enables the fulfillment of expectations that the highest UN political organ will objectively investigate these allegations to bring a convincing closure to the Douma file.

Even though the International Court of Justice is available to provide Advisory Opinions (Article 96), neither the General Assembly and the Security Council nor the Secretary-General and other organs of the UN and its specialized agencies have made use of the Court even though a wide range of legal issues involving human rights, laws of war, territorial sovereignty, false flag operations, and other reputed disinformation have arisen during the Syrian civil war, including serious allegations of institutional fraud in the official reporting on the use of chemical weapons in Douma.

Secretaries-General Ban Ki-moon and António Guterres both held the view that there cannot be a military solution to the Syrian conflict. They continuously interacted with the General Assembly, with the Security Council as a whole and with individual P5 members, and with the Human Rights Council to find peaceful ways to resolve the Syrian crisis. Additionally, Secretary-General Guterres and Michelle Bachelet, the UN High Commissioner for Human Rights, have encouraged the Security Council to refer the Syrian crisis in its entirety to the International Criminal Court.

Meetings have also taken place between Secretary-General Guterres and OPCW DG Arias to review the general state of Syrian chemical weapons disarmament. Whether these also involved the Douma controversy has not been disclosed. Unlike Secretary-General Kofi Annan, who in 1998 traveled to Baghdad, against the advice of some P5 member countries, to meet President Saddam Hussein and, using his moral authority, negotiated an improved humanitarian program for the Iraqi people living under UN sanctions, neither of the two subsequent Secretaries-General chose to make use of such authority and travel to Damascus for meetings with Syria's President Bashar al-Assad.

Because the issue of chemical weapons has stalemated the Syria debate in the Security Council for the past three years, for Secretary-General Guterres to raise the major controversy about OPCW's investigation in Douma with the Security Council, the General Assembly, and the Human Rights Council became an increasingly tempting option—see UN Charter Articles 12 and 99. The Secretary-General has chosen not to do so. There is no evidence that external pressure explains his decision.

The Secretary-General's Special Envoy for Syria Geir O. Pedersen; the High Representative for Disarmament Izumi Nakamitsu; and the Chair of the Independent Commission on Syria Paulo Pinheiro, three senior UN civil servants, have followed developments in Syria in accordance with their respective mandates in the areas of constitutional change, human rights, disarmament, humanitarian assistance, and more generally, the cessation of a decade of armed conflict.

In compliance with the Security Council's directives, Special Envoy Pedersen has been reporting regularly on his consultations with all relevant parties involved in the Syrian conflict, including developments in disarmament. His accounts make it clear that his mandate, like that of his predecessors, involves a protracted and difficult political mission in the UN Secretariat's efforts to contribute to crisis mitigation given the polarized nature of the conflict. In separate statements in early 2022 to the Security Council and the EU, he informed the UN that suffering in Syria was at its highest level since the war began eleven years ago and a political solution to the conflict was not in sight. In such briefings, Pedersen could have addressed disarmament issues including the specific OPCW Douma controversy, which continues to divide the Security Council and hamper the peace process. He chose not to do so.

The High Representative for Disarmament has the mandate to assist all parties in their efforts to eliminate weapons of mass destruction and to provide substantive and organizational support for norm setting in relation to such disarmament. In the context of Syria, the current High Representative for Disarmament, Izumi Nakamitsu, has rightly reminded the government of Syria and other parties that there remain "gaps, inconsistencies and discrepancies in Syria's declaration of its chemical weapons stockpile" and that "the OPCW has yet to receive a declaration from the Syrian authorities of undeclared types and quantities of various nerve agents." These statements have also consistently reflected her confidence in the "professionalism, impartiality, and dedication" of the OPCW and in the "robust and long-standing UN-OPCW partnership." She also has expressed repeatedly her gratitude for the support UNODA, her office, has been receiving from the Arms Control Association, a "US national non-partisan organisation, dedicated to promoting public understanding of . . . effective arms control policies." At the same time, there is no public record that the High Representative for Disarmament has ever taken any position with regard to the allegations that OPCW had manipulated scientific evidence involving the final fact-finding mission report for Douma and the public demand to reassess the validity of the published report, even though it is part of a High Representative's formal remit to "foster disarmament measures through dialogue, transparency and confidence building on military matters" and to liaise "with permanent missions to the UN and civil society." Her statements provide no evidence that she has visited Syria or maintained any dialogue with the Syrian government. As a senior representative of the UN, which is perceived by citizens to be a "we the peoples" organization, she also decided not to respond to the Statement of Concern presented to her by twenty-eight people as their expression of profound public unease about the Douma allegations and the consequent expectation that she would take up this matter with the concerned parties.

Five months after pro-democracy demonstrations had erupted in Deera, southern Syria, in March 2011, the Human Rights Council passed resolution A/HRC/S-17/1 establishing the Syrian Independent Commission of Inquiry on the Syrian Arab Republic to monitor the humanitarian situation in Syria and report to the Security Council, the Secretary-General, and others on alleged violations of international humanitarian law in the country. Throughout the eleven years of civil war in Syria, the chair of this UN Commission has continuously presented the Commission's findings to all UN bodies, often with critical conclusions whenever internal and external parties had violated international law. About chemical weapons issues, the Commission confirmed that the alleged chemical weapons attack of April 7, 2018, on Douma was not included in its list of thirty-eight established cases of the use of chemical weapons but added that the "Commission's investigations are ongoing."

In its most recent report, dated June 29, 2022, the Commission points out that the Syrian people in all parts of the country are confronted with serious levels of violence, grave violations of human rights, illegal detentions, and disappearances. The crisis in Syria, the report points out, has been aggravated by the presence of five foreign militaries (Iran, Israel, Russia, Turkey, and the US), non-state armed groups and terrorist entities. The Commission believes that currently more than 90 percent of the Syrian population is living in poverty and concludes that it is "unconscionable" that the Security Council is not able to get more involved. Given that the Commission stresses that chemical weapons in Syria "remain high on the agenda," the case of Douma should be included, since civilians died in the alleged chemical attack and a public request has been made to investigate this incident. There is, however, no indication that the Commission has been investigating Douma or has any intention of doing so. There is also no public evidence that the UN Human Rights Commission, as a commission, or its president Ambassador Nazat Shameem Khan, who received the Statement of Concern regarding Douma, have ever seriously considered the public request to investigate this human-rights-related incident.

## The Significance of Douma

UN bodies, UN member governments, and the UN civil service have one responsibility in common: to adhere to the Purposes and Principles of the UN Charter. We have reviewed the controversy about the alleged use of chemical weapons in the town of Douma in 2018 to obtain a detailed insight into how the UN as an institution, governments as members of this institution, and the Secretary-General and his team have dealt with the Douma chemical weapons file in the context of UN Charter obligations.

Our understanding, which does not purport to be a judgment, is as follows:

The UN System at all levels has been able to quickly introduce policies, recommendations, and mechanisms to manage chemical weapons disarmament in Syria as a serious issue for international peace and security, and most importantly, for the protection of the Syrian people.

As the specific issue of Douma became embroiled in international partisanship and confrontation right from the beginning, unified positions in the Security Council and the General Assembly have failed to materialize, which explains the failure to pass any unanimous Security Council and General Assembly resolutions on Douma.

The Human Rights Council, with its focus on human rights issues, rarely took positions on chemical weapons in Syria and did not pronounce on Douma.

UN civil servants led by the Secretary-General have responded to the demands of the Security Council and the General Assembly with efforts to implement their disarmament mandates, albeit with substantially different degrees of commitment:

1. The Secretary-General's Special Envoy for Syria has maintained contact with all parties concerned and presented his conclusions, but without specific reference to Douma.

2. The High Representative for Disarmament has justifiably reminded the Syrian authorities that the Syrian government had yet to provide disarmament information in general and about Douma in particular. At the same time, she did not promote, as part of her mandate, dialogue and confidence-building measures between the parties. Her involvement in the Douma controversy was limited to defending the OPCW management's contested decision rather than supporting the

call for bringing disagreeing OPCW parties together to investigate allegations of the manipulation of scientific evidence with the objective of achieving closure to this still prevailing threat to international peace and security. As a senior UN official, she also chose not to respond to the Statement of Concern on Douma, which she had received from the public.

3. The Chair of the Independent Commission investigated the human-rights-related impact of the use of chemical weapons in Syria but inexplicably excluded the contested case of Douma. Following the publication of the Statement of Concern, the Commission had an option to add Douma to its agenda. This did not happen.

4. There is no public evidence that the Secretary-General himself has discussed in any detail the Douma controversy, either with his Special Envoy, the High Representative for Disarmament, or the Chair of the Independent Commission. There are also no records in the public domain that the Secretary-General in his interaction with the General Assembly, the Security Council, and the Human Rights Council discussed Douma with these three bodies. It appears that Douma was also not a subject of the Secretary-General's meetings with the OPCW Director-General. He also chose not to react to the Statement of Concern he had received through a former UN colleague on behalf of the twenty-eight signatories.

What emerges in the context of the UN Charter is that the example of Douma, as a genuine peace and security concern, has remained a marginal issue in the General Assembly and the Human Rights Council and continues to be a divisive and stalemated crisis in the Security Council. The UN Charter's Purposes and Principles have been largely ignored by all three policymaking UN bodies. The Secretary-General and his team had options to lobby for solutions for peace in Syria and did use them but not consistently or with equal measure, and they mysteriously excluded Douma without any explanation. Neither the UN policymaking bodies nor UN civil servants have been prepared to engage with the OPCW to bring about clarity regarding the allegations that the public and several governments have made about Douma and the failure of the OPCW to protect its institutional integrity in view of incriminating evidence. By refraining to do so, the UN has put into fundamental question its own integrity and seemingly avoided exposing the truth about an issue that would embarrass the Western P5 members.

Even if all UN entities but the Security Council had taken steps to find solutions for a crisis such as Douma, only the P5 in the Security Council possesses the authority to bring about a closure consistent with the mandate and ethos of the United Nations. The present UN's constitutional reality is such that the permanent members of the Security Council, especially China, Russia, and the United States, reserve for themselves the discretion to apply their combined power according to the principles of the UN Charter for the benefit of all wherever they live or practice. Unfortunately, the diktat of national power and the primacy of geopolitics has been dominating the overall UN treatment of the Douma controversy, giving rise to a crisis of trust for those who have followed the controversy or have been trying to induce the UN to act responsibly on a most delicate issue of peace and security.

Douma constitutes a dramatic example of one seemingly "small" case in the wider context of global geopolitics, but it has significant implications for international relations and global peace and security. It is for this reason that we decided to include this case study in the book.

# PART THREE

## OBSTACLES TO MITIGATE

# EIGHT

# Responsibility to Protect (R2P), National Sovereignty, and Geopolitical Ambition

### Idealistic Ambitions versus Realistic Limitations: The Decline of War Prevention with Reference to International Wars

Much of the explanation for negative impressions of UN performance arise from its inability to control the behavior of its largest members, three of whom are P5 veto powers. Such states were never meant to be controlled by the UN in relation to peace and security. Reliance was placed on the dynamics of responsible self-governance of geopolitical actors, aware of the dangers of the nuclear age and the ravages of war. This Faustian bargain with the P5 was also a recognition that these governments would not transfer sufficient capabilities to enable UN enforcement, exposing the weakness of the UN if a geopolitical crisis emerged. And finally, this way of proceeding took some account of the frustrations arising from the inclusive approach adopted by the League of Nations after World War I. In fact, the Charter provided for a greater peace and security role for the Security Council, based on intended coordinating and standby capabilities, which never materialized due to Great Power tensions and an underlying reluctance of all states to erode the primacy of sovereign discretion with regard to national security.

A public sense that the UN was a failure took hold during the Cold War and for some observers, was highlighted first by the inability and seeming unwillingness to induce the two adversary superpowers to engage in nuclear disarmament negotiations or for the UN to exert enough pressure to overcome US and Soviet reluctance. It should be remembered that hopes and expectations relating to the UN were formed as much around the terrifying imagery of Hiroshima as by the prolonged devastation wrought overall by World War II. Feelings of disappointment, then, shifted focus from the seeming irrelevance of the UN in relation to international wars to its inability to play even a moderating role in the contexts of what came to be called "internal wars." This perception of UN impotence reached a climax during the decade-long Vietnam War starting in the early 1960s and resurfaced again during the Syrian War that began in 2011 and dragged on for more than a decade.

The Ukraine War, raising anew the fear of nuclear warfare, again sidelined the UN except in the symbolic domain of condemning Russian aggression and the Secretary-General's warning that the play of forces was raising the risks of human catastrophe to unacceptable levels. In contrast, the West condemned the Russian attack and backed the Ukrainian response with massive military and economic assistance and did little to support a diplomatic off-ramp.

Anxieties about a new major war spiraling out of the Cold War dominated the political and moral imagination of both diplomats who conceived of the United Nations and a worried public. These anxieties were intensified by the fresh memory of the devastation caused in World War II through strategic bombing campaigns and even more by the atomic bombing of Hiroshima and Nagasaki at the end of the Pacific War and after the UN Charter had been drafted and adopted at San Francisco. Such concerns were underscored after it became clear that the cooperative wartime antifascist alliance would not hold up in peacetime. Diplomatic friction between the wartime allies precluded agreement on peace arrangements in Europe and East Asia, resulting in the instability of the divided countries of Germany, Korea, and Vietnam and the makings of future troubles. In the background was a newly emergent central international conflict configuration that became known as the Cold War. It gave a post-1945 structure to geopolitics in the form of bipolar security governance, a historical development of the greatest significance, further accentuated by the 1949 victory of the Communist insurgency in China. The worsening of relations among the victors in World War II had an overall negative effect on internationalist aspirations, including hopes for a robust UN war-prevention role. This development was reinforced by a loss of confidence in the West that market-oriented constitutionalism was the universal wave of the future. This combination created widespread anxiety about the future of world order, which had the immediate effect of limiting prospects for the UN, whose war prevention potential depended on sustaining an atmosphere of geopolitical cooperation and friendly relations throughout the world.

From a constitutional perspective, this deepening split among the five permanent members of the Security Council immediately heightened the salience of the veto power to constrain UN action whenever the P5 failed to reach agreement on a global policy issue. It is notable that the vision of UN effectiveness held by the US wartime leader Franklin Delano Roosevelt was premised on a naïve confidence that the winners in World War II would continue to cooperate in the post-1945 world to keep the peace. The two other prominent wartime leaders, Winston Churchill and Joseph Stalin, were more realistic. They were cynical about maintaining cooperation among ideological adversaries absent a common enemy. These leaders accurately foresaw that the tensions at the end of the prior war would create a world order beset by tensions and distrust posing strategy and war prevention challenges of a magnitude that was new to international relations.

In an extraordinary shift of mood, instead of seeing nuclear weapons as a menace to the future of humanity, leading members of the UN deployed this weaponry and treated it as a strategic necessity and, ironically, the keeper of the peace. The weaponry came to be regarded as the indispensable feature of a geopolitically managed war-prevention system based on fear rather than cooperation or disarmament. The UN did reinforce this morally questionable foundation of world peace by providing the auspices for the negotiation of the Nuclear Non-Proliferation Treaty (NPT) that entered into force in 1962. The treaty was seen as a stabilizing development by mainstream realists, who were worried about the breakdown of nuclear management arrangements if many additional governments came to possess nuclear weapons or if public pressure for nuclear disarmament was ever taken seriously. The viability of the NPT as a global arrangement was structured around core ideas of reciprocity between nuclear and nonnuclear states. In exchange for states agreeing not to acquire nuclear weapons, the nuclear weapons states agreed to negotiate nuclear disarmament in good faith, and beyond that even to seek general and complete disarmament, as well ensuring these nonnuclear states that as parties to the NPT, they would still enjoy the supposed benefits of access to peaceful uses of nuclear energy.

The bargain was never implemented in the manner prescribed by the NPT text. The nonproliferation commitments were generally, if selectively implemented, but the promised disarmament negotiations never happened. The disarmament provisions were silently ignored or dismissed in foreign policy circles as "useful fictions," helpful to achieve nonproliferation goals without impeding retention, development, and discretion of the weaponry by the leading nuclear weapons states, which turned out to be none other than the five veto powers.[1]

Unsurprisingly, what followed was the non-implementation of the disarmament dimensions of the treaty coupled with the selective enforcement of the nonproliferation dimensions (as with Iraq War of 2003 and threat diplomacy directed at Iran, while Israel's covert acquisition of nuclear weaponry was deliberately overlooked). In effect, the UN gave its blessings to a global managerial regime that as an operational arrangement possessed the hierarchical features of "nuclear apartheid," which defied the Charter affirmations of the equality of sovereign states.[2]

Not until 2017 did nonnuclear-weapons states, with a strong push from peace activists around the world, awaken to this perversion of the bargain at the core of the NPT. Nonnuclear states are mounting a normative challenge against nuclear apartheid by their support for a UN Treaty on the Prohibition of Nuclear Weapons (TPNW), which entered into force in 2021 after fifty governments deposited certificates of ratification. Of related significance was the formal statement issued in response by the three Western nuclear weapons states expressing their outright rejection of the TPNW on the grounds that global security threats are better addressed by deterrent nuclear capabilities.

Nuclear weaponry and the dangers of nuclear war continue to be major concerns of the UN, but now it is clear that within the organization are two divergent paths to peace and security: the geopolitical path of the leading Western nuclear weapons states and possibly all nine countries possessing nuclear weapons and the international law path of the mainly non-Western states that seek prohibition, denuclearization of international relations, and eventual disarmament. This juridical pushback seems to lack sufficient political traction on its own to overcome this geopolitical resistance, yet both world-order strategies cohabit within the UN System. As with the establishment of the International Criminal Court (ICC) and the Anti-Personnel Mine Ban Treaty, challenging geopolitical positions requires a robust coalition that joins international member governments to a strong activist movement of global scope rooted in transnational civil society, and even then, these counter-hegemonic forces will struggle to achieve operational effectiveness. In a telling instance, the ICC managed to be established in 2001, despite a failure to obtain the participation or even support of several important UN members, including leading geopolitical actors. So long as the ICC concerned itself with the crimes of sub-Saharan Africa, its existence was tolerated, even affirmed. However, when it dared to propose investigations of alleged crimes by the United States in Afghanistan or by Israel in Occupied Palestine, the pushback was immediate and intense.[3]

The message was clear. A direct and determined repudiation of ICC independence would occur if this judicial tribunal dared challenge geopolitical practices directly. It is this paramount tension that has adversely affected UN performance and reputation throughout its existence, except for a momentary flourish of agreement at the end of the Cold War that allowed the UN to act cooperatively in effectively nullifying Iraq's attack and annexation of Kuwait in 1991. Such recourse to the UN was soon forgotten as the US led the way to projecting its own power globally in a manner that again marginalized the UN. By 2003, George W. Bush declared that the UN would be "irrelevant" if it refused to go along with US plans to attack Iraq. UN approval of US-UK war plans was not forthcoming, and the aggression against Iraq occurred, proving Bush correct to a degree but also showing the gaps between geopolitical behavioral norms and relevant international law prohibitions.

## Decline of War Prevention: Internal Warfare

Aside from geopolitical obstacles, there was another important reason why public disenchantment with UN arose in recent decades. As the avoidance of World War III became subject to geopolitical management handled almost totally outside the UN by way of deterrence arrangements and bipolarity, Washington and Moscow sought to avoid direct confrontations in light of the near outbreak of nuclear war in the Cuban Missile Crisis of 1962. An accompanying adjustment in the configuration of active international conflict occurred, involving a pronounced geographic move away from the European center of political rivalry to the peripheries of international conflict in the global South. Competitive interventions by the antagonistic superpowers in struggles within states largely, yet not completely displaced wars between states.[4] As a result, internal wars became a major preoccupation in international relations. The central idea was to carry on the ideological struggles between East and West within prudent limits and thus try to avoid escalations of engagement that might lead to combat confrontations between the United States and the Soviet Union, especially, but not only in decolonizing settings.

The United States was awkwardly situated, being normally aligned with the European colonialist establishment forces, while the nationalist challengers were correspondingly more often influenced by Marxist thought and Soviet anti-colonial perspectives. International law, as codified to meet the requirements of a divided world order, formulated under UN auspices the Declaration on Principles of International Law concerning Friendly Relations and Cooperation among States in accordance with the UN Charter (A/RES/2625[XXV], October 24, 1970), highlighting the norm of self-determination as a fundamental element of world order. The UN formulation definitely supports the anti-colonial consensus by specifically endorsing the intention "to bring to a speedy end to colonialism" in accord with "the freely expressed will of the people concerned." The text of this important UN resolution goes on to say "that the subjection of peoples to alien subjugation, domination and exploitation is a denial of fundamental rights, and contrary to the Charter." Beyond this, a right of such a subjugated people to resist is also affirmed, although the UN text reflects sovereignty concerns by declaring that the principle of self-determination cannot be validly exercised if it leads to the territorial dismemberment of an existing state. Again, from the perspective of symbolic politics, the alignment of the UN lends legitimacy to anti-colonial struggles and strengthens the will of global solidarity initiatives. In effect, the substantive realization of self-determination is beyond the direct reach of the UN, but not its encouragement in general and on occasion in specific circumstances. Chapter 5, devoted to Palestine/Israel relations to the UN, vividly illustrates the practical obstacles to exercising the right of self-determination and gaining relevant UN support when geopolitical actors use their leverage to frustrate such aspirations, and there is nothing the UN has been able to do about it, yet it keeps trying.

These internal wars and struggles for control of the state attracted various forms of intervention, ranging from diplomatic support to covert and overt interferences with the dynamics of self-determination. Such interventions raise international tensions, especially if the internal war is strategically situated geographically or in a resource-rich country, particularly if the conflict is articulated along ideological lines. There was also an important normative inhibition on UN war-prevention missions in these contexts due to the Charter's self-imposed limitations on its authority with respect to internal strife and warfare (see Article 2[7]). In general, prior to the establishment of the UN, the principle of territorial sovereignty led almost automatically to the emergence of a customary legal norm prohibiting intervention in the internal affairs of sovereign states. Although such a norm existed, it achieved at best the status of "soft law," which meant that it was habitually violated in a variety of ways by imperial practices and geopolitical actors.[5]

The UN Charter incorporates the principle of nonintervention as a limitation of its own competence, with the single exception of a situation in which an internal war poses a threat to international peace and security as determined in accordance with Chapter VII. Article 2(7) of the Charter sets forth in strained language the principle of domestic jurisdiction—that is, within the sovereign domain of an international state: "Nothing contained in the present Charter shall authorize the United Nations to intervene in matters which are essentially within the domestic jurisdiction of any state or shall require the Members to submit such matters to settlement under the present Charter; but this principle shall not prejudice the application of enforcement measures under Chapter VII."

The main point is that the UN gives legal reassurance to states that it will not intervene, but this reassurance has two major flaws. First, the UN has been operationally helpless to control sustained and large-scale interventions in internal wars by geopolitical actors and has lost credibility with respect to war prevention with respect to public opinion. Such wars as those in Indochina, Afghanistan, and Syria that lasted more than a decade, are often referred to as "forever wars," producing massive death and destruction. These "forever wars" or "frozen conflicts" have underscored the sense of UN irrelevance.[6]

It is not that the UN was entirely insensitive to the world order dilemma caused by promising war prevention in its Preamble yet withholding authorization to take responsibility for mitigating or stopping internal wars. Various attempts over the years have been made to authorize force, perhaps most notably in contexts where a so-called humanitarian intervention enjoyed widespread international support due to the severity of abuse being experienced by a portion of society victimized by the state, as has recently occurred in Myanmar with respect to the Rohingya or earlier in the conflicts in Bosnia and Kosovo.

In the aftermath of the Kosovo War (1999), the UN implicitly modified the Domestic Jurisdiction inhibition by adopting the norm of responsibility to protect (R2P). As pointed out in a previous chapter, the application of R2P to Libya in 2011 produced a bitter controversy when the operational reality, delegated by the UN to NATO became less a humanitarian instrument (to save civilians under threat in Benghazi) than a policy instrument facilitating NATO's pursuit of geopolitical regime-changing goals. When it came to Syria, the distrust generated by the Libyan experience led the UN being unable to reach even a minimal consensus by which to mitigate the terrible humanitarian tragedies experienced by the Syrian people. Once again, the UN was wrongly blamed for this apparent hands-off approach.

The real responsibility for the failure in Syria should be attributed to the geopolitical clash of priorities in the setting of internal wars and the distrust that was generated by seeking a limited humanitarian authorization that was operationally expanded in Libya to achieve unauthorized geopolitical goals. Given the veto power enjoyed by the permanent members of the Security Council, it is naïve and misleading to suppose that the UN is capable of acting autonomously on the high politics of peace and security.

When the UN is deprecated in such high-profile contexts, there is a tendency to overlook its multiple achievements outside the domain of war prevention that have made global governance more humane and made the lives of billions of people throughout the world safer and more satisfying. World public opinion should come to appreciate that even taking full account of the regrettable shortcomings of the UN, which need to be addressed, the returns on investment in its budget are on balance an incredible success for the world order, and such a record could be further enhanced by a larger budget and greater support from the peoples of the world and their governments.

It is important to realize that the veto built into the constitutional structure of the UN has acted as a debilitating limitation on the war prevention capabilities with respect to violent conflict between sovereign states. The point here is that the failures and disappointments of the UN with respect to war prevention should be related to the architecture of the organization that accepted the idea that operational responsibility for major instances of international war prevention would be dealt with by way of geopolitical management, and internal war prevention through the territorial management of political violence as a matter of sovereign rights. It is not the UN that should be blamed for wars, militarism, and nuclearism, but the unwillingness of the geopolitical actors to respect international law and seek nuclear disarmament and the failure of many governments to respect the basic human rights of their citizens and to become vigilant in insulating their sovereign space from intervention.

Part of the blame for this kind of unsatisfactory situation precedes the formation of the UN and arises from the nature of Westphalian world order that adapts to the coexistence of state sovereignty and geopolitics, a reality that was not frontally addressed in the UN Charter or the operations of the organization. Another part of the blame relates to the way international law deals with internal wars, allowing governments, however abusive, to receive military support if facing internal rebellion while also providing a variety of moral and political justifications for helping anti-government movements overtly or covertly. There are no clear standards or procedures to implement and interpret the norm of nonintervention. Beyond this, geopolitical actors have developed skillful means by way of covert interventions in ongoing struggles for control of states often in violation of the declared wishes of national populations and their leaders and hence in operations to hide their violations of the spirit and substance of the norm of self-determination. The Soviet overt interventions to suppress democratizing movements in Eastern Europe during the Cold War are illustrative of the suppression of the basic rights of a people, as are the US anti-left interventions in Latin America to uphold ideological alignments and lend military and diplomatic support to uphold the economic interests of foreign investors.

## Universality of Membership, Conditionalities of Participation

The larger lesson regarding the UN is clear. In relation to peace and security but not necessarily in other policy domains, the UN can establish norms and procedures, but their implementation is subject either to a Security Council veto, or if not applicable, then to a geopolitical veto. Geopolitical actors, especially the United States, can be more or less supportive of the UN, but whatever its outlook, it will resist crossing certain red lines. There are significant differences in political style ranging from the liberal internationalism of the Kennedy or Obama presidencies to the illiberality and ultranationalism of the Trump presidency. In either case, Israel will be insulated from UN censure and accountability, and the impunity of the US government and its personnel will be jealously guarded. What this means, in practice, is that the UN must restrict its peace and security activism to those settings where a sufficiently supportive geopolitical consensus exists, and even there, the devil is in the details, and what initially appears to be a policy consensus can easily fall apart, as in two high-profile post–Cold War undertakings: Iraq in 1992 and Libya in 2011.

These problems pertain not just to matters of peace and security. Issues of legitimacy may also occasion certain geopolitical responses. The United States withdrew its membership from the UN Human Rights Council in Geneva on two separate occasions because it was unable to protect Israel from criticism and policy recommendations within that veto-free arena. Because there is no veto outside the Security Council, geopolitical leverage takes different forms, including defunding threats and suspension of membership. What is clear and points to the importance of the UN, even when its judgments are unable to modify behavior in accord with the Charter, is the degree to which legitimacy issues matter. Thus, when the HRC criticizes Israel for the expansion of unlawful settlements or for the use of excessive force in Occupied Palestine, it matters, and Israel suffers a defeat in the ongoing legitimacy war that influences reputation and international standing.

Recognitions of geopolitical leverage within the UN constitutional structure and by way of influence with respect to budgetary support and political efficacy led the UN to pivot away from the war-prevention vision of the Preamble of the Charter and even from the more far-reaching peace-keeping expectations that were left unrealized in the Charter itself, such as the earmarking of standby peacekeeping forces and a P5 command mechanism within the UN structure.[7] During and after the Cold War, it became obvious that neither superpower was motivated to give effect to the Charter's Chapter VII expectations, thereby leaving conflict and its management where it had been since the establishment of the Westphalian statist framework of international relations. Even after the fall of the Berlin Wall in 1989, signaling the end of the Cold War, there was not the slightest impulse by the victorious West to implement a more ambitious war-prevention role for the UN despite the momentary claim that collective security mechanisms could now function as intended due to geopolitical harmony, supposedly supportive of "a new world order."

There was a temporary and rather artificial show of unity in 1990–91 in response to Iraq's attack upon and annexation of Kuwait. After the UN authorized a coalition of countries, led by the US, to restore Kuwaiti sovereignty, first by sanctions and then by a military operation, there were second thoughts about entrusting the UN with such an expanded global security role. Above all, the US did not want to be burdened with global peacekeeping responsibilities disconnected from its strategic and material interests or lose its geopolitical discretion in war/peace contexts by so strengthening the UN. Such reluctance created an impression that it was not the Cold War that was most deeply to blame for the disappointing UN performance in relation to war prevention, but the refusal of P5 members to limit their discretion to privilege strategic interests in relation to peace and security.

But there was one crucial development that allowed the UN a measure of effectiveness. It was not a result of formal rules but reflected some imperatives of an interdependent world, including the benefits of cooperation within international institutions. The UN succeeded where the League of Nations had failed. It kept its implicit promise of being a universal organization encompassing the whole of humanity, and it made itself sufficiently valuable that even its most disgruntled and defiant members maintained their UN membership. Especially the United States has periodically expressed its frustrations in the context of the Human Rights Council and the two specialized agencies UNESCO and WHO by its petulant temporary withdrawals from participation.

Such behavior has not caused the collapse of these important actors within the UN System, but it has highlighted how much less vulnerable the UN would be if its budgets were funded by an independent form of taxation and points to an area where reformist energies might be best concentrated. Of course, as with other efforts to make the UN more independent of geopolitical pressures, those members that benefit from a status that exaggerates their importance and accompanying leverage would be resistant, highlighting that one of the constitutional weaknesses of the UN is the difficulty in achieving reform. Concretely, it makes no sense to retain both France and the UK as permanent members of the Security Council, yet their removal or replacement by an EU seat has proved impossible to negotiate. Arguably, if the UN became more independent, it might weaken the stakeholder ethos of participation that has sustained near-universal membership for three-quarters of a century. Such a pushback against reform should be taken seriously, especially so long as the mood of ultranationalism prevails in so many leading member states. What this mood encourages is a purely transactional view of the UN, which means that if membership costs more than the political payoff, states could withdraw as a further demonstration of their nationalist priorities or simply as a backlash against censure or sanctions.

The Soviet Union learned a lesson about the costs of nonparticipation in relation to the authorization by the Security Council of backing the defense claims of South Korea in the Korean War. At the time, 1950, the Soviet Union was boycotting the Security Council in protest of the UN's refusal to allow the Beijing government to represent mainland China in the organization despite the fact that the Taiwan government had lost complete control of China in 1949. If the Soviet Union had been present in the Security Council, its use of the veto would have prevented the UN from taking sides in the Korean War. The Soviet delegate publicly declared that such a mistake would never be made again by Moscow, and it never was, not only by the Soviet Union but by any of the veto powers or for that matter, by any member of the Security Council.

The one occasion on which a state did exercise its right of withdrawal was back in 1965, when Indonesia, under the leadership of its founding leader, Sukarno, withdrew in reaction to the UN's condemnation of the country's Crush Malaysia campaign. Indonesia not only withdrew but proposed the formation of a new world organization composed of non-Western decolonized states that would be an alternative to the UN, which he charged was dominated by the old world order historically imposed on the world by the West, now disintegrating under the impact of decolonization. It is significant that despite considerable support for Sukarno's radical critique of the UN, not a single state joined the effort to establish a parallel organization. Throughout its existence, the UN has been coping with ultra-nationalist hostility to more globally oriented civil society advocacy in the US and elsewhere.

It should be appreciated that the Charter contains no provision conferring a formal right of withdrawal, possibly to avoid a repetition of the experience of the League of Nations. In addition to important countries, most notably the United States, not joining the League, Japan withdrew in 1933 when criticized for its aggression against Manchuria, and later the fascist states of Germany and Italy were expelled or withdrew. Jurists have speculated that UN members have no right of withdrawal once committed to the treaty, although this assertion has never been tested. What is clear politically is that UN has weathered many storms during its existence without fracturing the organization or diluting its claims and achievement of universal membership. While being proud of this exceptional record of participation, there should be a corresponding sense of disappointment when it comes to the UN's record of implementation, which is overall far more mixed and decidedly poor when it comes to compliance by members enjoying a right of veto or protected by veto-wielding members. The question to be asked is whether universal participation has been worth the price of according geopolitical actors a right of veto. An unanswerable corollary question is whether the League pattern of nonparticipation would have been repeated had the right of veto not been given to the five winners in World War II. Because of Western domination of the UN prior to decolonization, it seems likely that the Soviet Union would not have joined, making the UN resemble a Western alliance more than an organization dedicated to representing the interests of humanity and operating according to neutral principles of law and morality.

We cannot look to a peaceful, much less a just world order without a far greater respect for the authority of international law and of the Charter as a lawmaking treaty that extends its norms on the use of force to all states, regardless of power and size. The degree to which the war-prevention norms of the Charter are part of contemporary international law was convincingly affirmed in by the World Court in its *Nicaragua* decision of 1986.[8]

As matters now stand, the potential peacefulness of the world depends on far greater willingness of geopolitical actors to show respect for international law with regard to the use of force and on the willingness and ability of national governance structures to respect the human rights of all their citizens, including economic and social rights.[9]

## What the UN Can Do

This universality and continuity of participation encouraged the UN to shift its agenda priorities to areas of behavior where political impediments were less pronounced than those with respect to peace and security or sovereign rights within territorial confines. These shifts in emphasis were especially pronounced in relation to *symbolic politics*, which primarily concerns norms and standards of legitimacy, rather than *substantive politics*, which is preoccupied with modifying targeted behavior. Many crucial areas of international life are primarily shaped by symbolic politics or at least where non-substantive leverage can exert a great indirect influence. Some of these will be examined in relation to UN effectiveness and contributions to the underlying purposes of the UN, which in addition to peace, are set forth in Article I of the Charter, which calls for not only peaceful behavior but also for global cooperation and friendly relations in addressing common problems and disputes, as well as mandating the observance of human rights, which was understood as connected with the maintenance of peace.

Part of the reason that the UN is undervalued results, in our opinion, from the failure of the public and sometimes governments to appreciate the importance of symbolic politics in the modern interconnected, digitized world of intense communication networking.[10] If we grasp the counterintuitive reality that the anti-colonial wars against superior military capabilities were won by the weaker side, we can begin to appreciate the significance of symbolic politics. The US lost the Vietnam War not by military defeat in the combat zones of substantive politics but in the symbolic domains of Vietnamese perseverance and through escalating public perceptions hostile to the US mission of denying the people of Vietnam their postcolonial right of self-determination.[11]

Another aspect of this agenda shift needs to be appreciated. In the domain of substantive politics, the non-Western members of the UN were much less preoccupied with war prevention. They were concerned above all with achieving a level playing field in the world economy, coming forth with proposals for a new international economic order in the mid-1970s that led to the awareness of a North/South split that became in the 1970s and 1980s as intense within the UN as the East/West Cold War confrontation. The dynamics of decolonization and Cold War gave rise to the Non-Aligned Movement, which confronted the market-driven ideologies of the West with a common front and created strong tensions within the organization. It also led to the formation of reactive civil society initiatives such as the Trilateral Commission (US, Europe, Japan) to promote Western market-oriented and financial interests. Later, the World Economic Forum provided an influential unified platform for neoliberal globalist worldviews that provided an arena where heads of state, corporate and banking officials, and even civil society personalities and UN officials interacted to promote shared global policy objectives.

In the end, partly reflecting the rise of environmental concerns, a kind of compromise was reached that expressed itself by according the South victories in symbolic politics in exchange for backing away from challenging the world capitalist framework that was embedded in the prevailing norms and procedures addressing issues of trade and investment. In this regard the agenda shift occurred within the UN, according much greater emphasis on "development" and far less to "war prevention." The challenge with the development discourse, which was less threatening to the North and West than the earlier insistence on a new international economic order, purported to reconcile a market-driven world economy with developmental opportunities for less developed countries, and the results in Asia showed that under certain conditions of development, this could be done spectacularly.[12]

In this section, we attempt to show the degree to which the UN creatively adapted to its shortcomings, demonstrating institutional flexibility. We believe that this proves that not only the world but the UN is "greater than five." Due to space limitations, we discuss with extreme brevity illustrative UN activities other than war prevention, which combine to varying degrees symbolic and substantive contributions to a humane and just world order.

### 1. Normative Architecture

One of the most important contributions made by the UN is to strengthen and expand the international law framework applicable to international relations. This framework guides not only the conduct of international relations but also the internal governance of states through the development and codification of international law. Among the most notable institutional parts of the UN System that have this role are

the International Court of Justice: the highest judicial body in the UN available to decide legal disputes among states and to provide organs of the UN with authoritative Advisory Opinions on legal issues;

the International Law Commission: an expert body that works on areas of international law to impart a common understanding of its rules and principles, as well as to identify unsettled areas where agreements need to be reached; and

the Human Rights Council: with fifty-nine elected states drawn from the UN membership, administering a wide range of "special procedures," including the observance of international human rights treaties and appointing special rapporteurs and special envoys to report on human rights on themes such as the rights of women, the right to food, the right of free expression, poverty, religious freedom, indigenous peoples, and many other issues including situations that are particularly challenging with respect to human rights, perhaps most prominently, the Occupied Palestinian Territories.

This normative architecture is important not only to provide standards that are useful in setting limits on the international behavior of states but also to give some structure to the communications of claims and grievances in international relations, set boundaries on reasonable behavior, and provide decision-making procedures and criteria by which to resolve disputes. Such a normative architecture can also be useful in legitimizing civil society activism. International norms set standards by which to assess the behavior of states, including one's own state, thereby strengthening citizen and civil society participation in democratic and some nondemocratic states. This is most relevant with respect to human rights, including the right of self-determination. Opposition groups in Eastern Europe after World War II often invoked international human rights standards in formulating their demands for greater domestic freedom during the Cold War. Antiwar and antiracist movements in Western societies also benefited from supportive international norms.

The UN has provided a sense of normative entitlement to such aggrieved groups by giving their claims and demands a legal discourse. This was certainly the case for the Declaration of the Rights of Indigenous Peoples, as well as for peoples subject to oppressive denial of basic rights as in

Occupied Palestine, Western Sahara, and Kashmir. In other words, by the imprimatur of UN endorsement of nonviolent struggle and resistance is accorded to the most marginalized and vulnerable peoples in the world. It also encourages support for transnational civil society actors and solidarity initiatives, such as Amnesty International and Human Rights Watch. These respected organizations arrange their work of exposure of abusive behavior by reference to texts prepared within the UN, including the Universal Declaration of Human Rights, the Covenant of Civil and Political Rights, and the Covenant of Economic, Social, and Cultural Rights. It both legitimates and empowers this kind of transnational political action.

## 2. Normative Advocacy

In ways that were not anticipated, the UN, even in the midst of the Cold War, was able to promote certain partisan positions that legitimated governmental positions and civil society activism. Among the more prominent instances of such normative advocacy were the anti-apartheid campaign, permanent sovereignty over natural sovereignty, and the right to development. Such advocacy mingled moral enthusiasm with a sense of legal rights and duties in the postcolonial period. At times, the advocacy invoked existing norms but in a manner that encroached upon "domestic jurisdiction" of sovereign states, as was the case with respect to the UN support for the anti-apartheid campaign during the 1980s. At other times, the advocacy was itself an attempt to assert or generate a norm as with the right to development or the responsibility to protect (R2P). What seems clear is that the UN provided arenas where policy advocacy could legitimate claims relating to global justice, and these concerns were only indirectly related to war-prevention agendas. The relevance of normative advocacy by the UN depends on shaping a political consensus that extends to the geopolitical actors, or at least is not strongly opposed. A crucial context involves the efforts to extend individual accountability for international crime beyond the confines of "victor's justice" and geopolitical manipulation.[13]

## 3. Lawmaking Treaties

To bring order to an increasingly complex world, the UN provides a setting that respects the formalities of sovereign equality yet also allows global political leadership to overcome impasses among governments by negotiating compromises that offer win-win outcomes. A favorite example concerns the highly important Law of the Seas Treaty of 1982, which went a long way to produce a widely acceptable public order of the oceans, without which, a chaotic scene of conflicting claims and numerous disputes would exist. It was a context where rules and guidelines generally served the interests of differently situated states. This high degree of reciprocity and mutuality encouraged compliance by the strong as well as the weak. Even the geopolitical insistence on a broad scope for the norm of freedom of the seas so that navies and long-distance fishing fleets could roam the oceans rather freely was finally agreed upon by granting an exclusive economic zone (EEZ) to coastal states that protected access to marine resources far beyond the earlier notions of territorial sovereignty ending at twelve miles, or even three miles, which reflected the navigational and economic interests of maritime states. The compromise allowed "innocent passage" through waters beyond twelve miles without permission from the coastal state while prohibiting economic intrusions for two hundred miles unless the coastal state was unable to make full use of the EEZ. Comparable lawmaking treaties were negotiated to prevent conflict and expropriation of resources in Antarctica, as well as to ensure peaceful uses of space and the moon and many other spheres of international life.

Of particular importance over the course of the last half century has been the UN effort to lend auspices to meet environmental challenges by means of lawmaking frameworks. One notable treaty arrangement was the Paris Climate Change Agreement (2015), which at the time enjoyed near universal support, being hailed as a major breakthrough in the urgent effort to regulate carbon emissions and meet the threats posed by global warming. It must be admitted that weaknesses in this dramatic initiative were also evident—to secure widespread support, the agreement essentially rested on voluntary behavior. There was little that states were obligated to do beyond making pledges to cut their carbon emissions over time and continue the interactive process. There was also no enforcement procedure embedded in the agreement to implement the pledges or to prevent withdrawal. It came as a heavy blow when the United States, a lead negotiator of the agreement, announced its withdrawal from the agreement, as well as its refusal to abide by its terms. Fortunately, the withdrawal turned out to be temporary, as the US government again became a party in 2021.

It is evident that minimum requirements of world order depend on a robust UN role with respect to facilitating the lawmaking treaty process, which serves as a primitive legislative mechanism in the absence of a legislature. Again, the UN cannot engender global cooperation if the geopolitical will is not present. The decline of American global leadership in recent years has impaired the UN capacity with respect to lawmaking, and no geopolitical actor has so far stepped forward to fill this leadership vacuum, although there are some signs that China might be attempting to do so. The UN Secretary-General can give moral encouragement and stress the need for global cooperative undertaking for the public good, as António Guterres did during the COVID pandemic, but it became evident that such a plea could not by itself overcome the resolve of the US to handle the health challenge on a transactional and intergovernmental basis. By so doing, the UN was denied an opportunity to demonstrate its potential contribution to a more cooperative phase of world order that reflected the changing nature of security, which was tending to become for most countries more a matter of "human security" than "national security," which is focused on the defense of sovereign territory and meeting threats posed by "enemy" states.

### 4. UN Summits and Global Conferences on Policy Challenges

The UN in the less contentious atmosphere of the 1990s began to provide venues for gatherings of states, reinforced by energetic civil society participation, on policy issues of global scope. It added an informal prelegalization phase to the lawmaking role summarized in the previous section. Such events focused world attention on public concerns that were not receiving the kind of treatment that many governments and civil society activists felt appropriate. Controversial issues were discussed and often a consensus was reached that was more progressive than the existing situation, recommending reforms. This function of the UN to raise public awareness and influence public opinion reached a peak in the 1990s on such issues as the environment, human rights, women, population, and the social agenda. The final outcome of these events, taking the form of conference declarations, were significant contributions to the shaping of public opinion and civic activism. As might be expected, some leading governments did not agree with the declarations of the summits and calls of the conferences for more globalist policies and for greater economic and political commitments to the funding and realization of such reforms, inducing disillusionment and even criticisms to the effect that the summits were a waste of time and nothing more than talkfests challenging the established world order.

The highest profile contributions from the perspective of the UN's importance in symbolic politics occurred in the 1990s. It remains uncertain whether these events energized national, transnational, regional, and global constituencies and thereby exerted pressure on public policy and governance practices. What is known is that such events threatened to erode governmental dominance of global policy venues and thus produced a blowback effect that led the UN to become far more cautious in sponsoring such events. Perhaps a more innovative Secretary-General or restored interest in liberal internationalism by leading governments will induce a new cycle of global conferences on such hot-button topics as climate change, food security, health, migration, global and regional disarmament, biodiversity and global commons.

### 5. International Policy Domains Other Than War Prevention

There was always the intention to entrust the UN with promotional and problem-solving roles other than its primary mission of international war prevention. This breadth of coverage is set forth in Article 1 of the Charter, depicting the purposes of the new organization:

2. To develop friendly relations among nations based on respect for the principle of equal rights and self-determination of peoples, and to take other appropriate measures to strengthen universal peace;

3. To achieve international co-operation in solving international problems of an economic, social, cultural, or humanitarian character, and in promoting and encouraging respect for human rights and for fundamental freedoms for all without distinction as to race, sex, language, or religion; and

4. To be a center for harmonizing the actions of nations in the attainment of these common ends.

This emphasis originally exhibited an understanding that international peace and security would be indirectly benefited by global cooperation across a wide spectrum of human concerns if coordinated within the UN System and by a recognition that addressing the economic and social agenda of poor and less developed countries would contribute to international peacefulness. What gave this UN role outside of war prevention its special salience, however, was the combination of the geopolitical impasse brought about by the Cold War and the reluctance of leading states, especially the veto powers, to dilute hegemonic authority and control over war/ peace and security concerns. Overall, this explains the dual perception of the UN. Those who expected it to rise or fall by reference to war prevention were disappointed and tended to regard the UN as irrelevant, while those who valued the broader agenda may have wanted a more progressive approach at the UN but recognized how important the organization was, and not only in the legitimacy realms of symbolic politics. The UN was an invaluable source of guidance and information, offering many venues for symbolic politics and human well-being that strengthened transnational activism. This had behavioral consequences that brought many realities in the world into a closer conformity to the values enshrined in the UN human rights documents and the Charter itself.

We review here, in the spirit of illustrative confirmation, a tiny sample of valuable contributions of the UN outside the domain of war prevention.

### FOOD SECURITY

By way of the UN Special Rapporteur on the Right to Food and otherwise, the UN has served as an early-warning facility for alerting the world to threats of famine and various forms of food insecurity, including pesticides, nutritional deficiencies, obesity, and market distortions. The UN has also given some visibility to the many abuses of migratory farm workers, the excesses of industrial agriculture, and the importance of treating access to affordable, sufficient, and nutritious food as a right rather than as object of charity and voluntary governmental behavior. Such contributions have as yet not mobilized the political ambition of leading governments or the public to address food challenges in a responsible manner.

### DEVELOPMENT

The influx to the UN of former European colonies in Asia and Africa made issues relating to development far more prominent than was originally contemplated by drafters of the UN Charter. Among the signal achievements withing the UN were a series of UN General Assembly resolutions that legitimated claims to the right to development and permanent sovereignty over natural resources. In effect, developmental priorities of the non-West were challenging the established treatment of foreign investment, trade, and financial assistance, seeking to offset neoliberal capitalist practices by according greater weight to claims based on national sovereignty and overall considerations of equity. This developmental discourse also somewhat lessened the neoliberal orientations of the Bretton Woods Institutions, especially the World Bank and the IMF, giving more leeway to developing countries to promote the social and economic well-being of their citizenry with respect to formerly rigid demands relating to fiscal-discipline-setting conditions for credit and assistance.

## HEALTH

The positive role of the WHO has already been discussed with respect to the COVID-19 pandemic, as well as the dysfunctional US geopolitical push-back. The larger picture, however, includes the evidence created by earlier epidemics (such as Ebola and SARS) of the invaluable significance of a central coordinating capability in relation to health information, including evaluating the appropriate level of national responses. There is much that needs to be done, including the implementation of a global public-goods approach to vaccine development and distribution so as to restrict commercial, class, and nationalistic manipulations. Post-COVID reports confirm the worldwide threats of a series of contagious diseases.

## ENVIRONMENT AND CLIMATE CHANGE

Through its global conferences, the UN raised awareness of environmental challenges throughout the world that were posing a variety of serious threats to the future. Such consciousness-raising needed to overcome the skepticism of developing countries that Western concerns with global environmental standards were not being asserted in a manner that denied the benefits of industrialism to the latecomers to modernity. Capitalist interests were also threatened, leading an American president to send a message in 1992 to the UN Rio Conference on Environment and Development that "the American way of life," which meant the consumerist standard of living, was "nonnegotiable."

## HUMAN RIGHTS OF WORKERS, INDIGENOUS PEOPLES, WOMEN, CHILDREN, MIGRANTS

The UN has strengthened human rights far beyond original expectations, which tended to regard human rights as subordinate to sovereign rights and their international protection as aspirational rather than obligatory. Such modest expectations were confirmed by the formulation of a human rights framework as a declaration rather than a lawmaking treaty or covenant. The Universal Declaration of Human Rights (1950), despite its declaratory form, came to exert a growing influence as it provided transnational civil society with a set of authoritative standards. Under the impetus of the Cold War, human rights became a zone of ideological conflict with two consequences. First, governments on both sides of the ideological divide purported to take human rights seriously as integral to their legitimate political identity; second, the divide led the West to stress civil and political rights, while the East emphasized its commitment to economic and social rights. The questionable result was to split human rights in two, while making the transition from the permissiveness of a declaration to the obligatory character of a covenant. The latter resulted in two documents: the International Covenant on Civil and Political Rights (1966) and the International Covenant on Economic, Social, and Cultural Rights (1966). Despite embodying the UN framing of human rights in international law, the implementation of human rights remained largely a matter of self-enforcement at the country level, with the important addition that civil society actors could now invoke human rights claims as part of the rule of law.

Beyond this, the UN provided a venue for the negotiation of international instruments of both declaratory and obligatory character that were of importance in the domain of symbolic politics, as well as in support of civil society activism. The UN helped greatly to call attention to the grievances and needs of the vulnerable and victimized on a global level: workers, women, children, indigenous peoples, children, and refugees.

### CULTURAL HERITAGE

For most people, the cultural dimension of international relations is not understood to be an essential element of a viable world order, especially in the present complex and interconnected global setting. Entrusting "culture" to the exclusive control of sovereign states is short-sighted. Cultural affinities can serve to foster more cooperative regional relations, and cultural exchange can overcome many inter-civilization misconceptions and misunderstandings. The UN played an important role in conveying a sense that "an alliance of civilizations" is linked to moving toward a more peaceful world. This inter-civilizational approach emerged as alternative to the "clash of civilizations" hypothesis that gained such widespread acceptance after the Iranian Revolution in 1978 and seemed to prevail in the West after the 9/11 attacks on the United States.

In more practical and less salient ways, the UN by way of UNESCO contributes to inter-cultural understanding and dialogue. UNESCO is responsible for promoting cultural heritage sites throughout the world, an affirmation of the achievements of the past, a valuable resource for humanity.

### INFORMATION

It is rarely discussed and even more rarely appreciated that the UN, plays a crucial although sometimes contested role in providing the governments and publics of the world with trustworthy information on world economic data, environmental and health issues, and human rights hot spots. A reliable foundation for assessing factual claims is an indispensable precondition for the adoption of policy initiatives across the entire spectrum of the global agenda. Although many of the numerous UN reports gather dust on library shelves or in obscure digital files, many are relied upon to get a clear picture of reality at a time when social media and mainstream news outlets can be deceptive and the source of dangerous and inflammatory conspiracy theories, racism, and hate speech.

And yet, the UN role, as in most of its important undertakings, has some problematic aspects when it comes to providing the world with trustworthy information. As elsewhere, when important interests are at stake, geopolitics can take over, either suppressing or manipulating information, sometimes confounding the distinction between information and propaganda. A clear, telling example concerns the work of the UN Centre on Transnational Corporations, established to collect and make available information pertaining to the activities of these corporations. It critically considered their practices in contexts of foreign investment and thus became a thorn in the side of corporate and financial operations. Its very effectiveness turned out to be a liability, and in a blatant geopolitical intrusion, the UN Secretary-General fulfilled his pre-election pledge to abolish the Centre in 1991, shutting down a facility that had usefully allowed the Global South to better protect their national economic interests. An analogous interference with a valuable internationalist undertaking is the very inflammatory context of allegations of recourse to chemical weapons by a country engaged in combat operations was discussed in chapter 7 in relation to the contested alleged Syrian use of sarin gas in the Syrian town of Douma in 2018.

## Concluding Note

The preceding illustrative sketches of areas of international life where the UN complements the role of states in serving the global public interest should be part of an evaluation of its overall benefit to humanity. Each of these UN areas of activity deserve extended consideration in book-length treatments; there are many valuable studies available but not any that share our concern of situating the work of the UN outside war prevention contexts and in a broader framework of an evaluation of the UN's strengths and shortcomings. We have tried to make this case for an upgraded feature of UN success as a feature of world order, while noting its weaknesses that are mostly associated with an understandable susceptibility to a variety of pressures exerted by geopolitical actors, as well as from its limited mandate to intrude upon the sovereign prerogatives of its members. These weaknesses are magnified in the present era of autocratic leadership and resurgent nationalism in many of the most important member states and to some extent in all five veto powers. Not until the UN enjoys more budgetary and political independence can we expect these weaknesses to disappear. And as with any bureaucracy, there are internal issues of competence, integrity, and corruption that need attention. Because UN performance is often measured by satisfying governmental member states more than by producing desirable policy outcomes, the quality of the UN civil service is not as good as it should be, although there are within UN ranks many talented, dedicated, and uncorruptible civil servants.

The main point remains. The value of the UN cannot be judged by considering exclusively, or even principally, its experience in war-prevention contexts. Once stated, this probably seems obvious, but because public perceptions of reality have become so dependent on how the media reports the news, it is not surprising that the UN continues to be judged almost exclusively by reference to its record with regard to war prevention, especially in instances where humanitarian costs of prolonged combat are high and superfluous in relation to the underlying behavior and the violent conflict persists, especially in what are aptly being called "forever wars" (Afghanistan, Syria, Yemen, Republic of the Congo, Ukraine).[14]

Our principal assertion is that despite the obstructions associated with geopolitics and statism, the UN by its contributions in many spheres of international life has vindicated the claim of being an indispensable feature of a sustainable and positive world order. It is our belief that with more independent and increased funding, as well as greater forbearance by geopolitical actors and more appreciation by member governments, civil societies, and the media, the UN could enlarge these contributions and more convincingly demonstrate its relevance to world peace, global justice, ecological stability, and overall planetary sustainability. Such an assessment should not be confused with an expectation that the UN can address such basic structural problems as predatory capitalism, global militarism, and ecological unsustainability. The transformation of these underlying conditions depends on the rise of a progressive transnational movement of peoples that becomes strong enough to exert a benevolent influence on governmental and international institutional practices.

# NINE

# Civil Society Participation in the UN: Opportunities, Obstacles, and Pitfalls

## Early Days of Cooperation between UN Agencies

For many decades, villagers and slum dwellers and most UN civil servants in country offices around the world never met, nor did UN civil servants working in New York interact with diplomats accredited to the UN. There were exceptions, but few. In the field, UNICEF, FAO, WFP, WHO, and staff of other UN agencies worked with people in villages and poor urban areas in installing water-supply and sanitation facilities, introducing better agricultural practices, providing primary health care, and training teachers. At UN headquarters in New York, Secretaries-General and other senior staff interacted with government representatives to remind them about their responsibilities for peace, security, and people's well-being, but they seldom had contact with citizens to get a feel for their life, their hopes, dreams, fears, concerns, and ambitions.

In the early years, there was little cooperation between UN specialized agencies, the UN Development Programme (UNDP), the World Bank, and various UN funds and programs. Revealingly, prospective beneficiaries usually were not involved in the design and the implementation of programs. The UN would identify sectors suitable for assistance, but often with little input from governments or local authorities. This one-way street of cooperation changed over time as governments in the developing world gained experience and self-confidence and began to demand inclusion in determining priorities for project planning and execution. The UN role became more interactive and more receptive to the local context.

Cooperation within the UN System at the time, if there was any, had to do with links between UN agencies such as UNESCO, FAO, and ILO and UN sources of funding, which at the time was mainly the UNDP. While the UNDP was recognized by the UN System as the informal leader in the management of UN technical assistance, a UN System esprit de corps in any formal sense did not exist beyond occasional meetings—for example, to discuss security matters in response to coups d'état and national strife that often shook the developing world. A high visibility of coming together would occur only when a UN Secretary-General or other senior UN officials visited a country. Dialogue among UN entities in the field about a common development strategy was absent.

What was seen in the late 1950s and 1960s as a preferred splendid isolation to safeguard the turf of individual UN entities eventually led to a growing awareness that UN activities in those years often manifested flaws due to duplication, a disregard for the benefits of joint approaches, and insufficient consultation with governments of recipient countries. The UN System also failed to take account of local voices, grassroot knowledge, and environmental concerns. To partner was neither in the mindset of the UN System nor the wider, mostly Western donor community.

## Improved Program Coordination

In a subsequent phase of UN development cooperation (1970s–1980s), the complexity of UN System programs and projects increased significantly,[1] as did the diversification of funding sources. In 1985, the General Assembly had requested the Secretary-General to re-examine "all aspects of coordination in the UN System and to submit to the 42nd General Assembly session a comprehensive report with recommendations for enhancing coordination."[2] Meetings of UN heads of agencies, funds, and programs chaired by the Secretary-General took place at regular intervals in what was then called the Administrative Coordination Committee (ACC; as of 2001 renamed the Chief Executives Board). On these occasions, more time was used to improve program rather than administrative coordination. Costly substantive overlaps that had existed in many areas were gradually eliminated by this UN body, which increased from thirteen to thirty members in 2020, with fifteen UN specialized agencies, twelve UN funds and programs, and the International Atomic Energy Agency, the International

Organization for Migration, and the World Trade Organization, a non-UN organization.

The water sector serves as a good and successful example of coordination. WHO, UNICEF, the UN Industrial Development Organization, the World Bank, and the UN itself had each carried out their own water projects without consultation with other UN entities or local communities. Under ACC directives, however, it was decided to negotiate letters of understanding that would delineate boundaries of involvement and thus end counterproductive and costly parallelism. The Secretary-General also stressed the value of UN partnerships with established NGOs. However, there was still no effort either by the Secretary-General or the General Assembly to promote interactions with grassroots civil society organizations.

## Increased Participation of National Counterparts

It was in those years that national professional counterparts were becoming available to join international UN experts in project implementation. It was quickly recognized that the involvement of local staff would accelerate nation-building and furthermore establish links between the UN and people at the grassroots level. It was, however, no more than an important but modest first step. The role of UN experts was seen as containing both benefits and liabilities. This obvious conflict of interest between UN project personnel and national counterparts became a regular and sensitive topic of discussion between UN leaders and governments.

These changes occurred at a time when many governments of developing countries were anxious to demonstrate political sovereignty through postures of socio-economic self-reliance. As it turned out, global dynamics would show that the peoples of the South had overlooked the grim realities of power, greed, and corruption at national and international levels, as will be discussed later.

During the 1990s and beyond, UN activities remained detached from cooperation with local communities. Very little was done by the UN System to include the people, the ultimate recipients of external support, as indispensable partners and participants in the development process. Neither governments nor UN leadership at headquarters or in the field were ready yet to make the necessary policy changes and accompanying psychological adjustments. The following six examples from direct personal experience in the 1980s clearly confirm this assessment.

1. The San people of southern Africa, commonly referred to as "Bushmen," the hunters and gatherers of the Kalahari Desert, have learned to survive under the harshest of conditions. To do so, they often preserve precious water in ostrich eggs, which they bury in the sand to save their contents for times of extreme water shortage. When asked what they needed more than anything else, their answer was immediate: "Water, we need water." In response, UN staff found local carpenters to assemble small wooden boxes with glass tops that collected condensation water from morning dew in the desert. These were miniscule but helpful additional drops of water for these tribal people. This seemingly modest help was enthusiastically welcomed by these pre-modern tribal people and encouraged them to demand more support for their survival from the Botswana government.

2. The UN dispatched an expert to rural Mali to help villagers improve their beekeeping. On arrival, he told them to stop hanging their hives in the trees and instead deposit them on the ground. Beekeepers followed the advice of the expert. After several months of technical beekeeping assistance, the expert was satisfied with the local acceptance of modern beekeeping. He completed his mission and returned to the Malian capital Bamako on his way home to Germany. Due to a dust storm, air travel had to be postponed for two days, so he decided to return once more to "his" village. On arrival, he was shocked to see that the villagers had once again hung their beehives in the trees. Asked why they had done this, the farmers let him know that they had agreed to place the hives on the ground because they did not want to hurt their guest's feeling.

3. Ghana has beautiful sandy beaches, which foreign residents were eager to visit. There was an obstacle, however: the beaches were often covered with human excrement because villagers along the coast traditionally used the beaches as their toilets. Foreigners, including UN personnel, thought they had the answer: modern toilet facilities had to be built near the villages and away from the beaches. This was done. The problem was solved. But no! The local people did not feel comfortable at all inside the "fine" toilets that had been constructed for them. However, they were glad to make use of the toilet enclosures as storage facilities for their grain, while maintaining their habitual practice of using the beaches for intestinal relief.

4. In Pakistan, the UNDP and FAO had agreed with the government to support a large-scale apple research program in Baluchistan. Apples were an important source of income at the markets frequented by wealthy residents of Karachi, Lahore, and Islamabad as well as elsewhere in the country. In line with their poverty-alleviation policies, the UNDP and the FAO in cooperation with the government wanted to introduce new varieties of apples, better growing practices, and disease control and train poor Baluchi farmers so they could improve their earnings and escape from their lives as indentured servants. Unfortunately, the UN had failed to do its homework. At midpoint in the project, at a review meeting on site, the two UN organizations were horrified to find well-to-do farmers driving late model SUVs waiting outside the research farm. These were not the poor farmers that had been expected. It turned out that the project had been supporting rich landowners who benefited from a UN project while continuing to exploit the very farmers that the project was meant to assist.

5. During a visit to the mountainous Hindukush area of northern Pakistan where the UN, together with the Aga Khan Foundation, was introducing potato growing and fruit drying, we came across a poor, elderly villager. He was proudly showing us a few apple trees in his possession and spoke of these trees as if they were his children. This gave us an idea: we had the apple project in Baluchistan, and we wanted him to see it. We proposed this to the villager. He seemed at a loss, not knowing how to react. He had never been outside the hilly areas of northern Pakistan, let alone traveled in an airplane to a distant place away from his family. We convinced him to overcome his hesitation and spontaneously appointed him as a "UN trainee." A few weeks later, he was off to Baluchistan, in the southern part of the country. In six weeks, the UN project team in Quetta had taught him how to prune, fertilize, and propagate apple trees, carry out disease control, and store and market a harvest. He was a very astute observer, eager to learn from the UN project, but also anxious to go back to his home in the Himalayas. When the time came to leave, the UN project manager gave him 150 saplings with one condition: half of these would be for his orchard, the other half for other residents in his small village. A year later, the good news reached us in Islamabad that not a single sapling had failed to root.

6. In the 1980s, war was rampant in Afghanistan. The UN had launched Operation Salam, humanitarian assistance for all thirty-four prov-

inces of the country regardless of whether they were under control of
President Mohamed Najibullah and his government or the opposing
mujahideen. The UN office in Pakistan's capital, Islamabad, oversaw
UN operations in those parts of Afghanistan controlled by the opposition. The UN had agreed with all Afghan parties involved that support would be given directly to local communities based on priorities
decided by village councils. What emerged was an array of locally
selected micro-projects with budgets averaging $10,000, dedicated to
such undertakings as building farm-to-market roads and small health
centers, cleaning karees systems,[3] and constructing and repairing primary schools, along with other projects responsive to locally decided
needs. Villagers and UN staff would jointly monitor implementation
and expenditures. Keeping control over project activities and maintaining transparency with respect to resource utilization left little
room for misuse and corruption. This created an atmosphere of trust
within the communities. Villagers were confident that they would
get the full benefit of what they had been promised. It reminds us of
our experience with India's panchayats, the village council system,
through which grassroots development is managed locally. For the Afghanistan of today, the UN should remember Operation Salam of the
1990s and negotiate similar programs with the Taliban government.
This would reduce local suffering and help to build trust between local
communities and the central authorities in Kabul.

The above examples illustrate the crucial relevance of local participation in development planning and implementation. The UN has become
well aware that civil society must be involved when technical or capital
programs are implemented at the local level. In the past this had not been
the case at all. Major multibillion-dollar investments by governments, corporations, and international economic institutions, with life-changing
implications for communities, were often undertaken without consulting
those affected by such investments. In fact, not infrequently, the supposed
beneficiaries turned out to be losers exploited by such projects. The list of
such examples is long. Among the well-known cases is that of hydroelectric
dam construction in eastern Turkey, not to supplying electricity to villages
in the area but for the benefit of urban areas far away in central and western Turkey. Well known are also the hydroelectric dam projects in Zambia/
Zimbabwe (Kariba), Mozambique (Cahora Bassa), and India (Sardar Saro-
var). We cannot here detail the complicated debates about the ultimate

payoff value for local communities of such projects and only make the point that governments, institutions, and foreign investors often made decisions about multibillion-dollar investments without any involvement of local communities. In some instances, large numbers of local people were even forcefully resettled, deprived of their livelihoods, frequently without compensation. It was "a story of the powerful against the powerless" in which the UN was rarely able to play a constructive role. The human suffering associated with such activities could be attributed in whole or in part to regional and global institutions ignoring human security.

## Emerging Partnerships with Civil Society

In the 1990s, the winds of reform intensified and "swept throughout the entire United Nations system borne by the profound geopolitical and social changes in the world and affected the functioning of international organizations."[4] There were welcome pressures from some governments and from non-governmental groups for the UN to broaden its outreach and expand collaboration within the UN System and enter partnerships with national and international non-UN institutions. The UN Chief Executives Board, especially the Secretary-General himself, was anxious to use the propitious moment of political receptivity in supporting appropriate substantive and structural reforms, also involving the IMF and the World Bank as parts of the UN System. Its actual participation in more inclusive cooperation with civil society and grassroots-level organizations, despite its rhetoric, was sluggish at best.

The Economic and Social Council (ECOSOC), as a central UN policy-making body, was ready to intensify linkages between economic, social, and humanitarian, as well as peacebuilding programs within the UN operational system. Secretary-General Kofi Annan conveyed to the UN offices in the field that the fullest cooperation of UN agencies, programs, and funds with the UN Resident Coordinators/UNDP Resident Representatives was expected. UN leaders in the field had been given the task of forming UN country teams. These would be located, if possible, in shared premises, would prepare joint programs based on agreed development assistance frameworks, and would be financed, where feasible, through integrated program budgets. As these joint actions were not yet mandatory but voluntary, the results at the country level were mixed. Nevertheless, UN System country and inter-country cooperation, with a focus on civil society collaboration, expanded significantly during the 1990s. An increasingly integrated UN presence at the country level with "one chief, one premise, one program, and one budget" became the order of the day. An unfortunate gap between prescribed behavior and implementation, remains.

There were other encouraging improvements in UN System's teamwork:

1. Joint follow-ups to UN mega-conferences and summits devoted to health, education, gender, population, and other social issues took place.

2. UNAIDS, the UN program on HIV/AIDS created in 1990 by five UN organizations (UNICEF, UNFPA, UNDP, WHO, and the World Bank) were effectively cooperating and by 2020 involved eleven UN entities taking unified global action against HIV/AIDS.

3. The Global Environment Facility, a Washington-based foundation that tackles global climate change issues, including those at the community level, has been working closely with UNDP in coordinating small-scale poverty-alleviation grant programs throughout the Global South.[5]

These examples of UN interactions with local communities show that the UN System had discovered the importance of direct cooperation with grassroots partners. The 1990s saw a modest UN beginning of this crucial shift to people-centered assistance, but major obstacles remained. Among them, agreement on commonalities and a unity of purpose between the UN and the World Bank turned out to be difficult. Development strategies of the Bank in Washington and the UN in New York differed significantly. The best example of these differences has been the UN System response, led by UNICEF, to the structural adjustment programs of the IMF and the World Bank for developing countries. Their message to the UN's financial institutions was yes to structural adjustment but it has to be adjustment "with a human face." The UN insisted that significantly more attention be paid to global poverty issues, and economic concerns were to be linked to human concerns.[6]

All too often, a turf mentality of UN agencies prevailed at the country level, encouraged by national government ministries.[7] These links created difficulties for UN agencies at the national level as ministries expect compliance and loyalty when differences arise between "their" ministries and other national authorities. Constraints on cooperation were further accentuated within the UN System by the different professional backgrounds of members of the UN country teams. Sectoral specialists, such as those from

FAO and UNICEF, and program generalists from the UNDP and the World Bank often had fundamental disagreements on priorities, program content, and implementation strategies.

Despite some progress in mobilizing and coordinating contributions to the UN goals of poverty eradication and people-centered sustainable development, as the Administrative Committee on Coordination had requested in 1996, the UN System fell short in implementing an all-inclusive and people-minded agenda in which NGOs, and urban and rural community organizations would serve as full-fledged partners. Work overload, the lack of appropriate staff resources, insufficient financial means, and at times also an absence of organizational will led to disappointment at the level of performance.

## Linkages between UN Development, Peacekeeping, and Humanitarian Programs

Undeterred by these obstacles, Secretary-General Kofi Annan pursued an agenda of extensive structural and substantive reforms to improve linkages between the UN field-based development system, peacekeeping and conflict management, and humanitarian programs.[8] In recognition of the 1990s as a most volatile "decade of sanctions and disasters," he strengthened the UN Office for Coordination of Humanitarian Affairs.[9] He persistently reminded member governments that the operational UN could meet their expectations only when it received adequate and timely funding. At the end of his first four-year term, he presented to the General Assembly in 2000 his ambitious vision for the role of the UN in the twenty-first century. The timing could not have been better. The need for UN reforms had already been recognized by member countries, transformative actions by the UN were underway, and despite US resistance, there was widespread global acceptance of the importance of multilateralism. Multilateralism was no longer thriving but remained operative, especially in fostering development in the Global South.

Kofi Annan put people center stage rather than governments and institutions. No Secretary-General before him had done so. In the spirit of the UN Charter, he argued, globalization must be configured and regulated to benefit people instead of focused on maximizing profits. Freedom, equity, solidarity, nonviolence, respect for nature and joint responsibilities were values to be shared by all nations and not just as rhetorical endorsements, but through policies and practices. Annan insisted that the UN make every effort "to free men and women from abject and dehumanizing poverty, to free them from the scourge of war and from the danger of living on a planet spoiled by human activities and whose resources could no longer provide for their needs." His voice was that of a man who had the rare ability to feel with his mind and think with his heart—being at once both a pragmatist and visionary.

Kofi Annan in a Gandhian manner reminded us why the UN existed, for what and for whom. His advocacy was on behalf of men, women, and children, and local communities, with special attention given to the disadvantaged and marginalized, the poor and the poorest, and those victimized by globalization. He asked that every nation on earth, whether UN member countries or not, commit to a common mission to work toward the global mental, physical, and spiritual well-being of every person on the planet. This message, we believe, should inform future decision-making globally, regionally, nationally, locally, and individually.

It does not come as a surprise that Secretary-General Annan in his portrayal of the UN hardly mentions civil society and that similarly, the UN Charter makes no reference to it. Civil society is essentially a Western concept. Following the industrial revolution in Europe in the nineteenth century, its relevance concerned the role of peoples living in urban or semiurban areas of Europe and North America. Only when globalization accelerated in the second half of the twentieth century did the West-centric reference to civil society acquire an inclusive global relevance. Civil society, nevertheless, remains one of the "most enduring and confusing" of concepts. It is used internationally as a "convenient organizing composite of non-governmental circumstances involving citizens, community life, human rights, collective action and social change" that often have "nothing in common within or between regions and continents."[10]

## The Emergence of Human Development and Local Knowledge as UN Priorities

The last decade of the twentieth century was full of excitement within the UN System because of the signals from policymakers that they were ready to give much more authority to UN staff in the field and that they expected improved interagency cooperation of all UN programs under the leadership of a senior UN civil servant, the UN Resident Coordinator. Governments wanted to see more alignment between UN technical assistance and World Bank capital assistance. The debate at the UN and at the country level centered more and more on common development concerns such as poverty reduction, primary health, education for all, clean water, improved sanitation, and women's rights. The UN was moving closer to adopting an existential agenda responsive to "we the peoples."

Time was ripe for fundamental changes in international cooperation. In addition to the World Bank's annual development reports that focused on economic and financial aspects of development that the Bank had been issuing since 1946, the UNDP released its first annual human development report in 1990. UNDP administrator William Draper had invited Mahbub ul-Haq, former finance minister in Pakistan and Yale University–educated economist, to produce such a report in cooperation with Professor Amartya Sen, a friend of his from India. The intention was to provide a global perspective contextualizing development with human concerns that extended beyond an economistic preoccupation with GDPs. As such, these UNDP reports affirmed that the purpose of society was for its members to "lead long and healthy lives, to be educated, and to have access to resources needed for a decent standard of living." Through this UNDP initiative, governments, organizations, universities, and citizens are now able to obtain periodic updates providing insights into the social and economic conditions of life at the national, regional, and global levels.

There is wide agreement about the importance of knowing at least in aggregates how long people are living, how many years they attend school, and what their incomes are during a given year. Such valuable quantitative information has given rise to a better understanding of

the status of development within countries, the reasons why there are differences among countries, and what is needed to foster progress;

how better to target investments to accelerate national primary and secondary school attendance; and

the causes of poverty as reflected by levels of income and purchasing power.

Table 3.1 reveals an enormous gap in people's life expectancies, access to education, and individual incomes between the developed and the developing worlds and within countries. It is particularly revealing about education. While in countries such as the Netherlands, Canada, and Norway, practically all school-age children attend primary and secondary schools and prepare for adult life, the reality for children in countries such as Somalia, Burkina Faso, and Niger is the opposite. There, severely inadequate educational facilities leave the young totally unprepared for their future.

The UNDP acknowledged some serious limitations in their reporting, however. First, the data collected was frequently unreliable, especially about those most in need of support, the least developed countries. Second, such quantified comparative data obscures the wide range of differences in life chances within countries with respect to longevity, schooling, and income. The quantitative data does not identify the mental and physical quality of peoples' lives, the quality of health services they receive, the relevance of local cultural traditions in the "imported" educational curriculum, the status of adult literacy, the laborers' working conditions, the fairness of incomes earned, and the nutritional value of available food. Quantitative aggregates, while useful trend indicators, hide quality-of-life differences that needed to be known to adequately respond to national and local needs. In recognition, UNDP and the wider UN System have struggled to obtain quality-of-life information and adopt new indicators now considered essential for development programming. Therefore, the UNDP, together with UNICEF, UNFPA, WHO, and others in the UN System have strongly opposed giving primacy to economic growth policy and rejected the perception of some bilateral and multilateral institutions that "what cannot be counted does not count."

There were unexpected additional obstacles for UNDP that hampered its annual human development reporting. For some governments, this annual report was initially seen as just another UN report. They did not find it a worthwhile contribution to the development discourse; for others, it was politically controversial since it ranked countries according to the UNDP's perceived level of human development. To illustrate: In the late 1990s, the UNDP had agreed with Austria, Germany, and Switzerland, the three German-speaking countries in central Europe, to have a cost-shared German edition of the UNDP report. A few years later, the German Ministry of Development Cooperation refused to continue the co-financing of the German edition. For the ministry, the report was obviously not important enough to be translated. The UNDP was told to instead seek financial support from Mercedes Benz: "UNDP gets the money, and Mercedes the advertisement." The UNDP, of course, rejected this suggestion. When the 1996 edition of the UNDP report came out, Hans von Sponeck, serving at the time in New Delhi as the UN Resident Coordinator, was summoned to the Indian Ministry of Foreign Affairs and was told by the head of the UN division: "If UNDP shows once more a better country ranking for Pakistan with 134, compared to India's ranking of 135, than we do not want to have UNDP in India any longer." A year later, a "miracle" occurred: the 1997 report showed India ahead of Pakistan with a ranking of 138 and Pakistan 139.

It took many years for the UN System to become sufficiently aware that equitable and sustainable development programs could not provide adequate assistance without insights into quality-of-life conditions at the grassroots level and that local knowledge was required for meaningful needs assessments. At UN headquarters, *inclusive* suddenly became a standard part of the daily vocabulary to stress the importance of considering the immediate needs of the rural and urban poor.

With respect to development, the UN showed that it could adapt to global changes and be innovative. The UN System was able to rely on its rich institutional memory and cumulative experience. UN leaders repeatedly demonstrated that the UN had the capacity to assess the challenges of the twenty-first century and the ability to find new strategies and solutions for addressing the challenges that were unfolding. It did not need to be told by governments and outside think tanks what to do.

"Local" knowledge systems needed to be accepted as indispensable elements of inclusiveness. The UNDP, having become aware of this, decided to establish what it called the Accelerator Lab Network with global outreach.[11] Such a network would test new holistic approaches that combined international, national, and local knowledge for meeting sustainable development challenges. The objective was to move from "external thinking to a stronger focus on locally led solutions and from centralized planning and control to influencing outcomes with local accountability." In 2021 UN local knowledge labs operated in 115 countries. Knowledge labs worked on "crowd investing" in Armenia, Columbia, and Egypt; leveraging Islamic finance for public policy in Turkey, Malaysia, and Turkmenistan; and introducing basic income in Serbia, China, and Albania. The UNDP head for Strategy and Planning, Joseph D'Cruz, pointed out: "The biggest mistake we have made in international development for a long time has been that when we come into a context and assume that we have figured out a problem, we think we then have to solve the problem, ignoring the fact that very often on the ground individuals, households, and local communities have already been tackling the issue." No doubt, such an initiative has the potential to reshape and democratize the development process in favor of people and local communities.

The UN in the three-quarters of a century of its existence has become a valuable reservoir of knowledge and competence, which deserves to be recognized as an important global public good. The often-heard statement that the UN cannot be more than the totality of its member states is unfortunate. UN operations constitute additionality. It is wrong to describe the UN in the twenty-first century as being in a "mid-life crisis"; if anything, it suffers from a "mid-wife crisis." Secretaries-General and the system have managed slowly but continuously to improve UN programming, often against all political odds, in accordance with UN Charter principles. The transition from the Millennium Development Goals to the Sustainable Development Goals (2015–2030) for equitable socio-economic progress in harmony with planet Earth is another major milestone.

The number of NGOs with ECOSOC consultative status has continuously increased from 46 in 1946 to 6,343 in 2022. The World Social Forum with the motto "Another World Is Possible" was created in 2001 in Porto Alegre as an emerging global social movement with a mission that is opposite to the neoliberal globalization promoted by the World Economic Forum. In the words of its founder Chico Whitaker, a fervent Brazilian social activist and member of the advisory board of WikiLeaks, the World Social Forum aims "to co-exist with the World Economic Forum," founded in Davos thirty years earlier. Imbued with laudable intentions consistent with UN ideals, it has attracted thousands of people of all ages and from all corners of the world for its annual meetings. Unfortunately, the World Social Forum is managerially weak, has never achieved adequate funding, has only marginally influenced sustainable social change, has experienced a steady decline, and struggles to exist at all. The affluence of the World Economic Forum and its ties to the hegemonic heights of world power are illustrative of the weakness of civil society initiatives as contrasted to the potency of neoliberal corporate undertakings.

## Civil Society and UN Governance

Five years after Kofi Annan had presented his groundbreaking report *We the Peoples: The Role of the UN in the Twenty-First Century*, he submitted to the General Assembly in 2004 a sequel of equal importance entitled *We the Peoples: Civil Society, the United Nations and Global Governance*, sponsored by the UN and prepared by a panel chaired by Fernando Henrique Cardoso, former president of Brazil.[12] The panel's report defined *civil society* as "associations of citizens entered voluntarily to advance their interests, ideas, and ideologies." In proposing such a definition, the report clarified with whom the UN was interacting for the common good of all people. Cardoso and his team argued that "civil society is now so vital to the UN that engaging with it is a necessity not an option," something UN staff and outside observers had felt for some time. Anticipating criticism from governments, the Cardoso panel wanted to reassure governments that opening the UN to the "plurality of constituencies and actors would not be a threat to governments but a powerful way to reinvigorate the inter-governmental process itself." Knowing how the UN tended to react to reform pressures, he made the point that it was not about "how the UN would like to change but, given how the world has changed, how the UN must evolve its relations with civil society to be more effective and remain relevant."

Looking at the panel's recommendations from a multilateral perspective, we share the view of Secretary-General Annan that UN–civil society partnerships would be "one step further for the benefit of the organization and the people it was created to serve." In October 2004, when the General Assembly reviewed the panel's recommendations, no governments openly rejected the report. The EU praised Annan's response to the panel's report by stating, "The Secretary-General, sometimes in the face of opposition, has managed to introduce courageous and constructive changes to the organization." There was widespread agreement in the General Assembly that the UN needed to become more civil-society-minded and link the global and the local. The overwhelming majority of member states confirmed this, either through statements of their delegations or through the pronouncement of the Non-Aligned Movement, the Rio Group of twenty-four Latin American countries,[13] and twenty-eight EU countries. This common position was exhibited in a vote of support for linking "the global and the local."[14]

The General Assembly had realized that a more effective United Nations could no longer hope to succeed without a broadened and more productive outreach to new constituencies. There was a tacit acceptance that "global policy issues were no longer the realm of governments alone."

When it came to specifics, it should not be a surprise that some countries had reservations. To assert some control over civil society participation, the suggestion was made that NGO accreditation should come from the General Assembly. The proposal was right away rejected by the US delegation. Joined by India, the US felt that in broadening UN–civil society cooperation, there was no "compelling case for going beyond ECOSOC" and the General Assembly did not need to be involved. Many governments sought NGO accountability and performance monitoring, urging that general rules addressing UN-NGO engagement had to be taken much more seriously and advocated the adoption of a code of conduct.

Cameroun, Iran, Namibia, Pakistan, Singapore, and the EU insisted that accreditation of NGOs should be undertaken with great care. Zimbabwe expressed concern about the "growing numbers of NGOs and their motives, representativeness, and integrity." Similarly, Cuba, Israel, Jamaica, Venezuela, and Vietnam warned of the dangers of "hidden agendas of outside bodies," recommending to "proceed with caution." India called for due diligence in country-level engagement with NGOs to "ensure that UN mandates are not exceeded, and governments remain the main interlocutors" for UN operations. Singapore made the point that NGOs that "contribute nothing to the work of the UN" should lose their UN consultative status. The Holy See observer mission pointed out that the UN should listen more carefully to the needs and demands of the global community. South Africa recounted the valuable contributions made by NGOs at UN summits. Switzerland urged the UN to "identify best practices" in its efforts to reform UN–civil society partnerships.

Only a handful of countries chose not to express specific views on the Cardoso Panel report. Japan seemed hesitant to react to the report as it was still "opening up space for civil society."[15] Ecuador, with an authoritarian administration headed by President Lucio Gutiérrez, and the Philippines, a country with a long tradition of extensive non-governmental participation in social development, both chose not to take the floor. The Democratic People's Republic of Korea (North Korea) did not even join the General Assembly review. North Korea seemed to have no political space for civic action. The Republic of Korea (South Korea), on the other hand, expressed the idealistic view that "the UN is the sole global forum in which all nations and all peoples have a voice" and therefore, Seoul welcomed UN-NGO partnerships, as recommended in the Cardoso report. Among the P5 countries, France and the UK had agreed to a collective EU statement in support of enlarging UN–civil society cooperation; China "recognized the importance . . . of the participation of civil society in the work of the UN"[16]; and the US was ambivalent, as indicated above. The Russian Federation, normally not shy of stating its position, remained silent about the report. Such diversity of responses about state-society relations and the role of civil society actors should not come as a surprise but prepare the UN for a difficult debate on how civil society can be permanently integrated into the intergovernmental global-order debate.

The NGO community had much to say about the Cardoso report. NGOs were elated that after decades of modest cooperation with the UN, the General Assembly had at last recognized that links with civil society were important enough to be included on the agenda of the General Assembly. When the report became available, a wide array of non-governmental groups, individual citizens, and scholars reviewed its recommendations. An animated debate ensued, which twenty years later is still going on, but without clear results.

We have referred earlier to the importance of funding for the perennially cash-strapped and underfinanced UN operational system. We did so when we discussed the trends of government contributions for UNDP, which showed steep increases in recent years of earmarked funds with donor-imposed conditionality rather than unearmarked core funds that the UNDP could use freely in accordance with its policies. In 2021, only $647 million, a mere 12 percent of UNDP's total annual budget of $5.4 billion involved unearmarked core resources.[17]

While some NGOs also feared the link between funding and political pressures reflecting donor preferences, other NGOs were more "flexible" about accepting funding. Still other NGOs used funds as directed by their donors rather than in consultation with local beneficiaries. This underlines the importance of strict UN rules of accreditation and monitoring to ensure that UN–civil society partnerships are carried out in accordance with UN policies and the principles of the UN Charter. It must be remembered that in the early years, NGOs were almost exclusively of Western provenance and reflected Western interests. Today, local NGOs can be found in every corner of the world, yet within transnational contexts, Western-based and Western-funded NGOs still command the heights of influence, nowhere more so than with respect to human rights.

As we set out to prepare this chapter, we spoke about a global "NGO community" but quickly realized that such a community does not exist, just as there is no "international community" or "world community." The language of community is blithely used despite the absence of shared values and policy priorities. Apart from enormous diversities of purpose and objectives, there have been striking differences between the NGOs in the developing world concerned with national and regional priorities and NGOs in the developed world concentrating on the entire world. The former want to contribute to socio-economic progress in their communities but are often ill-equipped to do so in terms of both human and financial resources. There was certainly ample room for NGO-South and NGO-North partnerships. Circumstances have changed as Southern NGOs have become more professional, more self-reliant, and more autonomous, frequently receiving outside support from donor governments directly rather than as before via Northern NGOs.

This trend from dependence to independence and from largely welfare-oriented institutions to a much broader multifaceted network of Southern NGOs is not different from the trends of cooperation between donor and recipient governments that insist on national execution of their programs. Self-reliance has become the principal norm. The obvious message for the UN and other partners was to always keep in mind local priorities and to confirm that whatever was being transferred was not already nationally available.

As far as private sector corporations and banks are concerned, there is no formal accreditation procedure governing cooperation with the UN. It

is apparent that many enterprises have used cooperation with the UN as a
source of moral authority to legitimize and optimize their commercial interests but without necessarily "humanizing" their business practices. Reviews of the experience with Public-Private Partnerships (PPPs) involving
the UN present a confusingly mixed picture.[18] There is an unquestionable
and urgent need to replace existing UN guidelines for PPPs with detailed
rules of engagement. There should be full transparency to determine
whether agreed-on rules are adhered to and whether cooperation genuinely
contributes to the achievement of the UN's seventeen Sustainable Development Goals. If reviews confirm such contributions, partnerships should be
encouraged to continue. The UN should make sure that both its positive
and negative experiences are widely shared. Public-private partnerships
that fail to meet established standards should be terminated promptly and
the reasons for doing so be made public. An overall conclusion is that UN
PPPs to date have had little overall impact on the life of people at the grassroots level.

   *Promoting People First—Public-Private Partnerships* was the intriguing
title of a publication in 2016 by the UN Economic Commission for Europe
(ECE). The report discussed the Chinese One Belt, One Road initiative, a
mega-infrastructure investment program launched by China's president Xi
Jinping in 2013 in Beijing as a centerpiece of Chinese foreign policy.[19] The
ECE states: "To rebuild the old silk road by land and sea . . . giving a considerable boost to the prospective public-private partnerships in emerging
markets, can have a spill-over effect for the UN Sustainable Development
Goals, and by 2050 possibly advance 3 billion more people out of the low-
income category into the middle class." Leaving aside the politics involved
and the questionable projections regarding the number of people likely to
gain from such massive investments, we agree with the ECE that "people
should be the priority and main beneficiaries." The New Silk Road program
in which over half of UN member countries are involved could become
a model for the application of human rights-based and climate change–
sensitive PPP rules of engagement between NGOs, the private sector, governments, and the United Nations.

   In addition to NGOs and the private sector, there are foundations,
mostly American, that have become partners with the UN in the delivery
of people-centered development assistance. Among the first foundations to
establish a connection to the UN was the Rockefeller Foundation, which
in 1946 donated to the UN the land on New York City's East River where
the UN is headquartered. Today, the Turner Foundation is by far the largest foundation supporting the activities of the UN.[20] In 1998 it agreed with

Secretary-General Kofi Annan to establish the UN Foundation (UNF), a very misleading name since it is not a UN entity but a US-incorporated institution whose mission is to "demonstrate the value of investing in the UN, encourage new partners to work with the UN and promote strong US leadership at the UN." In the twenty years of its existence, the UNF has mobilized $2 billion for the UN System from various sources, including the Gates Foundation, the Rockefeller Foundation, the Vodafone Americas Foundation, and US companies. According to Ted Turner, the UNF currently focuses on "some of the greatest collective action challenges of our time, including achieving the Sustainable Development Goals and the Paris Agreement on climate change." As a driving force behind the opening of the UN toward the business sector, the UNF has cooperated with many US business partners.[21] There is nothing intrinsically wrong with such collaboration, as long as the UN fully protects itself against manipulation. The insistence on strict rules of accreditation and monitoring apply to UN partnerships with foundations, relying on similar standards to those applicable to UN cooperation with NGOs and the private sector.

Our general concern about UN vulnerability to manipulation exists, however, whenever the organization relies on outside funding to fulfill its mandate because of inadequate financial resources. It seems appropriate to refer once again to the iron chain of funding controls governing the UN's regular budget that were put in place by governments. After decades of prohibition, these controls need to be relaxed to enable the UN to have access to additional sources of revenue. One option would be to impose an international tax, for example, a "Sustainable Development Goals solidarity tax" levied on all international financial transactions. In one form or another such a tax has been proposed many times. When and if this happens, the humiliating yearly rounds of begging-bowl diplomacy by Secretaries-General and other UN leaders would no longer be necessary.

There is one other type of UN partnership: cooperation between the General Assembly, the Security Council, and the operational system of the UN with members of national parliaments (MPs). Such contacts, rare as they are, have existed for many years. MPs, including ministers, get briefed by UN country teams and visit UN projects. As one example, in 1993, the UN country team in Pakistan composed of thirteen UN entities, excluding the World Bank, presented an "open letter on human development" to political parties represented in the National Assembly and entered into a dialogue with MPs. Although these politicians appreciated this initiative, the Pakistani foreign ministry considered it inappropriate UN interference in Pakistan's national affairs.

UN policymakers also realize that when briefing visiting politicians, these contacts can make the difference between political and financial support. For them it is important to demonstrate that the UN implements locally what it has promised internationally whether it involves development, security, or peacekeeping. They emphasize no longer what the UN hopes to achieve but what it has achieved. "FAO will contribute to food security in northern Pakistan" is replaced by "FAO has introduced potato growing in the Himalayan valleys of northern Pakistan, and 629 villagers are now more food secure during the harsh winters in the mountains." The UN has learned that glossy booklets expressing infinite optimism about tomorrow's possible achievements are far less convincing than reports of progress. The UN System has come to understand that such reassuring messages of performance and achievement need to be transmitted regularly to parliaments, governments, NGOs, and most importantly, to civil society. The UN should respond to the admonition "do more with less," as has been suggested at times by major donors, with a convincing explanation of why it could "do more with more."

The long-standing partnership between the UN and the Inter-Parliamentary Union (IPU) constitutes a valuable bridge to improve the level of understanding and appreciation by members of national parliaments of the work of the United Nations.[22] The IPU points out that "working with the UN is a crucial and growing part of our work" and it therefore welcomes more interaction with the UN. At the same time, the IPU is worried that suggestions as made by the Cardoso Panel for more and possibly formalized General Assembly contacts with civil society could lead the UN to establish its own inter-parliamentary structures. The IPU sees this as a first step toward a UN global parliamentary assembly for international cooperation and rejects the efforts of the Campaign for a Parliamentary Assembly promoted by a global network of parliamentarians, NGOs, scholars, and dedicated citizens that advocate democratic representation of the world's citizens at the UN. This campaign, it is argued, would give elected citizen representatives, not only states, a direct role in global policy and "could contribute to overcoming the increasing [global] legitimacy gap."[23]

The argument for a people's assembly or parliament is to enrich the policy dialogue at the UN and to ensure that grassroots perspectives are given a venue to express grievances and aspirations. Proponents point to the role played by the European Parliament in adding a democratic dimension to the workings of the European Union. Opponents worry about encroachments on national sovereignty and a bureaucratic diversion from an already overburdened, under-resourced UN System.

## UN System Media Outreach

Following the leads by UN agencies, with UNICEF at the forefront, the UN has come a long way in broadening its media outreach to the public. Its Department of Global Communications (formerly the Department of Public Information) and the global network of UN Information Centres remind us that the UN has been communicating for some time with the world in the six official UN languages with a media outreach a people's organization should have.[24]

Over the years, the UN has opened more and more of its windows to inform civil society about how it functions and why it is relevant to civil society's needs, hopes, and even dreams. At the same time, citizens throughout the world in turn want to inform the UN about their lives, their needs, fears, grievances, and hopes. Our own UN experience confirms that the UN System, however, is still ill equipped to respond to public contacts. We have seen letters of appeal, communications that contained important political insights, requests from minority groups for UN mediation assistance, messages of despair, cases where former UN staff tried to intervene on behalf of individuals, and requests from whistleblowers for protection. These various civilian efforts to connect have two features in common: silence from the UN and resentment from people whose pleas have remained unanswered. This is clearly unacceptable and to the detriment of the UN image. No doubt, it has more to do with the UN System's structural incapacity to respond rather than with UN staff's deliberate lack of empathy, but it also has to do with a reluctance of senior UN officials, such as the UN Secretary-General or the UN High Commissioner for Human Rights, to deal with politically sensitive matters raised by outsiders, especially when they involve major UN member countries.

The General Assembly and UN executives need to find ways to end this serious communication barrier. The UN, as a people's system, must realize that communication facilitating direct contact with civil society is part of its fundamental institutional responsibility. The UN is failing to fulfill its prime mandate when it seems to be unreachable by grassroots voices. In this context, we find it curious that the UN website identifies civil society as "the third sector of society along with government and businesses." It would be more appropriate for a UN website to identify civil society as "the first sector of society followed by government and the private sector."

There should be no difficulty in finding the human and financial resources to establish UN-wide facilities that improve interaction with civil society, making it mandatory for the UN System to respond when civil society seeks help. It may be burdensome, but it is the foundation of UN legitimacy that is too often brushed aside as a meaningless impediment to the top-down mentality of UN officialdom.

## Civil Society as Institutionalized Partners

Over time, global citizenry has steadily moved from the sidelines to the centers of interaction. The intergovernmental debate about development and socio-economic progress is becoming more people-minded. More international law has been created to protect people's rights. Voices from the street and populist protest can no longer be ignored by governments and intergovernmental institutions. As we have shown, local knowledge has started to have impacts in political decision-making. Partnerships and consultations at all levels are growing, giving more weight to redressing imbalances between constituencies due to disparities of wealth, gender, ethnicity, and influence. Such encouraging developments have come a long way, but they also have a long way to go. The UN is still perceived, by and large accurately, as an organization only of sovereign states, especially in the context of security and the use of force.

UN concerns for people and concerns for the habitat in which they live have been incorporated into the Sustainable Development Goals to create a more balanced coexistence. Despite the slow pace, the UN has proved that as an institution, it is able to adapt and is not a dinosaur bypassed by evolutionary cycles. We want to emphasize that the UN, as an institutional network, constitutes a unique and additional dimension of world order that ensures that global security and welfare are greater than the sum of contributions by 193 member states.

The challenges that lie ahead for the UN as a "193 plus one" entity are formidable. In this third decade of the twenty-first century, there are many that require multilateral attention under UN auspices. Ultranationalism and toxic forms of polarization within countries; regionalism, fundamentalism, and extremism of all varieties; de-Westernization and Easternization; renewed militarization; the rise and fall of political actors, old and new; and of course, weaponry of mass destruction, climate change, and the devastating systemic impacts of pandemics, however, are interfering with constructive efforts to achieve higher quality global governance. Corruption and transnational crimes are omnipresent and are having disabling effects on problem-solving efforts of governments and international institutions. Therefore, political, social, and economic instability are on the rise in all parts of the world and are especially affecting the poorest sectors of societies around the world.

The impact of global wealth and global poverty on people's lives is sobering. "Global wealth jumped to a new high," the Allianz Global Wealth report for 2020 states, and it adds what can only be considered as a facetious aside, "but not everyone benefited." The wealth gap between rich and poor is immense, as the data in table 9.1 show. In these uncertain times, data such as these change continuously, sometimes dramatically, and the seriousness of the impacts of the COVID pandemic and the war in Ukraine have yet to become fully known. The constant reality that remains, however, is the profound disparity in the quality and quantity of life in global civil society aggravated by conflict and militarization, climate change, poverty, corruption, natural calamities, discrimination, and pandemics. What one social scientist has called the "precariat" (derived from *precarious*), a new social class of people who are acutely vulnerable, lacking minimal security, subject to severe mental and material deprivations, is emerging around the world.[25] A World Economic Forum analysis concluded that in 2019 at least 700 million people around the world were suffering from mental health problems because of violence, poverty, and loneliness, conditions that existed before taking account of the added burdens of the pandemic.[26]

Despite the many obstacles and unforeseen setbacks, people have finally "arrived" on the global agenda. Governments can no longer reject civil society's right of participation in the debate about life in the twenty-first century. Partnerships between the UN and the non-governmental world are a new normal and have become a standard consideration for the General Assembly. Local knowledge is appreciated as indispensable for inclusive development cooperation. "The mountains tried to divide people, but people climbed the mountains" in the words of an Afghan proverb. Human disappointment about the myriads of unfulfilled promises of governments and international institutions have become more difficult to ignore even as they remain daunting to fulfill.

## Closing the Global Gap

The gap between the haves and the have-nots constitutes unquestionably the most fundamental and pervasive of all global gaps. The goal of poverty reduction is posited as the first goal among the seventeen UN Sustainable Development Goals. However, given the COVID pandemic, worsening climate change, and global spillovers from the Ukrainian War, the challenges

TABLE 9.1.  The challenge of the wealth-poverty gap.

**THE WEALTHY**

- In 2021 global wealth amounted to $233 trillion.
- 1% of the world's population owned over 50% of global wealth (Credit Suisse).
- 2,153 billionaires had more wealth than 4.6 billion people; 21 billionaires came from the Middle East and North Africa, 73 from Latin America, and 614 from the US.
- Consumers in wealthy countries wasted as much food as the entire net food production in sub-Saharan Africa.
- The superrich avoided as much as 30% of their tax liability.
- Multinational corporations had tax havens in compliance with OECD or IMF standards in countries like Singapore, Ireland, Netherlands, and Switzerland. Many paid taxes at an effective tax rate of close to zero, saving them an estimated $100–$250 billion.
- Despite the COVID pandemic, massive dividends of around $1 trillion were paid out by corporations in 2020.
- For the largest 32 companies, "pandemic profits" jumped by $109 billion in 2020.
- By mid-year 2020, the G10 countries plus China made $15 trillion available to prevent COVID-19-related insolvencies and illiquidities in their countries.

**THE POOR**

- Almost half the world's population earned less than $5.50 per day, and in 2019 (pre-COVID-19) 8% of the global population made less than $1.90 per day.
- In 2014 and 2022, respectively, 22.4% and 29.3% of people were facing hunger; in 2020, due to locusts, violent conflicts, climate shocks, and COVID-19, there was a significant increase of hungry people; 379 million children were missing school meals because of the COVID pandemic.
- $1 trillion of food was lost or wasted; it could have fed 2 billion people, twice the number of undernourished across the globe.
- While good health and well-being had improved for many up to 2019, in 2020, due to COVID-19, childhood immunizations had to be interrupted and malaria deaths showed a 100% increase.
- 2.2 billion people lacked safe drinking water, 4.2 billion were without proper sanitation, and 789 million did not have electricity.
- Foreign Direct Investment (inflows) for developing countries increased by 29.9% from $644 billion in 2020 to $837 billion in 2021.
- Some 400 million people became jobless because of the pandemic. Many of the poorest lost their poorly paid jobs. There was 20% unemployment among the young.
- Migrant remittances, often the source of survival for families in low- and middle-income countries, decreased by 20% from $550 billion in 2019 to $445 billion in 2020.
- 39 million doses of COVID-19 vaccine had become available by mid-January 2021, according to WHO, for 49 richer countries, but in early January 2020, Guinea, a poor developing country in Africa, had enough doses to vaccinate only 25 people.
- Only 34% of global households showed an education completion rate; for the richest 20%, the figure was 79%.

*Sources:* Credit Suisse, Allianz, Reuters, Oxfam, UNCTAD, World Bank, World Food Programme, and the WHO.

of poverty will not decrease in the years ahead. On the contrary, they will worsen unless world leaders address poverty with a sense of urgency, reinforced by energetic job creation, for developing and developed countries alike. To meet this challenge requires a strengthening of the organization, including an unprecedented display of unity by UN members.

In 2020 some 800 million people, or one out of ten, had to live on less than $1.90. "Human rights for all" and "No one must be left behind" are important UN slogans, but they will acquire real meaning only if this ratio changes and the number of poor decreases by 2030, at the latest. Global wealth is such that the problem is not one of resources, the problem is one of distribution. In 2019 the world ate $130 billion worth of chocolate, while the UN World Food Programme had a budget for feeding the poor of $11 billion! The level of development finance has always reflected a pittance compared to the needs. As a reminder, there are presently about 1.3 billion people living in 107 developing countries for whom OECD countries provided aid in the amount of $157 billion, or thirty cents per person per day.

Comprehensive national and international labor conventions and legal norms exist but have failed to prevent such abuses. The General Assembly should feel compelled to adopt a global social contract to guarantee workers a minimum income for dignified survival with no room for impunity for violations.

UN Secretaries-General and the General Assembly, as an assembly of representatives of the people, have a moral responsibility to appeal to governments to show greater respect for the poor and in this spirit, to reduce significantly the often-exorbitant levels of conspicuous spending of public resources by their high officials.[27] The challenge is the moral imperative of equity and justice based on human dignity, about which Dag Hammarskjold, the second UN Secretary-General, spoke in these mysterious words: "Humility before the flower at the timberline is the gate which gives access to the path up the open."

Many of these recommendations have partly found their way into the policies and operations of the UN. The UN has become readier to involve all relevant constituencies in its field operations. Fostering multi-constituency processes and networked governance by bringing people from diverse backgrounds and beliefs together is now consistently encouraged by UN System leadership. While not welcomed by some governments, investment in UN–civil society partnerships and corresponding structural changes in parts of the UN System continue to take place. The Security Council, it should be noticed, has yet to agree to a more institutionalized interaction with civil society.

We cannot end this chapter without reminding readers that support for these moves to enhance the relations of the UN to civil society is endangered by adverse trends in geopolitical relations among the P5 and intensified by the prolonged Ukraine War and by the spread of ultranationalist populism around the world, which goes hand in hand with a decline in compassion for the suffering of others and a distaste for all forms of internationalism. Our hope is that the dangers to all posed by unmet global challenges will help reverse these trends in the years ahead, that is, before it is too late.

# PART FOUR

## TOWARD THE FUTURE

# TEN

# The Unmet Challenge of UN Reform: Institutional and Operational Perspectives

We believe there is a great deal of confusion surrounding the issue of whether the UN is flexible enough to keep up with rapidly changing historical circumstances. Our response is at first no followed by a more positive yes. The no derives from a formal structure, especially apparent in the operations of the Security Council, an impression reinforced by the virtual exclusion of civil society participation. The veto power given to the P5 maintains a hammerlock on the capacity of the Security Council to reach decisions that clash with the interests of any of the five permanent members. It has also blocked needed initiatives to amend the Charter or to reconstitute permanent membership in the Security Council by acknowledging that major changes in the geopolitical landscape of world order require changes in the structure and procedures of the UN System. In this spirit it seems to us that India, Brazil, and Nigeria and South Africa should have the same status as that enjoyed by the persisting anachronistic composition of the P5. Alternatively, or in conjunction, maybe it is time to diminish the influence of geopolitics by eliminating or at least limiting the veto and permanent membership. Such steps, although not likely be taken in the foreseeable future, would at last be responsive to the frequent and deserved Turkish admonition "The world is greater than five."

Yet this pessimism, fortunately, is not the whole story. As this chapter attempts to show, the UN System as an operational reality has found ways to circumvent the formal rigidity of its limitations. The operational UN has been innovative and adaptive, reflective of the normative predispositions of the peoples of the world, who are often victimized by geopolitical priorities. By shows of flexibility and innovation, the UN has contributed to the de-legitimation and eventual collapse of European colonialism and South African racism. Ways were found to enhance the peacekeeping role of the UN even in the midst of the Cold War, and it became clear that the Secretary-General held a post that permitted a creative and independent leader to expand the activities of the operational UN in new directions consistent with the Purposes and Principles of the Charter and the spirit of the Preamble.

It is our hope that this gap between the formal UN as depicted in the Charter and the operational UN can be reduced in the years ahead, especially with respect to the Security Council and the participation of civil society. Enhancing the roles of the International Court of Justice and International Criminal Court in the context of promoting the peaceful settlement of disputes, giving aggrieved countries peaceful remedies, and strengthening accountability for international criminal wrongdoing by those acting on behalf of sovereign states would be necessary preconditions. Also helpful would be more autonomous funding of UN programs by way of an international tax and a selection process for the Secretary-General that diminished P5 influence in the selection process.

The overall goal is to gain respect for the legitimacy claims and performative effectiveness of the UN as the world's optimal governance structure in reaction to the growing severity of global scale challenges in the twenty-first century.

## Constitutional Amendments, Political Context, and Evolving Circumstances

More than other legal instruments, constitutions framing the operations of governmental and intergovernmental institutions confront the most challenging dilemmas of keeping faith with a hallowed framework that was agreed upon to set limits on and guidelines for governance without foreclosing adaptations to fundamental changes over time. This challenge of balancing clarity about what is being agreed upon when the new ordering arrangements, such as the UN, are established against the flexibility needed to cope with altered and evolving realities seems almost impossible to overcome. This near impossibility is further stressed in the UN setting by the extreme reluctance of the 193 political actors that claim national sovereignty to accept limitations on their freedom of action or obligations of accountability with respect to their undertakings. Such concerns are reflected in the constitution-making process that produced the Charter of the United Nations. The salience of global-scale challenges—most notably addressing extreme poverty, global health, climate change, and threats to biodiversity—makes it of continuing importance to lessen the leverage exerted by sovereignty and geopolitical forms of resistance to the establishment and implementation of emergent global norms and procedures adopted in response to changing historical circumstances.

As might have been expected, the UN Charter, as drafted and endorsed in 1945, leaned heavily toward clarifying what was being undertaken by becoming a member and sacrificed the kind of needed and desirable flexibility that future developments throughout the planet have come to require to ensure the well-being of humanity. Conferring the veto power on the victorious states in World War II was a further acknowledgment that the sovereign prerogatives of geopolitical actors could not be curtailed beyond their will whatever the circumstances and was thus an overt recognition of the hierarchical nature of international society and the limits of governance in accord with international law. This feature was complemented by procedural rules that made it difficult, if not impossible, to introduce changes in UN structure and practice over objections from any one of the P5 that might otherwise have allowed the organization to become more effective, self-reliant, and legitimate over time—or contrariwise, that might have led the UN to fall apart or prove less effective in relation to the satisfaction of an array of world order needs, especially those challenging the poorest and most vulnerable countries.

The fresh memories of the devastations of the World War II played a part, as did anticipations of worse to come if a future major war occurred, but so did lessons learned from the past, most relevantly by the failure of the League of Nations after World War I. These concerns preoccupied the political leaders in 1945. This helps explain the stress on war prevention as operationally embedded in the Charter by the unconditional prohibition on aggressive recourse to war in Article 2(4) and the restrictive delimitation of self-defense to situations of "prior armed attack" in Article 51. It proved politically impossible to reconcile geopolitical accommodations with this war prevention imperative. As a result, the Charter conveys a mixed and confused message that over the years has pleased neither realists skeptical of the UN role in world affairs nor satisfied the overwhelming plea of civil society for a stronger UN that could bring peace, justice, and ecological stability to the whole of humanity.

Two factors were very instrumental in giving these prominent features their knife-edged contradictory character: first, the felt urgency of address-

ing wars of aggression both to reinforce the moral claims associated with
the outcome of World War II and to alleviate worries about the dangers of
the recurrence of a war involving major states; and second, avoiding and
overcoming the features of the League Covenant blamed for its disappointing performance, particularly its deference to the norm of the juridical
equality of sovereign states, whether large or small. This insistence on the
equality of states was widely believed responsible for inducing geopolitical
actors either to stay out of the League of Nations, to be expelled for violating
the basic norms of state behavior set in the League Covenant, or to withdraw when their behavior was under serious challenge within the League.
And so, the drafters of the Charter squared the circle by unconditionally
condemning war but giving the most dangerous potential warmakers a
right of exception by way of the veto. What might better serve humanity
and the UN at this time is a right of exception to the veto itself to be exercised in situations of violent international conflict and severe assaults on
human rights by way of crimes against humanity, genocide, and in the near
future, ecocide. There was also the realist sentiment that given the state-
centric nature of global order, the management of power was necessarily
subject to the behavior of the so-called Great Powers, and no written text,
however widely subscribed, could overcome this salient feature of international relations.

Despite the Cold War and rogue behavior by several permanent veto
powers, the UN has managed to prove its value to all members, large and
small, but not primarily in the manner set forth by the Charter Preamble
or Articles 1 and 2 specifying the guiding purposes and principles of the
organization. The UN has succeeded in making itself indispensable so
far by proving useful to governments mainly in ways not stressed in the
Charter, while at the same time disappointing peace-oriented international
public opinion that has watched wars come and go over the years with the
UN on the sidelines, losing confidence in the relevance of the UN to the
all-important war/peace agenda. The Global South, with its focus on facilitating development, is far less disappointed than the West, which initially viewed the UN exclusively through a war/peace optic given further
relevance for OECD countries by championing market orientations with
respect to trade and investment.

Raising the UN profile has also been difficult given a series of global challenges largely unanticipated in 1945, including the growing importance of
climate change, global migration, and borderless health hazards such as
the COVID pandemic, as well as countless other issues that have raised
public awareness of the need for more centralized and effective global gov-

ernance structures that rely on multilateral problem-solving frameworks, which only the UN is presently capable of providing. Yet, despite these globalizing pressures, there is a recent trend for an increasing number of governments to espouse ultranationalist outlooks that reject most forms of global cooperation and accountability. This unfortunate development has further diminished the reputation of the UN whether measured by the promotion of Charter goals or the attainability of the seventeen Sustainable Development Goals by 2030 or its response to the growing global migration crisis, largely a manifestation of prolonged civil strife, extreme poverty, and threats to livelihood brought about by global warming. Few members of the UN regard upholding global public goods as an important enough objective to alter national policy and behavior, despite the pressures of presently challenging circumstances. Additional policy concerns are related to intensifications of geopolitical rivalry, generating prospects of a second cold war and an accompanying arms race, resulting in a further reduced willingness to engage in cooperative problem-solving and to accord the attention and resources required to avoid irreversible damage to the earth's most basic ecosystems, including the natural habitat. To this must be added the emergence of nationalist worries about the reliability of global supply chains upon which neoliberal globalization had come to depend. With China and others, worried about food challenges in the future, leading the way, there appears to be a resurgence of economic nationalism, partly as a reaction to the vulnerabilities of globally dependent countries during the COVID pandemic and partly in response to dissatisfactions with neoliberal globalization that gave rise to a search for greater national economic resilience.

It is obvious that several UN reforms would strengthen the organization, allowing it to serve better the needs of its members and the peoples of the world, promoting the global public good for present and future generations, and meeting those distinctive challenges of the present era that can be successfully addressed only through collective action on a global scale. Such a recognition makes us aware of three kinds of UN reforms:

1. changes that are needed to reflect changes in international developments in the more than seventy-five years that the UN has existed, including a changed geopolitical landscape with altered alignments, the developmental priorities of a postcolonial world, and human security concerns such as climate change, natural habitat, biodiversity, food and energy security;

2. changes in voting rules, funding, and the autonomy of the UN
   Secretary-General that center on strengthening the politically independent constitutional foundations of the UN beyond what was established in 1945; and

3. changes that would ensure greater UN responsibility and capabilities to protect vulnerable peoples, especially migrants and victims of
   severe repression presently and in the future.

In effect, these three reform pathways involve a combination of responses to structural limitations in the original UN design, emergent unanticipated global challenges, and ongoing efforts to have an ongoing mission
to adapt as needed to future developments, including changing values and
policy priorities, increased and more independent funding, and altered
perceptions of global challenges, as aggravated by dangerous patterns of
geopolitical confrontation.

Against this background there arises a central question: can the UN be
changed to better serve humanity given the interplay of current crises of
world order? Several approaches to generate desirable changes in the role
and capabilities of the UN will be considered in this chapter:

—formal amendment of the UN Charter;

—creative and constructive interpretation of the Charter by the UN
  System, especially the Secretary-General and the International Court
  of Justice;

—violation of norms embodied in the Charter by geopolitical actors in
  response to changed strategic perceptions of national, regional, and
  global security;

—reduced reliance on the right of veto by permanent members on an informal basis, reflecting the reemergence of more internationalist leadership in key countries exhibiting greater sensitivity to longer range
  global challenges;

—increased respect for international law and human rights by sovereign
  states, including by the P5 due to a more globalist, empathetic, and
  norm-guided understanding of national interests; and

—greater influence of independent sectors of transnational civil society
  not captive to corporate control, through more direct participation in
  UN affairs and indirectly through expanded roles in many facets of how
  the operational UN goes about meeting human needs and aspirations.

We know what the problems of the UN are and have fairly widespread agreement on what needs to be done by way of strengthening the effectiveness and legitimacy of the organization, but we remain puzzled and distressed by the inability to gain the political traction needed to overcome resistances to change that reflect the leverage of vested economic, national, and geopolitical interests and a constitutional structure and tradition that have proved inflexible in key policy areas. We consider the pathways to reform by reference to their amenability to structural and interpretative change achieved by indirect developments at the level of national governments and civil society, and finally as a result of pressures mounted by ecological, economic, cultural, and political trends that cannot be successfully managed except through dedicated global efforts. We also take note of geopolitical noncompliance with Charter norms due to the persisting strategic ambitions of P5 members as reinforced by overly militarized, unilateralist, and dysfunctional conceptions of national and global security, anarchically lingering in the NATO West.

In the sections that follow, our attempt is to show how the issues raised above can be and to some extent are being quietly addressed at the UN, including by structural reforms via Charter procedures, global cooperative multilateral initiatives, creative executive interpretations of Charter constraints, General Assembly activism, geopolitical noncompliance that can sometimes serve as a form of adaptation, and demilitarization of global security.

The UN is challenged from several different angles to be more relevant with regard to the wider human security agenda; to take account of the rise and fall of regions and countries; to constrain the rogue behavior of and confrontations between P5 members; to be more attuned to changing world conditions, priorities, and values; and to confront the absence of reliable procedures to achieve political accountability, especially by P5 states and their protégés.

### Reforming the UN by Amending the Charter: The Prescribed Mode of Adaptation to Change

The difficulty of amending the Charter can be easily appreciated from simply reading Article 108 addressing the issue:

> Amendments to the present Charter shall come into force for all Members of the United Nations when they have been adopted by a vote of two-thirds of the members of the General Assembly and ratified in ac-

cordance with their respective constitutional processes by two-thirds of the Members of the United Nations, including all the permanent members of the Security Council.

The two procedural obstacles are the requirements of a positive vote and ratification by national constitutional processes of two-thirds of the membership in the General Assembly, including the five permanent members of the Security Council. Often, as in the American case, with treaty obligations, the chief obstacle occurs in the process of seeking a national formal endorsement, which requires a two-thirds vote of the US Senate in support of a resolution favoring ratification of an international treaty. Such approval is likely to be difficult to obtain if the Charter amendment is perceived as encroaching on US sovereign rights, unless it falls within the domain of the "bipartisan consensus" in the US Congress—that is, overarching support for foreign policy positions that are not determined by affiliations with either of the two political parties. Similar difficulties throughout the world at this second national stage of the UN amendment procedure help us understand why there have been so few amendments to the Charter over the course of seventy-five years despite dramatic changes in the global setting and in the character of the challenges facing the UN. One almost comic illustration of UN reformist paralysis is the Security Council's perpetual reliance on "provisional" rules of procedure.

Indeed, despite these procedural obstacles, it is astonishing that the only amendments over the entire history of the UN have been to increase the membership of the Security Council from eleven to fifteen in 1968, or more than half century ago, and to increase the membership of Economic and Social Council from eighteen to twenty-seven in 1965 and from twenty-seven to fifty-four in 1973. This sparse record by itself exposes the structural rigidity of the organization and makes the prospect of changes in such fundamental issues as the veto, funding, or mandatory recourse to the International Court of Justice unlikely to occur except in response to catastrophic international developments of scope and severity comparable to a war between geopolitical actors.

An indirect acknowledgment of the organizational need to address longer-term issues of change is made in Article 109 of the Charter:

1. A General Conference of the Members of the United Nations for the purpose of reviewing the present Charter may be held at a date and place to be fixed by a two-thirds vote of the members of the General Assembly and by a vote of any seven members of the Security Coun-

cil. Each Member of the United Nations shall have one vote in the conference.

2. Any alteration of the present Charter recommended by a two-thirds vote of the conference shall take effect when ratified in accordance with their respective constitutional processes by two-thirds of the Members of the United Nations including all the permanent members of the Security Council.

3. If such a conference has not been held before the tenth annual session of the General Assembly following the coming into force of the present Charter, the proposal to call such a conference shall be placed on the agenda of that session of the General Assembly, and the conference shall be held if so decided by a majority vote of the members of the General Assembly and by a vote of any seven [amended to nine in 1968] members of the Security Council.

So far, such a General Conference has not been held, and even if it had been, the amendment process calls for ratification in Article 109(2) by all permanent members of the Security Council, which would likely nullify prospects for adoption of almost any significant UN reform proposal, especially if, as is likely, it encroaches on sovereign rights or diminishes geopolitical leverage. Interestingly, if an Article 109 conference does not take place after ten years, then its occurrence is supposed to be put on the agenda of the General Assembly, provided such an action is supported by a majority of UN members in a General Assembly vote and any nine Security Council members. It is one of the few provisions of the Charter that partially circumvents the veto, but since the provision has not been acted upon, it has so far had no demonstrable effect of enhancing the adaptive capability of the UN. Article 109 is a potential mechanism for raising consciousness about UN reform priorities that will be considered in chapter 11.

Because the P5 retains the option of blocking the adoption of any amendment to the Charter by a refusal to ratify (Article 109[3]), this path to flexibility does not seem promising. On formal issues of representation, there have been difficulties from time to time, none greater than after the controversial change in government when the Communist movement took control over the governance of continental China in 1949 but was denied UN representation for more than twenty years. After much diplomatic wrangling, an agreement with China was finally reached in 1971 to bring Security Council representation into harmony with political realities. A degree of adaptability can be achieved by heightened public pressure, common sense, and pragmatism among the P5, reflecting their shared outlook that an operationally effective and legitimate UN can often serve their purposes better than can an ideologically congenial grouping of major states.

Experience indicates that changing the Charter to achieve desirable UN reforms seems constrained by vested interests in the status quo and the obstructive availability of the veto to the permanent members of the Security Council that blocks what might have been a useful pathway to reform. It is now limited to unusual circumstances when geopolitical interests converge or can be reconciled on an ad hoc basis. What makes this observation particularly persuasive has been the failure to make any significant formal changes to the Charter over the course of seventy-five years despite the pressures to do so.

So far in its history, support for formal changes in the UN's constitutional framework have not been backed by a strong enough political will to achieve meaningful results. There are few signs that this will change in the near future given the turn away from internationalism and multilateral cooperation in response to problem-solving challenges of global scope. Yet in this period of uncertainty, unforeseen developments may change the present outlook.

There is no doubt that the Charter has a constitutional status with respect to the UN System and remains the foundation of support for legitimate action bearing on many global issues, especially recourse to force. Pope Francis in his important encyclical *Fratelli tutti* puts forward language that reminds us that even though the approach to Charter reform has hampered the growth and development of the UN, it is still a framework for making better global governance from the perspectives of peace, security, ecological stability, and justice: "The Charter of the United Nations, when observed and applied with transparency and sincerity, is an obligatory reference point of justice and channel of peace."

The challenge, then, facing those that believe the world needs a stronger UN and yet must be flexible enough to adapt to fundamental changes of global significance is not to be paralyzed by the present inability to legislate changes through amendments of the Charter. We need to look elsewhere to realize that the UN possesses a variety of other means to address new challenges and take advantage of opportunities. These achievements have reflected their creative application in concrete circumstances. In our judgment, crucial and major UN reforms reflected in the UN policy agenda and operations have occurred throughout the history of the organization. These "reforms" have not depended on amending the Charter. Their discussion and analysis is addressed in the remainder of this chapter. The essence of our view is there exists more potential for reform of the UN than meets the untutored eye.

### UN Auspices for Multilateralism: Agreements, Conferences, and Norms

The UN has played important roles in international life by providing convenient and legitimating platforms for various manifestations of multilateralism, which is better understood as using diplomacy to address issues of widely shared concern on the part of national governments. The UN possesses a globalizing framework of unlimited potential scope that supplements regional and bilateral efforts to reach mutually beneficial collective arrangements in harmony with Charter values.

In our Anthropocene age, a framework for collective action, while necessary, is beset by difficulties due to diverse and clashing interests, differing priorities and values, and widely divergent perceptions bearing on responsibilities for harm and endowments with respect to solutions. There is a problem-solving set of motivations and goals and also a quite separate array of issues relating to fairness, equity, and distributions of burdens and benefits, which also reflect the impacts of inequalities at all levels of international life. When multilateralism succeeds most dramatically, win-win outcomes occur for all participants in the process, and although geopolitical leverage exerts a strong influence that varies with the context, there is some leveling of outcomes due to the requirement that widespread agreement is necessary if negotiated arrangements are to become effective in practice. The absence of a formal veto also is an advantage of UN problem-solving when its mechanisms are situated outside the constraints of Security Council procedures.

There is no doubt that the UN's positive relationship to multilateral approaches with respect to global policy formation is a major underappreciated contribution to world order. It is not surprising that multilateralism works better when it is supported by geopolitical leadership. For the early decades of UN operations, the US and Europe shared a liberal internationalist outlook that tended to promote global cooperation in all forms, despite the obstruction of Cold War constraints. Between 2017 and 2021, this dimension of UN activities was situationally weakened by the concurrence of the Trump presidency with the overall rise of ultranationalist leadership in many important countries against the background of the pandemic, neoliberal globalization, and climate change crises. This inhibited all forms of globally oriented multilateralism and, as in the Cold War, accentuated

partisan forms of coalitions that were more inducive to conflict than cooperation on behalf of the common public good.

A positive example of multilateralism was the long process of negotiating a lawmaking treaty that established a public order for the oceans
that has stood the test of time. The Law of the Seas Treaty that entered
into force in 1982 exhibited the constructive potential of multilateral solutions achieved within a UN setting and benefiting from a self-interested
liberal global leadership orchestrated by the United States. There were
many tradeoffs and bargains that touched vital interests of diversely situated states: for instance, land-locked versus coastal, developed versus
developing, maritime freedoms and naval claims to "freedom of the high
seas" versus territorial self-defense, coastal seabed claims versus common
heritage, global commons versus geopolitical domain, island states versus
coastal states. To find enough common ground to satisfy the range of interests at stake required a combination of diplomatic skill and perseverance. It
also required and managed to include a dispute-settlement procedure that
depended on law rather than force. The resulting treaty did not gain formal
adherence by every state, and most notably and quite ironically not by the
United States, which had presided so determinedly over the negotiating
process. Yet, impressively, because the treaty did achieve beneficial compromises and provided for stability, its provisions have been observed even
by those states that did not formally become parties. The relevant observation here is that despite the US failure to ratify, the agreement was able to
fashion a world-order solution without worrying about an obstructive UN
veto. In fact, the treaty is now widely regarded as setting forth standards
that are part of customary international law, which means that they are
thought by many legal experts to be binding on all states whether parties
to the treaty or not.

The General Assembly gave its blessings to the process and the outcome
even though there are some shortcomings to the Law of the Seas approach.
For instance, its tolerance of unrestricted naval activity under the banner
of "freedom of the high seas" exhibited deference to maritime geopolitics,
allowing the United States to maintain a global naval presence by way of
a vast network of hundreds of foreign military bases. Some of these shortcomings are reviewed in the report of the Independent International Commission on the Oceans.[1]

The Climate Change Agreement reached in Paris is another example of
achieving positive results that are somewhat more obligatory for the UN
membership than General Assembly recommendations yet circumvent the
veto in the Security Council. Such ambitious ordering instruments are de-

signed to serve the global common good subject to constraints of negotiat-ing governments as to the limits of compromise and tradeoffs. To secure the widest possible participation in such an agreement, sacrifices are made with respect to verification, obligatory norms, and even implementation short of enforcement. Such a process is itself vulnerable to change as when ultranationalist leadership of sovereign states withdraw from participation or refuse to uphold what had been agreed upon. These weaknesses high-light fundamental concerns with a statist governing structure for world order in a historical context within which policy challenges can effectively be met only by more centralized and globally oriented mechanisms of con-trol that incorporate equity concerns. At present, the UN lacks this kind of capability and is limited to facilitating functional multilateral problem solving, being unable to decree the shape of solutions that are both effec-tive and fair. As suggested, enlightened international leadership by geopo-litical actors can, if they are so minded, mitigate this structural deficiency of global governance.

Despite these limitations, there are many achievements of a practi-cal character under UN auspices that involve political compromises and tradeoffs, ordering arrangements that avoid conflict and wasteful expendi-tures, uphold global public interests, and do not depend on a P5 consensus to go forward. Related contributions have been made by adopting norma-tive standards that influence national behavior and lend legitimacy to the goals of civil society activism.

Among these achievements, we point to the Antarctica Treaty, the de-militarization of the moon, the elaborate UN human rights architecture an-chored in the Universal Declaration of Human Rights, the UN Covenant of Civil and Political Rights, and the UN Covenant of Economic, Social, and Cultural Rights. There are many more specialized and technical arrange-ments and mechanisms that depend on UN authority to achieve global outreach, including fact-finding missions, commissions, and "special pro-cedures" of the Human Rights Council entrusted with the task of develop-ing policy recommendations and influencing public understanding.

Such instances of multilateralism have not significantly addressed the internal workings of the UN, but there is no obstacle blocking such constitution-building initiatives in the future if a sufficient political will comes to exist among UN membership, preferably encouraged and strength-ened by a civil society movement that exerts pressures to achieve a more autonomous organization that can better withstand geopolitical manipula-tion and move more directly to promote the global common good.

*The Creative Potential of Interpretation: The UN Secretary-General*

In some important respects, needed flexibility with respect to organizational structure that has not been achieved by amending the Charter has been obtained through interpretation in relation to the role of the political organs in authorizing initiatives. There have long been debates about the proper way to interpret a constitutional text such as the Charter. There are two main views: the predominantly European approach, associated with a jurisprudential commitment to limit interpretation to the language of the norm, constructing the meaning of law without any contextual deference to political consequences or moral considerations.[2] The basic idea is that legal language is to be treated as clear on its own without taking account of extralegal considerations. This kind of sharp separation of law from politics and morality reflects the historical struggle centered in Europe to free the governing processes of society from the influence of religion, especially the Catholic Church. The American approach to interpretation was quite different, evolving without concern for insulating law from religious influences, and in any event, pluralist in relation to religious teaching and premised on the inherent ambiguity of law.[3] The adoption of contextualist approaches to Charter interpretations would allow more latitude in interpreting UN activities by going beyond the supposed plain meaning of the Charter text to take account of what kind of meaning under changing historical circumstances would best realize the Purposes and Principles of the Charter.

This ambiguity of legal norms has two main sources: the uncertainties of language itself and the contradictions associated with a legal order seeking to achieve clashing objectives. To overcome the uncertainties of language, the interpreter is obliged to look, whether admitted or not, beyond the language of the text to the intentions of the drafters of the text and, according to some thinkers, by reference to the Purposes of those who created and administer the text, which for the UN Charter is expressed in Article 1. The recognition of these clashing objectives can be conveyed by the relationship between the norm on the equality of sovereign states as members of the UN and bound by international law and the inequality accorded via permanent membership of the Security Council and the P5's veto privileges.

Another such clash embedded in the Charter is between deference accorded to the principle of nonintervention by the UN in matters within the domestic jurisdiction of states and the international commitment to promote human rights and, especially, to offer protection to people facing severe oppression from their own government. To resolve such a clash, the interpreter can pick and choose between applicable norms or have recourse to the socio-political context to determine an interpretation that is most consistent with the Purposes of the UN or with the reasonable expectations of the founders, which can be construed to take account of changing conditions and values. Thus, nonintervention may have meant one thing in 1945 and mean quite another after human rights norms were articulated in obligatory texts and given prominence in UN operations. A UN attempt, stimulated by civil society initiatives, to rely on postcolonial language that did not seem to be authorizing interventions overriding sovereign rights was developed in the aftermath of the controversial Kosovo War. It involved the adoption in 2005 of an emergent legal norm endorsing the right to protect (R2P), which seemed to validate a range of UN initiatives that were protective and humanitarian. The 2011 application of R2P authority in Libya by NATO, as discussed earlier, used a limited Security Council authorization for a no-fly zone protecting a single city to provide the limitless justification for an expansive use of force that resulted in a regime-changing intervention carried out by NATO military action. This behavior was not formally reprimanded but it undermined trust among the P5, inhibiting future uses of R2P for fear of giving a UN cover for controversial geopolitical undertakings.

In domestic legal orders, we entrust authoritative interpretation to independent judicial tribunals that often have sharp internal tensions involving various ways of achieving predictability by adhering to original meanings of norms versus seeking flexibility by taking account of changed conditions or, more problematically, of changed normative priorities of the judges. The situation is different internationally, including within the UN, as there is no regularly available means to achieve an authoritative interpretation. The International Court of Justice has a largely unutilized potential to provide the UN System with guidance as to the interpretation of the Charter and other legal questions that arise, but it is rarely used, and even when used, its authoritativeness is diluted by characterizing ICJ legal assessments as Advisory Opinions, which implies that they are subject to voluntary compliance and a political override. In effect, those acting under the authority of the UN have discretion to interpret along the lines that they see fit, although subject to political pushbacks by way of criticism and withdrawal of support for the renewal of election if part of the UN's administrative hierarchy. In other words, there is considerable discretionary room for interpretative creativity, but it is subject to political reactions and reflects the bureaucratic temperament of the political actor. Is that high civil servant willing to give in to geopolitical pressures and not make waves, or is that high civil servant prepared to take risks to fulfill the purposes of the UN? There are many ways that the ICJ could perform in a more integral and consistent manner that would help realize the Purposes and Principles of the Charter. Such measures could be adopted informally to referencing the ICJ for a quick assessment of a proposed UN authorization of force. If agreed upon, the ICJ would have to establish chambers of three judges, in the manner of the International Criminal Court, to process urgent inquiries from either the Security Council or the General Assembly on very short notice, rationalized in a provisional legal judgment to be put in final form at a later date. The UN could do more to establish the ICJ as a guidance mechanism for the assessment of international behavior by states and international institutions of all kinds. Such a mechanism would serve also as a confidence-building recognition of the importance of increasing respect for and the authority of international law.

Such a dynamic can be seen through the prism of the highest-ranking UN civil servant, the Secretary-General, although it applies throughout the operations of the organization and has illustrated over the course of UN experience both bureaucratic servitude and institutional creativity. The position of Secretary-General is highly sought by governments and individuals. The position has been rotated among regions although the first two Secretaries-General were Europeans, perhaps a parting gesture of deference during the last stage of colonialism. As yet, despite nine Secretaries-General, no woman has been deemed worthy of selection.

This awkward gender bias seems likely to change soon. The appointment of the Secretary-General is by the General Assembly on the basis of a recommendation by the Security Council (subject to the P5 veto; by informal agreement, there has never been a Secretary-General candidate from a P5 country). The Charter rather vaguely depicts the functions and powers of the Secretary-General beyond the authority in Article 99 to bring to the attention of the Security Council any question that the Secretary-General believes is a threat to the maintenance of international peace and security. Article 100 affirms the independence of the Secretary-General, prohibiting any transmission of instructions from a member government to the Secretary-General or interference with the selection of the civil service staff recruited to carry on the work of the UN. In practice, the Secretary-General has had to fight hard to uphold his political independence, illustrated by dealing with overt pressures brought to bear by the United States to deflect criticisms of Israel, as well with secret backroom pressures.

Undoubtedly, the most celebrated example of UN leadership and institutional creativity as it relates to adaptability was supplied by Dag Hammarskjöld, who was Secretary-General between 1953 and 1961 and died in a plane crash induced by sabotage while overflying the Congo on a controversial UN mission. Hammarskjöld established his own interpretative approach, which expanded the UN role beyond the Charter without violating the norms of the text, as construing capabilities that are "not contrary to the Charter, but are in a certain sense outside the explicit terms of the Charter."[4] This perspective offered Hammarskjöld the basis for his most celebrated "innovation," that of peacekeeping, which was a new, vital undertaking between mere observation (Charter, Chapter VI, Articles 33–38) and enforcement (Chapter VII, Articles 39–51), an extra-Charter source of authorization that became informally known as Chapter VI1/2—in effect, an amendment made operational by practice and precedent. This meant that what was not prohibited by the Charter could, if properly crafted and explained, achieve an extension of UN capabilities to fulfill its Article 1 Purposes in accord with its Article 2 Principles without recourse to the easily stymied amendment procedure. Such extensions of UN authority are far from automatic, generally requiring skillful navigation of geopolitical waters.

Peacekeeping became a major UN achievement in the form of the UN Emergency Force I (UNEF) that was configured in a manner that respected explicit Charter norms yet allowed for a flexibility of operations that helped maintain an armistice in a tense post-conflict situation in the Suez Canal area. With the consent of all parties involved, the General Assembly mandated UNEF I to secure and supervise the cessation of hostilities in 1956 between UK, French, and Israeli forces and Egypt over the nationalization of the Suez Canal. The operationalization of such a peacekeeping mission made clear its distinct character of augmenting the general mandate to promote the peaceful settlement of disputes by supplementing an observer presence with a detachment of unarmed UN peacekeeping forces with a clearly delimited mission: consent of the territorial government where troops deployed, UN impartiality as to the conflict, and nonuse of force by the UN except for self-defense and protection of the mission. UNEF I successfully monitored the armistice that brought fighting to an end in the Suez operation, stationing its forces in Egypt on both sides of the armistice dividing line. UNEP II after the 1973 Yom Kippur War also involved a UN peacekeeping mission in which UN-deployed forces in a buffer zone effectively administered the end of hostilities between Israel and Egypt.

Hammarskjöld also demonstrated that some UN contributions outside the explicit job description of the Charter could be made by informal means, what might be called "personal diplomacy." A famous instance was Hammarskjöld's successful negotiation of the release of American pilots captured during the Korean War by his appeal to the Chinese foreign minister, Zhou Enlai, which resulted in defusing a potential flashpoint in US/China relations at a time when Washington refused to accord diplomatic recognition to the People's Republic of China as China's legitimate government. Hammarskjöld also built a highly favorable public image, which made even powerful governments reluctant to criticize his expansive interpretation of his role, although angering the Soviet Union to the point of demanding Hammarskjöld's removal as Secretary-General. It may be that Hammarskjöld's success led governments both to be more cautious about selecting future Secretaries-General and more unabashed in exerting pressure directly by withdrawing support or indirectly through funding.

Hammarskjöld also exerted influence over the way in which international law functioned within the UN System. Although trained in the European tradition of law, he became a professional economist with strong interest and familiarity with religious and philosophic perspectives. Within the ambit of his leadership role, he urged the shift from a minimalist image of international law as a "law of coexistence" to a more multilateralist view, a "law of cooperation."[5]

Later holders of the position of Secretary-General proved to be weaker in their fulfillment of the expectation of geopolitical independence or were censured and their terms not renewed. Kurt Waldheim and Ban Ki-moon are examples of weak UN leaders, while U Thant and Boutros-Ghali did their best to uphold an image of geopolitical independence but paid the price of not being renewed for a second term.

What has become clearer in more recent years, with the decline of US support for multilateralism and its faltering role as global leader, is that the Secretary-General has an opportunity to play more proactive consciousness-raising roles as global challenges come to the surface. In other words, the UN, more than any other venue, enjoys a cosmopolitan identity that gives a Secretary-General a potential mobilizing capability. The current Secretary-General, António Guterres, exhibited a widely appreciated voice of universal devotion to the global common good during the COVID pandemic. This contrasted with Trump's obstructionism, crudely expressed by US withdrawal from the WHO and opposition to calls for global solidarity and humanitarian sensitivity that would have been forthcoming from the Security Council but for the US playing a spoiler role.

The US represents no more than the tip of a far larger nationalist iceberg that is generally making global cooperation for the common good so problematic during this period when its necessity has become so essential if global challenges are to be addressed effectively and empathetically. The post-Trump US administration immediately upon taking office in 2021 tried to restore earlier global leadership role of the US, but it found itself quickly distracted by geopolitical rivalry with China and Russia's Ukrainian attack. What remains a preoccupation is whether the militarized control over global security that created governance illusions of a unipolar world will persist or give way to the multipolar underpinnings of the post–Cold War world in the form of geopolitical realignment. The short-term fate of the UN will reflect the outcome of this still-unresolved struggle about global security, especially as to whether the management of military power is shared or remains subject to Washington's control. In the meantime, the UN is challenged to act creatively under these difficult circumstances.

It is not only the Secretary-General who can fill in the empty spaces in the Charter framework. A notable Security Council example of doing for international criminal law what Hammarskjöld did for peace and security was the establishment of ad hoc criminal law tribunals for former Yugoslavia and Rwanda in the 1990s. The mandate of these tribunals was to prosecute serious war crimes including genocide and crimes against humanity, violations of the laws and customs of war, and grave breaches of the Geneva Conventions.[6] The Security Council's only basis of authority was the claim to be "acting under the authority of Chapter VII of the Charter" but without any reference to a specific article and without any generalized grant of authority to establish international criminal tribunals. The enabling resolutions do try to anchor their initiatives in the generalized language of Charter VII, with the Yugoslav resolution stating that the establishment of the tribunal was necessary because the "situation continues to constitute a threat to international peace and security" and criminal prosecutions will "contribute to the restoration and maintenance of peace." There was no effort made to show the connections between the tribunal and the Charter role of the Security Council. These initiatives showed that the UN could encroach on national sovereignty and its procedures of legal accountability without limit if a political agreement was reached among the P5 plus and four or more non-permanent members. The resolutions also called upon the Secretary-General to "implement urgently" the resolution, which Secretary-General Boutros-Ghali did, by making "practical arrangements for the effective functioning of the Tribunal." In this regard, the main organs of the UN can provide a more pragmatic approach to adaptation and change than could have been achieved by explicitly vesting authority by way of a formal amendment to the Charter.

The efforts to find alternatives to the amendment procedure to enhance the ability of the UN to change should be subject to one important caveat.

There are areas where the failure to amend the Charter encourages a nihilistic disregard of normative restraints altogether. Such a process of cumulative disregard is evident in relation to the core Charter norms on the unconditional prohibition of recourse to force except for self-defense strictly defined and, even then, only provisionally validated in Article 51 until the Security Council fulfills its Charter role by giving an authoritative response to a national claim of self-defense. As patterns of post-1945 conflict changed, with more emphasis placed on intervention and fighting terrorism, the requirements of Article 51 to disallow recourse to force except in response to a prior armed attack directly contravened geopolitical trends with respect to security threats and uses of force to uphold vital national interests. At the same time, an argument could be made that stricter canons of interpretation, if respected, would have served the world better than political insistence on flexibility to meet changed international circumstances.[7] In the context of the Kosovo War, an international commission came up with an influential distinction between *legality* (depending on Security Council authorization) and *legitimacy* (the morally compelling argument for protecting people facing severe humanitarian threats).[8]

In effect, the Charter regime on force would be more relevant to our world today if one of two alternatives had been adopted: if an amendment to the Charter had reaffirmed the anti- aggression norm while reformulating the self-defense exception to the prohibition on recourse to force to allow for anticipatory claims of self-defense placing the burden of persuasion on the claimant or, as an alternative, if the P5 could reach an agreement that precluded use of veto in evaluating "the inherent right of self-defense" to allow a more permissive interpretation of the "prior armed attack" language. This tension between the two parts of Article 51 has been used by less positivist interpreters to argue that the prior-armed-attack requirement was subordinate to the inherent-right phrase, especially those seeking to reconcile the Charter with Western P5 geopolitical behavior, such as Michael Reisman. Article 51 can be interpreted expansively:

> Nothing in the present Charter shall impair the inherent right of individual or collective self-defense if an armed attack occurs against a Member of the United Nations, until the Security Council has taken the measures necessary to maintain international peace and security. Measures taken by Members in the exercise of this right of self-defense shall be immediately reported to the Security Council and shall not in any way affect the authority and responsibility of the Security Council under the present Charter to take at any time such action as it deems necessary in order to maintain or restore international peace and security.[9]

*"Realism with Hope": Toward a Nonviolent Geopolitics*

As argued, a major explanation of the failure of the UN to meet the expectations that existed at the time the UN was established has been the refusal by the P5 to comply with international law with respect to peace and security, which amounts to a constitutionally grounded recognition of the primacy of geopolitics through the right of veto. This primacy could be formally abolished by amendment or mitigated by increasing the authority and role of the General Assembly, but for reasons previously explained, this seems highly unlikely to happen anytime soon. A favorable opportunity to make such adjustments arose in the early 1990s when the Soviet Union imploded, the US was led by internationalists, and prospects for a Security Council consensus on global policy issues seemed temporarily promising, yet nothing happened, even informally, by way of strengthening the UN through the elimination of the veto or by a sense by P5 governing elites that adherence to international law is strategically beneficial given the declining leverage of military power and the capabilities of national resistance movements to neutralize over time a militarily superior invading country.

Yet given the pressures of the times, including the realization that acting collectively and in conformity with the precautionary principle has become the rational alternative to drifting toward planetary catastrophe. The Precautionary Principle adopted in relation to environmental concerns, suggests that behavior should be prohibited if climate experts see it as risking serious harms even if scientific certainty cannot be demonstrated in advance. It may become more evident that militarized geopolitics is no longer affordable, as well as being nonviable. In its place, the reformulation of P5 national interests could make the benefits of achieving the global public good by cooperative problem-solving and greater adherence to the norms of international law more evident, which would also have a tendency toward demilitarizing geopolitics. Especially in the NATO countries, such a process would have to be preceded by a recognition that the exaggeration of security threats over the course of decades produced negative results in foreign policy and in fact induced confrontations due to an overinvestment in military solutions to political conflicts. It also hampered domestic public investment in socio-economic equity. In effect, the UN and member nations would benefit from a more realistic appreciation of the more limited role of military superiority and coercive diplomacy in the postcolonial age of statist world order. In effect, a variety of adjustments would be made in the course of shifting the axis of foreign policy of geopolitical actors toward behavior in accord with a New Realism that was more responsive to the dangers and characteristics of twenty-first-century global conditions, including nuclearism, war, pandemics, climate change, and ecological dysfunction. The Ukraine War and its effects undermined such hopes, leading the West to move toward confrontation reminiscent of the Cold War and leading the non-West to find ways to preserve its interests and resist unilateralism by organizing its own political and economic coalitions, as with the BRICS and the Shanghai Cooperation Organization.

### International Law from the Perspective of Human Security

Instead of awaiting amendments of the Charter, the brightest hope for UN reform rests, as always, on transformations of political culture within major sovereign states and civilizational structures. When the P5 governments respect the constraints of the Charter and the political will of a majority of the Security Council, we might come to expect P5 states to abstain rather than to block action by casting a veto. It could be argued that UN reform may be achieved by a dramatic shift in geopolitical practice, reflecting a reformulation of national and geopolitical interests in favor of adhering to international law rather than continuing recourses to aggressive force to satisfy traditional strategic ambitions. Respect for international law and international procedures would accept the need of the strong to be as accountable and compliant as the weak. To be sure, this might strike realist readers as a distracting detour by way of utopia fantasy, yet we insist that this is "a necessary utopia" if the human species has any plausible prospects of avoiding future catastrophes. Geopolitical prudence and responsible crisis management, while desirable, are unlikely to be enough. The COVID health crisis gave the entire world a foretaste of a catastrophe arising from climate change or nuclear war or the destruction of biodiversity, but it will only help political elites adapt if they view the pandemic as a metaphor as well as a worldwide calamity endangering their own lives and interests in the future. That the pandemic originated in China yet impacted the West most heavily is both a reminder of interconnectedness and a stern lesson that often in human experience, wealth and military capabilities no longer make the human condition more secure. The Ukraine War, a flaunting of the UN Charter and international law on all sides, is a further demonstration of how much the peoples of the world need to stop handing get-out-of-jail-free cards to P5 and act upon the urgency of adhering to a Westphalian Charter framework by rejecting a geopolitics of impunity and even non-accountability.

Given the complexity and fragility of world order in the age of climate change, aggressive wars, and nuclear threats, the future of humanity depends on establishing a global legal order sensitive to legitimate grievances and needs of vulnerable peoples, the stability requirements of ecosystems, and responsibility to future generations. Such a legal order presupposes a robust global governance underpinned by international law applicable to all sovereign states, which, to repeat, is not the design embedded in the Charter back in 1945.

Yet to affirm the need for international law is not enough. We should have learned that autocrats use law mercilessly to impose their will on the public, suggesting that law in the service of oppressive and exploitative power is not compatible with UN values or the human interest. We call instead for law rooted in human security, the security and well-being of people and their habitats, for law linked to fairness, justice, and an ecologically viable future. And for law that is sensitive to the imperatives of the age of climate change, warfare, and nuclear threats, along with reliable accompanying accountability procedures. We also urge diligent adherence to the precautionary principle of reducing risk by timely responsiveness to the warnings of history, the guidance of experts, and the wisdom of spiritual leaders and indigenous peoples, voices of moral authority, and representative worldviews of pre-modern indigenous peoples.

### The Mobilization of Civil Society

Complementary to geopolitical demilitarization would be an activist mobilization of transnational civil society demanding reforms in geopolitical actors in line with priorities that stem from "human security," in all probability focused on human well-being and ecological stability, rather than from "national security," grand strategy, chauvinistic nationalism, militarist imaginaries, and ecological irresponsibility. Above all, political action that relies on hard power and imperial approaches to dominance, development, and order in foreign and domestic political life must be delegitimized and sidelined. Such a populist mobilization would seek not only reductions in carbon emissions by respecting the consensus of climate experts but also insist on increasing support for climate justice in allocating the costs of adjustment nationally, regionally, and globally. If the operational UN became receptive to such political messaging, it would instantly become what the Charter envisaged and not the instrumental geopolitical mechanism that took over the management of peace and security. As we have suggested throughout, the UN has over the decades proved its value to a humane future in many ways, yet not yet in relation to war prevention, and so it might return to its animating vision of preserving the peace as the world teeters on the precipice of geopolitical confrontation. People every-where are growing aware of the abiding dangers of living with the nuclear weapons and of the immense opportunity costs of enduring a second cold war at a time when the resources, attention, and problem-solving acumen of the world need to be focused on global challenges arising from climate change and destructive effects of ongoing warfare in several parts of the planet.

One role of civil society is to exert pressure on UN members to live up to the Purposes and Principles of the Charter, which includes a commitment to seek peaceful settlements of international disputes and a cooperative approach to shared challengers of global scope. This kind of fundamental shift away from militarism involves a call for "amending" the operational UN so that it acts in the spirit of the Charter itself, especially the Preamble and the first two Articles. This has started to happen as a result of units of the UN System interacting increasingly with non-governmental institu-tions and civil society and benefiting from specialized repositories of rel-evant experience and knowledge. What the peoples of the world appear to desire and expect from the UN, as expressed in a global survey made as part of the observance of its seventy-fifth anniversary, suggests less of a focus on war prevention and more attention to cooperative approaches to health for all, food security, equity with respect to the allocation of the ben-efits of economic and social development, and climate change.[10]

## Adapting to the Changes in the Geopolitical Landscape

As pointed out earlier, the UN as established was above all responsive to the interests, proposals, and beliefs of the nations that had won World War II, which included the two European colonial powers, the US, the USSR, and China, a country then in the midst of a civil war. The legal arrange-ment at the Security Council was less reflective of power relationships than the geopolitical designation assigned by international relations scholars who focused on the predominant military power of the US and the Soviet Union and described the world political order as one of "bipolarity," featur-ing what became the standoff between these two superpowers with antag-onistic ideologies and strategic ambitions.

Large countries, such as India, Brazil, Nigeria, and Indonesia were not considered as belonging to the victorious coalition or important and rich enough or traditionally prominent enough to enjoy a privileged status within the new organization. Colonialism persisted in Africa and Asia, and Latin America was treated as falling within the US sphere of influence. In this regard, the UN governance structures as of 1945 were not durable for several reasons: the anti-fascist coalition was superseded by the Cold War rivalry and European entitlement claims to geopolitical status collapsed with the end of the colonial order as new geopolitical claimants achieved political independence, an outcome historically evidenced by the failure of the 1956 British-French-Israeli Suez operation.

More than most reforms, it seems difficult to accommodate changes in the geopolitical hierarchy either by way of expanding the P5 to P10 or reconstituting P5 as P2 or P3, limiting permanent membership in the Security Council and the right of veto to the frontline geopolitical actors, which at this time means the US and China, to be sure, and maybe Russia, and downgrading the UK and France, yet possibly finding justification by regarding the European Union as a political actor entitled to permanent Security Council representation. A different approach would not alter what exists but add the most qualified candidates exhibiting a blend of geopolitical and representational perspectives, thus making a strong case for India, Brazil, Japan, and Nigeria.

Far more innovative and potentially more constructive would be a selection process in the Security Council based either on regional voting or on the basis of contributions to the public good as assessed by a commission composed of living Nobel Peace Prize winners, taking account of a country's record in terms of human rights, environmental footprint, and peaceful settlement of disputes. This kind of scheme might prove difficult to operationalize, but resting membership on a normative selection process that takes account of national records relating to respect for international law and pursuit of justice would be a big step toward accepting the tutelage of the new realism.

Of course, these are conceptual possibilities that illustrate different possible structural and ideational alternatives. There is no present support for achieving such reforms because geopolitical adaptation now totally depends on amending the Charter. Yet, examining these alternative reform ideas points both to present weaknesses and ways of strengthening the UN as a political actor that serve the needs and values of people rather than governments and transnational elites, provided it doesn't repeat the experience of the League, which lost credibility by both being weak with respect to capabilities and being ambitious with respect to preserving world peace, generating a sense of futility that diminished the benefits of belonging to the organization.

## Empowering the UN General Assembly

The UN General Assembly, composed of all member states, is overtly dis-
empowered in the Charter, being confined to making recommendations,
and in Article 12(1) disallowed even to discuss and recommend as long
as the Security Council is considering a dispute or situation endangering
international peace. This fundamental distinction between these two political organs of the UN was to ensure that geopolitical management of world
order would not be challenged from within the organization itself. By
drawing the basic constitutional distinction between decisions in the Security Council, where the P5 could block actions, and the General Assembly,
where they could not, any outcome was reduced to rhetoric, a mere recommendation, expressing the ambivalence toward the relations of power
and law that surrounded the founding of the UN, infusing its high-profile
operations ever since. Overgeneralizing somewhat, the governments of the
world, considered as a whole, seek peace with justice, while the P5 seek
order, geopolitical prerogatives, and advancing internationally their visions of justice free from the burdens of externally imposed constraints.
In this regard, whenever the P5 are split, the institutional consequence is
inaction or, at best, an ambiguous compromise. If the General Assembly
were endowed with the authority to make binding decisions, then it would
face the challenge of effectiveness if P5 or other Great Powers opposed and
refused to participate in funding and implementing the UN approach. In
this regard, this core constitutional compromise meant that the UN would
be limited in the contributions it could hope to make in view of geopolitical divisions but would be durable as a genuine global actor in ways that
the League of Nations had not been. The General Assembly, so far stripped
of real power, became perceived as a "talk shop" that embellished debates
about world politics without significantly contributing to the realization
of such transformative goals as ending aggressive war and nuclearism
or achieving peaceful settlement of disputes among states and equitable
development.

As time passed in the latter decades of the twentieth century, the powers
of the West grew wary of endowing the General Assembly with increased
influence because it was perceived as mounting concerted challenges to
a market-dominated world order. The shifts in membership following the
collapse of European colonialism, starting soon after the UN was established, meant a gradual decline of Western control, perhaps most starkly
expressed by the call of the recently independent states in the 1970s for
a new international economic order that would reframe world trade and

investment in a more equitable fashion. The atmosphere of the General Assembly began to be perceived in the West as dominated by the priorities of the Non-Aligned Movement, consistently supported by China, which sought to remain detached from the Cold War while making the overall work and policies of the UN more friendly to the aspirations of the Global South. Such developments produced panic in the North, prompting on one side a backlash against General Assembly activism, given strong leadership during the Thatcher-Reagan championship of neoliberalism and the formation of the Trilateral Commission (North America, Europe, and Japan) to give coherence to the interests and values of the capitalist West. It is significant that the Trilateral Commission, established on David Rockefeller's initiative with the mission of offsetting the influence of the Non-Aligned Movement, sought to deflect UN attacks on market-oriented economies. It did this primarily through encouraging a greater emphasis at the UN on the goals of economic development. In this global setting, exhibiting postcolonial realities, both sides began to elevate the role of global economic policy to the same level of prominence as the Charter gave to war prevention.

What became increasingly evident was the retreat by the West from its efforts to empower the General Assembly to circumvent the frustrations associated with the Cold War impasses in the Security Council. This retreat has persisted almost thirty years after the end of the Cold War, giving rise to two antagonistic views of the world economy, one built according to the precepts of neoliberal globalization and the other reflecting demands for an equitable world economy that is receptive to the developmental priorities of the Global South.

### The Unfulfilled Use of the International Court of Justice

The Charter attempted to strengthen international judicial decision-making without stepping too hard on sovereign toes. First of all, it made all members of the UN automatically parties to the Statute of the ICJ, but then came the fine print that deferred to state-centrism. The compromise UN formula consisted of a general pronouncement that states were not required to submit disputes to the ICJ unless they gave their consent in one of three forms: by agreement with the government of the other party; by inserting in treaties "a compromissory clause" that stipulated in advance that any dispute arising under the treaty would be submitted to the ICJ; or by submitting a voluntary acceptance of the "compulsory jurisdiction" of the ICJ in any dispute, subject to reservations and to a rule that the other party to a dispute was similarly reciprocally committed. In effect, the ICJ, like the

General Assembly has limped along without being called upon to adjudicate international disputes involving Great Powers or to provide guidance to the main organs of the UN System when important issues of competence or legality arise.

UN members are bound by Article 94(1) of the Charter to comply with ICJ decisions, and in the event of non-compliance, Article 94(2) gives the winning party the right to seek help from the Security Council in achieving compliance. An obvious reform would be to extend compulsory jurisdiction without reservations to the conditions of membership, although such a sweeping change would require a Charter amendment, which presently seems to be a decisive obstacle. Another course would be for governments to decide if it was to their advantage to comply with the compulsory jurisdiction option and thereby become more committed to resolving disputes by agreeing to adjudication either in treaties or in relation to disputes on a case-to-case basis. Leading states, indeed most states, are not willing to subject their vital concerns to compulsory international adjudication, insisting on an essentially voluntary relationship to international adjudication, which for most countries is what currently exists and explains why there is not much political traction outside the circles of professional international lawyers for enhancing the role of the ICJ.

Few cases are put before the Court and decided by the ICJ, and the most visible international disputes almost never become resolved by judicial action, although there is some evidence that recently more states are willing to take their chances with international adjudication. Although the ICJ is not regarded as nearly as significant a part of the UN System as is the Security Council and the General Assembly, it has often been overly demeaned. The ICJ, in a manner similar to other UN organs has found ways to be a valuable dimension of the UN's role in constructing world order. For one thing, the decisions and advisory opinions presented to the ICJ have been few and far between, although the ICJ has been adept, when given the chance, at making important contributions to the development of international law. This has generally taken the form of long, detailed majority opinions in the cases that come before it, often coupled with Separate Opinions and Dissenting Opinions. Also, the ICJ's pronouncements on international law can be useful for civil society efforts to challenge the policies of their own state or other states, especially its Advisory Opinions on large questions bearing on peace, security, and justice, such as human rights and self-determination claims in Palestine, Kashmir, Puerto Rico, and Western Sahara or on the legality of nuclear weapons. Like other reformist ideas, the ICJ, while respecting its jurisdictional limits, can evolve without requiring a Charter amendment, although formal action would certainly help to upgrade the ICJ's role and practice.

There is a parallel role given to the ICJ with respect to pronouncing on international law relative to issues that are on the agenda of the political organs of the UN, and with authorization of the General Assembly or Security Council and of other UN organs and the various specialized agencies in the UN System for matters within their institutional domain. This effort to bring guidance of international law to bear on issues of concern to the UN authorizes the ICJ to respond to requests by issuing Advisory Opinions. Such interpretations have been sought for a variety of issues ranging from the legality of nuclear weapons to Israel's construction of a separation wall that encroaches on Occupied Palestinian Territory to various infringements by autocratic regimes on the rights of journalists and dissenting activists. As might be expected, the ICJ is respectful of sovereignty, claims not to allow the Advisory Opinion route to overcome the absence of consent to jurisdiction by a party to a dispute, and is careful to acknowledge the limits of prescribed law. An interesting question is whether the ICJ should be respectful of geopolitical realities, especially pertaining to the P5, when issuing Advisory Opinions, as it seemed to be in 1996 when analyzing entrenched international policy in the context of examining the legality of threats or uses of nuclear weaponry. The dissenting opinion of Christopher Weeramantry certainly developed this line of critical response to the majority opinion.[11]

The Western nuclear weapon states unsurprisingly indicated their unwillingness to accept the international guidance of international law as set forth by the ICJ, but nonetheless, the majority opinion and the even stronger dissenting opinions encouraged and legitimated antinuclearism around the world and undoubtedly contributed to the civil society–Global South momentum that produced the 2021 UN Treaty on the Prohibition of Nuclear Weapons, which is formally opposed by a consensus among nuclear weapons states. In light of the Treaty on the Prohibition of Nuclear Weapons, as entered into force in 2021, it could be argued that the development, deployment, and even the possession of nuclear weapons had been rendered not only unlawful but criminalized and, controversially, that even non-parties can be held accountable by the application of principles of customary international criminal law that view the treaty as enjoying a status of universal applicability.

Increasing recourse to the ICJ in both its decisional and guidance roles would definitely contribute to a more effective and just structure of world order and improve the character of the UN role in global governance as measured by Charter Purposes and Principles. Yet this overall raising of respect for international law would have to come mainly from the shifts in the internal political consciousness of member governments, especially the P5, involving a recognition by political elites and more globally oriented publics that under present conditions, national interests are better served by compliance with legal norms than by their purely volitional acceptance or outright violation, given present realities.

Consideration needs also to be given to proposing an operational rule of practice that whenever an issue of international law arises anywhere in the UN System, it should be referred to the ICJ for resolution, including a finding that the impact on a particular question is unresolved. To avoid unacceptable delays in UN undertakings, it would be desirable to have ways of obtaining prompt and provisional legal opinions with limited authoritative weight. Perhaps a panel of international legal experts could be given such assignments to balance expediency of response against authoritative decisions as to the law.

## The UN Secretary-General

Article 97 declares that the Secretary-General elected by the General Assembly upon a recommendation from the Security Council is "the chief administrative officer." The role as the leading voice of the operational UN is not set forth, but it gives the Secretary-General an opportunity to take account of changes in the global setting that affect not only international peace and security but the full spectrum of UN concerns. It is also significant that the Secretary-General is given the authority in Article 99 "to bring to the attention of the Security Council" any issue that he or she believes poses a threat to international peace and security, while Articles 100 and 101 seek to insulate the Secretary-General from pressures exerted by members to underscore the autonomy and independence of the office. We know in practice that despite these Charter assurances, the operational UN has seen many thinly disguised efforts to exert pressure on the Secretary-General to adopt certain positions or else funding will be withheld and support withdrawn for reelection to a second term of six years. From the beginning of the UN, there has even been something that approaches geographical ownership of certain posts to ensure the presence of US citizens in the Secretary-General's advisory inner circle as well as dominating, along with Europeans, the upper echelons of the Bretton Woods Institutions. In recent years, this manner of privileging the nationals of certain UN members has lessened somewhat, but it still continues. Against such a background, it is not surprising that the leadership skills, public reputation, and principled character of the Secretary-General deeply influence whether the essential role is to serve as a kind of handmaiden of the P5 or rise up to become the world's most powerful voice of conscience and policy guidance. The nine Secretaries-General since 1945 have been assessed to have very mixed records when it comes to independence, institutional creativity, and articulating the conscience of humanity.

On the negative side are occasions when P5 bullying seeks to nullify the independence of the Secretary-General. On other occasions the Secretary-General has been able to light a fire or at least keep a fire burning, which encourages action that promotes UN values, purposes, and principles. Part of what the Secretary-General is potentially capable of doing is to call attention to challenges arising from changed circumstances, facilitating existential adaptation without formal amendment. This has been particularly evident as human rights have risen from their status as moral sentiments and remote aspirations to obligatory concrete commitments of UN membership. It is also true that highlighting respect for UN responsibilities with regard to environmental protection and ecological stability has allowed the Secretary-General to be perceived as a dynamic voice of reason who is not a de facto partisan or a captive to the "political realism" that shapes the behavior of many UN members.

As with other aspects of UN performance with respect to changing circumstances, the encouragement by or opposition of the P5 plays a large role in determining the significance and impact of Secretaries-General and shapes how they publicly or covertly carry out the duties of the office. With P5 backing, reinforced by public opinion, the Secretary-General can contribute a strong informal consciousness-raising capability to the UN as new issues arise or old concerns are allowed to lapse, causing serious adverse human consequences.

## UN Funding

Ever since the UN was established, there have been concerns about leaving its funding in the hands of member states, with a realization that allocating assessed dues on the basis of GDP as of 1945 would give richer countries disproportionate influence inconsistent with juridical promise of the equality of sovereign states affirmed in Article 4 of the Charter, already severely diluted by the geopolitical exception. The familiar folk saying "Who pays the fiddler calls the tune" has proven an accurate approximation of relative US influence and power.

During recent years, three issues have dominated financing concerns: (1) an annual cash shortfall due to members failing to meet their financial obligations, which creates recurrent budget crises that limit the capacity of the UN to meet its obligations, much less to expand its operations; (2) advocacy and continuing exploration of alternative financing schemes that would give the UN greater financial stability as well as increased insulation from what has sometimes been described as "financial blackmail," or the refusal to pay arrears unless certain actions are taken and certain priorities observed; (3) increased attention to defunding threats and policies, influencing the conduct of the Secretary-General and even the political organs of the UN System. This has made staff even in peripheral venues of the UN such as the Human Rights Council reluctant to take positions or support initiatives that will provoke anger from a major funder of the organization. Our experience of holding positions within the UN confirms this disillusioning reality.

Reforming the UN financial system has been on the agenda of the organization since its founding, yet little has happened because major states do not want to lose their leverage. Also, alternative revenue schemes to governmental contributions meet resistance from entrenched private sector interests and political objectives. Among the schemes that have been proposed for funding reform are the following: various ways of taxing currency exchange transactions; levying a tax on such harmful activities as carbon emissions, tobacco sales, and hydrocarbon fuels; levying fees on certain uses of the global commons; a tax on international travel by plane; and even a UN-administered lottery.

As matters now stand, the financial condition of the UN is unlikely to change through extensive reforms of the sort proposed over the years, and improvements will depend on the voluntary good will of major member states, and to some extent on controversial public-private partnerships with corporate donors. As mentioned previously in contexts other than reform, such a prospect has dimmed in recent years in response to the rise of ultranationalist shifts in attitudes toward the UN. As in other sectors of UN activity, the behavior of the US is of great significance, given its peculiar status as leading donor and leading defaulting debtor. Although there has been a gentle swing of the American pendulum from Trump's anti-globalism, most dramatically signaled by the defunding of the WHO in the midst of the pandemic, to a somewhat more liberal internationalist engagement by the Biden presidency, it would be wishful thinking to expect much of a shift, except possibly with respect to climate change. There is every indication that in the peace and security and even human rights areas, the US values the UN primarily as a policy instrument to be used against adversaries, and if turned even slightly against its strategic interest, the US uses its leverage as a shield. Additionally, the intensity of current geopolitical confrontations seems likely to diminish interest in and support for the enlargement of UN capabilities through funding increases or independence.

## Concluding Remarks

This chapter has sought to emphasize the tensions between constitutional rigidity and operational flexibility when it comes to UN reform, whether motivated by adapting to changing circumstances or achieving greater legitimacy for the UN as a whole and for its constituent elements in the form of principal organs and specialized agencies.

As Secretaries-General and governmental leaders have demonstrated, many of the silences or gaps in the UN Charter can be responsibly filled intermittently by well-crafted and creative initiatives that enjoy widespread support in relation to the role of the UN. Another source of adaptability involves the adoption of contextual styles of interpretation that take seriously the de-limitations of Principles and Purposes in Articles 1 and 2 of the Charter, as well as responding to emergent unforeseen challenges. It is important for the healthy evolution of the UN that neither members nor the UN become prisoners of narrowly conceived textual interpretations that refuse to look beyond the language of the norm or the literal contours of past precedents and fail to take account of contextual factors and precedents.

A major source of disappointment over the years with respect to the performance of the political UN has arisen because of the inability of the P5 to act more frequently in concert and avoid the paralyzing impact of the veto. When the Cold War ended, there was a brief period when it seemed possible that the UN would have the consensus that had been hoped for when the organization was established, but this hope was dashed partly by renewed geopolitical tensions, rising distrust among leading UN members, and the unanticipated rise of ultranationalist governments. Not only has the UN suffered from these developments, but this decline has also spilled over to limit multilateralism and global problem-solving frameworks generally. The US retreat from its former position of leadership when it came to globalizing initiatives has had an overall negative impact on the UN.

This disappointing assessment of the UN as the world advances into the third decade of the twenty-first century can rapidly change. We look with favor at the following possibilities:

the revival of a globalizing spirit to meet challenges that cannot be addressed by states acting on their own; the renewal of more globally minded national leadership;

the rapid decline of the present influence exerted by ultranationalist members;

a more militant pressure from national publics, with growing transnational links to apply more energy and resources to achieving global solutions to global problems;

greater opportunities for civil society representatives to participate within the UN;

and more governmental acceptance of political ownership of and accountability for adverse global developments.

Overall, we view the historical situation as conducive to greater relevance for UN activities, although this expectation is far from assured. How the urgencies of the present will be addressed by governments, regions, and civil society is one of the great uncertainties of our time, and the possibilities of ultranationalism, extremism, warfare, chaos, famine, and ecological catastrophe to interfere with the functioning of solution-oriented, UN-centered diplomacy should not be overlooked. These issues will be more fully considered in the final chapters, although we acknowledge at this point that radical uncertainty clouds our expectations about the future of the UN, making prediction hazardous and yet giving those of us hoping for a stronger UN sufficient incentive to carry on and even intensify our struggle for a more effective and legitimate UN. As the relevant futures are unknowable, every person on the planet has the responsibility and opportunity to endow hope with action and belief.

# ELEVEN

# Institutional Reforms: Amending the Charter, Prospects and Options

### What If? But If?

What kind of a UN would exist if recommendations made over the years by a majority of UN member states in the General Assembly had resulted in actual reforms?

In the preceding chapters, we have described some of the UN achievements during the past seventy-five years. The UN sapling of 1945 has become a mature tree with many branches. The institutional experience, changing policy challenges, and socio-political pressures have led to the emergence of a significantly more nuanced and elaborate organization. Today the UN has many of the capabilities needed to carry out its Charter-based mandate and is readier to deal with complex structural and substantive challenges arising from global developments, provided it enjoys the support of a consensus among the geopolitical powers, which are the P5 in the UN context by virtue of their special status in the Security Council.

However, achieving consensus has proved over time to be a big obstacle, especially with respect to the peace and security agenda. Besides, the P5 is no longer reflective of the geopolitical landscape in the 2020s as the European states are less important, and countries such as India, Brazil, Nigeria, and Japan are geopolitically more influential than either France or the UK. The failures of the UN to prevent or even to play a significant role in the brutally waged, prolonged proxy wars in Syria and Ukraine have had disastrous humanitarian consequences as well as underscoring the weakness and inadequacy of the UN as it currently functions. Such a pattern also exhibits the limited normative authority of the Charter and of international law generally, especially with respect to war prevention.

Such a comment is not meant to neglect some signal achievements of the UN. Universality of membership has almost been achieved since only a few territories remain without formal UN participation, and even these will likely seek membership in the UN once they attain statehood. It is also relevant that not a single UN member has withdrawn from or been expelled by the UN. Such an impressive record is somewhat clouded by a few instances of uncertainty about the territorial integrity and political independence of existing member states. As in the past, there could be in the future national breakups or the merger of two or more sovereign states into a single state. Such developments to the extent they occur would enlarge or contract the size of the General Assembly. Postcolonial imperial encroachments on weaker states also raise concerns about the political independence of some members, including the capabilities of their governments to serve as legitimate representatives of the nation and its people.

Among major UN achievements is the large body of UN law that has been developed and codified, covering many aspects of human life and environmental sustainability. The General Assembly and the Security Council have become over time more willing to interact with the UN operational system and civil society actors on global issues. UN-sponsored summits devoted to many key areas of human concern and their follow-up have created road maps for advancing global well-being with respect to various topics, such as human rights, gender equality, environmental protection, population balances, and social and economic policy.

All nine Secretaries-General, despite the diversity of their socioeconomic, political, and geographical backgrounds, have displayed varying degrees of sensitivity to the relevance of geopolitical changes. Within the constraints of their executive roles, they have provided moral and operational leadership to encourage multilateralism and to the extent politically possible, have maintained the organization's overall relevance in the areas of peace, security, and development even when confronting strong geopolitical resistance to actions and policies in accord with Charter values. Efforts along these lines have included establishing linkages between UN operational units involving political, humanitarian and development affairs; the integration of UN System programs with their growing focus on human and sustainable development; and bringing UN System operations "closer to the people" by expanding inclusivity through UN partnerships with civil society organizations, NGOs, civically minded foundations, and the private sector. The UN and the UN System as a whole has significantly broadened its media outreach globally and in many languages. This has helped to keep people everywhere, in urban and rural areas, better informed about the contributions of the United Nations to a more peaceful, just, and sustainable world order. The improved dissemination of news about UN activities has encouraged feedback, facilitated media access, and contributed to somewhat more transparency with respect to UN activities.

It is to be regretted that there have also been serious UN regressions. Following the collapse of the Soviet Union and a brief period of P5 cooperation, geopolitical confrontation within the UN again deepened due to adverse reactions in the West to the rise of China as a political and economic superpower. Additionally, revived concerns about Russian pressures on countries along its borders, especially in the Caucasus. The United States no longer seemed able to play its increasingly controversial post–Cold War role of the unopposed leader of a Western alliance of global scope. This further complicated and agitated the global setting. The quality of debate in the General Assembly and the Security Council between Washington and Beijing and their respective allies has grown more belligerent and has been aggravated by Russian assertiveness. Clashing national interests and geopolitical policy priorities have replaced the spirit of cooperation that seemed to be growing among P5 members in the years immediately following the end of the Cold War. Instead of the appearance of cooperation and consensus, there emerged once again an atmosphere of tension in the Security Council that recalled the Cold War years of distrust, confrontation, and paralysis.

These developments have given rise to the militarization of the debate in the Security Council and have led to the formation and growth of regional alliances operating outside the Charter framework. Such developments have produced increasing defense budgets and arms races in the pursuit of strategic interests. Illegal wars and prolonged military interventions have taken place without any UN pushback. UN resolutions are frequently ignored or misused, and false flag operations are carried out by states to justify and build public support for their recourse to military action. Neither the International Court of Justice nor the International Criminal Court (formally independent of the UN) have been able to assert any relevant authority in the spirit of the universality of law and justice to address these deviations from the UN Charter or international law. Non-accountability and impunity enjoyed and relied upon by the most powerful countries continue to be characteristic of international relations and thus undermine the major premise of the rule of law: juridical equals should be treated as equals. In effect, geopolitics, with its political norms, enjoys primacy over adherence to international law, including the UN Charter, whenever perceived to be clashing with the strategic interests of a geopolitical actor.

Another step backward has been evident in the financing of development support to low-income countries. The UN suggested a level of 0.7 percent of GNI to be earmarked for international development assistance by OECD countries.[1] This target was never reached. Donor contributions to UN System budgets, which are woefully inadequate for the tasks assigned to the UN, are further hampered by increasingly taking the form of earmarked funds for sectoral use that reflect donor priorities rather than UN preferences or the greatest needs of recipient governments. Earmarking funds subverts the UN System's programmatic goals and its autonomy, inserting a state-centric bias into the basic authority to decide on the use of funds at its disposal.

For many years, the integrity of the UN international civil service was not questioned. Just as in national foreign services, the core of UN personnel consists of men and women who pursue UN careers after receiving permanent appointments. These long-term appointments have been increasingly replaced by "continuing" contracts, which have injected an element of job insecurity, discouraging many qualified individuals from applying for UN positions and making others vulnerable to manipulation due to fears that their UN contracts might not be renewed.

Besides the matters of UN progress and regression that we have identified, there are complex structural, substantive, and procedural UN reforms still awaiting the attention of the General Assembly and the Security Council. It is a matter of urgency for the General Assembly to accept belatedly its responsibility to comply with the terms of the constitutional review mandated by the UN Charter in Article 109. Such a review process is intended to give UN member states an important opportunity to reconsider how the UN might better fulfil its role as a peacemaker, peacekeeper, problem-solver, and arbiter of disputes in the twenty-first century. Unfortunately, this review process that looked so promising on paper has been nullified in practice. It has been resisted at the level of implementation by member states that fear a loss of status and leverage in the UN System if reforms consider changing power ratios and standards of representation in the organization.

Without questioning the juridical equality of sovereign nations, the UN must review the one-country, one-vote approach that presently prevails in General Assembly decision-making and consider the possible adoption of weighted voting as the EU member states have successfully done on a regional basis. The Security Council, the UN's main policy- and decision-making authority, has yet to alter the composition of permanent membership established in 1945, despite major changes in the geopolitical, demographic, and developmental changes over the course of seventy-five years of experience in a turbulent historical period. The General Assembly should make appropriate recommendations for institutional reforms and deliberate on whether regional rather than national representation in the Security Council should become, as we would recommend, a desirable alternative. Of course, the General Assembly could not make its recommendations mandatory without amending the Charter, a process itself subject to a veto by any current P5 member. For this reason, such structural adjustments are highly unlikely to happen soon, no matter how much such operational adjustments would enhance the legitimacy and effectiveness of the organization.

Globalization has brought about a significant increase in worldwide social networking and a much greater awareness of the importance of civil society and local knowledge for the work of the UN. As a result, over time many ways have been found to increase ad hoc and informal participation of civil society representatives in shaping and implementing the UN agenda. The inclusion of civil society, however, has yet to become a consistent feature of UN operations. Confirmation by the General Assembly that such a level of participation is the preference of most member countries would be a helpful sign of receptivity to reform, but there are no present indications that a greater role for civil society will soon become a UN reality. There are also dangers that arranging increased influence for civil society actors will mostly benefit of large-scale private-sector interests.

At present, there are 193 UN member countries. The UN's contribution to global developments is judged on that basis. Forgotten is that the UN as an institution contributes significant additional benefits through its work, apart from providing a legitimate venue for multilateral cooperation. This 193+1 reality should be formally recognized and explained by the General Assembly as a way of educating people and government bureaucrats about the real value of the UN.

We are aware that many recommendations for UN reforms have been made during the past seventy-five years by the UN General Assembly and by the nine UN Secretaries-General, but most have not been adopted or even seriously considered. Given this background of frustration and failure to adopt sensible reforms at the UN, we try to fill the gap by envisioning the kind of UN organization that would now exist had the best of proposed reforms been adopted and implemented. We do so without pretending that the political obstacles to the UN reform process can be overcome merely by a demonstration of the UN benefits that would result. Governments have ingrained beliefs and a variety of interests that often are opposed to taking the steps to construct a more capable and independent UN. This opposition to a stronger UN is often vaguely explained as a matter of attachment to the prerogatives of national sovereignty and geopolitical discretion, which tends to obscure more concrete material interests of state power and private wealth.

We have chosen to focus on major General Assembly proposals that seek to overcome or at least mitigate deficiencies in UN capabilities and operational efficiency. Our focus is on UN reforms that aim to make the organization more substantively, structurally, and financially independent and effective. During the reform process, the UN would improve its reputation as a more legitimate, respected, and relevant institutional framework that is actively seeking to meet growing global challenges facing humanity in a constructive manner. We discuss these proposals from a prescriptive viewpoint, considering them integral to our ultimate conclusions regarding the world order imperatives of multilateralism, global solidarity, and greater UN autonomy. It is necessary to keep in mind the conjectural nature of what we set forth. Our principal intention is to encourage discussion and debate from different perspectives throughout the world as to desirable and necessary ways forward in light of intensifying global challenges.

## What If?

Let us imagine that one day a UN press conference is held in which the global public is informed by the Secretary-General that the General Assembly has just concluded a long-overdue conference in accordance with Article 109 of the UN Charter. On this occasion, the General Assembly has agreed, the Secretary-General reports, to initiate a long-overdue, wide-ranging review of the operations and mandates of the United Nations. The intention is to determine what reforms are needed for the organization to become an institution more capable of responding to the challenges of the twenty-first century in keeping with the Principles and Purposes of the UN Charter.[2]

Suppose the public were informed that the Security Council and the General Assembly had decided to make it mandatory that these two main UN bodies work together whenever an issue had been deemed by them as a TMI, a topic of major importance. When a concern has been identified as such, the Security Council and the General Assembly would meet in appropriate working groups, with the Secretary-General in attendance and expected to play an important executive role in implementing TMI-related decisions. An expert body composed of international law experts representing the major regions of the world would be invited to comment on these TMI-related initiatives, either in the International Law Commission or in selected ad hoc bodies set up by General Assembly and Security Council.

We further conjecture that a subsequent UN press release identifies nine TMIs as areas where UN reforms are needed (table 11.1). Each of these topics has been classified as "work in progress" intended to take into account the most recent relevant resolutions adopted by the General Assembly for each of the TMIs. The UN Department of Global Communications confirms that it will regularly provide public briefings on progress in relation to each TMI. Such briefings would increase the transparency of the UN and give the interested public greater knowledge of what the UN is doing and how it could affect their lives.

A year after the end of the review conference, the Secretary-General presents his first special report on the progress in dealing with these nine TMIs. In the introduction, the Secretary-General notes the fact that this new consensus-forming and decision-making process has been working well. The General Assembly and the Security Council have met regularly to make progress in addressing individual TMIs, which now includes more systematic consultation with the international law expert consultative body. To illustrate, the Secretary-General refers to nuclear disarmament as a major TMI, a General Assembly agenda item for decades, which has been subject to extensive and difficult deliberations in relation to trends in military spending, arms trade, and modernization of nuclear weaponry.

Over the years, more and more UN member countries ratified the Comprehensive Nuclear-Test-Ban Treaty (CTBT) and supported the resolutions

TABLE 11.1   Selected UN topics of major importance (TMIs).

1. UN Charter reform
2. Nuclear disarmament
3. Decolonization
4. Environmental protection, including climate change
5. Regional participation (UN Charter, Chapter 8)
6. Multilateral mechanisms
7. International Economic Order
8. UN finances and funding
9. Civil society

for the establishment of nuclear-free zones around the world and for decreasing the trigger-alert readiness of nuclear weapons systems. Pressures
had been mounting on the P5 to act in unison with the rest of the Security
Council, the General Assembly, and the ICJ to comply with these initiatives, including, above all, the commencement of negotiations under UN
auspices for a treaty of phased nuclear disarmament that would be reliably
monitored and verified to ensure continuing compliance. Also reported
upon was the acceptance by the UN of the important contributions of existing nuclear-weapon-free zones, the ratification of the CTBT by the permanent members of the Security Council, the reactivation of the Disarmament
Commission, and an agreed timetable for the progressive elimination of
all nuclear weapons and the reductions of and limitations on conventional
weapons. These risk-reducing steps had been urged by the General Assembly for many years but were totally ignored. Now the situation was more
encouraging. The UN Secretary-General in his report took note of the fact
that these disarmament-related measures had resulted in gradual global
demilitarization, reductions by most countries of military budgets, and corresponding enhancements of human security.

During the year under review, the Security Council, the General Assembly, and the body of international legal experts also dealt with residual
issues of decolonization. The General Assembly had passed its first resolution on decolonization in 1960, and since then resolutions were repeated
almost annually. In the twenty-first century, granting independence to territorial dependencies, as we have pointed out in earlier chapters, remained
on the UN agenda although there were not many such entities left.

The Secretary-General observed that a consensus had emerged between the Security Council and the General Assembly that granting of
political autonomy should be determined by plebiscites administered by
the UN. The Secretary-General expressed the view that an important step
forward in decolonization had been facilitated by the much-improved
global cooperation. The Secretary-General recalled that since 2002, when
colonial Portuguese Timor became the independent state of East Timor,
no non-self-governing territory had become independent. Most peoples in
the remaining non-independent territories were situated in the Caribbean,
West Africa, the Southern Atlantic, and the North and South Pacific. These
communities reacted enthusiastically to UN support for supervised local
elections to determine their future. The grievances of entrapped minorities
in sovereign states should also be addressed by the UN as urgent matters
of humanitarian and normative concern. Palestine, Western Sahara, and

Kashmir are among the most crucial unresolved self-determination grievances deserving of more effective UN attention cases.

The Secretary-General in presenting his report also stressed that the
General Assembly and the Security Council recognized that the ICJ was
an integral part of UN System and urged coordination of work on the TMIs
with independent international law experts. The absence of cooperation
between the three main sources of UN authority in the past had been a
serious UN shortcoming, expressive of the weakness of international law
in relation to UN operations, especially bearing on peace and security. In
the context of the TMIs, the General Assembly and the Security Council
acknowledged that the ICJ was a potentially valuable resource for the interpretation of UN Charter Law. These political UN organs significantly
agreed that there existed a Charter responsibility to encourage members
with legal disputes to have recourse to the ICJ to obtain a binding legal
judgment. The Secretary-General also pointed out that in the past, the
views of the ICJ were rarely sought by other entities in the UN System,
and even then, were authorized only to issue judgments that were formally categorized as Advisory Opinions, indicative of their discretionary
status, implying the option to disregard them. In effect, these carefully rea-
soned legal assessments had no obligatory weight. The Secretary-General
expressed the hope that this new spirit of coordination among the main
organs of the UN would lead to appropriate changes in the statute governing the authoritativeness of all international pronouncements by the International Court of Justice. In the past, ICJ Advisory Opinions exerted some
influence on civil society discourse and activism on such issues as nuclear
weaponry and contested uses of force but have been largely ignored by the
actors whose behavior was being challenged.

The Security Council and the General Assembly had added to their TMI
agenda a review of the extent to which governments had made use of UN provisions and procedures when dealing with regional and internal conflicts. Over
time, more and more inter-country arrangements were established that often
violated the provisions of Chapter VIII of the UN Charter devoted to regional
arrangements.[3] Major regional alliances such as the North Atlantic Treaty Organization (NATO) and the Shanghai Cooperation Organization (SCO) representing twenty-nine Western and eight Eastern countries respectively, had
even signed agreements of cooperation with the UN Secretariat, giving the
misleading impression that regional alliances enjoyed an equal footing with
the UN itself rather than being important but subsidiary partners.

The Secretary-General noted that the inclusion on the list of TMIs of the UN's role in resolving regional and local conflicts was a clear sign that there was recognition of the value of regional arrangements as partners of the UN in matters calling for conflict resolution. The Secretary-General stated further that there should no longer be any regional alliances primarily dedicated to military security. Regional arrangements equipped with special knowledge and local experience should be considered an important part of the global peace and security structure and as such be encouraged to coordinate their work with that of the UN in crisis management and regional crisis prevention as prescribed by the UN Charter. As a formal participant in the Security Council and General Assembly deliberations, the Secretary-General would continue to carefully monitor developments of this TMI and inform the public about how well regional arrangements were responsive to the UN's call for cooperation and coordination.

In the past, UN member states had never fully considered the value added by the United Nations as a system for peacebuilding, the maintenance of security and human development, and norm development. The Security Council and the General Assembly, in adopting the TMI agenda, were seeking to overcome this UN weakness and affirming that the UN System, as an institution, was an important contributor to stability, peace, and justice in the world. The annual human development reports of the UN Development Programme described progress that had been made in the delivery of UN assistance, while duly noting persisting problems. In general, the reports showed that the UN had improved its sensitivity and responsiveness to local conditions and, in doing so, enhanced significantly the impact of and appreciation for the UN agencies, funds, and programs on human and sustainable development. This allowed the Secretary-General to convey to the Security Council and General Assembly that the UN System was ready to get involved as an integrated system in development cooperation and crisis mitigation within an international law framework and subject to political approval and oversight at the level of national authority. As a model outline of UN System involvement, the Secretary-General presented to these UN bodies an illustration of what an integrated UN approach could accomplish: an Arctic Zone of Peace support program with provisions calling for implementation by the intergovernmental Arctic Council, to be carried out in accordance with international law. The participation of selected intergovernmental organizations (IGOs), non-governmental organizations (NGOs), and civil society organizations (CSOs) illustrated the UN's sophisticated and broad outreach to civil society actors in this particular setting, as shown in figure 11.1.

Our analysis of annual General Assembly resolutions shows that ever since 1964, most member states have regularly passed resolutions favor-

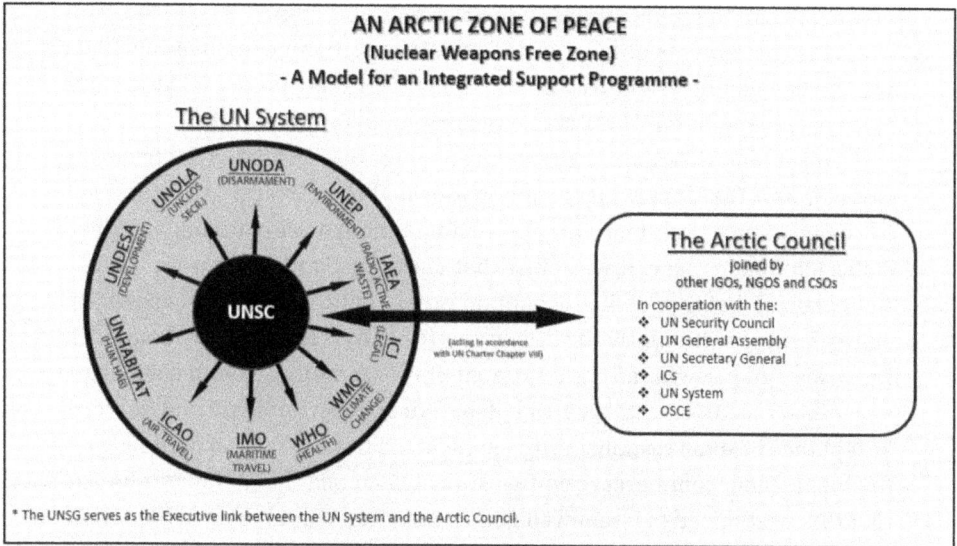

FIGURE 11.1    An example of a possible integrated UN System support program.

*Source:* Hans von Sponeck.

ing a reformed international economic order with more equitable trade relations, especially for developing countries in contexts of foreign direct investment.[4] Developing countries, hoping for economic justice, expected that such a new order supported by the United Nations, UNCTAD, and hopefully by the World Trade Organization, which was established outside the UN, would create a level playing field for trade and commerce involving all countries. The Western-oriented regulatory mechanisms of the World Bank and the International Monetary Fund, entrenched capital interests, excessive protection of intellectual property rights, and the weak negotiating power of the South, however, have prevented developing countries from overcoming opposition from richer countries and private business interests to the establishment of a more equitable world economic order. Deregulated markets, privatization, and tariff and non-tariff barriers, key elements of the Washington consensus, continue to exist.

Eighteen years of the so-called Doha Round of trade negotiations between developing and developed countries nevertheless did yield a slightly more equitable trade environment.[5] Nevertheless, the West joined by Japan had neither agreed to a major demand of the South, the reduction of developed countries' farm subsidies, nor put an end to high tariff and non-tariff barriers for agricultural and non-agricultural products from developing countries. At the same time, industrialized countries insisted on free access to the markets of low-income countries without concurrently offering the developing world free access to many of their products. Mutuality was absent, and bitter resentments resulted and have remained.

The Secretary-General in reviewing the progress of work of the Security Council and the General Assembly confirmed that extensive discussions of the economic, commercial, and financial cooperation among member states had taken place. It was clear that more time and effort were needed to bring into being a global economic order that took greater account of equity issues, particularly the difficulties faced by less developed countries in Africa and elsewhere. The treatment of this complicated and controversial subject as a priority TMI was itself encouraging evidence of the UN acceptance of some responsibility for ensuring fair conditions with respect to global trade, commerce, and investment. The Secretary-General hoped that this would lead to a renewed global push that would reverse the failed attempts of the 1970s to restructure the world economy along fairer lines.

Throughout the years, the annual funding of the UN operational system had been another ongoing concern. Assessed (mandatory) annual contributions, especially on the part of major contributors, were frequently paid after considerable delays while many smaller and least developed countries, despite their economic plight, paid their dues on time. The funding of peacekeeping operations and other urgent UN projects was also often problematic due to delays in payment or nonpayment. These funding uncertainties undermined confidence in UN efforts in the vital area of peace, security, and humanitarian emergencies.

As we pointed out earlier, the UN costs the world very little if objectively compared to what it contributes. The regular annual UN budget of $3.4 billion (2023) amounts to less than 45 cents per person on the planet. Some wealthier governments have described their financial contributions to the UN as a "sacrifice." This observation is pretentious and simply false and applies only to the poorest of countries that, at times, cannot even meet minimum obligatory contributions due to special circumstances beyond their control, such as climate-related droughts as in Somalia and countries in the Sahel. The Security Council and General Assembly, the Secretary-General noted, had agreed that countries get a net benefit from their UN funding commitments, and where possible, should demonstrate this by increasing their financial support to the UN.

It was further agreed that the humiliating and time-consuming efforts of Secretaries-General to induce governments to make timely payments had negative consequences for UN operations. Flexible payment of annual dues should be replaced by obligatory transfers to take place during the first six weeks of the new year. The introduction of punitive measures if member states failed to meet their financial obligations was under review. It was also confirmed that General Assembly and Security Council requests to the UN System to implement new initiatives would be given a go-ahead by the Secretary-General and other CEB members only after full funding had been secured. An exception to this policy would be made to enable UN interventions in emergency situations such as major humanitarian crises or natural catastrophes for which UN assistance would be provided as funding became available. The wider issue of compliance with the recommendations of the General Assembly arose as long ago as 1970. Some weak efforts were then made to obligate OECD member countries to make international development finance available at 0.7 percent of their GNI. However, failure over the years to live up to these modest funding expectations led to widespread disillusionment with the political will of the UN when it came to development assistance.

The Secretary-General told the audience with a smile that in a recent meeting each newly accredited ambassador to the UN was given a copy of the UN Charter to stress the importance of the normative framework in discharging the responsibilities of the organization to the peoples of the world. It was the Secretary-General's duty to remind member governments that the United Nations provided venues for peacefully resolving crises among states by recourse to diplomacy, trade-offs, and compromises. Representing the interests of "we, the peoples," the Secretary-General conveyed to government representatives that they must never forget that the UN ultimately receives its mandate from the peoples of the world and in the end remains accountable to them.

The Security Council and General Assembly had realized that over the years, civil society and the non-governmental community had become an influential global voice with important messages for governments working at the United Nations. These messages sought solutions in all areas of global relevance, from peacebuilding to climate change, sustainable and equitable development, human rights for the benefit of all, and more recently, natural habitat protection. ECOSOC in cooperation with the General Assembly had concluded partnerships with NGOs in all parts of the world, including increasingly in low-income countries. Local community knowledge became a major element in the formation of inclusive agendas of cooperation between the UN and member countries.

It was not a surprise that the further strengthening of relations between the UN and "civil society" was listed as a key TMI. The challenge to the

UN was to establish structural arrangements that regularized civil society participation. The purpose is to ensure that civil society has regular opportunities to take part in global decision-making involving the General Assembly, the Security Council, and other entities within the UN System. Considering past General Assembly resolutions calling for greater UN cooperation with civil society, UN bodies were now actively working toward the meaningful inclusion of civil society as a genuine partner in the activities of the organization.

The Secretary-General concluded an outline of the work of the Security Council and General Assembly by affirming the conviction that UN reform efforts for the first time had achieved a holistic review of all key concerns that member states had repeatedly voiced but had not been able to implement. This meant that the persistent General Assembly efforts, often dismissed in the past, supported by citizen movements around the world had not been in vain after all. Multilateralism was receiving new and expanded shows of support through a strengthened United Nations that was becoming better equipped to deal with global needs and threats, which themselves were increasing. The Secretary-General wanted the public to know that a sense of trust in the organization and respect for international law was beginning to permeate meetings of the Security Council and the General Assembly. This was a new beginning with exciting prospects that "the global community" was at last becoming a reality, available to undertake fundamental reforms, including adaptations of the UN Charter so that it might be regarded as a genuine people's constitution for the twenty-first century.

International and national media prominently and sympathetically reported this generally welcome news about these impressive global reforms that enabled better and better performance. Governments at last were taking concrete structural, substantive, and financial measures that allowed the UN to meet the formidable global challenges confronting the whole of humanity. The media made special reference to the UN's work in such areas as the reduction of human poverty, climate change, and habitat protections, and the bringing to life of the long-deferred dream of a genuine "global community" based on shared values and concerns that complemented, and if necessary, transcended the national interest and geopolitical ambitions of specific countries.

## But If?

The above sketch of what might have been and should be is illustrative of a UN that could be existing today if the requisite political will had been present, and it still might be brought into being tomorrow, if powerful governments, especially the P5 (particularly China, Russia, and the US), joined the majority of member states in accepting and implementing proposals and procedures for a more responsive, empowered, autonomous, law-abiding, and legitimate United Nations.

We would like to shift our attention from a "what if" UN back to the "as is" UN and reflect on what lies ahead both by way of obstacles, opportunity, and world order imperatives. Specifying the potential of the UN as we have tried to do in plausible terms in no way relieves us of the challenge of dealing with what is presently deficient and why it is so hard to do what the peoples of the world need and want.

# TWELVE

# The UN of the Future:
# The Grand Challenge—Realism with Hope

After eight decades of existence, it is undeniable that the United Nations has persisted through tumultuous times, but the organization has survived and even flourished in certain respects. There have been major failures as well as valuable political and operational accomplishments despite fundamental systemic obstacles, including those embodied in the original UN design. We have discussed the limitations on the UN's ability to fulfill its broad promise as resulting from the veto power given to the five permanent members of the Security Council; the privileging of national and statist over global and human interests by most members; the constraints on the International Court of Justice by restricting international law guidance to Advisory Opinions rather than legally binding decisions; and the disregard of international law by autocratically governed states and geopolitical actors.

This concluding chapter considers what could and should be done to empower the UN to better serve the needs and desires of humanity at a time of critical global conditions with respect to peace, security, and development, as well as unprecedented challenges associated with nuclear dangers, climate change, biodiversity, natural habitat, global migration, food security, world health, and artificial intelligence.

We recall that in 1945 the primary holders of global power and victors in a devastating world war, as represented by Roosevelt, Stalin, and Churchill, reached an agreement for a multilateral institutional structure that would be constructed in such a way as to avoid a repetition of the disappointing experience of the League of Nations. At the same time, these leaders were determined to uphold the national interests of their states, considering the ideological, economic, cultural, and geopolitical dimensions of their political reality. Whatever their differences, these leaders of East and West were united in their resolve to maintain global leadership in the postwar world. Joseph Stalin seemed convinced that communism would be welcomed by the still colonized peoples of the South while Franklin Roosevelt and Winston Churchill, believed in the global appeal of free trade, economic development, and political liberalism. What resulted was a pragmatic yet tenuous power-sharing compromise that provided political space for the pursuit of geopolitical goals without which the United Nations could not have been established.

It is helpful to appreciate that even before the UN started to operate, the seeds of big power conflict were sown, which over time would grow into towering toxic plants that increasingly hampered the work of the organization. After almost eight decades of experience, both within the UN and in relation to the behavior of member governments, an appraisal of the impacts of Great Power politics and their concurrent geopolitical influence on the legitimacy and effectiveness of the UN System needs to be evaluated.

Our analysis is presented in two parts. The first part covers the UN's political, legislative, and juridical responsibilities that are allocated among the Security Council, the General Assembly, and the International Court of Justice. The second part deals with the UN executive system, the UN administrative structures, the specialized agencies, programs, and funds.

## The General Assembly and the Security Council

The Great Powers had not anticipated the major impacts of decolonization and the postcolonial pressures exerted by newly sovereign nations on the UN, taking the initial form of determined efforts to level the economic playing fields in North/South relations, especially bearing on trade, investment, and development. This pressure on the established order caused governments in the North to fear being confronted in the General Assembly by a "tyranny of an evolving majority" that was distrustful of the existing market-driven policy framework. This perception promoted, in turn, a range of reactions by the five permanent members of the Security Council to protect their institutional dominance within the UN System and to oppose all moves to increase the authority and role of the General Assembly. Majority demands of global relevance, often in a manner paralleling the South/North divide, for example, on denuclearization or in relation to a new international economic order, were either ignored by P5 countries, or individual member countries were put under great pressure, mainly of a political and financial character, to abandon their transformative demands.

Until this day, the primacy of geopolitics and Great Power nationalism have remained the decisive forces in global decision-making bearing on matters of peace and security, as well as the management of the global economy. In the early years, the Soviet Union made clear, especially in the Security Council, that its national and regional interests took precedence over support for global multilateralism. Additionally, many countries, especially in the Global South, were reluctant in the Cold War atmosphere to back policies emanating from the West. While the United States generally supported UN membership of newly independent countries, the USSR tried to block admission of any country believed to have a Western orientation. The USSR believed that most new admissions to the General Assembly would further marginalize its role within the UN. In the end, the USSR was forced to accept the fact that the General Assembly would have a Western face and that decisive economic and financial power continued to be situated in North America and central Europe and would likely remain so indefinitely. These trends meant that the UN was increasingly dominated politically, financially, and operationally, by the US and its European allies as the Cold War narrative unfolded.

Three qualifications of the above assessment should be noted. First, this image of Western dominance of the UN has been weakened by the impact of decolonization and challenged by the Non-aligned Movement that sought to detach itself from the East/West struggle at the UN and elsewhere. Second, at the end of the Cold War in the early 1990s, the US engaged in a series of regime-changing interventions, which undermined respect for the global rule of law and tarnished its reputation as global leader. Third, the unexpected rapid rise of China both challenged and diluted US unipolarity and exhibited a nonmilitary path to Great Power status that impressively rejected realist assumptions about the militarist core of international power relations and status.

A review of the voting record of the General Assembly reveals deep and pervasive cleavages between the developed and developing countries, with China remaining aligned with the developing countries despite its economic and technological ascendancy. With equivalent consistency, the United States has been voting against key resolutions, often the only country to do so, that called for nuclear and nonnuclear disarmament, for social and economic equity in relations with the developing world, for decolonization, for more equitable North/South trade relations, and even for female and gender-based human rights. Progressive changes in these critical areas of global life were perceived as endangering US supremacy as well as its sovereign and geopolitical prerogatives and the market-driven interests of capitalist economies.

The rise of China at the end of the twentieth century, the repeated failures of military interventions and attempted state-building by the United States in Asia, Africa, Latin America, and the Middle East, and in recent years, the shifts of economic and commercial power from West to East have intensified a process of de-Westernization and promoted multi-polarization with significant implications for global governance, multilateralism, and the future orientation of the UN.

It is of interest that the United States and other Western countries have begun to admit publicly their realization that neither a single country, not even the most powerful, nor an alliance of countries can adequately meet challenges of global scope such as climate change, migration, religious extremism, transnational crime, and pandemics on their own. We consider this still-emergent awareness that international problem-solving depends on global mechanisms capable of engendering global solidarity as a hopeful sign of reinvigorated appreciation that human betterment depends on a stronger UN with greater lawmaking and policy-implementing capabilities. These meta-national imperatives contain important messages for governments, peoples, and private sector interests: nationalism as well as regional unilateralism perpetuate division, conflict, and confrontation and have prevented the United Nations at political and operational levels from achieving many of its objectives with respect to world peace, security, ecological stability, and socio-economic progress for all. The UN and the WHO have reminded the world that COVID-19, the most recent and highly dramatic example of a truly global crisis, can be handled effectively only by a worldwide integrated effort. The pandemic vividly demonstrated that highly contagious viruses respect no borders and during the crisis, harmful effects could have been mitigated by less statist and conflictual, more cooperative and equitable international responses.

The Ukraine War (2022) revived the original preoccupation of the UN with the prevention of aggressive warmaking. Although the UN was limited to endorsing a General Assembly Resolution condemning the Russian aggression, the inability to exert a restraining influence on geopolitical violations of basic Charter norms exposed a dangerous gap in world order. The alternative to passivity was geopolitical confrontation, which contained highly dangerous risks of escalation, including the approach to the thresholds of nuclear threat or use. A geopolitical strategy of response has endangered turning the UN into a geopolitical propaganda tool for P5 actors that can command majority support in the General Assembly. This accomplishes little and may give the UN a reputation of being a rubber stamp for Western priorities.

In our efforts during several years of research and reflection to understand why the UN, in particular the Security Council and the General Assembly, evolved in the way they have, we have come to a fundamental conclusion for the period since the end of the Cold War. Evidence and assessments, which have been set forth in previous chapters of this book, show that the US in pursuit of its worldwide geopolitical interests by way of a unilateralist foreign policy makes use of its military and economic power as a matter of national discretion rather than subject to the rule of law. This pattern of behavior has been the single most clarifying explanation of both the turbulence of international relations and the often-disappointing performance of the United Nations.

Despite deficiencies in overall performance, the General Assembly and the Security Council have succeeded over time in narrowing their isolation from the non-governmental world of civil society. As we have pointed out, the General Assembly via ECOSOC has significantly expanded its links to Southern and Northern non-governmental organizations and today is partnering with civil society in ways that until recently were inconceivable. Western governments, but also other states such as India, however, insist that General Assembly cooperation must "fully respect the intergovernmental nature of the Assembly,"[1] a stand that reflects a fear that civil society could endanger the independence, public interest goals, and nationalist orientations of governments and political elites. This fear relates especially to well-funded NGOs that are vehicles for the promotion of private-sector business interests.

Such anxieties help explain why the Security Council has staunchly refused, until well into the second decade of the twenty-first century, to engage significantly with civil society. Nevertheless, some progress has been made. The Security Council today at least maintains, although with noticeable reluctance, informal contacts with civil society. This recent Security Council approach involves inviting selected NGOs, CSOs, and individuals to participate, even in some politically sensitive Council debates. A related positive development is associated with the increased reliance by the Security Council on UN special envoys, political affairs officials, and senior UN field staff in its briefings and deliberations. The Security Council has furthermore agreed that operational staff participating in mediation, peacekeeping and peacebuilding, humanitarian intervention, and development issues can work at the country level as integrated teams. These are positive steps that improve cooperation between the Security Council and the executive arm of the UN but fall far short of the structural adaptations that are required if the UN is ever to become an effective facilitator of peace and sustainable human development.

The UN, in carrying out its legislative functions, has over the years also given rise to the development of international law with the potential to improve global community-mindedness and human rights. We have depicted this contribution to world order in prior chapters. We also observed that governments have often ignored or broken the very laws they had helped establish, further diminishing respect for international law.

The emerging geopolitical changes due to global redistributions of power and the concurrent multiplication of international threats make UN engagement in genuine global dialogic processes a matter of growing urgency. For this to happen, a series of constitutional changes in the UN Charter are needed to enable the UN to fulfill its potential to cope with global challenges. Political leadership in the world, especially leadership associated with the five permanent members of the Security Council and state groupings of such as the G7, the G20, the Shanghai Cooperation Organization, and BRICS can no longer ignore the dramatic realities imperiling the well-being, indeed the survival, of the human species and its natural habitat.

We want to believe that given these circumstances, most present and future governments will become willing not only to support but to facilitate a constructive international debate on what must be done to ensure an enhanced role for the UN. US President Biden reassured his audience in 2021 at the UN General Assembly with these words: "Instead of continuing to fight the wars of the past, we are fixing our eyes on devoting our resources to the challenges that hold the keys to our collective future." Promising rhetoric of this sort induces cynicism unless acted upon. We would hope that the US, along with other countries, can be persuaded to act in this spirit, but it will not happen without strong populist pressures that insist on such a reorientation of foreign policy. If this spirit gains ascendancy, dysfunctional unilateralist policies would come to an end and a start would be made toward building global trust among countries that would encourage greater cooperation in addressing vital issues, including peace and security. It is crucial that not only the P5 countries but also other leading UN member countries such as Brazil, Mexico, India, Indonesia, Germany, Japan, Nigeria, South Africa, and the Scandinavian countries become again actively supportive in bringing about basic UN reforms.

There can be no doubt that a P5 foreign policy pivot is a precondition for a new global governance paradigm. Without it, multilateralism will continue to stagnate while the challenges grow ever more severe. Political leaders must remember that the United Nations was never meant to be an autonomous actor but rather to serve as a vehicle for the pursuit of common goals in a still predominantly state-centric world order. As a result, no matter how serious the concern, the UN will not be able to fashion a helpful response without a consensus among its leading members and constructive involvement by its overall membership. It is our hope that the UN gains greater operational self-reliance by becoming less dependent on receiving the green light from the Security Council and exclusively governmental funding for its regular budget.

How realistic and achievable such proposals are for a comprehensive constitutional and structural UN renewal would become clearer if a long overdue General Conference of the Members of the United Nations is finally put on the General Assembly agenda. According to the UN Charter, such a conference should have been held in 1955, ten years after the organization was established in 1945.[2] This unbelievably long failure to hold such a conference, given the momentous changes in the global setting, can only be explained by the reluctance of the P5 to weaken their position within the UN System. Further delay has become intolerable. This delay of sixty-five years should be ended as soon as possible. Nevertheless, despite this urgency, it will take concerted efforts to make this conference take place.

At best it will be a daunting, lengthy, and complicated undertaking. We expect that it will encounter similar resistances to what so long obstructed UN efforts to respond to the climate agenda. Significantly, the UN, after many warnings from climate experts, did sponsor initiatives that led to the 2015 Paris Climate Agreement and the 2021 Cairo COP26 and the 2022 Glasgow COP27 sequels. Perseverance by some governments, supported by civil society, especially youth leaders, briefly gave the world a glimmer of hope a decade ago that global warming could be contained within manageable limits set by an expert consensus on what policy adjustments on carbon emissions were necessary within given time intervals. The national commitments were essentially voluntary; the attention of governments was distracted by COVID and the Ukraine War; and global warming has grown more menacing that ever.

In seventy-eight years, the number of UN reform challenges have continually increased for the Security Council and the General Assembly, the two organs serving as the legislative bodies of the UN. Should member governments act to maintain the UN's present status quo, that would probably allow the UN to persist at best as a generally ineffectual institution when it comes to spearheading responses to major strategic and ideological issues that possess the greatest relevance to the future of human well-being. The General Assembly needs to transform itself into an assembly of all for all, mustering the political will to close ranks and finally agree to discuss and decide on the future of the United Nations by a belated insistence on convening the General Conference. On such an occasion, world leaders would be given a singular opportunity to demonstrate that they are becoming responsibly globalist in outlook and disposed to multilateral solutions to the problems of humanity because an understanding was taking root that such an approach would be of benefit for everyone. If such a disposition were to emerge, it would immediately encourage dialogue, cooperative problem-solving, and compromise with respect to the complex and diverse UN institutional constraints that have given rise to the frustrating ingrained practices of both the General Assembly and the Security Council.

"Structural engineers" charged with UN reform will have the dual task to ensure, first, that a Security Council whose membership reflects the geopolitical realities of the day is converting to engage in decision-making based on majority preferences rather than reflecting the interests of a few major states that won an important war back in 1945, and second, to make it possible for the General Assembly to exert greater influence on Security Council decision-making. Such an empowered General Assembly would no longer operate in only advisory and recommending roles. As we have discussed, the General Assembly did acquire in 1950 a "uniting for peace" mandate with the authority to act in a peace and security context when the Security Council was unable to do so. Such a narrowly defined mechanism, however, was the product of a Western attempt to circumvent the Soviet veto power and convert the UN into a policy tool of the transatlantic alliance. This authority, rarely used in recent years because the West was not any readier than the East to empower the General Assembly in conflict situations, needs to be revisited in this changed global setting.

The reconfiguration of the legislative dimension of UN decision-making is almost certain to be the most difficult part of international efforts to reform the UN in a manner enabling the organization to address the problems of the twenty-first century and performing in a world that is vastly more complex and challenging than what existed in the immediate post-WWII years. We purposely refer to "international efforts" because we expect that the reform process, if successful, will involve not only governments but also a robust transnational civil society movement empowered by playing participatory roles within the UN.

There also is the need for a collective Security Council/General Assembly reassessment regarding the composition and the size of the Security Council and the use of the veto by its permanent members. Security Council permanent membership consisting of three Western countries plus the Soviet Union (now Russia) and China was already problematic in 1945 but has become anachronistic in the 2020s. The demographic, geographical, and geopolitical realities of the twenty-first century suggest major adjustments in the geographical distribution of permanent seats in the Security Council. They call for permanent representation for Africa and Latin America, which at present have none, and increased representation for Asia. The necessary downgrading of the role and status of the US, UK, and France, as three Western permanent members of the Security Council, representing just 8 percent of the world's population, is an indispensable component of the reformist proposals that we advocate. We fully realize that potent interests will do their best to block such a reform project, however appropriate it is. This dysfunctional opposition is enabled by the legal framework of the Charter that allows states that possess an unrestricted veto power to protect their entrenched institutional interests, however detrimental such obstructive behavior is to a more effective UN. To circumvent this obstacle will be a major challenge for UN reforms.

The composition, size, and voting rules of the Security Council have remained a topic of disagreement among members for many years. In the early 1990s, a UN report stated that the Security Council with only fifteen states gives rise to a claim of underrepresentation of the world on whose behalf the Council acts.[3] In the eyes of the developing world, there is a prima facie case that the Security Council does not reflect today's global reality. A situation of resentment and discontent has developed that undermines respect for the work and authority of the Security Council.

Despite mounting pressure for Security Council reform, the only change that occurred was in 1965 in response to the growing number of countries becoming independent. The Council membership was increased from eleven to fifteen members by adding four seats for non-permanent members.

During this third decade of the twenty-first century, there is general agreement in the Security Council that reforms can no longer be delayed. Voices for Security Council reforms are growing louder during these times of extremely tense relations. There is little agreement, however, about details regarding key issues such as categories of membership, the veto, regional representation, enlargement, and the relationship between the Security Council and the General Assembly. It is important to distinguish recent efforts arising from the Ukraine War to abridge the use of the veto to contain and punish Russia from a UN reform movement aimed at making the organization more effective and legitimate globally.

The Chinese government concedes that Security Council membership needs to expand "when the time is ripe" and that "the overrepresentation of developed countries must end"; the French government argues that "an increase of permanent members must consider the relative weight acquired by certain states." Both countries understand that geopolitical change demands Security Council adaptation. The US supports expansion of the numbers of both permanent and non-permanent seats. Russia supports the expansion of the Security Council to include new permanent members from Africa and Latin America. For the UK, Security Council reform is "today more relevant and important than ever; momentum for change is building around the UN."[4] The P5 pronouncements, positive as they seem to be, do not dispel the impression that these five countries continue to adhere to an anachronistic and dysfunctional Faustian bargain, which is expressed by a refusal to replace in the functioning of the Security Council the primacy of geopolitics and a willingness to live within the limits of the Charter and international law. The hope of 1945 that the wartime alliance among the five permanent members of the Security Council would morph into an alliance dedicated to keeping world peace disappeared before it was even tried.

The dangerous current stalemate produced by the Ukraine crisis and other global challenges requiring major cooperative initiatives makes the reform debate even more urgent. Many UN member states have become understandably impatient with prolonged failure to make those governance adjustments that take account of changes in the geopolitical atmosphere and the geographical distribution of economic and political influence, as well as radical shifts in priorities on the global policy agenda. In 2016, a General Assembly working group concerned with the role, authority, and effectiveness of the General Assembly reaffirmed "the central position of the General Assembly as the chief deliberate policymaking and representative organ of the UN," pointing out that the "revitalization of the work of the General Assembly is a critical component of the overall reform of the UN." We share this view and believe that there exists a growing demand by governments and informed public opinion for a thorough review of the structural relationship between the Security Council and the General Assembly as set forth in the UN Charter and reflected by more than seven decades of institutional experience. Such an early debate and dialogue for reform is desirable and overdue.

An aspect of this reform challenge is to include revised expectations for non-permanent Security Council members, perhaps stressing the election of states that would undertake to represent their region's as well as their nation's interests. This proposed shift in identity might seem insignificant, but it could be part of an overall transition from a UN dominated by geopolitically guided statism to a UN that is more globally oriented and operationally independent, as well as more disposed to rely upon multilateral cooperative mechanisms to solve global scale problems. From the vantage point of the present, such radical reforms seem unlikely because they presuppose that dominant states will voluntarily give up their geopolitical and statist prerogatives to form a more viable UN. The Ukrainian crisis, the future geopolitical roles of Russia and China as major powers inside and outside of the UN, and the concurrent global-order adjustments, however, will no doubt have a profound impact on the future of multilateralism. Western permanent Security Council members may be persuaded, although reluctantly and not assuredly, to accept such reformist objectives as the lesser of evils.

Should the Security Council not be adapted, it would remain incapable of discharging its primary responsibility, "the maintenance of peace and security," making the UN virtually irrelevant at a time when the world order faces increasing conditions of disorder and is faced with urgent needs for multilateral cooperation. What if the P5 despite this reality holds stubbornly to their selfish national interests? If this happens, various initiatives will almost certainly be put forward for bypassing the UN, including forming new polarizing alliances and coalitions, and might even lead to attempts to form a new global organization, more legally and financially empowered to act on its own, with the goal of inventing an institutional tool with better prospects of serving the needs of peoples of the world than is the present UN. Yet, we should ask, if countries are unwilling to renounce their prerogatives within the UN, why would they be willing to join an organization that subordinated geopolitics? In response we can observe that the mere effort of a group of countries to form a new organization might be just the push the P5 needs to finally obtain their support for UN reform, and further, without some sort of threat, it would likely remain harder to induce the P5 to make these sensible adjustments.

As we have pointed out, vetoes by permanent members of the Security Council have frequently been cast in furtherance of national interests and geopolitical ambitions, including the privileging of their political alignments over the global public interest. Such a serious misuse of authority has prevented the Council from functioning in accord with international law and the idealistic hopes of the strongest supporters of the UN. The General Conference foreseen in the Charter, to which we have referred, would potentially be able to invoke some important recommendations made over the years by the General Assembly and by individual member states and UN Secretaries-General to adopt arrangements that decrease the likelihood of future veto-related breakdowns in fulfilling the mandated role assigned to the Security Council by the Charter. Such recommendations would focus, in all probability, on limiting the uses of the veto. An attractive compromise approach could be to replace the veto with a two-thirds or three-quarters majority on all Security Council actions, although with the caveat that such voting is not used as a geopolitical tool to isolate a given P5 member.

Few supporters of an effective UN doubt the need to change the voting rules in the Security Council, but fewer still are unaware of the difficulty of inducing the P5 to renounce or even alter this constitutional prerogative that they have enjoyed ever since the UN was founded. To be clear, burdensome as the veto has proved to be, it was part of the original Charter design, including the crippling condition that the veto powers must themselves agree on its curtailment. Reformist zeal should not overlook the risks arising from getting rid of the veto power, which might produce a repetition of similar failures to those experienced by the League of Nations, which became irrelevant due to nonparticipation by several of the most influential states.

In the case of Iraq there have been two key so-called consensus resolutions during thirteen years of comprehensive economic sanctions, stating that sanctions would be lifted only if "Iraq has completed all actions contemplated" and "Iraq has cooperated in all respects."[5] Council members obviously could not agree on whether Iraq had "completed all actions" and "cooperated in all respects." Almost nine years passed between these two resolutions and even during this long period, no agreement was reached by the P5 on how to achieve Iraq's disarmament while at the same time protect the innocent Iraqi civilian population from the harsh effects of sanctions. In both instances, the Security Council's consensus approach did not overcome the disagreement. On the contrary, it aggravated the conflict, victimizing civilians and interfering with UN efforts to fulfil the humanitarian responsibilities assigned to it.

Consensus resolutions can also be misused by P5 members, as previously observed, to support actions not within the scope of the Security Council mandate but in furtherance of national interests and geopolitical ambitions. Two such resolutions, one for Iraq, the other for Libya, provide examples. The Security Council decided in 2002 that "if Iraq is in material breach of its obligations, it will face serious consequences."[6] With regard to Libya, the Security Council authorized member states "to take all necessary measures" in circumstances where P5 members were divided as to the preferred course of action and interpreted the imprecise wording unilaterally rather than collectively.[7] The result in both instances was unlawful military interventions producing significant harm to civilians and serious violations of UN Charter law as well as international humanitarian law.

The UN Charter has given the Security Council the authority to establish subsidiary bodies that include sanctions committees. These committees, with a membership that reflects the composition of the Security Council, are intended to oversee sanctions policies and facilitate the implementation of humanitarian exemptions. The management of sanctions was supposed to be left in the hands of the operational organs of the UN. However, just as with the Security Council itself, these committees, operating under provisional rules of procedure, adopted a practice of relying on consensus-based decisions. This meant that sanctions committees were being controlled by the P5 and, as von Sponeck, who attended Iraq Sanction Committee meetings witnessed, policy and implementation monitoring degenerated into various forms of damaging micromanagement reflecting antagonistic P5 interests at play. In this way, consensus-based decisions frequently undermined humanitarian assistance earmarked for Iraq, obstructing efforts by experienced UN personnel to keep faith with the humanitarian mission entrusted to the UN. It became obvious that consensus resolutions should be used rarely and briefly.

For many years, a wide range of other issues concerning the functioning of the Security Council has been left unattended. Security Council rules of procedure have become problematic. The UN Charter directs that the General Assembly and the Security Council "shall adopt their own rules."[8] While the General Assembly from the beginning has worked in accordance with formally approved rules of procedures, the Security Council has failed to do so, and quite deliberately. Until now, it has failed to adopt definite rules. Instead, the Security Council conducts its business according to "provisional" rules first identified as such in 1946. P5 member countries have seemed comfortable with this arrangement, insisting that "rigid rules would interfere with the flexibility the Council needs to do its work."

It would have been difficult to argue with these five countries that the Security Council, as an intergovernmental entity, should indeed have *formally* established rules in accordance with Article 30 of the UN Charter rather than provisional ones because the latter do not provide assurances that they are consistent with UN Charter objectives. The record of the Security Council shows that what was justified as needed for the sake of "flexibility" to carry out UN operations was instead often used to provide the P5 "protection" for their political activities, which were frequently carried out in a manner that defied the constraints of international law.

These rules of procedure and the use of consensus resolutions may seem technical and of no general interest, but such concerns are integral to understanding public disappointment with the performance of the UN. The example of the Security Council's handling of Iraq sanctions unequivocally illustrates this point. The UN Charter declares that a country "party to a dispute under consideration by the Security Council, shall be invited to participate . . . in the discussion relating to the dispute."[9] The provisional rules of procedure assert that "unless it [the Security Council] decides otherwise . . . it shall meet in public." A confidential report to the Security Council related to Iraq argues that "due to a grave change of procedure, it is now the other way around."[10] The Council meets more often than not, in so-called "informal consultations" behind closed doors, inaccessible, even if the topics to be discussed are of direct relevance to a government not a member of the Council. Von Sponeck witnessed the frustration of Iraqi diplomats who wanted to join such Security Council meetings to discuss matters involving their country but were barred from participation. The General Assembly should express its opinion that the Security Council discontinue operating under provisional rules and instead adopt formally agreed rules of procedure.

The range of fundamental structural, substantive, and procedural adaptations needed to equip the UN Security Council to tackle global challenges is broad and incredibly complex. Most importantly, members of the Security Council need to be persuaded to become more responsive to an operational paradigm that is oriented toward global-mindedness, trust-building, greater equity in sharing resources for the welfare of all, and increased sensitivity toward global environmental protection. Furthermore, the five permanent nations in the Security Council need to understand that their privileged status of leadership and discretionary action in relation to the other 188 UN member countries, besides being outdated and controversial, is conditional. Whenever P5 members do not vote in accordance with the Purposes and Principles as defined in the UN Charter (Article 24) and act in violation of Charter law, we wish to propose that either the President of the Security Council or the General Assembly under special authority (A/RES/377/1950) or both be authorized to declare such voting out of order and void. This sweeping reorientation of Security Council practice presupposes a willingness to govern UN undertakings in a manner less reflective of stat-ist and geopolitical realism and more in keeping with a globalist paradigm. We are fully aware that such conditions do not presently exist, and insuf-ficient political traction now exists for this reorientation of UN practice to occur.

To adjust the governance structure is undoubtedly the most demanding act of change for any institution of governance. Global conditions of life are currently extremely fragile, and people everywhere need protection, making these recommended changes in the UN urgent and nonnegotiable. We have pointed out earlier that existing mega-crises of climate change, weaponry of mass destruction, pandemics, poverty, extremism, and human migration, affecting almost all nations and peoples in the world, offers uniquely strong incentives for far-reaching solutions based on ambitious of problem-solving and cooperation. We are aware that it is a giant task to turn this rational imperative into a viable political project.

The struggle of nations, especially between the poor and the wealthy, to find common ground for global survival (as at COP meetings in Copen-hagen, Glasgow, and Sharm El Sheikh) is a stark reminder of the immense challenges facing humanity for which the entire UN System is called upon to respond in effective and humane ways. China and the US, the two larg-est $CO_2$ emitters, have at various times expressed their willingness to work closely together in reaching climate change targets, a glimmer of hope that governments, including P5 countries, are realizing that current global crises require global solidarity and that the UN offers the strategic plat-forms for global cooperation, equitable adjustments, and trust-building.

Generations of older people have a moral obligation not to forget that they will be replaced by future generations. The young, in developing and developed countries alike, are uniting in their awareness that getting the global house in order ecologically, socially, politically, and economically is a precondition for their security in the future, regardless of where they live or their class or race. The voices and protests of youth at COP meetings and in the streets around the world for the UN to declare a "system-wide cli-mate emergency" highlights their demands. Future generations preparing for their future will not relent in pressing for responsible change. Unless governments fully understand this, protests, often violent, will increase dramatically from Europe to Central Asia and from Africa to Latin Amer-ica and Australia. In response to this global reality, the UN, especially the Security Council, will need to abandon its insular non-transparency and open its doors to public dialogue and interaction in a search for fair and just solutions for all. It is encouraging that most UN member states increasingly understand this crucial need for UN reform. This understanding is reflected in a progressive UN decision in 2022 that "living in a clean, healthy, and sustainable environment is a universal human right."[11]

The UN Charter, despite granting special powers to the Security Council, nevertheless gives the General Assembly the right to debate issues that "endanger international peace and security" and to alert the Security Council accordingly. In cases of emergencies, the General Assembly has the underused uniting-for-peace authority to overcome impasses at the Security Council that imperil world peace. What is further required is a two-thirds majority in the Assembly to agree on a way forward. We believe this authority should be further extended to give the General Assembly more authority and responsibility to intervene in all areas of global public concern. This would be a momentous change in the operational logic of the UN, substituting the will of a super-majority of states in the General Assembly for the current grudging acceptance of the primacy of geopolitics in the Security Council.

Across the South/North divide in the General Assembly, many governments and increasingly the informed public complain about the overall persistent ineffectiveness, indeed behavioral irrelevance of the General Assembly in dealing with global matters. This disappointing record partly reflects the unwillingness of General Assembly members to find solutions through compromise, as well as the absence of a leadership capable of brokering agreements. Another reason for General Assembly ineffectiveness is that it and its subsidiary organs have not developed the ability to handle the increasing workloads resulting from a plethora of agenda items. UN working groups have on several occasions come up with long lists of steps the General Assembly should take to increase its effectiveness and efficiency. These include improving working methods, streamlining agendas, shortening speaking time, clustering or deleting program items, applying sunset clauses, and eliminating overlaps. Unfortunately, to date, these internal housekeeping reforms have not been implemented and the General Assembly is more diminished in stature than ever, with its recommendations being seldom acted upon and rarely even reported to the public.

A review of annual UN reports has confirmed that the General Assembly and its subsidiary bodies devote an inordinate amount of time to annual reconsideration of recommendations and resolutions, with texts often repeated for decades in such areas as disarmament, decolonization, global trade, socio-economic development, and crisis management in different parts of the world, especially the Middle East and South Asia. These General Assembly initiatives, redundant as they are, do not set forth any corrective course of action in such areas as disarmament, decolonization, and socio-economic justice. At the same time, these resolutions are tools of antagonists in legitimacy wars, especially reflecting counter-hegemonic forms of resistance directed at the primacy of geopolitics. Although of minimal intergovernmental consequence, such General Assembly initiatives may underpin civil society activism regarding human rights, civil strife, and environmental degradation.

In this regard, our criticisms of the substantive irrelevance of the General Assembly when it comes to mandating constructive action by governments, should acknowledge the positive symbolic impact that General Assembly resolutions have upon the legitimacy balance in the liberation struggles of repressed peoples. Although this UN relevance to domains of symbolic politics should not go unappreciated, greater support needs to be given to General Assembly undertakings that have realistic chances of producing substantive agreements and becoming operational. If this were to happen, it would create more of an impression that the UN is putting a practical stress on problem-solving. This would help overcome the widely held skepticism that the UN, especially the General Assembly, is "nothing but a talk shop" that substitutes utterances of state propaganda for real dialogue and shared problem-solving.

The General Assembly relies currently on six main committees to assist it and member states in dealing with a broad spectrum of concerns ranging from political, disarmament, security, environment, to economic, financial, social, human rights and cultural heritage as well as administrative, budgetary, and legal issues.[12] The General Assembly should carefully review whether the existing committees adequately cover or wastefully duplicate the treatment of priority issues of global, regional, national, and institutional importance to allow the General Assembly to adapt better its operations to global developments. For instance, the committees on disarmament and international security could be merged, and so could the special political and decolonization committees, the economic and financial committees, and the social, humanitarian, and cultural committees. At the same time, we believe that an additional subsidiary General Assembly working group should be added to cover issues of climate change, sustainable development, ecological stability, environmental protection, and governance. The status and progress of reforms of the General Assembly, the Security Council, and the operational system could be made the primary responsibility of a General Assembly Monitor, a select committee established to exert pressure on high-level UN leaders to implement UN System reforms, including agreed steps to lessen geopolitical back-channel pressures that have in the past weakened reforms of the UN.

The UN legislative dimension is unquestionably in urgent need of overhaul. The pressure for change is being expressed in many forms. What is being sought is an institution that helps to advance global justice and promotes and protects people's well-being and at the same time contributes to ecological safeguarding and, more ambitiously, the healing of our wounded planet. On November 9, 2021, Mexican president López Obrador delivered a notable message to the UN Security Council, declaring that the UN, "the most important caucus of the international community, must awaken from its lethargy and routine . . . to reform itself and to denounce and to fight global corruption and to combat inequality and social unrest with more commitment and more depth, with insistency and more leadership." We fully associate ourselves with this almost desperate plea for UN reform, although we regard "international community" as reflective of an aspiration for shared values rather than a presently existing reality.

There is, of course, an extensive UN reform agenda beyond the Security Council and the General Assembly, involving the International Court of Justice and the many institutional components of the UN's operational system.

## The International Court of Justice

Arguably, the judicial dimension of the UN System is the least utilized and least evolved element in the overall scheme of governance that it was hoped the UN would provide when it was established. The International Court of Justice (ICJ) has been hampered in serving the visionary perspectives of the Preamble to the UN Charter, as well as in upholding the Principles and Purposes of the Charter set forth in Articles 1 and 2, by two principal design features of the UN. First, international law guidance sought from the ICJ by organs of the UN results in "advisory opinions" rather than enforceable UN decisions emanating from the Security Council or conceivably from the General Assembly. Second, recourse to the ICJ by states embroiled in legal disputes is mainly a matter of their mutual agreement rather than automatically obligatory. True, states can opt to accept the "compulsory jurisdiction" of the ICJ, but this voluntary alternative has been ignored by leading states or has been discredited by noncompliance and impunity from adverse political consequences for the wrongdoer. Also, the compulsory jurisdiction is accepted by few states, and even then, it is subject to major reservations and a requirement that it is applicable only if both states to the dispute accept it on a reciprocal basis.

Reform priorities would attempt to address these intentional design limitations. Treating ICJ authoritative guidance about international law as "advisory" sends a message that compliance with even a strong majority opinion is voluntary rather than obligatory. The nuclear-weapons states encountered no friction when they chose to disregard the Advisory Opinion in 1996 on the legality of the threat or use of nuclear weapons nor did Israel when a near unanimous ICJ Advisory Opinion in 2004 decreed the dismantling of those portions of the separation wall built in Occupied Palestine. In effect, despite the ICJ being less political than other organs of the UN, with judges largely selected on their credentials as jurists, its international law assessments are subject to what amounts to a "political veto" by any member of the UN. The main role of the Advisory Opinions has not been to alter behavior on the ground but rather to influence world public opinion and civil society activism—that is, to exert influence in the symbolic domain of legitimacy politics.

As far as the present limitations on the ICJ jurisdictional authority is concerned, it would greatly strengthen the relevance of the UN judiciary if members of the UN could be persuaded to make compulsory jurisdiction mandatory once remedies within the respective states have failed to resolve the dispute. This kind of deference to judicial authority would still be dependent on discretionary compliance unless the veto on implementation by the Security Council was suspended. Such a drastic reform would not be realistic unless there was overwhelming support to lessen the leverage of the P5 and, more generally, to weaken deference to the state-centric features of the original UN design. Enhancing the authority of the ICJ is a challenge both to geopolitical prerogatives and to the sovereign rights of states.

## The Operational System of the UN and Its Specialized Agencies, Funds, and Programs

The UN operational system has continuously expanded its presence everywhere on planet Earth, even in the face of persisting polarization and nationalism. We have observed UN agencies, funds, and programs and their decentralized systems impressively overcoming their organizational isolation of the late 1950s. A hopeful pattern of increasing integration has been evident in recent years. During the initial decades, the focus of individual UN entities was on implementing their own programs rather than cooperating with others. Technically difficult communications between field offices that were distant from UN headquarters created an additional dimension of isolation. These were the days of dependence on pouches or diplomatic bags, often causing long delays in the transmission of information.

These delays were not totally unwelcomed in many overseas UN offices. Serving in remote countries such as Bhutan, Botswana, or Fiji, UN personnel often welcomed delays because "they left us alone for a while" or meant "freedom from bothersome and unpersuasive directives from UN Headquarters bureaucrats." Later came more efficient tools of communication, such as fax machines followed by email, Skype, and Zoom. These technological mainstays of the digital age ended the isolation of field offices. Now interactive communication networks have enabled the UN operational system to promote higher quality output and greater inclusivity. Distance and remoteness have become operationally less relevant.

Elements of the current organizational configurations had been created long before the UN came into existence: the International Telecommunication Union (ITU) in 1865, the Universal Postal Union in 1874, the International Labour Organization in 1919, and so on. Others—for example, UNICEF, FAO, WHO, UNESCO, and the World Bank—were established in the late 1940s and 1950s to respond to post-WWII emergencies and focused upon children, food, education, and national reconstruction. As the range of needs of the developing world became better understood and more widely accepted as entailing global responsibilities, the UN System responded by diversifying its organizational networks further to provide a wider assortment of new services. The UN Development Programme (UNDP), for example, was established in 1965 to coordinate multilateral technical assistance. Organizations with sectoral responsibilities appeared, such as the UN Industrial Development Organization (UNIDO) for industry, the International Maritime Organization (IMO) and the International Civil Aviation Organization (ICAO) for sea and air traffic, the UN Population Fund (UNFPA) for population, the UN Development Fund for Women (UNIFEM) and UN Women for gender equality, the UN International Drug Control Programme (UNDCP) and the UN Office on Drugs and Crime (UNODC) for drugs and crime, and the World Food Programme (WFP) for food supply.

The World Trade Organization (WTO), a non-UN institutional complement to the UN Conference on Trade and Development (UNCTAD), was established in 1995 to lessen friction with the Global South while promoting trade and investment. Institutional parallels of this sort tend to undermine the authority of the UN System. This pattern of avoiding UN institutional attachments, as with the WTO and the ICC, erodes and weakens the UN's valuable and important actual and potential role of providing unified global governance.

We acknowledge that non-UN institutional innovations can on occasion have a progressive impact as was the case of the International Criminal

Court, which could not be established within the UN System. The ICC could only be outside it. The existence of the ICC, despite disappointing aspects of its record, has strengthened prospects for accountability by perpetrators of international crimes despite its current limits in asserting jurisdiction or implementing its findings, especially with respect to major geopolitical actors. The positive contributions of the ICC to date are principally confined to the domain of symbolic politics. As stressed earlier, it is a mistake to dismiss symbolic contributions as worthless, given the degree to which legitimacy perceptions influence public opinion, civil society activism, and sometimes even intergovernmental behavior, as the UN anti-apartheid campaign waged against South Africa illustrates.

This mix of UN bodies with vastly different specializations and distinct sectoral interests, and at times overlapping objectives, needed strong leadership at the UN Secretariat to convert them into a system in which parties were willing to coordinate their mandates and cooperate as UN teams. It was a slow and frustrating but persistent process complicated by geopolitical interferences exerted by the World Bank and the International Monetary Fund, two major UN agencies underpinning global economic policy and dominated by the US and its Western allies. There was an undeniable clash between the neoliberal market ideology of the World Bank and the IMF and the moral authority of most of the UN operational system. Over time, this clash has moderated and led to more effective relations between the UN and the Bretton Woods Institutions.

In the initial decades of UN operational activities, both donor and recipient governments were the UN's exclusive partners. These patterns of cooperation have changed significantly in recent years. In implementing its programs, the UN outreach has broadened to include more and more citizen involvement and partnerships. We are confident that this trend will continue as the value of local knowledge and participation in decision-making and policy implementation is almost everywhere greatly appreciated. Today non-governmental and civil society organizations participate routinely in UN summits devoted to human well-being on subjects ranging from health to education, population and housing to human rights, including gender, climate change and eco-protection and rehabilitation. In chapter 9, this relatively new and important role of civil society in multilateral policymaking has been discussed. We regard civil society not only as a partner but as an essential collaborator with the UN and governments in the development of a worldwide discourse related to peace, security, human rights, climate change, and sustainable development. How the private sector fits within this push for greater civil society participation is a controversial conceptual issue, with policy implications. It would not be desirable to open the UN to well-funded lobbying campaigns in such domains as arms sales, energy, pharmaceuticals, or food.

During the years when the UN operational system was making good progress in combining human and financial resources for the delivery of integrated development assistance, there was relatively little intervention from donor governments, except at the annual meetings of the various UN governing boards at which policies and funding were determined[13] or when UN System activities touched on matters of political interest such as refugee, migrant, and internally displaced person movements, narcotics, transnational crime, or security issues. At UN headquarters in New York, accredited governments, the Secretary-General, and senior UN staff were constantly preoccupied with acute political and security matters and tended to overlook the linkages between political crises and inadequate development, giving scant attention to the work of UN agencies, funds, and programs.

However, as more UN agencies, funds, and programs established joint programming and linkages between development, environmental protection, humanitarian support, peacekeeping, and security operations, the Security Council and the General Assembly began to appreciate the value of their cooperation with the work of the UN. This was unquestionably a significant step forward. We hope that General Assembly and Security Council outreach will become a standard feature of UN activities rather than still being selective, reflecting discretionary choices. This cooperation should only have to do with the sharing of experience between policymakers and implementers and not impinge upon funding arrangements or UN policy. A trend toward earmarked funding by donor countries to support their preferred UN development initiatives is problematic for reasons previously considered. It also challenges the judgment and professionalism of UN leadership by exhibiting doubt when it comes to determining policy priorities. Government earmarking is also inconsistent with the provisions of the UN Charter.[14] In the case of the UNDP, for example, in recent years, up to 80 percent of its finance have been earmarked, resulting in the disproportionate influence of richer countries.

The inadequacy of the financing of the UN operational system more generally has been discussed earlier. Any serious reform in this area must include a willingness of OECD countries and other governmental authorities to significantly increase their levels of support.[15] This means that the General Assembly should redefine the formula of assessed contributions from member countries and insist that governments adhere to making payments at the beginning of each year or face penalties. While for 2022, four of the permanent members had paid in full their assessed contributions for the UN regular budget, the US, as of December 2022, had not only major arrears from previous years but had made no payments at all for that year. The US had also significant arrears in making payments of its assessed contributions to the UN peacekeeping budget.[16] The US government even owed $203 million to the World Health Organization as of early 2021, and this despite the special needs of this UN organization during the COVID pandemic.

The annual deliberations in the General Assembly's administrative and budgetary committee about assessed contributions for the UN regular and peacekeeping budgets have become an embarrassing display of dereliction of fiscal duties by member states, tainting further the already poor UN citizenship record of some P5 members.

The strengthening of the UN depends crucially on persuading the US and other P5 members to approach the UN in more law-abiding and fiscally accountable ways that manifest a growing sensitivity to adopting global approaches to global problems. Persuasion will not be easy. The US approach to the UN has been consistently responsive to narrowly defined national interests, geopolitical ambitions, and domestic pressures that take precedence over international needs and ethical standards in American foreign policy.

The UN Secretary-General and his team should not be humiliated in the future by being forced to travel the world with begging bowls, asking governments to pay their mandatory share and pleading for voluntary contributions to fund programs that the General Assembly has expressly approved. As we have pointed out, it should become an iron rule of practice that the operational system will implement new UN initiatives only when resources are reliably forthcoming and without earmarking strings attached. The UN of the future, if it to fulfill its potential and expanding world order expectations, will need to become free of geopolitical and other corrupting manipulations. We realize that this is easier said than done.

There is also the question of non-governmental sources supplementing funding of the UN System's regular annual budgets, an issue that has been raised repeatedly over the years but without a resolution. The idea of an international solidarity tax for supplementary resources—for example, to underwrite the UN's seventeen Sustainable Development Goals for 2015–2030 or to meet climate change targets—currently lacks support from major governments that fear a loss of control over UN activities.

The good progress the UN operational system has made over the years, despite many obstacles identified in various chapters, does not mean that there is not room for further improvement. The "one house, one chief, one program, one budget" plans for the UN's field presence are yet to become mandatory without disruptive delays. In this context, adequate training and preparations for country assignments of UN staff to field duty stations have never been taken seriously, even when politically sensitive posts are involved. The costs of this institutional failure have often been significant. Many governments and non-governmental organizations want to make sure that staff serving abroad are carefully prepared for assignments and equipped with knowledge about national and regional governance and the political, cultural, sociological, and historic context and learn the basics of the language spoken at their assigned duty station. The UN System does not presently have any such mandatory preparatory training programs. We are confident that the value added to UN field offices performance would be substantial.

Some governments, at times, have even questioned the need for a permanent UN civil service, suggesting instead employment arrangements on a contract basis and with limited duration. We consider this a misguided and short-sighted proposal. The United Nations System, just as national administrations, could not function effectively without a permanent civil service. Personnel that have grown professionally within the UN and display the benefits of many years of multilateral experience and time-tested commitment to the values of the UN Charter and the practices of the organization are a core resource for tackling the increasingly complex tasks entrusted to the UN and constitute a valuable public good. The General Assembly and the Security Council, therefore, should express their unconditional commitment to rely upon a permanent UN System civil service and ensure that it is made up of personnel meeting the highest standards of dedication, efficiency, competence, and integrity.

Through digital and print media, international conferences, and public webinars, the UN has come a long way in offering the public high-quality insights into a wide range of UN activities in all areas of life. Unfortunately, communications have seemed very much a one-way process from the UN to the public, without the public being given an adequate opportunity to offer reactions and proposals to the UN. We have come across many examples of individuals and groups who reached out to the UN in the belief that the UN was "their" organization but they often received only silence in response, even when there were serious, sometimes political, social, or life-threatening matters that they wanted to bring to the UN's attention. It is a harsh but verifiable conclusion that despite the UN purporting to be a "we, the peoples" organization, it has failed from the outset to feel an obligation to listen to the people's voices and offer advice. "There is no capacity for such a response mechanism" is a lame excuse often heard to explain this serious deficiency. It is totally a matter for senior UN officials to becoming genuinely more people-minded.

As the UN System, especially the UN Secretariat itself, continues to be forced to accept political appointments under pressure from member governments in violation of UN Charter norms, we consider it significant that the General Assembly, governments, and the Secretary-General reiterate that all UN staff, particularly at senior levels, should meet the highest standards of competence and integrity,[17] which was often severely lacking in the past. The remit of the UN Ethics Office should be expanded beyond concerns about individual staff to also include institutional issues. At the time of entering UN service, staff at all levels were once asked to take the following oath of office: "I solemnly declare and promise to exercise in all loyalty, discretion and conscience the functions entrusted to me as an international civil servant of the United Nations, to discharge these functions and regulate my conduct with the interests of the United Nations only in view, and not to seek or accept instructions in regard to the performance of my duties from any government or other source external to the organization." This oath should again become mandatory for all UN staff and, as a reminder, be repeated whenever a staff member is promoted. UN ethical issues involve not only the UN's civil service but also officials and staff of government missions to the UN. We are fully aware that currently, it is unlikely that they will be subject to ethical accountability, as they should be.

Prior chapters have dwelled upon the strengths and weaknesses of the UN as a political and operational institution. As outsiders who were once insiders, we have offered a picture of change and reform that the United Nations system requires to become a credible and effective institution able to promote the well-being of all people wherever they live and to enhance the human security and ecological stability of the planet. Our understanding of the dangerous and confrontational political reality in which we live in the twenty-first century does not inhibit us from putting forth admittedly visionary proposals for governance structures conducive to a world of peace, justice, and ecological stability. Such a vision cannot be realized unless and until states become truly committed to the promotion of the common good of humanity and function far more in accordance with the legal and moral standards laid down in the UN Charter, the two UN Covenants on Human Rights, and some version of an Earth Charter. Such revisioning of national interests would enable the UN to become a more independent, trusted, and vital component of a sustainable and equitable world order. If this were to pass, the UN would be less beholden to the statist and geopolitical architectures of world order that evolved from their

European experience and better able to provide the world with a global framework in the postcolonial era but one yet to be adapted to reflect the global solidarity needed to offer the twenty-first-century human and equitable security to the peoples of world.

Governments have been impressed by the operational system's improving response capacities in dealing with unforeseen natural disasters as well as a variety of catastrophes associated with human behavior, whether deliberate acts (genocide) or unintended byproducts of ordinary behavior, as in industrialization and extractive mining. Today, the UN operational system is generally appreciated as a system with worldwide capabilities and a helpful willingness to cooperate with many actors including governments, non-governmental organizations, and civil society in the course of implementing programs to better people's lives and the public good. Despite this notable progress, the capacity of the operational UN needs further improvement, structurally and financially. A General Assembly reform debate should determine what needs to be done to further strengthen the operational system to meet the challenges depicted throughout this book.

The UN's legislative and policymaking bodies, the General Assembly and Security Council, have faced a far wider range of political and structural obstacles than the operational system. These most prominent organs of the UN System have largely failed to fulfill fundamental UN Charter objectives to strengthen peace, promote people's welfare, and prevent war, and therefore, they have disappointed public expectations.

Despite important achievements, the General Assembly has had considerable difficulties in prioritizing its agenda and promoting practical results whenever its attempts run contrary to P5 strategic interests. The General Assembly invests substantial time and energy in efforts that members additional to the P5 have consistently opposed, as well as often failing to find bridges to overcome or minimize the divide between the developed and the developing world.

The Security Council, regrettably, has largely remained a collective of fifteen countries preoccupied with maximizing their national and regional interests rather than being a team acting on behalf of all UN member countries, especially on vital issues of war and peace, human development, and global crises such as COVID, Ukraine, and global warming. We have cited examples to show that cooperation between the five permanent Security Council members has rarely taken place when the Council sought to respond to intrastate and interstate conflicts for which unanimous agreement in the Council was required. However, when there was voting unanimity—for example, condemning and responding to Iraq's 1990 invasion of Kuwait or more recently the genocidal aftermath of the 2021 military coup in Myanmar—joint action confirmed the normative authority of the Security Council, especially if reinforced by existentially congruent P5 strategic interests. Even when action is authorized by Security Council decisions, the results may still be counterproductive either by way of doing too much (Libya, 2011) or too little (Myanmar, 2021), reflecting either the presence or absence of strong strategic incentives on the countries supplying the peacekeeping firepower.

The UN has demonstrated its ability to distinguish between the legal and illegal uses of force, although its performance is marred by double standards because unlawful behavior by allies is not condemned as it is for adversaries. The same assessment can be made in cases of UN peacekeeping—for example, along the borders between Israel and Syria, between Pakistan and India, and in Cyprus along the green line dividing Greek and Turkish areas of control. In these settings, sufficient Security Council unity has been present to moderate and contain underlying conflicts. Nevertheless, the 1945 spirit of Yalta granting primacy to geopolitics within the political UN has continued to dominate UN responses at the top of the global agenda, although configurations of power along with the magnitude and nature of international threats have drastically changed.

It would be naïve to suggest that normative, structural, and substantive reforms, necessary as they are, would suffice to confer on the two political organs of the United Nations the legislative authority needed for the UN to provide the world with the necessary degree of equitable global governance. The General Conference and subsequent periodic reviews of the UN's constitutional framework, we argue, would provide opportunities for the UN System to make necessary reform decisions to enhance the UN's effectiveness and legitimacy. Such reviews could also be occasions to reconfirm that member countries remain willing to give the needed political and material support to demonstrate their intention to take steps to reach the sustainable development goals set by the UN. If the peoples of the world are to have any realistic hope of meeting global challenges, an ambitious UN reform process must soon get started with the genuine backing of most, if not all, the members of the organization.

## Inspirational Declaration and Forum

The outcome of the General Conference should include an inspirational declaration describing the envisioned UN governance reforms and the urgency of their robust implementation. Such a statement would then form the basis of the UN's contribution to a Global Forum, which we propose to be held to mobilize public opinion in support of the UN reform process. Such a Forum would not resemble a climate-change type of summit but would be a summit focusing on the metaphysical and spiritual as well as the physical conditions of our planet in which all nations, including the few non-UN countries and territories not yet independent, would be invited to participate. It would be the first planetary summit of human solidarity with the lofty aim of adopting a unique global compact bonding governments and international institutions with a hypothetical world citizenry.

In recognition of the need for such a global compact, governments; non-governmental organizations; and local, regional, national, and global formal and informal leaders would come together to work out plans for safeguarding the planet, for protecting the well-being of future generations, and for envisaging how a United Nations of the Future could be empowered to act on behalf of humane values, ecological imperatives, and global goals, while becoming more mindful of reestablishing sustainable patterns of coexistence between human activity and natural habitats.

At the Forum, a Declaration would also be presented to affirm the view that unilateralism and geopolitical exceptionalism can have no place in a world that strives to become a genuine community for the first time in human history. The Declaration would outline ambitious goals, above all an overarching commitment to forms of global life in which equity, the rule of law, and harmony between the needs of the people and the needs of the environment prevailed in the process of creating and maintaining a global community of nations, territories, and peoples guided by an overarching goal of safeguarding of human dignity of all peoples and operationalizing a revolutionary respect for the rights of nature.

The Forum would furthermore focus on global and local changes of particular benefit to youth, advocating life-relevant education and cognitive training and curricula in schools that included at all levels such subjects as ethics, cultural anthropology, multilateralism, ecology, history, and militarism, as well as subjects dealing with local knowledge and traditions. Admittedly, this is a radically ambitious undertaking that might seem utopian and that under the most favorable circumstances would take a long time to accomplish, but if once started and widely affirmed as desirable and necessary, it might benefit from an accelerating momentum.

The Global Forum's conclusions would also be intended to impart a sense of direction and a spirit of urgency for the UN reform process. An ombudspersons' group would be set up, chaired by the UN Secretary-General and consisting of an equal number of women and men from civil society and governments representing all regions and constituencies. It would prepare a comprehensive annual assessment of progress toward the attainment of the global order, with an emphasis on the extent to which the United Nations has been able to contribute positively. It would identify setbacks, disappointments, and recommend modes of redress.

We would not have devoted the energy to reflecting on the future of the UN if we did not believe that it possesses the potential to play a large role in the development of a necessary and desirable global order. At the same time, while affirming our faith in such an endeavor, we are under no illusion that a global political atmosphere of trust and empathy, convergence, compromise, and accountability will, as if by magic, emerge to replace the current features of world order such as global polarization, confrontation, inequality, exploitation, disinformation, violence, militarism, and distrust. We are also mindful of the resistance that would arise during the transition from the present "culture of selfishness," "short-termism," greed and corruption, competition, and autocratic governance to our preferred future of vision, perseverance, courage, global-mindedness, truthfulness, and patience and resilience, emboldened by struggle for overall decency in human relations and ecological stability.

As visionary realists, we believe that the day can come when nations are sufficiently transformed to be patriotic members of a true global community as partly fashioned by a more global United Nations, substantially liberated from geopolitical manipulation and short-sighted nationalism. Such a UN would open wide its doors to enable officials, diplomats, and international and national civil servants to carry out an agenda reflecting the priorities of peace, justice, and human development for all, within the limits of ecological stability, coordinating as a team of like-minded women and men inspired by their transformative mission.

It becomes crucial to appreciate that the stakes for humanity have never been this high and without our vision achieving success, the prospects for humanity are bleak. It is with this awareness that we take it upon ourselves to articulate a new humane and ecologically sensitive realism for international relations that opposes the tenets of "political realism," which continues to act based on anachronistic beliefs and an outmoded secularist worldview. It is dangerously shameful that the political class of advisors and experts that guide most national leaders continues to premise national and human security on militarist calculations as well as to consistently privilege the efficiencies of capital over the well-being of people.

Were the transformative change not to come through the collective acceptance by at least two-thirds of the 193 nations comprising the UN

General Assembly, civil society leaders from around the world should be emboldened to declare a state of emergency pertaining to global governance. Such a declaration, reflecting fear and desperation, should be coupled with a statement setting forth a program of UN reform formally delivered to the UN Secretary-General as the peoples' representative, entrusting this woman or man with the formidable historic role of acting as mediator on behalf of humanity between people and the General Assembly. At the same time, we would implore civil society leaders to turn to the many thinkers from all world civilizations, including those of indigenous traditions, and to intellectuals and scholars, spiritual and religious leaders, living on all five continents to share their knowledge, experience, and wisdom for the benefit of humanity in constructing a new cosmic survival life model configured from a planetary perspective. This unquestionably is an intergenerational project, one that we fervently hope will not be dismissed as naïve and non-implementable. It is a daunting undertaking, but given the state of our global reality, it can be regarded as "a necessary utopia" responsive to the precarious fragility and ethical shortcomings of present modes of organizing complex societal and inter-societal life systems and ultimately finding the place for planet Earth in the wider cosmic setting of all life.

Quite naturally, we are unsure whether this evidence of precariousness and danger will lead public opinion in the directions we have recommended or instead will lead to extremist and escapist solutions animated by delusional beliefs that normalcy can be preserved through autocracy and weaponry. We are sure, however, that inclusive forms of human security are the best possible basis and protection for global peace and positive coexistence in harmony with the natural habitat.

## Concluding Thoughts

We are almost too aware that envisioning a UN that fulfills the Charter Purposes and Principles seems a dream from the perspective of the present. There does not seem to exist sufficient intergovernmental political and ethical commitments to push hard enough to circumvent or even to marginalize the influence of entrenched private-sector interests and anachronistic public-sphere realism. We are quite certain that necessary reformist initiatives will fall on deaf ears in the present atmosphere, which is a discouraging conclusion for us to reach.

If necessity is truly the mother of invention, political traction for UN reform should be forthcoming in the years ahead, spurred by dire concrete manifestations of global warming as reinforced by documented warning from scientists and climate experts. A turn toward more responsible and prudent leadership not only in P5 countries would make a difference and likely express itself by seriously curbing militarism coupled with a reallocation of public resources to finance an equitable global approach to a sustainable future, emphasizing massive cuts of greenhouse-gas emissions to address in the nick of time the adverse effects of climate change, especially on the least developed countries, and a radical approach to ending the curse of extreme poverty.

An additional impetus for change is a revived anxiety about nuclear weapons, their possible use in conflict situations, and their proliferation in the wake of the understanding that their possession may have a deterrent effect on hostile adversaries. The irony is that nuclear weapons make greater sense for middle and smaller states such as Iran, Ukraine, and North Korea exposed to threats that normal military capabilities cannot hope to address than they do for the P5 that control most of the existing nuclear warheads. Comprehensive denuclearization leading through a phased treaty process dedicated to the elimination of all weapons of mass destruction would depend on successfully operationalizing a global approach that might set a hopeful precedent encouraging modifications relevant to restoring the ecological balance of the planet.

If the UN is ever empowered to meet those fundamental moral, legal, peace and security challenges that gave rise to its establishment, it will have to overcome or at least minimize persisting state-centrism and geopolitical rights of exception. This presupposes a transformed internationalist mindset that is much more committed to shaping a global order based on a reformed UN Charter than has existed previously. For this to happen will require political honesty, patience, courage, and cooperation between states and civil society and, most importantly, accountability at all levels.

In this spirit, we are fully mindful of the current absence of political traction to move in directions that promote the future well-being of humanity but refuse to be paralyzed by this awareness. We continue to believe that what needs to be done and is desirable to do will happen, and to envision reform credibly is to make this prospect somewhat more likely to occur without awaiting reformist pressures resulting from catastrophic shocks activated by a nuclear war, an ecological collapse, or worldwide riots by people feeling betrayed.

# REFLECTIONS

# Nine Young Leaders and Their Visions about the UN of Tomorrow

The UN has come a long way in its global outreach. In its early days, cooperation involved almost exclusively links to governments. Gradually, non-government partnerships were formed, especially between ECOSOC and Western NGOs. UN leadership in convening summits to raise global awareness in areas such as population, education, gender, human rights, and sustainable development led to the increasing and enriching inclusion of civil society groups from around the world in these events.

The UN and its membership had begun to realize that strategies for global change would benefit greatly from civic knowledge, different kinds of societal circumstances, and diverse civilizational traditions and values. The impact of climate change and the resulting demand for making development sustainable further expanded the role and participation of civil society in formulating global arrangements, as we have discussed throughout our book. More recently, following the 2015 Paris Climate Agreement and the Glasgow Climate Pact (COP26) adopted in 2021, the UN finally acknowledged the important role of "indigenous people, local communities and civil society including youth and children" in addressing climate change. At the same time the organization seeks to ensure that there will be "meaningful youth participation and representation in multilateral, national, and local decision-making processes."

This is to us a significant confirmation by governments and the United Nations that intergenerational collaboration has become an integral element of the multilateral agenda. With this mind, we have invited nine young persons from different parts of the world to give their perspectives about the kind of UN they believe will be needed for the world to live in peace, ecological stability, and human security. We did not try to impose our template on how they chose to respond, but we are pleased to report that our invitees accepted the challenge of our invitation, and we are convinced that their presence in our book enriches and globalizes its perspective on the work and promise of the UN.

---

### Saw Omer Nuradeni
*Iraq (Kurdistan)*

## THE UNHERALDED UN

My family spent much of the 1990s in the mountains and different villages of Northern Iraq because our home was constantly being attacked by the former Iraqi regime. As a result, my siblings and I were born in different parts of Iraqi Kurdistan. After running away from Erbil, the family settled for a while in Shaqlawa, a small town northeast of Erbil, where I was born. One day, as we walked past the Marew Hanan Christian church with my Muslim grandmother, she stopped in front of the church door, let go of my right hand to raise her hands from her black abaya, and started sending prayers in Kurdish to UN Secretary-General Kofi Annan. I thought if my grandmother who brought me up and whom I love and respect sends prayers to this person, he must be doing something good. I later realized that during the Saddam conflict, we were receiving rice, wheat, flour, oil, and other necessities from the UN, and in return, my grandmother sent prayers to the man in the UN whose name she constantly mispronounced as كۆفی عەنان.

During my first day at Binar Basic School in Erbil, some people walked into my class and started to distribute notebooks, pencils, backpacks, and grain cookies. At first, I was afraid of them because I had learned at an early age that, where I am from, safety is never promised. The notebook I received was light blue in color and had a circular mother-holding-a-child logo. Our smiles filled the empty-walled classroom as we received these surprises. From then onward, whenever I saw the logo elsewhere, I would feel special because I was once cared for by the mysteriously powerful people with their blue UN logo. I felt I was the child on the logo. This school-supply distribution continued into the second and third grades. In a childhood that was shaped by political conflict and economic instability, these were among my most precious memories. Throughout my childhood in North Iraq, the UN was my version of Santa Claus.

My pleasant childhood memories are closely tied to the name of the UN. As a young Kurdish Iraqi girl growing up in a land of constant conflict, I have always dreamed of peace and have always searched for it in small and large ways. I soon learned that the UN did even more to contribute to this dream. I could learn and speak Kurdish, wear Kurdish clothes on Newroz, and simply could exist as an Iraqi Kurd because the UN Security Council Resolution 688 condemned the oppression of Iraqi Kurds and gave us UN protection. This resolution responded especially to the ethnic cleansing operations the Saddam Hussein regime had carried out against the Kurds.

Ever since UN Resolution 688, the rights of Kurdish Iraqis, which should never have been violated, were restored. Consequently, as a Kurd I was able to share the same classroom with an Arab, a Yezidi, and an Assyrian. And my mother was able to make Kurdish clothes for my secondary school Turkish teacher to wear on Kurdistan Flag Day. I was able to be in an environment where I could proudly express my Kurdish identity while celebrating the ethnic and faith backgrounds Iraq has to offer.

Every day I witness the impact of this resolution, which protects the basic human rights for which my Kurdish Iraqi ancestors sacrificed their lives. Every day I witness what capabilities and authority the UN truly has. I hope the delegates and representatives of this organization are aware of the power they have to create a better world.

From my own experience, I think this world needs a UN that not only can restore human rights when they are violated but also can act in advance to prevent such violation. So the innocent children and families can live and enjoy freedom. So in the future, the soil of Halabja would be farmed again just as it had been before the 1988 chemical attack. So future generations can feel less pain in mourning their history.

Because I was raised in an environment of conflict, I grew up too fast. I felt the burden of always thinking about how to help my people. Hence, I felt I should deny myself personal satisfaction. That is too much responsibility to place on a child. The world needs a UN that with its capabilities and moral authority can act on behalf of suffering people wherever they live. This world needs a UN that is more inclusive. With more than 35 million Kurds, we are the biggest stateless nation in the world, but our voice has yet to be represented at the UN. Our world needs a UN capable

of extending fair, unbiased, and equal authority within the structure of
the organization to meet the needs of a global society. The UN needs the
authority to ensure peace and security without restriction from the permanent members of the Security Council and their power of veto. This world
needs UN leaders to keep representing the UN mother-child logo and for
the big powers to replace their national interests with efforts that benefit all
peoples in equal measure.

**SAW OMER** is a United World Colleges, Robert Bosch College alumni and
received her bachelor's degree from the College of Idaho. Her areas of interest include peacebuilding, negotiation, and conflict resolution.

---

## Gonca Oğuz Gök
*Turkiye*

## (UN)FINISHED JOURNEY? FUTURE OF THE WORLD
## ORGANIZATION IN A WORLD OF CRISES

**Everything will turn out right, the world is built on that.**
—MIKHAIL BULGAKOV, *The Master and Margarita*

The United Nations continues to be the only hope of humankind for contesting and resolving issues of common concern to all people. While threats
such as nuclear war still exist in the twenty-first century, climate and food
crises are getting more urgent than ever. Therefore, the idea of cooperation
of "the peoples of the United Nations" to cope with the pressing problems
and "avoid hell" is more relevant than ever. In other words, we need the UN
more than ever. Nobody can deny that the intergovernmental mechanism
of the world organization has proven ineffective, if not failed, in realizing
its purposes on many aspects. The UN does not have a proud record in
peacekeeping operations—for example, in Srebrenica, Rwanda, or Haiti. On
the other hand, throughout almost eighty years of its history, it has been
the UN mechanisms themselves that provided the space for "normative
innovations" with input from many and varied actors. It is the only truly
universal platform where we, the peoples, have had the opportunity to con-

test "what ought to be." In fact, many rights that we take for granted today have been contested, realized, and codified in the UN platform. The world organization is broken in its present form and needs "re-form," but the UN will continue to exist as long as our collective will for constructing a sustainable environment of peace for all persists.

The UN was established with three main purposes after the Second World War: "to save succeeding generations from the scourge of war," "to reaffirm faith in fundamental human rights," and "to promote social progress and better standards of life" (UN Charter). These three areas correspond to the three core pillars of the UN: peace and security, human rights, and development. The UN's effectiveness in realizing these aims may be evaluated from two main aspects: the organization's normative role versus its operational one.

From a normative role perspective, the UN's diffusion, and construction of ideas on issues regarding peace and security, development, and human rights have helped to alter how global issues are perceived and thus, to quote Thomas Weiss, "changed history."[1] Conceptualized largely as the "Second UN," the UN's specialized agencies and programs introduced a wide array of innovations in global governance, including among many others global commons, sustainable development, and responsibility to protect. The legitimacy of these specialized UN agencies largely derives from their rational-legal authority based on their technical expertise and perceived impartiality on issues with which they are concerned. Additionally, contributions by individual experts, NGOs, activists, and academicians—who comprise the "Third UN"—have helped the UN "think" by advocating, analyzing, and operationalizing various ideas since 1945.[2]

However, as Barnett and Finnemore noted long ago,[3] this technical functioning of the bureaucracies of the Second UN is also the very source of their ineffectiveness. Today, failures in various specialized agencies and programs are widespread and arise out of slowness or incompetency on various missions and tasks as well as lack of professionalization.[4] Examples are to be found in all three pillars. For instance, while the UN has come to be considered a significant actor in shaping the global normative development agenda—exemplified by the latest Sustainable Development Goals—it has flourished much less as an implementer of development programming, and its development pillar has been criticized for its failure to create a more "egalitarian system."

In human rights, the UN has been a significant actor, expanding its role from human rights promoter to implementation agent. Yet, although many human rights conventions are championed on the UN platform, its record has been criticized on many grounds for not being effective in terms of preventing small- or large-scale human rights violations. Failures of peace-keeping missions such as in Srebrenica and in the Rwandan genocide are well-known cases. Most recently, Blue Helmets have been accused of acting with impunity in sexual exploitation in Africa and bringing cholera to Haiti while under the protection of immunity. As Richard Falk asserts, the legitimacy crisis arises out of not only the ineffectiveness of the political organs of the UN but also out of a normative decline concerning the authority of human rights norms, international law, and the UN at large.[5] So, what should be done, and can the UN be fixed?

One of the most pressing challenges facing the legitimacy and authority of the UN in global governance centers on two questions: Whose interest do the rules serve? And who are the winners and the losers with the rules?[6] These form the basis for a very fruitful discussion of a new "contestation" of the normative and operational role of the world organization. Recent studies demonstrate that states do mostly care about the procedures of the UN,[7] while publics at large do mostly care about the performance of the UN—that is, its effectiveness in realizing its aims.[8] Therefore, unproductive efforts to foster UN legitimization through minor procedural reforms do not seem to be a long-term solution for public legitimacy at large. Furthermore, since the UN's response to the 1993 Rwandan genocide, adherence to principles, rules, and laws to protect the organization and avoid failures have resulted in a further loss of legitimacy, because of ineffectiveness.[9] Hence, it is time to think more radically about the problems associated with the effects of the laws of the UN themselves on the real life of individuals.

Considering the crises faced by its intergovernmental mechanisms, there is a historic opportunity for the Second and Third UNs to provide more space for proposing "normative innovation." As Debre and Dijkstra found in their most recent study, international organizations with large bureaucracies may be better able to resist member state challenges.[10] However, this necessitates strengthening, professionalizing, and reorganizing the Second UN, given that the UN may at times be a "bureaucratic monster," trying to engage with countless subjects with limited professionalization and countless rotations of staff and using a one-size-fits-all approach.[11] Therefore, with intergovernmental mechanisms having proven largely ineffective in times of crises, for the future relevance of the UN itself, it is time to place more emphasis on strengthening the Second UN and further exploring the Third UN.

Last but not least, although the UN was the product of a normative universal consensus of both global North and global South, its functioning, especially since the 1990s, has generally been tied to the liberal international order, marginalizing Southern voices and being ineffective in opening up a genuine contestation over the main issues of peace and security, development, and human rights. Therefore, inputs from rising and middle powers might also serve as a trigger for renewed commitment to multilateralism on the UN platform, uniquely universal as it is. The recent COVID-19 pandemic and the UN Security Council's paralysis over the Russian invasion of Ukraine are both a crisis and an unprecedented opportunity to open up a new contestation on the UN's 3Ps (purposes, procedures, and performance) for creating a more egalitarian and fair system. One should note that issues such as mitigation of the crises arising out of climate change may not be achievable without a stronger UN. There is enormous potential and opportunity for input from the Second and Third UNs, and this should be better materialized in the future for a more effective and legitimate organization. Despite the current pessimism about global governance, the demand for multilateral action is more intense than ever before in supporting the future role of the only true world organization. Therefore, it is now time to talk genuinely about fundamental "re-form," not only "reform" of the UN System, a re-form that might also have the potential to modify the centrality of interactions among sovereign states in the future.[12]

In conclusion, with its present structure and functioning, the UN's intergovernmental organs like the Security Council prove ineffective, if not destructive each and every day. However, if there is to a be a change, *it will again come from the UN System itself*, since it has the unique capacity to provide *multiple spaces for the progressive leadership* of various kinds of actors. After all, the UN System provides the only truly unique universal forum for "contesting future new orders" and "alternative visions" of global politics with input from many and varied actors. Change for re-form might result from *a coalition of new generation of visionary national leaders*, norm entrepreneurs of various kinds and normative innovation of advocacy networks, NGOs, experts, and academicians, among many others. The issues of common concern to all people, such as pandemics, climate change, and food crises, continue to increase. Thus, the UN's journey is not finished, but yet to begin, hopefully in a new, better form.

**GONCA OĞUZ GÖK** is Associate Professor in Marmara University, Department of International Relations. Her research interests are global governance, Ios, and the UN. Her most recent edited book is *The Crises of Legitimacy in Global Governance* (2021).

---

## Nyana Yoni
*Myanmar*

### ENVISAGING THE UN AS A MECHANISM OF THE WORLD'S COLLECTIVE LIBERAL LEADERSHIP TO FIND NONVIOLENT SOLUTIONS FOR HUMANITY

On the first of February 2021, my country's democracy suffered a blunt assault by the Myanmar Military (Myanmar Sit Tat). It staged a coup on the very day when the country's Union Parliament was to commence its third session with its newly elected members following the 2020 general election. Myanmar's people responded with massive but peaceful demonstrations in cities and villages across the country. People of all walks of life participated in these protests. It is estimated that over 400,000 civil servants and some 3,000 army personnel expressed their civil disobedience against this coup by the Myanmar Military.[1] The people resisted the army mainly because they felt their rights and their justice had been assaulted. The resistance of the people became a revolutionary movement not just to remove the Myanmar Military's rule but also to establish a new society that would bring justice, freedom, democracy, and self-determination for all religious and ethnic groups within the country. A political analyst named the current mass resistance in Myanmar "the multi-layered revolution which is calling for the removal of the military institutions, militarism, and military dictatorship, which has been founded on extreme nationalism, patriarchal values, and religious fundamentalism." In a pursuit for a just and democratic society, many people, particularly the young expressed their apologies to the ethnic minorities in the country including the Rohingya people for the nation's failure in responding to the human rights violations and the genocide committed by Myanmar's military and government as well as civil society's support of state-sponsored crimes. The Myanmar military, however, responded to these peaceful means of resistance with violent and brutal force, killing many people across the country.

Myanmar people, without realizing that the UN currently is largely ineffective because of the power of the veto of the five permanent members, two of which are also undemocratic illiberal powers, wrongly expected that UN would step in with peacekeeping forces, particularly in view of its responsibility to protect (R2P) mandate. Many youth demonstrators protesting in front of the UN offices in Yangon carried posters asking, "How many people are to die before the UN steps in with security forces?" On April 26, 2021, over four hundred civil society organizations in Myanmar also issued a statement calling for the UN leadership to intervene instead of ASEAN with its unfeasible and unacceptable "five-points consensus" initiative, which is giving implicit endorsement of the coup leader Min Aung Hlaing, who in fact is a criminal and has committed crimes against humanity. However, to date, the UN has failed and keeps failing Myanmar's people, leaving them with no choice but forcing them to choose armed struggle against the junta. In other words, Myanmar's people, faced with the lack of nonviolent solutions, are forced to choose killing other people. It cannot be that in this way the people of Myanmar are being damaged morally and ethically in their everyday life. It is a very painful reality that people at this time of the twenty-first century must opt for violence because of the lack of peaceful solutions. This constitutes a failure of humanity and a failure of the United Nations.

The purpose of the UN, as mentioned by Article 1 of the UN Charter, is "to maintain international peace and security," which seems all right if it is primarily for peace and security of the world's people rather than the unity and security of nations. Many people in the world are suffering from dictatorships and the brutality of geopolitical self-interests of powerful nations. In this way, the UN is confined merely as an arena of international politics in which the UN itself is responsible for the suffering of people.

When we look at the case of Myanmar, the role of UN is determined by the power politics of China and Russia on the one hand and the United States and some Western democratic countries on the other. This makes it clear that the UN has significant conceptual and structural flaws if it focuses primarily on nation-states and their international relations in order to address these flaws. The institutional responsibility of the UN is to act as the collective balancer of power games played by world's superpowers rather than providing platforms for the power games.

The current world's crises in fact reflect the ramifications of the clashes of liberal and illiberal forces. With the benefits of the digital and intellectual age, civil societies begin to show the strength of bottom-up interventions, reducing the power grid of the powerful who are opposed to the expanding open society. Regrettably, illiberal backlashes are clearly visible internationally and intranationally. Myanmar's democracy and opened society have long been challenged by such illiberal forces within Buddhist nationalist movements developed and manipulated by the military. Having failed to stop the momentum of the opened society, the military finally bluntly assaulted it with armed power. The international illiberal forces have significantly blocked the international liberal forces who want to help Myanmar's people to free themselves from domination by national illiberal force.

Myanmar is not the only example of people who suffer from the clashes of liberal and illiberal forces. Myanmar society is just a part of the world's humanity suffering from such clashes. Humanity currently is at serious risk of being defeated by illiberal forces as they are highly powerful economically and militarily. If illiberal forces prevail, there will be no justice, no security, and no peace for humanity. The world needs a highly robust platform for collective liberal leadership to effectively counter the illiberal forces. The platform of collective liberal leadership, however, cannot be achieved through hosting only the governments of nation-states but must include civil society as an integral partner for global decision-making. The world urgently needs a powerful collective liberal forum. The United Nations must realize that it is painfully lagging far behind and introduce the reforms that are needed to make it effective.

**NYANA YONI** is a co-founder and Executive Director of Enlightened Myanmar Research Foundation (https://www.emref.org). She has over fifteen years of experience in doing research and teaching in Myanmar. Her work has been published in *Modern Asian Studies*.

---

## Franziska M. Benz
*Germany*

## A UNITED NATIONS THAT REMEMBERS

The world needs a powerful, strong, and resilient UN with a flexible framework where its diversity finds common ground and expression to set agendas and act in service of humanity as part of nature and, therefore, nature itself. This means openness to worldviews and related legal frameworks of all cultures, particularly Indigenous cultures, that have always defined nature as part of their community. Being part of nature is a core principle that has to find its representation clearly in the UN Charter and legally binding instruments.

Considering recent severe global challenges, it is essential to rebalance, and rebalancing starts within. The world needs a UN that remembers that it is part of nature and is willing to shift toward an entirely genuinely embedded serving organization. Based on this more profound knowledge and understanding, existing capabilities will be embedded and connected, and new ones will be created. For general well-being, capabilities that align with nature's elements and its caring and supportive interactions are required.

The world needs a UN that practices understanding and allows itself to heal—a UN that provides space for the healing of fragmentation, dissociation, perfectionism, purity, and colonial structures as part of its dominant Western mindset that is still represented in its structures. The world needs a global institution that simultaneously acknowledges and celebrates its existence as a unique creation and that can learn—an organization that is not denying its Western part but provides safe spaces and platforms to bridge worldviews and find meaningful ways of integration.[1] A truly holistic existence of the UN requires the understanding and related actions that the Western part is only a part of all.

The world needs a UN that provides safe spaces where people can tell and share their stories and where female and male energy create value in harmony, guided by love, trust, and respect.

It is the principle of Mother Earth's caring in serving. Working and operating with the same principles as Mother Nature is essential. She acts in symbiosis.[2] It means mutual relations of the principle of nourishing and getting nourished. Structures that can be shifted toward the same principle internally will create a reflection externally; it will create a robust global interaction between the local and the global level that is strongly needed to entirely create an impact in the service of humanity and nature. Carrying the awareness of being powerful, strong, and resilient like a mountain and grounded like a tree, aware of its roots, flexible in its substance, and nourishing its branches and leaves, the UN will form an embedded organization that is strongly connected to its entities and constructive life cycles on earth.

I imagine the UN as a place where local and national interests can find common ground with multilateral intentions, and love is given priority over hierarchies and bureaucracy. A spoken word with the clearest intention that goes in line with the highest values of the institution will be taken for granted and will be truly heard.

Moreover, in my opinion, the world needs a UN that offers space for humans of every age to face the world's challenges and create impact together, where creativity can flourish, visions and dreams are present, and responsibility is taken on while history and past and future generations are always taken into consideration and represent an essential part of the discourse.

An aligned UN System acts in support always. It communicates always. At this point, I want to acknowledge the diverse and flourishing channels and platforms already established. Nevertheless, some parts of the UN remain powerless and hold on to hierarchies. The world needs a UN System capable of producing analysis on a global scale and knowing how to use it wisely. To visualize the integration of holistic worldviews and a paradigm where humanity is part of nature, I imagine an intertwined Sustainable Development Goals development based on a nature-based framing.

I imagine a United Nations that always remembers where it comes from as a people's-based organization—a UN that allows its Western structures to become more fluid to generate integrative outcomes. I imagine a thoughtful, reflective authority where all humans will be consulted and the transformative spirit of water can fully unfold within the UN.

Additionally, to the UN's reflective function, a reconnection and rebalance of its water, fire, and earth elements are crucial to generating a powerful impact. Transformation can only fully flourish when every part is taken into consideration.

The world needs a UN that can remember its roots. Through that, the UN will be stronger, and integration will be more likely to happen. Strength and integration that are a requirement of drafting and ratifying a declaration on Natural Rights and, as a crucial second step, capable of implementing the declaration while withstanding the strong winds of selfish capitalistic interests.

I imagine a UN that inspires because its flame of high values and passion never stops burning. A strong flame is necessary to strive toward "unity in diversity"[3] and a world where love, respect, trust, and honesty prevail.

The UN is on its pathway to healing, coming home, being complete, and setting holistic, interconnected agendas based on service for humanity and Mother Nature. I am full of hope that the UN will entirely enter the flow of live long transformation. There is guidance, awakening, and understanding, and understanding will expand.

Humanity needs the UN and its process of remembrance to realize and apply the understanding that all humans are part of nature. It is a mutual process that has already been started. Engagement is already happening on diverse levels, and Indigenous people's presence and worldviews are entering the UN increasingly. The world needs a UN that constitutes the most flourishing, global celebration of life, in its highest expression based on the highest values and ideals in the service of humanity as part of nature.

FRANZISKA MARIE BENZ is a student of Indigenous Science and Peace Studies at the UN-mandated University for Peace in Costa Rica. She holds a BA degree in Social Work and an MA degree in Peace and Conflict Studies. Ms. Benz is passionate about UN system change, transformative education, and the bridging of worldviews. Currently, she is based in Ulm, Germany, working on recovering her Indigenous roots.

---

## Ana Tawfiq Husain
*Pakistan*

## THE UN'S DANCE WITH SUBALTERNITY

A bold Habib Jalib—one of the most celebrated revolutionary poets of Pakistan—thundered his famous *Dastoor* (which roughly translates to "system"/ "structure") against the ruling military dictatorship in 1962. At its core, Jalib sought to capture the resentment held by the masses over an illusory sense of democracy and promises of equitable justice that were offered by the ruling elite but were really a prop for repackaging a system built on disparities. Just how long is too long before the cracks of such systems finally begin to surface?

I view Jalib's refusal to accept (let alone acknowledge) a system whose structures only allowed for cosmetic concessions rather than tangible reforms as a principled stance—whose moral basis can serve as a tool for the critique of structural, institutional, and systemic global injustices. By the word *global*, one would think of incidents, events, matters, and crises that concern and are felt by each of us and all of us. But why then do we often find that institutions which champion the causes of the global are only able to offer the very same illusory and cosmetic concessions that leave one more agitated than assured? Of this dilemma concerning the global, I would like to touch upon a selection of cases in point.

On April 7, 2022, the United Nations General Assembly tabled a resolution that sought the suspension of the Russian Federation from the Human Rights Council following the global outrage over the discovery of civilian bodies in the Ukrainian town of Bucha, near Kyiv. As ninety-three members proceeded to vote in favor of the motion while twenty-four stood against it and fifty-eight abstained, the resolution met the required two-thirds majority criteria for passing. This development was immediately hailed by Ukrainian foreign minister Dmytro Kuleba, who tweeted "war criminals have no place in UN bodies aimed at protecting human rights. Grateful to all member states which supported the relevant General Assembly resolution and chose the right side of history."[1] Such a proclamation should surely be welcomed. However, upon closer examination, one comes to observe that Israel, among other member states, had also voted in favor of the resolution. By sidelining the resumed continuum of violence at the Al-Aqsa Mosque in the West Bank as Israeli forces killed sixteen Palestinians between April 6 and 22[2]—a tragedy whose wounds from May 2021 are still all too fresh—the de facto inclusion of Israel being on the "right side of history" puts the transparency of the resolution into question.

Looking at Israel's increasing number of human rights violations, whether in Palestine or onward to Syria and Lebanon, one is beckoned to question the institutional and structural dynamics of the UN bodies and their criteria for inclusion to human rights councils where some cases of state-sanctioned violence are viewed as more "justifiable" than others. As such, this essay poses the following questions for consideration with regard to the UN and its subsidiary bodies: Why is it that certain conflicts, wars, and crises are given secondary importance despite each case having civilians caught in the crossroads of violence? How is the criterium set for deciding which case merits immediate collective action via financial, diplomatic, or even militaristic mechanisms as opposed to those which receive only the occasional expressions of "deep concern"? Why, despite how far we have come in human history after witnessing, challenging, and healing from all kinds of global tragedies, do we still hold the view that some struggles matter more than others?

A helpful starting point in the form of an analytical device that may unconceal the power relations underpinning this disparity in responses is Antonio Gramsci's notion of subalternity. The subaltern may allude to a figure of exclusion[3] as well as those groups who do not have the privilege of possessing political power—a notion that Jalib's *Dastoor* also incidentally highlights. Gayatri Spivak, however, sought to deepen this discussion. She contended that in addition to being silenced by the established order, the subaltern was defined by its exclusion from representation in both political and aesthetic senses.[4] As such, Peter Thomas notes that the subaltern "thus appeared to be a category suited to analyse and to problematise the experiences of marginalised, oppressed individuals and groups."[5] This is especially key for navigating through our postcolonial conditions to understand some lingering colonial legacies around us.

In our incumbent and, arguably, still rather state-centric political landscape, who gets to represent the "subaltern" is a question that continues to be tossed around. Whether Kashmir or Palestine—two of the most seemingly intractable crises of our times—we see how there remains a perpetual political vacuum where political elites who may even be detached from the ground realities are deemed the representatives of their struggles. Each "subaltern," then, is made to depend on other "established" voices to lend support for their causes in order to be better heard on global, intergovernmental, or regional platforms. The same logic, it may be argued, is extended to how these crises are tackled at the UN.

Keeping in mind that the UN was formed following the end of World War II during the age of colonialism, it is worth noting that that the current composition of the Security Council includes four out of five former colonial powers and/or states exhibiting empire-building ambitions. One is compelled to ask how the "subaltern" entities situated in the "third world" (a non-white, formerly colonized world that apparently seems to invite conflict, according to racist and ahistorical narratives pushed by Western journalists from various global media outlets) may then be heard. Coming to the General Assembly, should states which have resolutions centered on the breaching of human rights be allowed to cast votes on who should and should not retain membership in the Human Rights Council? If the answer to the last question is in the affirmative, does this indicate that some violators of international law and human rights can afford to simply shrug off these charges? Such a thought is as agitating as it is disturbing.

One could say that we find ourselves caught in the reform-versus-revolution debate in relation to the structural and institutional changes that the UN so urgently needs to address the dilemma of the "global." Is it feasible to deconstruct an entity whose existence was informed by the currents of Great Power politics? How long would it take for workable alternative arrangements to actualize? The questions are mammoth, and the answers are sticky. If we are to revisit Jalib's words to get a sense of the importance of placing social justice at the very heart and soul of a system, one message is clear: context matters; transparency matters; every life—from one corner of the Earth to the other—matters. They mattered yesterday, they matter today, and they should matter tomorrow if we are to retain hopes for a truly global solidarity.

ANA TAWFIQ HUSAIN is a Dean's Fellow and Lecturer at Habib University, Karachi, Pakistan, based in the Social Development and Policy program. She has an MA in International Relations from King's College, London.

---

## Heela Najibullah
*Afghanistan*

## THE UNHERALDED UN

I come from a country that has been embroiled in conflict for the past four decades. Afghanistan is landlocked, poor, and one of the oldest members of the UN. Afghanistan has been a dutiful UN member state since November 19, 1946, and unlike its South Asian or Central Asian neighbors, it is a signatory to many conventions. One such example is the Geneva Convention of 1951 for refugees and its Protocols, while many countries in South Asia are yet to sign the treaty.

Geographically, Afghanistan is located as a crossroad between the East and the West. Its geography can be an asset for the region and the global world; however, it has become a curse, shaping its political, economic, and social trajectories. Afghanistan's geopolitical conflict is central in demonstrating the dysfunctionality of the United Nations.

The UN's policies and actions as an institution were tested at the peak of the Cold War in Afghanistan. Continued superpower rivalries took further momentum in 1979 when the Soviet Union invaded Afghanistan. The UN got the mandate in November 1981 by adopting General Assembly Resolution 36/34 to negotiate the withdrawal of the Soviet troops from Afghanistan. It took ten years for the UN to negotiate the Geneva Accords, which were signed in April 1988, prompting the withdrawal of the Soviet troops. Even though the Geneva Accords were signed between the governments of Afghanistan and Pakistan, and the Soviet Union and the US were the signatories, the focus of the agreement was what the members of P5 wanted and negotiated, and it failed to bring a durable political solution to the Afghan conflict.

This episode from Afghan history (1981–1992) is a perfect case of a member state of the UN from "the global South" that engaged the UN to find a peaceful political solution at two levels. At the national level, the Afghan government pursued the policy of reconciliation, and at the international level, it worked with the UN to build consensus among the countries involved in the Afghan conflict. The efforts of the Afghan government and the UN to achieve peace in Afghanistan failed because of the political interests of powers involved. The UN failed to ensure that with the change of government, peacekeeping forces would be deployed in Afghanistan. The emphasis that peace could be obtained if the president had resigned, or government change is brought.

April 1992 was the start of vacuum of power, bloodshed, and radicalization that the Afghan government wanted to prevent because of the institutional limitations of the UN, such as P5 rivalries and its veto power.

Despite the UN's idealistic constitution and mandate, the case of Afghanistan demonstrates that the institution serves the interests of P5 and the powerful countries. Realpolitik dictates the fate of millions of people in developing countries, making them feel helpless, unseen, and unheard. The UN is not an organization where each member state has an equal say and where citizens of the poorer countries are seen as equal. Therefore, *Liberating the UN: Beyond Geopolitics, Realism with Hope* is well-timed to explore the possibility of making the UN a more accountable and accessible organization for all its member states and its citizens. This is possible by reforming the institutional structure of the UN, specifically dissolving P5 and allowing poorer nations and civil society to be a part of the decision-making.

One of the main reasons for not deploying peacekeeping forces in Afghanistan was lack of funding; the UN as a structure is dependent on member countries' donations. In the globalized world we live in, the UN must diversify its source of funding to be able to meet its constitutional obligations and objectives of global security not from a place of dependency but rather independence.

In trying to achieve the purpose of the UN, which is to maintain international peace and security, and achieve its preamble in safeguarding future generations from wars, the reformed UN can introduce demilitarized UN memberships and instead focus on how a global militarized force can curb arms production and instead support citizens of the world in common agendas that are set every decade (such as Millennium Development Goals or Sustainable Development Goals, corruption, access to resources, and climate change).

In ensuring the future UN is more accountable and equal for its people, the organization must introduce instruments where civil society can be strongly represented in decision-making, and that decision-making is transparent. Civil society can have as much of a role in choosing their representatives at the General Assembly as the national governments do, and this can be topic- or agenda-driven. For example, voting of individuals globally can take place based on climate change agenda, reducing arms race or production, prevention of future viruses, strengthening health care, or lack of access to resources.

With the current structure of the UN, civil society is neglected. I say this with a recent development in March 2022 on the extension of the UN mandate after the fall of the Afghan government. While member state representatives met behind closed doors with chosen groups of civil society, what the new mandate of the UN in Afghanistan should look like remained a mystery for the Afghan civilians and civil society till it was adopted. For months, the Afghan women's groups and other civil society members inside the country tried to seek information on the development of the mandate and to contribute to shaping the mandate but were unable to do so. In a globalized world where viruses, the economy, migration, and wars are border transient, the UN can be relevant as an organization when it considers and reforms itself, understanding that the twenty-first century is about connecting the people of the world and the common issues. It is the kind of UN that would impact on all people everywhere.

**HEELA NAJIBULLAH** is a PhD student at the University of Zürich and did an MA in Peace, Conflict Transformation, and Security Studies at the University of Innsbruck. She has authored the book *Reconciliation and Social Healing in Afghanistan* and has extensive humanitarian work experience on migration issues with the International Federation of the Red Cross.

---

## Lina Yu
*China*

## MY UN JOURNEY

Working as an international civil servant for United Nations has been my dream since I first read a book that describes how life on the planet would work best if it operated like a well-run village—people with different beliefs and cultures living and working together under certain rules and regulations to achieve a good life for everyone while respecting the differences that make the world diverse and more interesting. Amazingly, the UN plays a central role in this effort to unite people together toward a peaceful, just, and sustainable world through the fulfillment of its mandate.

I take this opportunity to describe my UN journey because I want young people throughout the planet to be drawn to such altruistic careers that not only contribute to a better future for all peoples but has been for me a source of fulfillment and continuous learning and satisfaction.

My UN journey started as an associate professional officer at the Food and Agriculture Organization of the United Nations (FAO). Transferring the career from laboratory-based professionalism at the national level to a global context, I was deeply inspired by the people I worked with while developing a number of technical documents and guidelines, the knowledgeable supervisors and mentors who drew a growing path for me; I was also amazed by the beauty of working in a diversified environment and the sense of jointly making some changes. All these laid a sound basis to further develop my UN career.

My professional areas were antimicrobial resistance (AMR) and One Health, which are cross-cutting by nature. The interface between human, animal, and environmental health concerns share threats to well-being, welfare, and sustainability to a healthier future; therefore, collaborations among sectors and levels are of critical importance. With my background in pharmacy and public health, I was fortunate and privileged to provide my contribution to these two important global topics, together with many people who share the same goal.

Starting in 2015 with the publication of the Global Action Plan on AMR by the World Health Organization (WHO), the world has witnessed the fast development of joint efforts against AMR and increasing awareness at all levels and sectors. To date, more than 140 countries have developed a multi-sectoral One Health national action plan[1]; a global governance structure and a multi-partner trust fund were established. These have paved the way for better policies and allocation of resources to be focused on AMR for further progress.

Fighting against AMR is a vivid demonstration of how different stakeholders—including international organizations, governments, civil society, financial institutions and philanthropic donors, and private-sector partners and individuals such as farmers, veterinarians, and doctors—work together to achieve a common goal, to achieve the sustainable development goals, beyond SDG3 (Health).

Working in the development environment and at specialized organizations and traveling around to implement programs, I clearly saw the need for support from the UN, particularly in resource-limited countries, and the urgency for development, I believe the key is to strengthen the capacities at country level through evidence- and science-based guidelines and projects for development from a sustainable perspective.

In the global context, I observed the imbalance of development among different countries, which shows the need for and benefits of hand-to-hand collaboration between countries. To facilitate such cooperative arrangements, the UN often plays a vital, central role, providing the bridge over which mutually beneficial arrangements among sovereign states improve cost efficiency.

In the fourth year of my UN journey, I am now working at the World Health Organization and dedicating myself to health-security preparedness, with a focus on building resilient health systems. My experience confirms that this is another cross-cutting area that requires different disciplines of expertise and brings together capacities required for the international health regulations (IHR) and components of health systems and other sectors for multisectoral, multidisciplinary, and effective management of health emergencies.[2]

Moreover, COVID also exposed various problems politically, economically, and technically, which also lead people to think about the changes that could make the world better for humanity and the lives of individual people and their communities. Facing all the emerging global threats that are challenging human well-being, the expectation for a stronger and more effective UN is well placed technically and politically.

Our endeavors in such areas as agriculture and health offer valuable experience that can help every participant in the global context to think how to position themselves, to fulfill their specific mandate, to complement each other in ways that lead to a better and sustainable world. As a young professional working in UN, I think my bit in this is to further enhance my technical expertise and better understand the needs at different levels, so to strengthen the support and contribution. By sharing different solutions for transformation, by working together, we all become stronger.

LINA YU, a pharmacist by training, an MPH candidate, has working experience in three UN agencies, including the Food and Agriculture Organization, the International Atomic Energy Agency, and the World Health Organization, supporting member states for capacity development in the area of antimicrobial resistance, One Health and health security preparedness.

## Ekaterina Postnikova
*Russia*

## THE UNITED NATIONS TRANSFORMATION: A VIEW ON REFORM FROM ANOTHER PERSPECTIVE

Discussions on how to reform the United Nations have been held since the late 1990s. The most vocal proposals are devoted to transformation of the UN Security Council to make it more productive, up to date, and aligned with global balance of powers. There are plenty of ideas on how to extend the Security Council's membership, how to modify permanent representation, and what to do with the veto right. Nowadays some regions remain underrepresented in the Security Council, so the reform of the Council seems necessary by default—thus, we will abstain from outlining the best possible options of its membership extension.

At the same time, we do not need changes for the sake of changes. What we must do is to outline what crisis the modern UN organization is currently facing and pave the way toward dealing with it.

The problem is that nowadays the UN is not as authoritative and powerful as it was at the beginning of its existence. For many years, the Security Council had had an exclusive mandate to impose sanctions on the UN members in case the majority decided to do so. However, history of the twenty-first century shows that this exclusive right is being dismantled: states neither need the Security Council's approval of military interventions and operations on the territory of sovereign countries nor do they depend on the UN mechanism of sanctions. Why would they do so if they can introduce sanctions on their own without asking anyone for permission?

History shows that the most prosperous and productive period of every international organization is at the beginning of its existence: the League of Nations after the World War I (if we can say so, a demo version of the United Nations, which could not prevent the World War II) and then the UN, which after all the hostilities and horrors of WWII was perceived as the only way to prevent such catastrophes in the future. Other examples are the EU, the OSCE, the Council of Europe, and so on. States were ready to listen to some "supranational authority" and to consider the interests of others. But as time goes by, post-WWII traumas become a thing of the past, and states do not consider it of vital importance to reach common understanding.

This shows that we live in the paradigm of realpolitik when everything depends on the political will of national states—the work and influence of the UN depend completely on their behavior. The UN cannot make countries act 100 percent in accordance with its Charter and other agreements once approved by all the member states; we see that when a state violates common norms, the UN has nothing left but to condemn this violation.

The only real leverage the UN can use is its authority and credibility in the eyes of member states—they should understand that there are extremely important areas where the UN is indispensable. The UN has formed a vast system of dozens of funds, programs, specialized agencies, and bodies. It means that the United Nations has enough resources to strengthen its authority and credibility.

In 2017, the UN Secretary-General António Guterres proposed three pillars for the reform:

1. Development (bold changes to the UN development system, focusing on the 2030 Agenda);

2. Management (empowerment of the UN managers and staff, simplification of processes, transparency);

3. Peace and security (conflict prevention and sustaining peace, enhancing the effectiveness and coherence of peacekeeping operations and special political missions).

The UN must reinvent its ideology, putting forward a sphere that in the current context is of vital importance. Given the number of conflicts, the ongoing arms race, and the threat of nuclear confrontation, a pillar that could become the UN's priority and core sphere of its activity is peace and security; the UN must prove its effectiveness in this direction. António Guterres's plan implies four steps: (1) prioritize prevention and sustain peace; (2) enhance the effectiveness and coherence of peacekeeping operations and special political missions; (3) continue moving toward a single, integrated peace and security pillar; (4) align it more closely with the development and human rights pillars to create greater coherence and cross-pillar coordination.

The UN must become a *global mediator*—a "global trader"—who considers the interests and aspirations of every actor. Conflict prevention is the key: UN managers and experts are present in almost every country of the world; they have access to national decision-makers, know the region and, thus, can assess the perspectives of armed conflict. The UN should become a leader in shuttle diplomacy, taking on the role of indispensable mediator. Backroom dealing, nonterminating dialogue, persuasion (not begging)—result-oriented, the UN should transparently use all the legal instruments, not hiding anything from any side of potential conflict.

States are still the key actors in international relations, but we cannot deny the presence of transnational corporations whose authority and influence in some countries is even higher than the state ones. When it comes to armed conflicts, businesses are the actors that lose a lot and gain nothing (except in several spheres such as weapons trade); thus, the UN should communicate with this sector to elaborate approaches that could prevent wars and provide win-win conditions both for states and businesses.

The UN has already enough elements and mechanisms to operate such work: special envoys, political missions, peacekeeping operations, regional offices, rapidly deployable mediation expertise, UN resident coordinators and country teams, analytical capacities, and so on. The organization should use these instruments more actively, regularly, creatively and in accordance with concrete circumstances and conditions.

Time is passing, and the world order is changing. It is time for the UN to transform from the object of world politics to subjects that possess a wide range of contacts in different spheres and with different actors—to an organization that is more flexible, agile, and ready to take the initiative. Such a transformation closely correlates with the second pillar outlined by António Guterres (Management). It seems to be purely technical and, thus, can be optimized in line with management strategies already elaborated—in this regard, the help of the Big Four accounting firms, for example, seems relevant.

Another problem multilateral organizations face is politicization. Many UN bodies and organizations working closely with it are focused on the subjects which are to be discussed without political rhetoric (e.g., purely cultural UNESCO, social WHO, or economic WTO). Nevertheless, political contradictions still affect the work of these bodies. In this context, it seems necessary to conceptualize the term *politicization*, outlining criteria for it in the rules of procedure, so that every time the discussion comes to a standstill because of political clashes, the moderator/president of the body could regulate it, putting communication back on track in accordance with subject on the agenda. Even though it is a purely technical solution, it could relieve tensions inside one body, making its work more focused and productive.

**EKATERINA POSTNIKOVA** is a diplomatic correspondent at the Russian media group RBC (RosBusinessConsulting) specializing in the areas of international security and post-Soviet space. Previously, she worked at the IZVESTIA daily newspaper and the news agency RIA Novosti. She is a graduate of the Moscow State Institute for International Relations and holds a master's degree in World Politics.

---

### James Altman
*USA*

## IMPROVING HUMANITARIAN INTELLIGENCE: BETTER COLLECTION AND USE OF INFORMATION BY THE UN IN EMERGENCIES CAN HELP SAVE MORE LIVES

Knowing what is happening in an emergency is crucial to mounting an effective humanitarian response. Yet precisely this—data collection and the use and dissemination of information on the situation—is often one of the most overlooked and poorly managed issues in emergency assistance. Although most people instinctively understand the need for providing medicine or repairing a damaged school, I find that few immediately grasp how critical it is to gather relevant, accurate, and timely information about an ongoing humanitarian emergency. Yet, in the most basic sense, nothing can be done in an emergency if you do not know what is happening. For example, if you are tasked with protecting children in a conflict, you need to know what areas are affected, what issues are affecting children (such as malnutrition, psychosocial distress, lack of safe water, forced recruitment by armed groups, etc.), how many children are in need, where exactly these children are, which of them are most vulnerable to which specific issues, whether any aid is reaching them (and if not, why not), is the aid having the intended effect, and dozens of other critical questions. Although there has been a serious push toward more "data-driven" humanitarian response in the past decade, much assessment data is still of questionable accuracy and not always helpful in designing and implementing humanitarian response.

Procuring accurate and timely data in an emergency is challenging. Security, access restrictions, resource limitations, and various cultural issues often make data collection difficult. For example, how do you find out how many children are in need of life-saving support, where exactly they are, how different subgroups of them are being affected differently, and what type of interventions are needed to support them if they live in territory held by an armed group that does not allow free access for UN personnel or their partners? Each unique situation usually requires equally unique and innovative approaches to collecting data. Although many methods of collecting data have already been used in past assessments (such as surveys, collection of water samples, analysis of satellite images, focus groups, or interviews with key informants), unfortunately, very little of it has later been reviewed to answer three basic questions: Was the data accurate? Was it actionable? And what are the best practices that can be recommended for future assessments?

Aside from recurring assessments with standardized methodologies (which are rare and often do not respond to urgent information needs in a crisis), most assessment methodologies are created largely from scratch and in highly difficult emergency situations. The responsibility for assessment design usually falls either to national staff in field offices—most of whom are primarily concerned with urgent program implementation and often have no experience or training in designing and conducting assessments—or to consultants brought in specifically for the task, but often with little or no prior experience in that specific conflict scenario or with the actual provisioning of humanitarian aid. What becomes evident to almost anyone who has worked long enough in the field (at least during my time in humanitarian response in the 2010s and 2020s) is that while much assessment data is at least accurate enough to facilitate humanitarian response and save lives without wasting or misdirecting resources, a lot of assessments produce contradictory conclusions and are highly inaccurate. This error can come from an enormous array of sources, including an assessor's unfamiliarity with a region, poor quality of interviews, badly tailored survey questions, inadequate training of field workers, not using appropriate delicacy and sensitivity or developing trust when inquiring about certain issues, using highly unrepresentative samples or sources, relying on anecdotal observations, and many other issues.

Another perennial issue with data collection is that information produced in assessments is often not of any practical use to humanitarians. Data must be "actionable," meaning that it can be used to inform and guide programming (for example, knowing how many people are without water and where they live in order to design emergency water provisioning) and/or be used for higher-level advocacy (such as pointing out the scale of recruitment of children by armed groups when advocating for an end to the practice). Data collection is often designed and conducted by people with little connection to or experience in the implementation of humanitarian programming response and therefore little understanding of what information is and is not useful. We used to joke that some assessments give you data as useless as knowing the colors of children's shirts but fail to provide actionable data that can be used to provide assistance such as total number of children out of school due to a shortage of teachers or the number of children with special needs in a community. Similarly, receiving data that may be relevant but is incomplete in such a way that makes it impossible for the reader to understand if it is representative of a situation can be problematic. For example, an assessment of one or two small informal IDP camps can be highly misleading if these camps are outliers on a large number of parameters and if assessors do not explain potential limitations of the methodology or if they give no indication as to the total number of people affected. Again, this data is either not actionable or if used for action may lead to inefficient or poorly targeted response.

It can be hard to collect data in an emergency and immediately assess its accuracy, but revisiting the region after the acute phase of a crisis to review the data and see if it appeared to be accurate is possible though rarely (if ever) done. Although UN agencies have a long history of conducting situation assessments, in very few cases have best practices of assessments—both in terms of their accuracy and actionability—been reviewed and their results compiled and disseminated. This may be particularly difficult since much short-term, emergency assessment data remains internal within organizations and is not published.

Even with a very competent assessment team and an effective data collection methodology, there is often a large structural gap between data collection and the parts of the organization that design and implement humanitarian programming. This is often evident in early assessment phases where not enough coordination occurs with program teams to find out what data they need and what they think would improve their sector's response. This can be as simple as a WASH team explaining that they could use data on which schools have drinking water and which do not, or an education section member explaining that it would be helpful to know how many students per teacher there are in a set of IDP camps. There are many ways to overcome these challenges, but ensuring that consultants or staff hired for situation assessments have some program experience (and therefore have a clear idea of what information is relevant and actionable) and providing resources to train relevant field staff in basic assessment design, data collection, and information management is an important start. Country-level leadership must also prioritize the deep integration of data collection and programming.

This builds to one of the most important issues where there can be poor alignment between situation data and operations: decisions about in which regions of a country to provide aid. The principle of greatest need should drive humanitarian response, but unfortunately political and security issues often hinder this. For example, maybe a non-state armed group controls a region and threatens to kill any UN worker or their local partners that enter the group's area of control. Obviously, this can greatly limit an organization's ability to help those in need. Other times, national governments of crisis-affected countries are uncompromising in their restrictions on letting UN personnel access certain areas (this is a major issue that can compromise the UN's neutrality and which should be a book in and of itself). But sometimes there may be an unfounded perception among risk-averse parts of an organization's leadership that a region is "no-go" when in fact it is very possible to operate there, either with appropriate caution (due to security) or with strong advocacy with governments (for removing political impediments). Although there are many substantial benefits to rotating staff to different countries every several years, one of the huge drawbacks is that it is rare to have organizational leaders that are experts in the political and social context of the country they are working in. I have been in situations where nearly all the national staff as well as most of the international staff operating in field offices are fully aware that it is not only possible (both in terms of security and political viability) but also mandated to do more to help children in non-government-controlled areas, but the leaders do not have a strong understanding of the situation and block implementation in these regions. Not only was this terribly demoralizing for much of the team, but much more importantly, it meant many children did not receive the potentially lifesaving support they needed. On the other side of this, I have been involved in situations where highly capable and data-driven leaders have been able to operate in challenging regional contexts that most other agencies had deemed impossible, when in fact most regional specialists could have explained from the beginning that this was viable if done properly and cautiously. Decisions like this should not be made largely based on the perceptions of country representatives and regional offices without further analytical justification. This can be professionalized through more detailed risk analysis and risk management assessments of situations and made at least partially transparent, thereby mitigating accusations of bias, incompetence, or inaction.

A last but crucial point is that data collection and information dissemination tools have advanced rapidly and very little of this has been incorporated in a meaningful way into most UN agency-level situation assessments. For example, GIS software makes tracking and visualization of humanitarian data more effective than ever, but few staff members have these skills. This could be combined with greater cooperation with agencies such as UNOSAT/UNITAR to have up-to-date satellite imaging and related analysis for field and country offices to greatly improve tracking of emergencies as they unfold. Other innovations such as short digital surveys[1] can allow, for example, a team that is distributing Mine Risk Education materials to all schools in a region to take a few extra minutes to get a GPS point for each school, ask the school director a few short questions such as numbers of children, availability of drinking water, and whether the school was damaged to later have a complete map of schools, locations of schoolchildren, and geographic distribution of issues affecting them. Employing well-designed data collection tools like these is generally inexpensive and allows aid to be much more efficiently targeted, also potentially lowering costs. This does not mean that "old-fashioned" methods of data collection can or should be entirely replaced. For example, in-depth interviews with a wide range of key informants by a well-trained assessor is almost impossible to replace for its ability to pick up unexpected issues that need addressing and their nuances. But if we use best practices and quality training to ensure that traditional assessment methods are employed as effectively as possible and couple this with newer tools, we can generate much more accurate and useful data on humanitarian needs. And if we ensure that data collection, programming, and advocacy operate in close alignment, all efforts can be targeted to ensuring that aid is directed to the most vulnerable people in any emergency.

My dream is that the UN should be so widely acknowledged and respected for the high quality and timeliness of its data and the transparency of its methodologies in emergencies that it should be hard for anyone to question its relevance and accuracy. Some specific areas are slowly moving in this direction—such as reporting of grave violations against children—but in general, these goals are not yet consistently met. The process should be fast enough that, for example, rapidly verified and incontrovertibly documented human rights violations can be used to immediately put pressure on abusers and not allow them or their political allies to avoid or deflect blame for the situation. Furthermore, I dream of seeing UN agencies operating with such timely and high-quality humanitarian intelligence data that they can dramatically cut response time—being on the ground with astonishing speed and greatly mitigating the worst effects of an emergency. Additionally, I suspect that better data on humanitarian needs will change what aid is provided and how. Institutions often change only slowly and sometimes it seems that many classic responses (such as the provisioning of hygiene kits or the giving of bags of rice) are simply not the most effective or efficient ways to direct resources to those in need. More and better information on humanitarian needs could lead to major innovations in the way we provide relief and save lives.

I understand that many may view this, or really any humanitarian response, as something like a small bandage for a large wound. And I agree that the UN should be a forum for preventing the "wound" in the first place, whether it be a war or a human-influenced environmental emergency. But until we move to an era where conflict, dire poverty, and manmade disasters are a distant memory, emergency humanitarian aid will be a lifeline for some and a chance at recovery and a brighter future for many others. It needs to be guided by the highest quality of data to ensure that it is effective and that none of those who need it most are missing.

**JAMES ALTMAN** is a specialist in collecting and utilizing data to protect vulnerable populations in complex humanitarian emergencies and has worked for UN agencies and NGOs in Syria, Iraq, Ukraine, and Chad. He holds an MA in Global and International Studies and is currently completing a PhD in Global Studies at the University of California, Santa Barbara.

# AFTERWORD

## by Ahmet Davutoğlu

*Former Minister of Foreign Affairs and Former Prime Minister of Turkey*

There is no doubt that the United Nations is one of the greatest achievements in human history in terms of the ideal of establishing an order on the basis of the common destiny and common values of humanity. However, like every living organism and every institution, it has to renew itself in order to maintain its effect and validity.

As the title of this book, *Liberating the United Nations: Realism with Hope*, suggests, we have to be realistic when considering the structural problems and challenges facing the UN. But this realism should lead us to hope, not pessimism. The way to do this requires putting forward a visionary perspective in the normative and structural reform of the UN.

This approach is very important because the psycho-methodological dilemma created by the swing between "utopic optimism" and "nihilistic pessimism" has made it difficult to understand the dynamic change in the post–Cold War international system and to develop creative solutions for the challenges. I believe that the authors' conceptualization of "realistic hopefulness," which is very consistent with the "realistic optimism" I have suggested as an alternative approach against "nihilistic pessimism" and "utopic optimism,"[1] is the most effective and visionary approach in understanding and overcoming challenges.

I have read it with great appreciation and enthusiasm because it brings together realistic determinations and hopeful vision in a consistent synthesis in the context of the reform and the future of the UN. Almost every part and every line of it corresponded to my previous theoretical works as an academic and to my practical experience as the Ambassador/Chief Advisor, Minister of Foreign Affairs, and Prime Minister of the Republic of Turkey in the context of the UN.

As the authors underline, "the United Nations is more needed than ever before, and yet less relevant as a political actor than at any time since its establishment in 1945." They declared their intention in this book as "to interpret this disturbing paradox, and what may be done to overcome it." They have accomplished these intentions with astonishing success. They successfully "document the failures of the UN without overlooking its positive contributions to peace and justice" and impressively "make a case for supporting the UN as an indispensable feature of twenty-first-century world order."

The basis of this success lies in the fact that both authors have theoretical depth and vast practical experience and can transform these two features into a creative synthesis.

Richard Falk is not only a great theorist who has established his own school of thought in the fields of international law and international relations but also a fervent activist who does not hesitate to step forward to fight for human rights and human dignity, which are the normative foundations of the UN.

The main characteristic that sets him apart is his ability to integrate the talent for theoretical analysis with a visionary approach. Even just by looking at the titles of his books, one can easily sense these two strands. His work reflects both theory and vision, like this book. To illustrate, in his books *Legal Order in a Violent War*, *This Endangered Planet*, *Predatory Globalization: A Critique*, and *Chaos and Counterrevolution*, Falk provides insightful theoretical analyses of the contemporary state of the world and the various threats it faces in the future. In his books *On Humane Governance*, *The Promise of World Order*, and *Human Rights Horizons*, he provides a visionary approach and detailed road maps on how to address these challenges and threats, which builds upon his brilliant theoretical analyses. His countless list of books and papers are a testimony to his analytical and visionary thinking.

Falk is a *public intellectual* flowing through history and a *citizen pilgrim*[2] traveling mentally, conscientiously, and physically through various societies and civilizations.

When opposing the Vietnam War and exposing its illegitimacy, when questioning the policies of the post-9/11 era and standing against the Iraq War, when defending Palestinians' rights as the UN Special Rapporteur on Palestine and resisting all the pressures by Israel and the Zionist lobby, when taking an active stance to counter existential threats to humanity like nuclear warheads and the global climate crisis, he always put forward both his analytical vision and his humanitarian consciousness.

He is not a theorist living in an ivory tower or an activist driven only by strong emotions. He is a pioneer in synthesizing a rational stance of understanding reality without surrendering to it and a visionary stance of offering solutions without falling into the traps of utopian thinking. He has witnessed the trials and turbulences of the twentieth century and has taken a courageous stance on every issue, while envisaging the dynamics of the twenty-first century and planting the seeds of ideas for the future by providing solutions to future challenges way before they actualize.

We met Richard Falk about thirty years ago. For nearly ten years, we have held intellectual debates in academic meetings on various occasions and in long sessions when he visited Turkey.

Later, our meetings provided us with opportunities to discuss whether theory holds true in the face of reality, as I shared my experiences with him first as a chief advisor to the prime minister, later as a foreign minister, and finally as a prime minister. Our paths frequently intersected during these periods.

Right before the US invasion of Iraq, I became the chief advisor to the Turkish prime minister, and I opposed both the US invasion in general and the use of Turkish lands for the attack on Iraq. At the same time, my dear friend Richard Falk was taking the clearest and most fierce stance against the invasion in the international intellectual community by asserting the illegitimacy of this occupation.

In 2008, he became the UN Special Rapporteur on the issues of human rights in the Palestinian territories occupied since 1967. Around the same time, I was mediating the peace talks between Syria and Israel. Just before the direct talks between Syria and Israel would begin, Israel launched a devastating attack on Gaza, against which Richard put the forward the most determined stance as a Special Rapporteur, while I was doing shuttle diplomacy between Israel and Hamas in order to stop those attacks.

During his appointment, he was extremely influential in documenting and publicizing the human rights abuses in the Palestinian territories through his ardent work on the ground. The reports he wrote were fully consistent with our observations. Unsurprisingly, Israel fiercely attacked

Falk because of his reports that perfectly reflected his moral integrity and courage.

When I became the Minister of Foreign Affairs, our relationship involved an even more direct collaboration. He made critical contributions to the mediation/conciliation/peace conferences that Turkey led and to the UN Conference on Least Developed Countries. During this time, one of the most striking examples of our common approach to integrate theoretical analysis with practical diplomatic processes was on the topic of nuclear threat. When together with Brazilian Foreign Minister Celso Amorim, who was a mutual friend of Richard's and mine, we operated the mediation process and signed an agreement between the IAEA and the P5+1 countries, and Richard provided the most fervent support. Our earnest relationship continued when I was Prime Minister, during which time he closely followed and commented on Turkish politics.

In short, we don't have only a common philosophical, moral, and political approach to contemporary issues like geopolitical risks, human rights, and international relations but also a common path of integrating theory and practice on these very same topics.

Hans von Sponeck, on the other hand, is one of the leading diplomats and intellectuals who can make the most accurate assessments and recommendations about the future of the UN, due to his thirty-two years of experience in the UN and the duties he has undertaken in very critical regions from Botswana to Pakistan, from Ghana to India.

In particular, his uncompromising humanitarian stance during his mission as UN Assistant Secretary-General for humanitarian assistance (Oil-for-Food Programme) in Baghdad provides an admirable example of how the UN humanitarian mission should be carried out in the field.

Although we do not have a joint work with him, Hans von Sponeck's views on the sanctions against Iraq and on the US occupation of Iraq in 2003 are the views I completely agree with. The striking aspect of the matter is that I, a Turkish diplomat, Hans, a UN diplomat, and Falk, a public intellectual, expressed the same concerns and thoughts in different fields, especially regarding the invasion of Iraq in 2003.

His resignation as a protest against UN policies in the context of the effects of the sanctions against Iraq on the civilian population[3] is the result of an exemplary stance showing that assimilation of UN values is more important than the balance of power within the UN. The process of sanctions against Iraq and Hans von Sponeck's attitude should be considered as a case study in UN training programs especially in these days when UN sanctions are on the agenda again.

Written by two wise men who have lived through the critical processes of the UN from the Cold War to the present and defended UN values under all circumstances, this book deals with the challenges faced by the UN and its normative and structural reform processes. It is a must-read contribution for UN diplomats, concerned statesmen, their advisors, and academicians.

I would like to take this opportunity to bring to the attention of esteemed readers a summary of my analysis in my above-mentioned book in the context of global order and UN reform as a modest contribution to this very valuable work.

The systemic crisis we face today imposes the need for a new paradigm of global order and governance that takes into account the dynamics brought by globalization. The various components of the current international order handed down from the twentieth century and grounded on the philosophical and institutional structures of pre-globalization modernity are struggling to manage the rapid dynamics of a globalization-fueled oceanic wave and to contain the associated risks.

The fate of mankind as a whole now faces a series of very large-scale threats. These threats require an endeavor beyond just optimizing nation-states' self-interests, because they are by their nature transnational, not international. Issues such as climate change, ecological stability, environmental problems, cybercrime, the proliferation of weapons of mass destruction, pandemics, health, human rights, regulating trade and investment, global migration, poverty alleviation, sanctions, and demilitarization/denuclearization and terror have now reached a scale that presents a challenge to everyone everywhere and are becoming increasingly difficult to resolve purely through inter-state relations based on "territorial sovereignty and hegemonic geopolitics" as it has been described by Richard Falk.[4]

One of the principal reasons for today's systemic crisis is the logjam created by the failure to enact UN reform, the political framework of which was drawn up after prolonged debate at the 2005 World Summit. The fact that virtually no progress has been made up to now is a leading factor in the increased level of insecurity and the spread of pessimism in the international system.

In the seventy-eight years since the establishment of the UN, global geopolitical, geoeconomic, and geocultural relations, technological communication tools, and the nature of inter-state and transnational relations have undergone a radical change. The founding texts of the UN were typewritten, the post–Cold War UN reform efforts were carried out on computers, and it is likely that artificial intelligence will be used effectively in many UN processes in the coming years. The question asked by the authors,

"Would it be the same if the UN had been established in 1995 or today?" is very valid in this sense.

So, the UN's ability to maintain its effectiveness and validity in the global order necessitates a comprehensive reform process. The UN system is already affected by all fragmentary global and regional balances of power as it becomes a technocratic mechanism without the tools or indeed the will to mobilize the shared values that enabled its establishment in the first place. International problems are now resolved (or not) according to the course of balances of power in the field rather than on the UN platform.

By dissolving the rapidly evolving environment of pessimism in the international community, gaining time for rational negotiations, marginalizing irrational actors and reactions that feed on an atmosphere of international uncertainty, and redefining the counterparts involved in prevailing issues as well as methods of resolution, a well-defined and time-framed UN reform process will be significant in terms of motivating decision-makers and opinion leaders to contribute to the formation of a new international order.

Today, like the international order, the UN is at a crossroads: either it will be the locomotive of a participatory and egalitarian humane world order based on inclusive global governance that requires a three-legged restructuring of the political, economic, and cultural global orders, or it will turn into a passive structure dependent on the power balances of the second Cold War period, which is likely to break out between the US and China. As it has been underlined by the authors, "there are growing signs of a second cold war with China and possibly Russia as adversaries of the US."

In order for the first option to be realized, the restructuring of the UN in a new world order architecture to respond to global challenges is a priority.

The fundamental question we face then is clear: What are the main obstacles to reform and restructuring of the UN and how can they be overcome?

As an academician in the field of international relations, as a diplomat/politician who has had the privilege of participating in various capacities in almost all the UN General Assembly summits from 2003 to 2015; as a Minister of Foreign Affairs (2009–2014) who was involved in UN Security Council processes when Turkey was a temporary member (2010–2011); who chaired or co-chaired many UN initiatives, such as the Alliance of Civilizations, the Friends of Mediation, and the LDC summits; and as a Prime Minister (2014–2016) who has participated in many UN fora, I have come to the opinion that four main factors underlie the inability to enact reform.

The first concerns the reform process's methodology. This methodology, which seems technical but is in fact entirely political, has been tied to a series of steps that render internal change impossible. The resistance mechanism observed in nation-state constitutions whose self-imposed rules make change impossible are also valid in the case of the UN Charter. According to the current charter, any change to the structure of the UN Security Council can be implemented only by amending the Charter itself. Article 108 defines how this can be accomplished: "Amendments to the present Charter shall come into force for all Members of the United Nations when they have been adopted by a vote of two-thirds of the members of the General Assembly and ratified in accordance with their respective constitutional processes by two-thirds of the Members of the United Nations, including all the permanent members of the Security Council."[5]

In and of itself, the fact that any reform is subject to the approval of the permanent members of the UNSC, who may use their privileged position in the current UN system to maximize their national self-interest, constitutes the greatest procedural barrier to change, because these countries do not see the UN reform process as an opportunity for the creation of a new international order but see it as a risk factor to their own privileged position. In this context, it is hardly surprising that permanent members with widely divergent interests share a common platform on the question of resisting reform.

While this state of affairs is open to criticism in terms of idealist values, it is an entirely comprehensible reaction in terms of realpolitik, because no country wants to lose its privileged status. Yet these countries need to read the decline in the UN's performance and effectiveness in recent years accurately. The UN is progressively moving away from its positive mission as the founder of international order, and its role is being debased to that of a braking mechanism against any process that might affect permanent members' own national interests. If this continues, the UN will turn into an increasingly irrelevant organization alienated from developments in the field. Having a privileged position of power within such an organization will become more and more devoid of meaning, at least for peace and security functions.

The second factor is that UN reform has not been seen as part of a comprehensive reform of the international order; on the contrary, it has been reduced to the issue of reforming the UN Security Council. This has served to dislodge the reform process from being a necessity that concerns the entire international community and turned it an power struggle area, especially with regard to the veto power. Countries like the G4 (Brazil, Germany, India, and Japan) are involved in a struggle to gain permanent membership, while those who see no chance of attaining such status oppose the expansion of this category. The justified demands of the African continent, widely seen as a victim of the UN system, have become a tactical trump card exploited by parties to this struggle. The UN Security Council permanent membership structure and representative capacity is truly very far from being any kind of reflection of today's balances of power. And the debasement of the issue to a question of which country should obtain a new privileged status has blocked the development of a comprehensive reform process.

The third factor is that the imposition of particular conditions by some P5 member countries has turned the reform process from a time-limited mission into an open-ended mental exercise. And in spite of the intensification of crises during this period, the failure to bind the reform process to any kind of schedule has cast a long shadow over the seriousness of the entire process. Like all routine international processes, UN reform has turned into a recurring agenda item in a succession of technical meetings.

The fourth factor is P5 members' reluctance especially on the issue of Security Council reform and the role that their tacit alliances to conserve the status quo play in depriving such a difficult process of political will. This has made the expectation and process of change more important than change itself; a routine and technocratic process recognized as unachievable from the outset has turned into a merry-go-round diplomatic exercise whose perpetuation is useful to all. Discourse and rhetoric has thus prevailed over the will actually to change the status quo.

I think that the main elements of a viable reform process that will minimize the effects of these obstacles can be defined as follows:

First of all, there is a need for a thorough reassessment of the UN reform process in the light of the experiences of the past quarter century in terms of its principles, methodology, and implementation processes. A reevaluation unaffected by political and conjunctural concerns is key to identifying bottlenecks in the UN reform process and developing a method capable of delivering results.

The most fundamental principle with respect to the legitimacy of the entire process should be the inclusion in these working groups of representatives from all elements of the world community and cultural and civilizational basins, as well as groups from all continents and regions at different levels of development. For the proposed institutional reforms to be realized, work that is going to be carried out must be based on the idealist foundation of inclusiveness and integrity and the realist framework of interest optimization and implementation of power.

Second, a common international will needs to be shown by extract-
ing the reform process from the field of tactical maneuvering and lifting
roadblocks based on P5/the rest, status quo/change, or center/periphery
dichotomies.

Third, a participatory and results-oriented method must be adopted for
a genuine, comprehensive reform process, and this method linked to a reasonable but not open-ended schedule.

Fourth, the reform process must be absolved from any impasse arising
from debate over which power is to be a permanent member and based
on common principles applicable to all. Representation and participation
principles should be reconsidered within a rationale of inclusivity, and the
question of how these principles are reflected in the UN structure must be
based on objective criteria.

Fifth, the relationship between the UN Security Council and the UN
General Assembly should be redefined as one of the most critical areas of
the UN's institutional restructuring process. Such a redefinition is the only
way to prevent the entire reform process from gridlock over the issue of
UN Security Council membership. The maintenance of the current kind of
relations between these two main structures without change will make it
extremely difficult either to overcome blockages in the reform process or to
argue convincingly for the prospects of a new participatory order.

Sixth, intermediate mechanisms should be set up in which regional
organizations and powers can engage with the concerned authorities in
parallel to formal Security Council meetings or come to decisions jointly
with the Security Council, regardless of the subject. The fact that countries
paying the price for global crises are out of the loop while, as a result, countries taking final decisions about these crises see negotiations as cards in
their own internal bargaining processes is an unsustainable state of affairs.

Seventh, international problems' increasingly transnational nature
should give ever greater weight to mechanisms and processes involving
non-state actors and civil society groups taking into consideration the
strength of interaction brought by developments in communication technology and the ever-spreading impact of non-state actors.

The most important principle for the success of this whole process is
*inclusiveness*. At a time when globalization is gaining momentum, it is not
possible for an international order without inclusiveness to be sustainable.
For example, can climate change and illegal migration issues be handled
without South's contribution, or can cultural conflicts be overcome with a
purely Western-centered approach?

The success of the UN reform process in terms of the global economic order can be achieved by including the countries that do not have a fair share in the global economic welfare, especially the least developed countries. Developing a special model of governance for countries and groups of countries that make up the periphery of the central economic-political stratum is of great importance in diminishing the domino effect of economic crises and ensuring a proper balance between productivity and equitable income distribution on a global scale. The most comprehensive arrangements must be finalized with respect to the third tier comprising a wide geographical area outside existing global economic-political dynamics that remains vulnerable to all kinds of crisis, scarcity, drought, and famine.

Likewise, the negative impact of the clash of civilizations thesis can be prevented by a global cultural order, where all traditional civilizations can interact in mutual respect. There has been a serious change of perception concerning civilizations and cultural pluralism in the period from the final years of the Cold War, when the first stages of transition from modernity to globalization occurred, to the present day.

A new mental paradigm that includes all civilizational and cultural legacies as honorable elements in a shared human history replaces the confrontational rhetoric based on the clash of civilizations concept with an interaction of civilizations conceptualization and invests new generations with the idea that we are walking from a common human past enriched by the legacy of different civilizations into a common future, once again with the contribution of different civilizational legacies, will bring with it a global cultural order worthy of human dignity.

I believe that this book, which was written on the basis of "the spirit of informed realistic hopefulness" with the correct expression of its authors, will be a real source and guide for decision-makers and leaders who sincerely want the UN reform to be carried out in the most fair, inclusive, and efficient way.

# NOTE OF ACKNOWLEDGMENT

It is our pleasure to acknowledge those who helped us at every stage to finish this book. Our collaboration was intellectually challenged by changes in the global setting within which the UN operates. It was also logistically stressed by our respective residences in Germany and the United States. These stresses not only led us to navigate the obstacle course of reaching consensus on many tricky substantive questions associated with our treatment of the UN but, against the odds, deepened our friendship. It also strengthened our commitment to this undertaking of "liberating" the UN so that it might better fulfil the hopes that accompanied its founding and establishment.

Although the UN was not "lost in translation," its performance has disappointed many people of goodwill around the world. We seek to identify crucial, debilitating flaws in UN design and practice, as well as to praise achievements and adaptations over the years of its existence, as well as to acknowledge the contribution of those within the UN whose often impressive efforts have allowed the organization to do more for the well-being of the peoples of the world than global publics, mainstream media, foreign policy experts, and political leaders acknowledge. In contrast, we contend that the world would have been worse off without having had the benefit of UN contributions over the course of the past seventy-five-plus years. At the same time, we insist it could be much better off if the shortcomings of the UN were overcome in a spirit of urgency, considering that we are living through a dangerous period of multiple global crises.

We take this opportunity to thank all those within the UN who have been our colleagues and friends in this continuing struggle to support the work of the UN System as well as encouraging UN reform efforts intending to improve contributions to peace, justice, human dignity, ecological resilience, cooperative problem-solving among states, and the peaceful resolution of international disputes. Over the decades we have both been involved in this work from within and without the UN as a matter of our highest professional and humanistic priority.

Richard Falk has been involved as a scholar, a participant in multiple international research projects and dialogues devoted to war prevention, human development, and protection of the natural habitat, and, for six stormy years (2008–2014), as UN Special Rapporteur on Israel's Violations of International Humanitarian Law in Occupied Palestine.

Hans von Sponeck devoted his career to civil service in the UN over the course of thirty-two years, with senior postings in Botswana, Pakistan, India, Geneva, and Iraq. In 2000 he resigned as the UN Assistant Secretary-General for Iraq on principle because of his strong opposition to geopolitical interference with the Oil-for-Food Program, the UN's humanitarian program in Iraq that he was directing at the time.

We are most grateful to Stanford University Press for agreeing to publish our manuscript and supporting our efforts at every stage. We benefitted greatly from Marcela Cristina Maxfield's warmly sympathetic and professional guidance throughout the process of preparing the manuscript for publication, who was ably assisted by her principal assistant, Sarah Rodriguez. Once the process of substantive revision was completed, Chris Peterson and his team were most responsive to our queries about how to complete the production stage efficiently and without mishaps. We are especially indebted to Barbara Armentrout, who with graciousness and great stylistic sensitivity proposed improvements and removed infelicities in carrying out her role as copy editor for the entire manuscript. We finally give thanks to the anonymous outside reviewers of Stanford University Press, who, despite giving us extra work, recommended publication after their valuable suggestions for revision were satisfactorily addressed. In the end we felt the additional work was well worth the effort.

Over the years Falk learned a great deal from prominent UN staff and executives with whom he came into contact and wants to thank them for facilitating and often improving on his written submissions. In the course of his primarily academic career, he first studied the UN as a graduate law student in 1957 at Harvard Law School, in a legendary course given by Professor Louis B. Sohn, which made him permanently aware of the troubled interface between the UN framework and international relations during the Cold War era and beyond. Several outstanding scholars/friends influenced his thinking about the UN over the years, including Saul Mendlovitz, Robert Johansen, Samuel Kim, Tom Weiss, and Michael Doyle. Hilal Elver, Falk's wife, herself immersed in UN studies and activities with a focus on the global food agenda, facilitated and encouraged our work, and at some sacrifice to her own valuable related work.

Von Sponeck would like to thank John Burley and Enrique ter Horst, two outstanding UN colleagues and friends whose sharp minds helped to alter faulty thinking; James Paul, former director of the Global Policy Forum, for his many years of outstanding analyses of UNSC affairs; Berthold Lange, founder of the Kant Foundation, who made sure that we would respect Immanuel Kant; Karin Leukefeld, the indefatigable Middle East expert and courageous investigative journalist; Helene Kyd-von Sponeck at the Danish Institute for International Studies in Copenhagen, my daughter-in-law, for her insistence never to forget academic rigor; Cornelis Klein and his wife, Namgay Dem, whose many years in the UN made them perfect commentators on our challenge to get it right when assessing the UN's performance; and Hans Bäumler, another UN friend, who enriched von Sponeck's understanding with his wisdom and humor, until he passed away in 2021. And most important, von Sponeck thanks his wife, Nelda, who has accompanied him through the decades of his UN life, for her infinite patience, his sons, Alexander and Mark, and their wives, Marie and Helene, and his daughter, Anna, an IT virtuoso, who stood by her neophyte father and Richard to overcome their fear of the digital unknown by assisting us in addressing the mystifying intricacies associated with preparing the final revised version of the manuscript.

As it happened, history did not stop evolving in this period between submission and publication, and the most relevant developments had a central bearing on the current limitations of the UN to address war/peace issues when the strategic interests of dominant sovereign states are involved. We refer not only to the continuation of the Ukraine War, but more dramatically to the controversies associated with Israel's response to the Hamas attack of October 7, 2023. Such an extreme pattern of violence both exposed the design weaknesses of the UN that paralyzed a response in accord with international law and humane values but also illuminated the institutional potentialities of the organization. In this respect, the South African initiative of invoking its status as a party to the Genocide Convention, by appealing to the International Court of Justice to pronounce upon whether Israeli violence constituted genocide, as well as whether to grant its emergency request for provisional measures. South Africa by so requesting was asking the Court to decree the suspension of Israel's behavior alleged to be of a genocidal character pending in ICJ final decision on the merits. The ICJ did issue an interim order on January 26, 2024, granting the main requested measures sought by the South African initiative. This itself was an extraordinary exhibition of judicial independence by the ICJ in which the judges somewhat unexpectedly followed the pathways of juridical conscience rather than the predilections of their governments of national affiliation. It was a glorious moment for the ICJ, for South Africa, and for those peoples and governments around the world that still believed in internationalism, international law, and the UN.

As positive were these achievements, the morning after illustrated the chilling performative deficiencies of the UN. By carrying on with its military operations Israel defiantly conveyed its refusal to comply with the UN orders. The well-being of the Gazan civilians was further jeopardized by Israel's day-after accusations that UNRWA staff members were involved in the October 7 attack, and the countries supportive of Israel joined in a shameless geopolitical response consisting of defunding UNRWA, thereby undermining its critical role in providing aid and shelter to the civilian population of Gaza facing survival threats of mass starvation and disease.

It is unclear how this configuration will impact on the UN, whether it will inflict lasting damage on its reputation, even to the extent of stimulating efforts by many countries in the Global South to pursue a new world order of their own free from geopolitical domination. Or, in the alternative, whether these frustrations to UN effectiveness will intensify previously mounting pressures for UN reform that will allow the organization to better achieve at last its purposes and principles as set forth in Articles 1 and 2 of the UN Charter. This seeming fork in the road will undoubtedly inform the Summit of the Future scheduled at the United Nations for September 22–23, 2024, and will likely clarify our assessments of UN reform based on an abiding vision of "realism with hope."

*Richard Falk (Yalikavak, Turkey; Santa Barbara, USA)*
*and Hans von Sponeck (Müllheim, Germany)*

# NOTES

**Epigraph**

"'Act on Your Ideals' Secretary-General Urges Young People at World Youth Forum," press release, SG/SM/6669, SOC/4460, August 7, 1998, https://press.un .org/en/1998/19980807.sgsm6669.html.

**Chapter 1**

1. See damning insider account by Daniel Ellsberg, *The Doomsday Machine: Confessions of a Nuclear War Planner* (Bloomsbury, 2017).

2. See influential critical assessments in Samantha Powers, *A Problem from Hell: America and the Age of Genocide* (Basic Books, 2013).

3. SC/RES/1973 (2011), by a vote of ten in favor, none opposed, and five abstaining (Russia, India. China, Brazil, and Germany).

4. And see Tatianna Carayannis and Thomas Weiss, "The 'Third' UN: Imagining Post-COVID-19 Multilateralism," *Global Policy*, 12, no. 1 (2021): 5–14.

5. A/RES/377 (1950), the still important Uniting for Peace resolution adopted in the 1950 Korean War, itself an early indication that the UN was not going to work to prevent the outbreak of wars between states as the founders of the UN had hoped and the Charter had envisioned.

6. See International Court of Justice, "Legality of the Threat or Use of Nuclear Weapons," Advisory Opinion of July 8, 1996, ICJ Reports 1996, 226–267; ICJ, "Legal Consequences of a Construction of a Wall on the Occupied Palestinian Territory," July 9, 2004, ICJ Reports 2004; and pending ICJ Advisory Opinion request, "Legal Consequences Arising from the Policies and Practices of Israel in Occupied Palestinian Territory, including East Jerusalem."

7. For further consideration, see Richard Falk and Andres Strauss, *A Global Parliament: Essays and Articles* (Berlin: Committee for a Democratic UN, 2011); Falk and Strauss, "Toward a Global Parliament," *Foreign Affairs* 80, no. 1 (2001): 212–220.

8. To be contrasted with the references to US adherence to "a rule-governed world" by US Secretary of State, Antony J. Blinken, "Virtual Remarks at the UN Security Council Open Debate on Multilateralism," US Department of State, May 7, 2021. See John Dugard, "The Choice before Us: International Law or a 'Rules-Based International Order,'" *Leiden Journal of International Law*, 36, no 2 (June 2023): 223–232; Stephen Walt, "China Wants a 'Rules Based International Order' Too," *Foreign Policy*, March 31, 2021, https://foreignpolicy.com/2021/03/31/china -wants-a-rules-based-international-order-too/.

9. Francis Fukuyama, *The End of History and the Last Man* (Free Press, 1992).

## Chapter 2

1. Robert O. Keohane, "Multilateralism: An Agenda for Research," *International Journal*, 45, no. 4 (1990): 732–764.

2. F. S. Northedge, *The League of Nations: Its Life and Times (1920–1946)* (Leicester University Press, 1986), 342.

3. The Soviet Union emerging from the Russian Revolution was eventually admitted as a member of the League in 1934 but was expelled five years later because of its illegal occupation of Finland.

4. Japan surrendered on September 2, 1945. Jason Ralph and Jess Gifkins, "The Purpose of UN Security Council," *European Journal of International Relations*, 23, no. 3 (2016): 630–653. See also W. Mattli and J. Seddon, *The Power of the Penholder* (Cambridge University Press, 2015).

5. Confidential report by German Ambassador Tono Eitel to the Security Council, November 14, 2000.

6. Stephen C. Schlesinger, *Act of Creation: The Founding of the UN; A Story of Superpowers, Secret Agents, Wartime Allies and Enemies, and Their Quest for a Peaceful World* (Westview Press, 2003).

## Chapter 3

1. The two covenants on civil, political, economic, social, and cultural rights had been adopted by the UN General Assembly in 1966.

2. US National Security Archive, October 26, 1962.

3. Kurt Waldheim, *Building the Future Order* (Free Press, 1980).

4. The first five Secretaries-General were Trygve Lie, Dag Hammarskjöld, U Thant, Kurt Waldheim, and Javier Perez de Cuellar.

5. Brian Urquart, *Hammarskjold* (Knopf, 1972).

6. UN CEB/2021, Human Resources Statistics, https://unsceb.org/human -resources-statistics.

7. The panel's report, *We the Peoples: Civil Society, the United Nations and Global Governance*, A/58/817, June 11, 2004, and the report of the Secretary-General to the General Assembly on follow-up, September 17, 2004.

8. A/RES/377 (1950).

9. Blue Helmets are UN peacekeepers that include soldiers, police officers, and civilian personnel.

10. Examples of such General Assembly resolutions include A/47/60A, A/48/28, A/49/427, A/49/149, A/50/39, A/50/29, A/51/17, A/52/78, A/53/39, A/54/54, A/54/200.

11. China Global Television Network, 2018; edu.sin.com.cn, August 22, 2014.

12. Address by Senator Jesse Helms, Chairman, U.S. Senate Committee on Foreign Relations, before the United Nations Security Council, January 20, 2000, https://www.govinfo.gov/content/pkg/CHRG-106shrg62154/html/CHRG-106shrg62154.htm.

13. In accordance with the UN Charter Article 17, annual contributions to the UN regular budget, payable at the beginning of each calendar year, are assessed for each country, mainly based on their gross national income. The GA had decided to cap the US contribution at 22 percent of the total UN budget since according to the UN assessment key, the US would have had to make an even higher contribution.

14. An Open Letter to Pakistan on Human Development from Heads of UN Agencies resident in Islamabad, September 1993.

15. Article 5 of the North Atlantic Treaty creating NATO in 1949 specifies that "an armed attack against one or more [member states] . . . shall be considered an attack against them all."

16. Examples of such US votes include A/RES/45/59B; A/RES/54/54G; A/RES/45/62C; A/RES/45/59D; A/RES/54/54L.

17. Boutros-Ghali, speech at UN 51st anniversary, Rome, January 11, 1996.

**Chapter 4**

1. There were 189 UN member countries in 2000; this number increased to 193 with Serbia (2002), Switzerland (2006), Timor-Leste (2006), and South Sudan (2011) joining the UN.

2. There have been other pandemics in recent years, such as SARS, swine flu, Ebola, and Zika, and it must be assumed there will new ones in the future.

3. Examples: "A Programme for Reform" (A/51/950, 1997); "The Role of the UN in the 21st Century" (A/54/2000, 2000); "Strengthening the UN: An Agenda for Further Change" (A/57/387, 2002); *A More Secure World: Our Shared Responsibilities: Report of the High-Level Panel on Threats, Challenges and Change* (UN Peacebuilding Commission, 2004); "In Larger Freedom: Towards Development, Security and Human Rights for All" (A/59/2005/Add.3, 2005); "Investing in the UN: For a Stronger Organization Worldwide" (A/60/692, 2006).

4. North and South Korea became UN member states in 1991.

5. Ban Ki-moon as South Korea's ambassador to Austria and Slovenia was elected in 1999 as chairman of the preparatory commission for the Comprehensive Test Ban Treaty organization.

6. The commission had been mandated by the General Assembly in 1952 to work for the "balanced reduction of all armed forces and all armaments including weapons of mass destruction."

7. Two Ban initiatives; see reports *Delivering as One* (https://www.un.org/en/ga/deliveringasone/index.shtml) and *The Post-2015 Development Agenda* (https://www.unodc.org/unodc/en/about-unodc/post-2015-development-agenda.html).

8. Letter of the President of the General Assembly, April 4, 2016.

9. Edith M. Lederer of the AP, June 20, 2017 (https://www.un.org/sg/en/content/sg/press-encounter/2017-06-20/secretary-generals-press-conference-un-headquarters).

10. Richard Falk and Virginia Tilley, *Israeli Practices towarwds the Palestinian People and the Question of Apartheid, Palestine and the Israeli Occupation*, no. 1, Economic and Social Commission for Western Asia, ESCWA/ECRI/2017/1.

11. A/58/317/2004.

12. In Pakistan and India, where one of us had served as UN Resident Coordinator, the only link civilian UN activities had with UNMOGIP, the military observer group in India and Pakistan, was through the UN's duty-free goods commissary.

13. S/Res/1645/2005.

14. Bernadotte was assassinated while on mission in the area.

15. A/67/123.

16. For a good review, see Shivani Singh and Manuel Herrera, "25 Years since CTBT: A Possible Bridge between Nuclear Powers?," Opinion Paper, IEEE.ES, Instituto Espanol, 127/2021, November 15, 2021.

17. In 1999 the US Senate rejected the ratification of the CTBT and in 2018, the US Trump administration, while initially indicating support for the CTBT, later confirmed that it would not ratify this treaty!

18. The fifteen judges of the ICJ , however, did not have a unanimous position on whether the actual use of nuclear weapons in extreme cases involving the survival of a state was unlawful. Additionally, two judges believed the court should have unambiguously concluded that the use of nuclear weapons would be unlawful in all circumstances.

19. US President Trump abrogated this agreement in 2018.

20. There were also ECOSOC resolutions on Palestinian women that only the US opposed.

21. In a change of policy, Canada supported for the first time in 2019 a resolution calling for the establishment of a Palestinian state.

22. See reports by B'tselem, an organization that was established in 1989 by a group of Israeli lawyers, doctors, and academics supported by members of the Knesset, the Israeli Parliament, to document human rights violations in territories occupied by Israel (https://www.btselem.org/).

23. UN Charter, Article 1/3.

24. Resolutions A/56/155/Dec2001 to A/74/149/Dec2019, covering a nineteen-year period.

25. US Department of State, *Digest of US Practice in International Law*, 2003.

26. Examples: A/61/146/2006 and A/62/141/2007.

27. A/60/230 and A/62/218.

28. A/74/3281, adopted by the General Assembly in 1974.

29. See A/62/183/2000.

30. A/57/5/2002 and subsequent yearly resolutions.

31. WTO emerged after many years of complex negotiations—see the debates in GATT, the forum for the General Agreement on Tariffs and Trade.

32. GA resolutions on decolonization; and related to the Chargos Archipelago, an NSGT, Philippe Sands, *The Last Colony* (Weidenfeld & Nicolson, 2022).

33. See A/73/295/2019.

34. UN Charter, Article 96 indicates that the General Assembly "may request the ICJ to give an advisory opinion on any legal issue."

35. US Embassy note verbale, February 3, 2020, to the Prime Minister's Office in Port Louis. See also Sands, *The Last Colony* (2022)

36. See A/64/104/2009.

37. Address to the UNCHR, April 7, 2005.

38. The FAO representative in India, Peter Rosenegger, in the 1990s told one of us in New Delhi that after a six-week travel throughout India, he was astonished to realize that most of the regional Indian departments of agriculture, forestry and fisheries had been established with UN technical assistance.

39. Often the experts were people who had emigrated but wanted to assist the countries from which they or their parents had originally come. One of us serving in Turkey at the time witnessed that UNDP had successfully promoted a special program called TOKTEN (Transfer of Know-How through Expatriate Nationals) through which specialists of Turkish origin who had a sense of commitment to their former country provided time-limited technical assistance and then returned to their "new" countries.

40. On one occasion in Islamabad, at a public function, the World Bank deputy representative in a conversation with a UN colleague about Pakistan's social action plan became so agitated about this distinction that he wanted to start a physical fight.

41. Between 2000 and 2021, there were thirty-two major UN global conferences on MDGs/SDGs, gender, climate change, finance, social development, food, development cooperation, and a range of other topics important for national, regional, and global development.

42. Different UN departments at the UN headquarters at times have also failed to engage in collaborative efforts and, in the absence of leadership, did so with impunity. One of us experienced this directly when a colleague from the UN Office for Humanitarian Affairs tried to contact the UN Office of the Iraq Programme and was told not to do so "because they are too political."

43. In 2020, there were fifty-six UN PDAs foreseen to cooperate, with a majority located in Africa and Asia.

44. To save money, no drinking water was served during meetings at UN headquarters, as one of us witnessed while visiting it in the mid-1990s.

45. For example, noncore contributions to UNDP have fluctuated in recent years between 75 percent and 80 percent.

46. UN Charter, Article 100.

47. This format is named for Ambassador Diego Arria of Venzuela. He had

suggested in 1992 that non-UN parties should be invited to express their views on matters of interest to the Security Council and the General Assembly. In recent years, this format has been increasingly applied by the UN.

## Chapter 5

1. The most definitive scholarly treatment of the themes of this chapter can be found in Ardi Imseis, *The United Nations and the Question of Palestine: Rule by Law and the Structure of International Legal Subalternity* (Cambridge University Press, 2023).

2. See John Quigley, *Britain and Its Mandate over Palestine: Legal Chicanery on a Global Stage* (Anthem, 2022).

3. The Peel Commission, formally the Royal Commission of Inquiry to Palestine, a distinguished group of British notables headed by Lord Robert Peel, was appointed in 1936 by the British government to investigate the causes of unrest among Palestinian Arabs and Jews. It issued a report in 1937 recommending partition within the British Mandatory, the typical exit proposal relied on by British colonialism after its divide-and-rule schemes collapsed. A year later the Peel recommendation of partition was rejected in the Royal Commission on Mandatory Palestine's Palestine Partition Commission Report, the so-called Woodhead Report. So the matter of the Palestinian issue rested until the UN acted by proposing partition plus the internationalization of the city of Jerusalem.

4. For a critical narrative of the period between the Balfour Declaration and the establishment of Israel based on archival research, see Thomas Suarez, *State of Terror: How Terrorism Created Modern Israel* (Skyscraper Publications, 2016). For general background, see also Rashid Khalidi, *The Hundred Years War on Palestine: A History of Settler Colonialism and Resistance* (Metropolitan Books, 2020); Avi Shlaim, *The Iron Wall: Israel and the Arab World* (Norton, 1988); and Illan Pappe, *The Ethnic Cleansing of Israel* (Oneworld Publishers, 2006).

5. John Mearsheimer and Stephen Walt, *The Israel Lobby and U.S. Foreign Policy* (Farrar, Straus and Giroux, 2007).

6. Israel's Basic Law of 2018, entitled Israel as the Nation-State of the Jewish People, July 19, 2018.

7. Of the many detailed reports, the following seem particularly notable on the issue of apartheid, and there is the lack of a common view of the extent of apartheid but not its existence. See Richard Falk and Virginia Tilley, "Report on Israeli Practices Toward the Palestinian People and the Question of Apartheid," *UN Economic and Social Council for West Asia*, 2017; Report, "A Regime of Jewish Supremacy from the Jordan River to the Mediterranean Sea: THIS IS APARTHEID," B'Tselem, Israel, 2021; *A Threshold Crossed: Israel's Authorities and the Crimes of Apartheid and Persecution*, report, Human Rights Watch, 2021; *Israel's Apartheid against Palestinians: A Cruel System of Domination and a Crime against Humanity*, report, Amnesty International, 2022.

8. See generally Richard Falk, John Durgard, and Michel Lynk, *Protecting Human Rights in Occupied Palestine: Working through the UN*, (Clarity, 2022; see especially the excerpt from Michael Lynx's March 2022 report, section en-

titled "From Occupation to Apartheid: Apartheid in the Occupied. Palestinian Territory," A/HRC/49/87, reprinted, 297–312). Although a civil society consensus alleges Israel to be guilty of establishing an apartheid regime, there is confusion as to date (embedded in Zionism from the outset or when the occupation became prolonged), as to territorial scope (Occupied West Bank, Jordan River to Mediterranean Sea), and as to extent of victimization (Palestinians under occupation, Palestinians in both the. OPT and Israel, the Palestinian people as a whole, including refuges in neighboring countries, exiles, and asylum seekers).

9. See Jonathan Schneer, *The Balfour Declaration: The Origins of the Arab-Israeli Conflict* (Random House, 2012).

10. See Suarez, *State of Terror*; Khalidi, *The Hundred Years War on Palestine*; and Pappe, *The Ethnic Cleansing of Israel*.

11. See General Assembly's condemnation of the US moving its embassy to Jerusalem, accompanied by US ambassador Nikki Haley's threats that the US would be "taking names" of those countries that voted in favor. Despite this crude attempt at intimidation, A/ES-10/L.22 was approved by a vote of 128–9 (with 35 abstentions), December 21, 2017. The issue was important because it challenged the UN consensus to deny validity to the proclamation of Jerusalem as the eternal capital of Israel and the Jewish people. The issue, vital for the Palestinian future, also illustrates the interplay of geopolitics and legality in the context of the General Assembly. At the Security Council, no threat was made because the US had used its right of veto to void a 14–1 decision on the same issue earlier in December 2017.

12. Rashid Khalidi, *Brokers of Deceit: How the U.S. Has Undermined Peace in the Middle East* (Beacon, 2013).

13. See Richard Falk, *Palestine: Legitimacy of Hope* (Just World Books, 2014).

14. The P5 reaction to the Treaty on the Prohibition of Nuclear Weapons (TPNW) is emblematic of geopolitical primacy in relation to UN initiatives bearing on strategic postures relative to nuclear weapons. (See "North Atlantic Council Statement as Treaty on the Prohibition of Nuclear Weapons Enter into Force," December 15, 2020; also Steven Hill, *NATO and the Treaty on the Prohibition of Nuclear Weapons*, Research Paper, Chatham House, January 29, 2021.) Omitted from the P5 reaction is any comment on geopolitical hypocrisy by calling for the full implementation of the NPT, including Article 6, which obligates parties to seek nuclear disarmament in good faith. In practice and offstage commentary, Article 6 is viewed as "a useful fiction" with a role limited to the appearance of a bargain with states foregoing the nuclear option.

15. John Dugard, *Confronting Apartheid: A Personal History of South Africa, Namibia, and Palestine* (Jacinda, 2018). Of particular relevance to recourse to the ICJ in the face of defiance by South Africa to international law norms is Dugard, *The Southwest Africa/Namibia Dispute: Documents and Scholarly Writings* (University of California Press, 1973).

16. See "Legal Consequences of the Construction of the Wall in the Occupied Palestinian Territory," Advisory Opinion, *ICJ Reports*, 2004; see also the pending General Assembly Advisory Opinion request, "Legal Consequences Arising from

the Policies and Practices of Israel in Occupied Palestinian Territory, including East Jerusalem." Also of symbolic relevance has been recourse by the Palestinian Authority on behalf of Palestine to the ICC as manifested by the harsh responses of the governments of both Israel and the United States.

## Chapter 6

1. See also Hans von Sponeck, *A Different Kind of War—The UN Sanctions Regime in Iraq* (Berghahn, 2006); and Hans von Sponeck, "The Politics of the Sanctions on Iraq and the Humanitarian Exception," in *Land of the Blue Helmets*, edited by Karim Makdisi and Vijay Prashad (University of California Press, 2017).

2. As a former UN Assistant Secretary-General who was responsible in Baghdad during 1998–2000 for the implementation of the UN humanitarian exemption, the Oil-for-Food Programme, von Sponeck discusses, as an insider, the roles that the United Nations, the wider UN System, and individual governments played during years of Iraq sanctions.

3. Resolutions S/660 and 661 (1990).

4. In 1998, renamed OCHA, the Office for the Coordination of Humanitarian Affairs.

5. S/1995/300.

6. S/706/1991.

7. S/687/1991.

8. S/705/1990. Under UN sanctions, Iraqi oil income was deposited into a UN escrow account in the Banque Nationale de Paris and closely monitored by the US Treasury Department's Office of Foreign Assets Control.

9. These two UN Humanitarian Coordinators were Denis Halliday (1997–98) and Hans von Sponeck (1998–2000).

10. At the time of Operation Desert Fox, the US air strikes against Baghdad, December 16–19, 1998, UNIKOM's liaison officer, Russian colonel Yuri Milyukin, supported us with valuable advice for the safety of UN staff living in the UN building in Baghdad.

11. S/RES/986.

12. A US report to the US National Security Council in August 1998 cynically stated: "Since 1991, the US has led the efforts in the [UN] Security Council to meet the needs of the Iraqi people."

13. The UNICEF representative, Philippe Heffinck, a colleague from Belgium, and Hans von Sponeck had decided that if a total evacuation were to take place, they would not follow this order and would remain in the UN office and accept the consequences.

14. SC resolution 688/1991 makes no provision for any foreign military involvement in Iraq's air space.

15. During the six and a half years of the OFFP, this post had been held by four different individuals.

16. During our time in Baghdad, the team of heads of UN entities was made up of nationals from France, India, Afghanistan, Sudan, Finland, Canada, and Germany.

17. We had discovered accidentally that $1 million was available at UN headquarters for mini projects in Iraq. This offers an additional insight into the careless management within the OIP. The amount was quickly disbursed to various NGOs for micro rural water supply, health services, and education projects.

18. Apart from Phase 8, the last OFFP phase, in 2002–2003, humanitarian revenue had always been less, sometimes significantly less, than the distribution plans required.

19. Iraqi deputy prime minister Tariq Aziz referred to the OFFP as a "refugee camp program."

## Chapter 7

1. For detailed background information on the role of UN envoys for Syria, see A/66/253 (2012) and S/2254 (2015).

2. See UNODA website for details: https://disarmament.unoda.org/.

3. The official name: Convention on the Prohibition of the Development, Production, Stockpiling and Use of Chemical Weapons and on Their Destruction, https://legal.un.org/avl/ha/cpdpsucw/cpdpsucw.html.

4. See also UN Commissioner Karen Abu Zayd's detailed statement of September 23, 2021, on conditions in Syria.

5. This is a reference to an alleged chemical weapons attack in Ghouta on August 21, 2013.

6. A/67/997 (2013) and S/2013/553.

7. S/2017/567.

8. White Helmets is a Syrian volunteer organization operating in opposition-controlled Syria and in Turkey; it concentrates on medical evacuations and search and rescue operations in war-torn areas. Over time White Helmets has become a target of a "systematic information warfare" and accused of alleged staged or fake rescues, misappropriating funds, working with al-Qaida and ISIS or the CIA and MI6.

9. www.couragefound.org.

10. A/RES/377 (1950). This is the only resolution that gives the General Assembly the authority to overrule the Security Council, provided a two-thirds majority of General Assembly members support it.

11. It consisted of Ambassador José Bustani, former director-general of OPCW; Professor Richard Falk, professor emeritus, Princeton University; Professor Piers Robinson; and Hans-C. von Sponeck, former UN Assistant Secretary-General.

12. The full text of the Statement of Concern and the list of signatories, published on March 21, 2021, can be found at www.BerlinGroup21.org.

13. S/2019/208, para. 9.12.

14. A/HRC/44/61, September 3, 2020.

15. A/HRC/39/65, August 9, 2018, paras. 92 and 93.

16. A/HRC/39/65, para. 31.

17. S/RES/2118 (2013).

## Chapter 8

1. NPT, Articles IV, VI, X. See also "Legality of the Threat or Use of Nuclear Weapons," Advisory Opinion, Separate Opinions, Dissenting Opinions, ICJ Reports, June 8, 1996.

2. The legal, political, and moral responses to chemical and biological weapons, which along with nuclear weapons, were also considered weapons of mass destruction but were treated quite differently. For chemical and biological weapons, presumably for reasons of managerial efficiency, dominant states sought to prohibit unconditionally their threat or use and even their development, negotiating international treaties to this effect. In practice, only limited success was achieved due to nonimplementation and violations of treaty provisions by non-nuclear states.

3. See Richard Falk, Introduction, in *Making Endless Wars: The. Vietnam War and Arab-Israeli Conflicts in the History of International Law*, ed. Brian Cuddy and Victor Kattan (University of Michigan Press, 2023). See also Oona Hathaway and Scott Shapiro, *The Internationalists: How a Radical Plan to Outlaw War Remade the World* (Simon & Schuster, 2017) for an unconvincing view that "law" created a new reality for international uses of force by virtue of the 1928 Pact of Paris (also known as the Kellogg-Briand Pact).

4. Pence Clancy, Richard Falk, and Susan Power, "The ICC and Palestine's Breakthrough and the End of the Road," *Journal of Palestine Studies*, April 2021.

5. Views on the status of intervention in internal affairs of states in contemporary international relations and international law are collected in Hedley Bull, ed., *Intervention in World Politics*. (Oxford University Press, 1984).

6. See H. Bruce Franklin, *Crash Course: From the Good War to the Forever War* (Rutgers University Press, 2018).

7. See Chapter VII, UN Charter.

8. See "Military and Paramilitary Activities in and against Nicaragua," *Nicaragua v. US*, ICJ Reports, 1986.

9. Justice Robert Jackson called for this behavior in his role as Nuremberg prosecutor, reminding the tribunal that the legal principles used to hold Germans accountable would henceforth bind those who sit in judgment.

10. See Anne-Marie Slaughter, *A New World Order* (Princeton University Press, 2004).

11. Not every winner of a legitimacy war will control the political outcome of a struggle if the substantive disproportion is too great—for example, China/Tibet, India/Kashmir, Russia/Chechnya, Morocco/Western Sahara.

12. See the cogent and still relevant analysis and assessments of Deepak Nayyar in *Asian Resurgence: Diversity in Development* (Oxford, 2019).

13. Richard Falk, "The Unresolved Struggle for International Accountability: From Nuremberg to the ICC," in *The Global Community Yearbook of International Law and International Criminal Accountability* (Oxford University Press, 2020).

14. See Franklin, *Crash Course*; Cuddy and Kattan, *Making Endless Wars*.

**Chapter 9**

1. A/RES/40/177.

2. A/42/232 and E/1987/68 (1987).

3. An ancient method of transporting water from underground channels to the surface for irrigation and drinking.

4. UN Joint Inspection Unit, *Review of the Administrative Committee on Coordination and Its Machinery* (1999), https://www.unjiu.org/content/review -administrative-committee-coordination-and-its-machinery-1.

5. Investments have ranged from $3,000 to $50,000 for initiatives such as mangrove management, waste disposal, biogas, herbal and medicinal plants, sealife protection, fuel-efficient stoves, barren-land development, use of traditional seeds, and cohabitation of wildlife and local communities.

6. See Jolly, Emmerij and Weiss, *UN Ideas That Changed the World* (Indiana University Press, 2009), plus Pogge, *World Poverty and Human Rights* (Polity Press, 2008).

7. Each UN agency has a major national counterpart, such as WHO with ministries of health, UNESCO with ministries of education, FAO with ministries of agriculture, and so on.

8. UN Secretary-General, *Renewing the United Nations: A Programme of Reform: Report of the Secretary-General* (UN, July 14, 1997).

9. Countries under sanctions in the 1990s: Iraq, South Africa, former Yugoslavia, Somalia, Liberia, Libya, Haiti, and Angola.

10. Michael Edwards, ed., *Oxford Handbook of Civil Society* (Oxford University Press, 2011).

11. In cooperation with the governments of Qatar and Germany.

12. A/58/817.

13. Succeeded in 2011 by the Community of Latin and Caribbean States.

14. Democracy Without Borders, an international NGO advocating the democratization and strengthening the UN; and United Nations, Office of the Secretary-General's Envoy on Youth, *Youth 2030* (UN, 2018), a UN report outlining a strategy for working with and for youth.

15. Frank Schwartz, "Civil Society in Japan Revisited," *Japanese Journal of Political Science* (November 2002).

16. "General Assembly Debate on UN Reform and the Cardoso Panel," Global Policy Forum, October 4, 2004 (https://archive.globalpolicy.org/reform/ initiatives/panels/cardoso/1004gacardoso1.htm).

17. Five countries (Germany, the US, Sweden, Japan, and Norway) contributed $400 million, or 62 percent, of these core resources.

18. Examples: US Council for International Business, *All In—Designing PPPs with the UN for Maximum Impact* (2019); Public Service International, *Why Public-Private Partnerships Don't Work* (2015), https://www.world-psi.org/en/ publication-why-public-private-partnerships-dont-work.

19. The Belt and Road initiative focuses mainly on power and transport sectors but also on water, sanitation, and telecommunications. OECD in 2018 estimated capital requirements of $1 trillion for a ten-year period.

20. Founded in 1990 by Ted Turner, former owner of the CNN and current chairman of the UN Foundation, with a commitment to protect the environment.

21. These include Exxon, Shell, Goldman Sachs, Caterpillar, Walgreen, Johnson & Johnson, Nike, Cisco, and Google.

22. The IPU was founded in 1889 and has had UN observer status since 2002.

23. Claudia Kissling, *The Legal and Political Status of International Parliamentary Institutions* (Committee for a Democratic UN, 2011); and Maja Brauer and Andreas Bummel, *A United Nations Parliamentary Assembly* (Democracy Without Borders, 2020).

24. The UN's six official languages are Arabic, Chinese, English, French, Russian, and Spanish.

25. Guy Standing, *The Precariat: The New Dangerous Class* (Bloomsbury, 2011).

26. See the World Economic Forum 2019 Annual Report, www3.weforum.org /docs/WEF_Annual_Report_18-19.pdf.

27. The General Assembly had decided in 1970 that donor countries should contribute 0.7 percent of their GNI. This target has never been reached. In 2021 a total of $185.9 billion, or 0.33 percent of GNI, became available from OECD countries. At 0.7 percent, the resources for development would increase to over $500 billion.

## Chapter 10

1. *The Oceans, Our Future*, Report of the Independent World Commission on the Oceans (Cambridge University Press, 1998).

2. See contrasting views of Lon Fuller and H. L. A. Hart. The first round of the debate, Hart's "Positivism and the Separation of Law and Morals" and Fuller's "Positivism and Fidelity to Law: A Reply to Professor Hart" can be found in the *Harvard Law Review* (vol. 71, 1958). The later rounds appear in Hart's *The Concept of Law* (Clarendon Press, 1961; Oxford University Press, 2012), Fuller's *The Morality of Law* (Yale University Press, 1964), Hart's review of Fuller's 1964 book (*Harvard Law Review*, vol. 78, 1965), and Fuller's reply to critics in the revised edition of *The Morality of Law* (Yale University Press, 1969). For jurisprudential background see Hans Kelsen, *Pure Theory of Law*, Max Knight, trans. (University of California Press, 1967).

3. See Myres S. McDougal, Harold D. Lasswell, and James C. Miller, *The Interpretation of Agreements and World Order: Principles of Content and Procedure* (Brill, 1994).

4. Ove Bring, "Dag Hammarskjöld's Approach to the United Nations and International Law" (www.cepal.org/sites/defaults/files/pr/files/44856-Anforonde -Ove-Bring.pdf); see also Ove Bring, "Dag Hammarskjöld and the Development of International Law," UN Web TV, 2008.

5. Wolfgang Friedmann, *The Changing Structure of International Law* (University Presses of California, Columbia, Princeton, 1964).

6. S/RES/827, May 25, 1993, dealing with former Yugoslavia, and S/RES/955, November 8, 1994, dealing with the Rwanda genocide, were supported unanimously.

7. See Franck/Henkin debate of the early 1970s about the status of the use of force under the UN Charter Article 2(4) and inconsistent practice re nondefensive pursuit of territorial claims by force (Korea, Cyprus, Suez Operation, Western Sahara, Kuwait, Russia, China): Thomas M. Franck, "Who Killed Article 2(4)?: Or Changing Norms Governing the Use of Force by States," *American Journal of International Law*, 64, no. 5 (1970): 809–837; Louis Henkin, "The Reports of the Death of Article 2(4) Are Greatly Exaggerated," *American Journal of International Law*, 65, no. 3 (1970): 544–548. See also Ian Hurd, "Permissive Law on the International Law of Force," *Proceeding of American Society of International Law* (2015): 63–67.

8. For elaboration see Report of Kosovo Commission, 2000.

9. UN Charter, Chapter VII, Article 51.

10. See António Guterres, *Our Common Agenda* (2021), https://www.un.org/en/common-agenda, Secretary-General's report on 75 years of UN activity and future prospects.

11. Judge Christopher Weeramantry's dissenting opinion in "Legality of the Threat or Use of Nuclear Weapons," Advisory Opinion, ICJ Reports, 1996, 433–555.

## Chapter 11

1. A/2626 (XXV), para. 43.

2. UN Charter Purposes and Principles, Articles 1 and 2.

3. UN Charter, Chapter VIII, Articles 52 to 54.

4. In May 1974, the General Assembly had adopted the Declaration for the Establishment of a New Economic Order with a focus on trade not aid.

5. These WTO-led trade negotiations, aimed at lowering trade- and non-trade barriers between high- and low-income countries ended in failure in 2018.

## Chapter 12

1. A/RES/71/323 (2017).

2. UN Charter, Chapter XVIII.

3. A/48/264.

4. Foreign, Commonwealth, and Development Office, January 26, 2023.

5. S/687/1991 and S/1284/1999.

6. S/1441/2002.

7. S/1973/2011.

8. UN Charter, Articles 21 and 30.

9. UN Charter, Article 32.

10. Confidential report to Security Council by German Ambassador Eitel, November 14, 2002.

11. A/RES/76/153.

12. See https://www.un.org/en/ga/maincommittees/index.shtml.

13. See UN System Chief Executives Board for Coordination, https://unsceb.org/.

14. UN Charter, Article 100(2)

15. During a visit to Bonn in 1998, UNDP Administrator Speth, German Minister of Finance Lafontaine, pointed out with a smile, "I would not spend 30 seconds a year on issues of UN finances."

16. US obligatory payments for the 2022 UN regular budget amounted to US$686 million (see GA/AB/4372); no US payment was made for 2022 (see GA Committee on Contributions for 2022). The total of US arrears for the regular budget as of September 30, 2023, amounted to US$930.291 million or 69 percent of all debts owed for the regular budget (see Catherine Pollard, "The UN Financial Situation," October 9, 2023). US obligatory payments for the 2022/23 UN peacekeeping budget amounted to US$1.6 billion (see GA/AB/4386). As of September 30, 2023, the US had peacekeeping debts amounting to US$1.494 billion or 46 percent of all debts owed for the peacekeeping budget (see Pollard, "The UN Financial Situation," October 9, 2023)

17. UN Charter, Article 101(3).

## Reflections
### Gök

1. Weiss, Thomas G., "How United Nations Ideas Change History, *Review of International Studies*, 36, no. S1 (2010): 3–23.

2. Carayannis, Tatiana, and Thomas Weiss, "The 'Third' UN: Imagining Post-COVID-19 Multilateralism," *Global Policy*, 12, no. 1 (2021): 5–14.

3. Barnett, Michael N., and Martha Finnemore, "The Politics, Power, and Pathologies of International Organizations," *International Organization*, 53, no. 4 (1999): 699–732.

4. Carayannis and Weiss, "The 'Third' UN."

5. Falk, Richard, "Legitimacy, Crises of Global Governance, and International Relations," in *The Crises of Legitimacy in Global Governance*, edited by Gonca Oğuz Gök and Hakan Mehmetcik (Routledge: 2021).

6. Hurd, I., "Legitimacy and Contestation in Global Governance: Revisiting the Folk Theory of International Institutions," *Review of International Organizations*, 14, no. 4 (2019): 717–729.

7. Binder, M., and M. Heupel, "The Legitimacy of the UN Security Council: Evidence from Recent General Assembly Debates," *International Studies Quarterly*, 9, no. 2 (2015): 238–250.

8. Dellmuth, L., and J. Tallberg, "International Organisations' Social Legitimacy: Interest Representation, Institutional Performance, and Confidence Extrapolation in the United Nations," *Review of International Studies* 41, no. 3 (2015): 451–475.

9. Cronin, B., and Ian Hurd, *The UN Security Council and the Politics of International Authority* (Routledge, 2008).

10. Debre, M. J., and H. Dijkstra, "Institutional Design for a Post-Liberal Order: Why Some International Organizations Live Longer than Others," *European Journal of International Relations*, 27, no. 1 (2021): 311–339.

11. Jain, D., "Where the UN Has Failed to Live Up to Its Mission: Looking Back to Look Forward," *Ethics and International Affairs*, 34, no. 3 (2020): 351–359.

12. Narlikar, Amrita, "From a Legitimacy Deficit to an Existential Crisis: The Unfortunate Case of the World Trade Organization," in *The Crises of Legitimacy in Global Governance*, edited by Gonca Oğuz Gök and Hakan Mehmetcik (Routledge, 2021).

### Yoni

1. H. M. Kyed, "Introduction to the Special Issues: Soldiers Defections since the 2021 Military Coup," in "Memories of Leaving the Myanmar Military," special issue, *Independent Journal of Burmese Scholarship*, vol.1 (August 2022); and "The Centrality of the Civil Disobedience Movements in Myanmar's Post Coup Era," *New Mandala Journal*, October 19, 2021, https://www.newmandala.org/the-centrality-of-the-civil-disobedience-movement-in-myanmars-post-coup-era/.

### Benz

1. The process of remembrance; healing, including dreams; and integration refers to Kremer and Jackson-Paton's *Ethnoautobiography* (Kendall Hunt Publishing, 2018).

2. Referring to the creation of an ecological civilization according to Jeremy Lent, *The Web of Meaning: Integrating Science and Traditional Wisdom* (New Society Publishers, 2021).

3. Mahatma Gandhi.

### Husain

1. Dmytro Kuleba (@DmytroKuleba), "Russia's rights of membership in the UN Human Rights Council has just been suspended," Twitter, April 7, 2022, 8:52 p.m., https://twitter.com/DmytroKuleba/status/1512095879037169665?s=20&t=goqml2-rH4oF-tT8iCzMXQ.

2. "Palestinian Wounded at Al-Aqsa Compound Slips into Coma," *Al Jazeera*, April 24, 2022, https://www.aljazeera.com/news/2022/4/24/palestinian-wounded-at-aqsa-compound-in-critical-condition.

3. Peter Thomas, "Refiguring the Subaltern," *Political Theory*, 46, no. 6 (2018): 861.

4. Thomas, "Refiguring the Subaltern," 862; Rosalind Morris, *Can the Subaltern Speak: Reflections on the History of an Idea* (Columbia University Press, 2010).

5. Thomas, "Refiguring the Subaltern," 862.

### Yu

1. Global Database for Tracking Antimicrobial Resistance (AMR), https://amrcountryprogress.org/#/map-view.

2. WHO, *Health Systems for Health Security*, June 25, 2021, https://www.who.int/publications/i/item/9789240029682.

### Altman

1. These are sometimes used, but often survey coverage is poor because the surveys are too long to expect a respondent to complete and questions are unclear or poorly designed.

**Afterword**

1. Ahmet Davutoğlu, *Systemic Earthquake and the Struggle for World Order: Exclusive Populism versus Inclusive Democracy* (Cambridge University Press, 2020), 1–6.

2. Richard Falk, *Public Intellectual: The Life of a Citizen Pilgrim* (Clarity Press, 2021).

3. Hans von Sponeck, *A Different Kind of War: The UN Sanctions Regime in Iraq* (Berghahn Books, 2006).

4. Richard Falk, *(Re)Imagining Humane Global Governance* (Routledge, 2014), 87.

5. www.un.org/en/sections/un-charter/index.html.

# SELECTED BIBLIOGRAPHY

Amorim, Celso, *Acting Globally* (Hamilton Books, 2017).

Andersen, Louise Riis, *The UN—A Half-way House between Nationalism and Cosmopolitanism* (Danish Institute for International Studies, 2020).

Annan, Kofi, *A Compact for a New Century* (UN Doc. SG/SM/6881, 1999).

——, *Interventions—A Life in War and Peace* (Penguin Press, 2012).

Arias, Oscar, Fundación Arias para la Paz y el Progreso Humano (www.un-ngls .org/spip.phppage=amdg&id_article=2592).

Archibugi, Daniele, and David Held, eds., *Cosmopolitan Democracy: An Agenda for a New World Order* (Polity, 1995).

Barnett, Michael N., and Martha Finnemore, "The Politics, Power, and Pathologies of International Organizations," *International Organization*, 53, no. 4 (1999): 699–732.

Baxi, Upendra, *Human in a Posthuman World: Critical Essays* (Oxford University Press, 2007).

Bello, Walden, *Deglobalization: Ideas for a New World Economy* (Zed, 2004).

Binder, M., and M. Heupel, "The Legitimacy of the UN Security Council: Evidence from Recent General Assembly Debates," *International Studies Quarterly*, 9, no. 2 (2015): 238–250.

Boutros-Ghali, Boutros, *An Agenda for Peace, Preventive Diplomacy, Peacemaking and Peace Keeping,* Report of the Secretary-General to the Security Council (https://digitallibrary.un.org/record/145749?ln=en, 1992).

Brown, Stephen, *UN Reform—75 Years of Challenge and Change* (Edward Elgar Publishing, 2019).

Cabrera, Luis, *Global Government Revisited: From Utopian Dream to Political Imperative* (Great Transition Initiative, Tellus Institute, Oct. 2017).

——, *Political Theory of Global Justice: A Cosmopolitan Case for the World State* (Routledge, 2004).

Carayannis, Tatiana, and Thomas G. Weiss, *The "Third" United Nations: How a Knowledge Ecology Helps the UN Think.* (Oxford University Press, 2021).

——, "The 'Third' UN: Imagining Post-COVID-19 Multilateralism," *Global Policy*, 12, no. 1 (2021): 5–14.

Césaire, Aimé, *Discourse on Colonialism* (Monthly Review Press, 2000).

Childers, Erskine B., and Brian Urquhart, *Renewing the United Nations System* (Dag Hammarskjold Foundation, 1994).

——, *Toward a More Effective United Nations* (The Ford Foundation, 1992).

Chimni, B. S., *International Law and World Order: A Critique of Contemporary Approaches* (Cambridge University Press, 2017).

Chomsky, Noam, *Hegemony or Survival? America's Quest for Global Empire* (Metropolitan, 2003).

Clark, Grenville, and Louis B. Sohn, *World Peace through World Law*, 3rd ed. (Harvard University Press, 1967).

Commission on Global Governance, *Our Global Neighborhood* (Oxford University Press, 1995).

Cronin, B., and Ian Hurd, *The UN Security Council and the Politics of International Authority* (Routledge, 2008).

Dante (Alighieri), *On World Government*, translated by Herbert W. Schneider (Griffin House, 2008).

Davutoğlu, Ahmed, *Systemic Earthquake and the Struggle for World Order: Exclusive Populism versus Inclusive Democracy* (Cambridge University Press, 2020).

Debre, M. J., and H. Dijkstra, "Institutional Design for a Post-Liberal Order: Why Some International Organizations Live Longer than Others," *European Journal of International Relations*, 27, no. 1 (2021): 311–339.

Dellmuth, L., and J. Tallberg, "International Organisations' Social Legitimacy: Interest Representation, Institutional Performance, and Confidence Extrapolation in the United Nations," *Review of International Studies* 41, no. 3 (2015): 451–475.

Falk, Richard, "Legitimacy, Crises of Global Governance, and International Relations," in *The Crises of Legitimacy in Global Governance*, edited by Gonca Oğuz Gök and Hakan Mehmetcik (Routledge, 2021).

——, *On Humane Governance: Toward a New Global Politics* (Polity 1995).

——, *(Re)Imagining Humane Global Governance* (Routledge, 2013).

Falk, Richard, Robert C. Johansen, and Samuel S. Kim, eds., *The Constitutional Foundations of World Peace* (State University of New York Press, 1993).

Falk, Richard, Samuel S. Kim, Saul H. Mendlovitz, and Donald McNemar, eds., *The United Nations and a Just World Order* (Westview, 1991).

Held, David, *Global Covenant: The Social Democratic Alternative to the Washington Consensus* (Polity, 2004).

Held, David, and M. Koenig-Archibugi, eds., *Taming Globalization: Frontiers of Governance* (Polity, 2003).

Hurd, I., "Legitimacy and Contestation in Global Governance: Revisiting the Folk Theory of International Institutions," *Review of International Organizations*, 14, no. 4 (2019): 717–729.

Ikenberry, G. John, *After Victory: Institutions, Strategic Restraint, and the Rebuilding of Order after Major Wars* (Princeton University Press, 2001).

——, *Liberal Leviathan: The Origin, Crises, and. Transformation of the American World Order* (Princeton University Press, 2011).

Jain, D., "Where the UN Has Failed to Live Up to Its Mission: Looking Back to Look Forward," *Ethics and International Affairs*, 34, no. 3 (2020): 351–359.

Johansen, Robert, *Where the Evidence Leads: A Realistic Strategy for Peace and Global Security* (Oxford University Press, 2021).

Jolly, Richard, Louis Emmerij, and Thomas Weiss, *UN Ideas That Changed the World* (Indiana University Press, 2009).

Kennedy, Paul, *The Parliament of Man: The Past, Present, and Future of the United Nations* (Vintage Books, 2006).

Kissinger, Henry, *World Order* (Penguin, 2014).

Kremer, Jürgen Werner, and R. Jackson-Paton, *Ethno-autobiography: Stories and Practices for Unlearning Whiteness Decolonialization Uncovering Ethnicities* (Kendall Hunt, 2018)

Leinen, Jo, and Andreas Bummel, *A World Parliament: Governance and Democracy in the 21st Century*, translated from German by Ray Cunningham (Democracy Without Borders, Berlin, 2018).

Lent, Jeremy, *The Web of Meaning: Integrating Science and Traditional Wisdom to Find Our Place in the Universe* (Profile Books, 2022).

Lopez-Claros, Augusto, Arthur L. Dahl, and Maja Groff, *Global Governance and the Emergence of Global Institutions for the 21st Century* (Cambridge University Press, 2020).

Mahbubani, Kishore, *The Chinese Challenge to American Primacy: Has China Won?* (Hachette Book Group, 2020).

Mazower, Mark, *Governing the World: The History of an Idea—1815 to the Present* (Penguin 2012).

McKeil, Aaron, *Cosmopolitan Imaginaries and International Order* (forthcoming, 2023).

Mehta, Vijay, ed., *The United Nations in the 21st Century* (Spokesman, 2005).

Narlikar, Amrita, "From a Legitimacy Deficit to an Existential Crisis: The Unfortunate Case of the World Trade Organization," in *The Crises of Legitimacy in Global Governance*, edited by Gonca Oğuz Gök and Hakan Mehmetcik (Routledge, 2021).

Paul, James A., *Of Foxes and Chickens—Oligarchy and Global Power in the UN Security Council* (Rosa Luxemburg Stiftung, 2017).

Pogge, Thomas, *World Poverty and Human Rights* (Polity Press, 2008).

Prasad, Vijay, *The Darker Nations: A People's History of the World* (New Press, 2007).

——, *The Poorer Nations: A Possible History of the Global South* (Verso, 2013).

Rachman, Gideon, *Easternization: Asia's Rise and America's Decline: From Obama to Trump and Beyond* (Other Press, 2016).

Ross, Carne, *The Leaderless Revolution* (Blue Rider Press, 2017).

Roy, Arundhati, *Power Politics* (South End Press, 2001).

Said, Edward W., *Orientalism* (Pantheon, 1978).

Sands, Philippe, *The Last Colony* (Weidenfield & Nicolson, 2022).

Schlesinger, Stephen C., *Act of Creation* (Westview, 2003).

Slaughter, Anne-Marie, *A New World Order* (Princeton University Press, 2004).

Schwartzberg, Joseph E., *Transforming the United Nations System—Designs for a Workable World* (United Nations University Press, 2013).

Talbott, Strobe, *The Great Experiment: The Story of Ancient Empires, Modern States, and the Quest for a Global Nation* (Simon & Schuster, 2008).

United Nations, Blue Book Series (https://www.ungeneva.org/en/blue-book, 1996).

——, Office of the Secretary-General's Envoy on Youth, *Youth 2030: The UN Youth Strategy* (UN Dag Hammarskjöld Library, 2018).

von Sponeck, Hans-C., *A Different Kind of War—The UN Sanctions Regime in Iraq* (Berghahn, 2006).

——, *Der Libyen Krieg—Internationale Schutzverantwortung—der lange Weg der UNO vom Konzept zur Norm* ( LIT Verlag, 2013).

——, *Human Development—Is There an Alternative?* (Capital Foundation, New Delhi, 1997).

——, *Sanctions and Humanitarian Exemptions: A Practitioner's Commentary* (Oxford University Press, 2002).

Walter, F. P., *A History of the League of Nations* (Oxford University Press, 1965).

Weiss, Thomas G. "How United Nations Ideas Change History," *Review of International Studies*, 36, no. S1 (2010): 3–23.

——, *What's Wrong with the United Nations and How to Fix It*, 3rd ed. (Polity, 2016).

# INDEX

Pages numbers with an *f* denote figures; page numbers with a *t* denote tables.

The authorized representative in the EU for product safety and compliance is:
Mare Nostrum Group
B.V Doelen 72
4831 GR Breda
The Netherlands

www.ingramcontent.com/pod-product-compliance
Lightning Source LLC
Chambersburg PA
CBHW030856270326
41929CB00008B/440